"Rosengarten, with [   ] as a spice grower in Guatamala, has harvested his knowledge and put it on valuable display in this book . . . [which] includes a planter's bushel of excellent recipes featuring spices of all kinds. . . . The special bonus . . . is Rosengarten's informative and extremely interesting discussion of the nature and history of spices from Egypt . . . to the modern Spice trade. The book rates A-1"

—*Publishers' Weekly*

"This is a magnificent volume from any of several points of view: as a source of fascinating historical information, as an account of basic botanical facts about spice plants . . . as a record of the economics of the spice industry, and as a catalog of tempting recipes in which the various spices are featured"

—*Garden Journal*
New York Botanical Garden

". . . skillfully satisfies the needs of the spice merchant, the economic botanist and the grower but, more important, [Rosengarten] has linked this most readably to the needs of the housewife, the chef, and the true gourmet."

George H. M. Lawrence, Director Emeritus
Hunt Botanical Library, Pittsburgh

FREDERIC ROSENGARTEN, JR., a native Philadelphian, is a graduate *cum laude* of Princeton University, Class of 1938. In World War II he served as a lieutenant in the Army of the United States (European Theater). From 1947 to 1959, he and his family lived in Guatemala where he managed three plantations devoted to the production of coffee, cinchona bark (quinine), essential oils and spices. Since then, as president of a Guatemalan spice-producing firm, his work took him many times to the spice markets of western Europe and the Middle East.

In 1960, in recognition of his developmental efforts in helping Guatemala to become the pre-eminent cardamom-producing country of the Western Hemisphere, the Guatemalan Government conferred upon him the decoration of the *Order of the Quetzal*.

More recently, Mr. Rosengarten has devoted considerable study, here and abroad, to the entire subject of spices, recognizing the need for a single illustrated work that would bring together the fascinating history of spices and accurate information concerning their place in the world of today.

THE BOOK
OF
SPICES

Frederic Rosengarten, Jr.

*Revised and Abridged by the Author
for This Edition*

PYRAMID BOOKS   •   NEW YORK

TO M.O.R.

THE BOOK OF SPICES

A PYRAMID BOOK

Second printing, October 1975

ISBN: 0-515-03220-4

This book was first published in a hardcover edition
by Livingston Publishing Company in 1969.

Pyramid Books are published by Pyramid Communications, Inc.
Its trademarks, consisting of the word "Pyramid" and the
portrayal of a pyramid, are registered in the United States
Patent Office.

Printed in the United States of America

PYRAMID COMMUNICATIONS, INC.
919 Third Avenue
New York, New York 10022, U.S.A.

(graphic design by anthony basile)

PREFACE

HAVING spent some years in the production of spices in Guatemala, the author has long felt the need for a comprehensive nontechnical book on spices. Reliable information is available on the botanical, agricultural, chemical, pharmaceutical, and other technical aspects of spices, but in general it is of difficult access to all except specialists.

A few years ago two meritorious illustrated books in German were published about spices: *Kostbarkeiten ferner Länder eine Gewürz—und Teepflanzenkunde von Alba,* compiled by H. Stender and published by Gehring & Neiweiser in Bielefeld, West Germany, in 1951; and *Das Buch der Gewürze* written by Roland Gööck and published by the Mosaik Verlag in Hamburg in 1965. Cordial acknowledgment is made of the courtesies of the authors and publishers of these two works, as well as to other authors and publishers in English who have permitted the use of excerpts and illustrations from copyrighted works, all of which are duly credited.

In the hope that the present effort will be of some use for reference in other parts of the globe, the Latin binomial of each spice is given, followed where possible by the name in eleven other modern languages.

The author has attempted to clarify the existing confusion concerning the identification and nomenclature of some spices and herbs—between, for example, cassia and cinnamon, marjoram and oregano, and the various types of "peppers"—capsicum (chili) peppers, black pepper, white pepper, and Jamaican pepper (pimento) or allspice.

5

Actually, it is difficult to determine where to draw the line when listing the spices, especially with reference to minor spices or herbs. It is hoped that the condimental plants selected for the thirty-five individual chapters will cover the international field adequately and fairly, and that this work may eventually prove useful to the housewife, to the student of economic botany, and to the producer, exporter and importer of spices. An effort has been made to tie in the practical modern culinary use of spices with their early history by the provision of proved recipes.

The author acknowledges his deep appreciation for the help given him by many persons during the preparation of this book. Whole-hearted thanks are due to Dr. George H. M. Lawrence, Director Emeritus of The Rachel McMasters Miller Hunt Botanical Library in Pittsburgh; to Dr. Richard Evans Schultes, Director of The Botanical Museum of Harvard University; and to Dr. John M. Fogg, Jr., former Director of the Morris Arboretum, Chestnut Hill, Pennsylvania, for their painstaking editorial criticism and helpful suggestions. The author is most grateful to Dr. J. I. Miller of Christ Church, Oxford, England, and to Dr. F. N. L. Poynter, Director of The Wellcome Institute of the History of Medicine, London, for their knowledgeable orientation concerning the history of spices; to the American Spice Trade Association, Inc., New York and Mr. Stewart P. Wands, Executive Vice President, for permission to make use of selected A.S.T.A. recipes and other reference data; to Mr. Bernard L. Lewis and his staff of New York City, for cooperation in the preparation of the recipes, and several helpful suggestions; to Mr. Ray E. Graham of McCormick and Co., Inc., Schilling Division, Salinas, California, for up-to-date information about the spice trade; to Dr. E. E. Leppik of the U. S. Department of Agriculture, New Crops Research Branch, Beltsville,

Maryland, for assistance with reference to technical information; to Dr. Bassett Maguire, Director of Botany of the New York Botanical Garden, for orientation on several botanical questions; to Mr. Dwight Ripley of Greenport, Long Island, New York, for the names of the spices and herbs in ten languages; to Dr. H. L. Li of Chestnut Hill, Pennsylvania, for information about Chinese history and names of the spices as reported in the Chinese literature; to Mr. Evan Guest of The Herbarium, Royal Botanic Gardens, Kew, England, for the names of the spices in Arabic; to Professor Philip K. Hitti of Princeton University for information relative to Arabic history; to Dr. Charles B. Heiser, Jr., Professor of Botany, Indiana University, Bloomington, Indiana, for information on the identity and nomenclature of chili peppers and for reading the chapter on them; to Dr. Donovan S. Correll of the Texas Research Foundation, Renner, Texas, for reading the chapter on vanilla; to Dr. Henry A. Jones of El Centro, California, for reading the chapter on onions; to Mr. J. S. Hemingway of Norwich, England, for information concerning mustard seed; to Dr. Rudolf Hirsch of the Van Pelt Library, University of Pennsylvania, for assistance in locating illustrations from medieval literature; to the Commonwealth Secretariat, Plantation Crops Section, London, for recent statistical data about spices; to Mr. Paul G. Stecher for precise information concerning several chemical references; to Mrs. Yanagi Toyokuni, Professor of Biology at Asahikawa University, Japan, for the names of many spices in Japanese; and to Mrs. Judith K. Benson for her competent collaboration in the typing of the original manuscript.

The author wishes to express his gratitude to the following, who have provided information, illustrations or otherwise assisted him during the course of the work: Dr. G. R. Ames and Mr. E. Brown of the

Tropical Products Institute, London; Mr. Donald E. Cooke and Mr. Jacob Dresden of Philadelphia; Dr. J. J. Duyverman and Mr. P. N. de Waard of the Royal Tropical Institute, Amsterdam; Dr. E. Esfandiari, Ministry of Agriculture, Teheran, Iran; Mr. Basil J. Freeman, Mr. Franz J. Ippisch, Mr. Federico Lüttmann E., Mr. Wouter Nicolai and Mr. Alberto Novella of Guatemala City; Mr. Peter Gavigan of San Francisco; Mr. Peter Goldberg of Basic Vegetable Products, Inc., Vacaville, California; Mr. E. Halfter of Copenhagen; Mr. Curd Küker of Hamburg; Mr. Robert Letendre of the New York Public Library; Mr. Einar Lindahl of Stockholm; Mr. Arthur J. McCarthy of London; Dr. Sheldon Margen and Dr. Susan M. Oace of the Department of Nutritional Sciences, University of California, Berkeley; Dr. Lloyd Miller, U.S. Pharmacopeia, Bethesda, Maryland; Mr. Frank C. Mitchell, Ministry of Agriculture and Lands, Jamaica, W.I.; Mr. Robert S. Renwick of the Grenada Cooperative Nutmeg Association; Mr. Donald A. Sayia of New York City; Mr. P. Schwab of Hamburg; Mr. Brian G. C. Smith, Mahe, Seychelles; The Spices Export Promotion Council, Ernakulam, India; Dr. W. H. Stahl of McCormick & Co., Inc.; Dr. W. T. Stearn, Department of Botany, British Museum (Natural History), London; Mr. G. E. Tidbury, Commonwealth Bureau of Horticulture and Plantation Crops, East Malling, Kent, England; Mr. Granville Toogood of Chestnut Hill, Pennsylvania; and Professor Fergus B. Wilson of Rome, Italy.

The author wishes to express his appreciation to the Livingston Publishing Company and the members of its staff for their diligent cooperation during the preparation of the original hardback edition of this book first published in 1969.

CONTENTS

THE SPICES

Part I

WHAT ARE SPICES?
A BRIEF HISTORY
OF SPICES

WHAT ARE SPICES?

Nose, nose, nose, nose!
And who gave thee this jolly red nose?
Nutmegs and ginger, cinnamon and cloves,
And they gave me this jolly red nose.

From *Deuteromelia* (1609)
by Thomas Ravenscroft

CHRISTOPHER MORLEY is said to have defined spice as the plural of spouse, but according to Webster spices are specifically, "Any of various aromatic vegetable productions, as pepper, cinnamon, nutmeg, mace, allspice, ginger, cloves, etc., used in cookery to season food and to flavor sauces, pickles, etc.; a vegetable condiment or relish, usually in the form of a powder; also, such condiments collectively." Figuratively, a spice is "that which enriches or alters the quality of a thing, especially in a small degree, as spice alters the taste of food; that which gives zest or pungency; a piquant or pleasing flavoring; a relish, as, variety is the *spice* of life."

An herb, as defined by the same source, is "a seed plant which does not develop woody persistent tissue, as that of a shrub or tree, but is more or less soft or succulent. Herbs are *annual, biennial,* or *perennial,* according to the length of life of their roots." It is also "a plant of economic value; specifically, one used for medicinal purposes, or for its sweet scent or flavor."

Generally speaking, when the aromatic or fragrant vegetable product used to flavor foods or beverages is from plants of tropical origin, it is considered a spice; when from plants of temperate regions, it may be considered a culinary herb. It is extremely difficult to determine where a spice ends and an herb begins, as culinary herbs are in reality one group of spices.

Today we think of spices primarily as condiments to use in cooking, but this has not always been the case. In ancient times they were valued as basic ingredients of incense, embalming preservatives, ointments, perfumes, antidotes against poisons, cosmetics, and medicines, and were used only to a limited extent in the kitchen. It was not until the first century A.D. in Rome that there was for the first time a notable increase in the utilization of spices as condiments in food. Medieval Europeans tried to obtain highly valued spices to flavor their drab, sometimes partially decomposed food—and to provide fragrant, and they hoped antiseptic, aromas to mask many disagreeable and noxious odors. The quest for tropical spices played a most important part in world history, stimulating the exploration of the globe and leading to the discovery of America and the opening up of the countries of the East to Western civilization and trade.

Most of the important tropical spices had their original home in the Orient, in a latitude belt of between 25 degrees north and 10 degrees south of the Equator, while other parts of the world have produced comparatively few. The Asian tropics have given us pepper, cinnamon, cloves, ginger, cardamom, turmeric, nutmegs, and mace; the only major spices native to the American tropics are allspice, vanilla, and the capsicum peppers (chilies).

The Mediterranean area, including North Africa and the Middle East, has supplied most of the culinary herbs: bay leaves, coriander, cumin, dill, fennel, fenugreek, mustard seed, rosemary, saffron, and sage. On the other hand, the colder regions of northern Europe and Asia have produced very few—for example, caraway seed and horseradish.

Local demand for spices has remained high in the less developed countries of the Far East. In the West, where improved refrigeration has resulted in less demand for spices to preserve foods or to camouflage the odors of decay, new uses for spices, essential oils and oleoresins extracted from spices have been developed in the frozen food, dehydrated food, and canning industries. A notable development of the past few years has been the marked increase in the use of dehydrated culinary herbs, especially of onion and garlic products.

Pepper alone normally accounts for over one-fourth of the total world trade in spices. In general it is difficult for the spice producer to sell his crop for future delivery to hedge his risks, as is frequently done in the commodity exchanges that exist for other agricultural products like sugar, cocoa, coffee, wheat, corn, and soybeans. With the exception of an inactive market in pepper on the New York Produce Exchange, no official commodity exchange exists for spices in the West, although limited private trading covering future sales and purchases of pepper (black and white), ginger, nutmegs, cloves, cinnamon, and cassia does take place in New York, London, Hamburg, and Rotterdam. In the Orient there is some exchange trading in pepper in Singapore on the Chinese Produce Exchange.

At the present time the volume of international trade in spices amounts to over $200,000,000 a year. Generally speaking, spices are far more important to the economies of the producing countries than to those of the consuming countries. Demand for most spices is fairly constant, but supply may vary because of weather, pests, diseases, or even political factors in the areas of production. Spice prices, therefore, are very unstable, and may fluctuate considerably from year to year. Saffron (from Spain) enjoys the distinction of being far and away the world's costliest spice—its average import price in the United States during 1971–1972 exceeded $100 per pound. Canadian mustard seed in recent years has been the least expensive of the spices and herbs—its import price in 1971–1972 averaged about 5 cents per pound.

In the United States there has been a growing interest in spices and condiments during the past twenty years. This country is by far the world's largest importer of spices, herbs, and condimental flavorings, importing in 1971–1972 over 295,000,000 pounds, with a value in excess of $80,000,000. In quantity, mustard seed is now the largest U.S. spice import, total imports in 1971 having exceeded 95,000,000 lbs.; black and white pepper rank as the most important in terms of value ($26.4 million imported in 1971).

Most spices are imported into the United States in unground or crude form. If ground, spices tend to lose their essential oil constituents and characteristic aroma more rapidly. Likewise, spice grinders can maintain stricter quality control and blend the spices more effectively in unprocessed form.

Per capita consumption of spices in this country has almost doubled during the past half century, having increased from 0.78 lbs. in 1920 to 1.41 lbs. in 1972. This growth in spice consumption may be due to various factors such as rising incomes, a greater demand for convenience and "gourmet-type" foods, and the increased use of spices in fast-food service facilities.

Available statistics concerning world production, exports, and prices of spices are summarized in the Appendix. Since many spices are cultivated on small holdings, especially in Asia, accurate data on acreage and production are very difficult to obtain.

The effect of spices on health is an intriguing subject that cannot be ignored, even though, unfortunately, few definite conclusions can be reached at the present time. Although no longer important in modern Western medicine, spices are nevertheless significant in some diets, particularly low-sodium diets. Research has been undertaken to determine the importance of spices as a substitute for salt in treatment of patients suffering from high blood pressure. Studies carried out in 1950 by C. A. Elvehjem and C. H. Burns in the Department of Biochemistry at the University of Wisconsin indicated that the sodium contributed to the diet by spices used in normal amounts is insignificant and that almost all spices can be safely used in low-sodium diets. All the spices tested, including those covered in this book, showed an insignificant sodium content (less than 0.1 percent) with the exception of allspice, celery seed, dehydrated celery flakes, whole mace, and dehydrated parsley flakes. These results showed that patients on low-sodium diets can flavor their food with most pure ground spices to compensate for the lack of salt; however, products such as garlic salt and onion salt, as well as other seasoning blends that contain salt, are to be avoided by these patients.

Aphrodisiacal properties have been ascribed to almost every spice at some time or other in various cultures. Modern medicine, however, questions these beliefs. Some urologists are of the opinion that because of irritating action which calls attention to these areas, certain irritating substances entering into the bladder or other parts of the lower genitourinary system may seem to stimulate sexual appetite and hence sexual activity. The limited amount of spices usually taken in food in this country makes it quite unlikely that these effects could be significant. But in certain Middle Eastern countries spices may indeed be ingested in large enough amounts to obtain more specific pharmacological effects as aphrodisiacs.

Recent studies to determine the influence of spices on gastric secretion have given contradictory and confusing results. Gastroenterologists now agree that the appearance and smell of food can have a decided effect on stimulating gastrointestinal function. The introduction of pleasing, flavorful material into the mouth may lead to increased salivary and gastric flow, whereas the reaction to an unpleasant odor or taste may lead to a rejection of the food and decreased fluid and enzyme production. H. Glatzel of the Max Planck Institute of Nutritional Physiology in Dortmund, West Germany, recently carried out an extensive investigation with human subjects and arrived at the conclusion that certain "hot" spices such as ginger, chili peppers, and mustard, when added in moderate amounts to a bland rice meal, will increase salivation to about eight times the "resting value," or normal rate. Other spices seem to have slightly lesser effects. Some evidence suggests that bile flow, essential to proper fat digestion, may be stimulated by some of the essential oils such as oil of caraway.

Additional research is necessary before any definite conclusions can be reached as to the effect of spices on cardiovascular functions, the blood-clotting process, and the growth of microorganisms normally residing in the intestinal tract; on the nutritional value of spices per se; on the carminative effect of spices; and on their effect as antioxidants to arrest rancidity in fat and in fatty foods.

The supposed food-preserving qualities of spices have also come under investigation. In the test tube, oils of cinnamon, clove, garlic, oregano, and sage have been found to have germicidal properties. Since the concentrations employed were generally so much larger than those normally used in everyday food, however, this research implies that spices were more likely used in ages past to disguise the flavor of spoiled and deteriorating foodstuffs than for their preservative qualities.

Further studies must be carried out before most of the traditional virtues attributed to spices in medicinal folklore can be verified or rejected. One may safely state, however, that spices can indeed make food more attractive and thus enable an ailing individual to fulfill a dietary prescription and make a faster recovery. Tests on hospital patients showed that cinnamon, allspice, mace, thyme, sage, and caraway seeds, taken in limited amounts, were all safe and in no way interfered with the healing process. Thus the spices may have helped the patient by making food acceptable that otherwise might have seemed unattractive.

Common salt, or table salt, although a mineral (sodium chloride—NaCl) and not a spice of vegetable origin, is nevertheless such an important seasoning and preservative of food that it must be mentioned in any book about spices. Salt has been used by man since the beginning of time. Biochemically it is so essential to the health of all humans and animals that it has played a vital role in the rise and fall of many civilizations. Used sparingly as a seasoning, it tends to enhance the flavor and aroma of most spices and herbs. It is often combined with ground dehydrated herbs to form herb salts such as celery salt, garlic salt, onion salt, and parsley salt.

Another well-known and widely used flavor enhancer is monosodium glutamate, or MSG. This crystalline salt of glutamic acid was first described as a pure substance in Japan in 1908. Although not a spice and possessing very little flavor of its own, MSG intensifies the flavor of other foods, especially that of meats, by causing the taste buds of the human tongue temporarily to become more sensitive.

There are several possible methods of classifying the spices and herbs. They could be grouped, for example, according to the *parts of the plant* from which the commercial products are taken. In this case, *dried flower buds* would include cloves; *fruits* would consist of allspice, black pepper, nutmeg, and vanilla; *underground stems* would comprise ginger, horseradish, and turmeric; *barks* would cover cassia and cinnamon; and *seeds* and *seedlike structures* would refer to anise, caraway, cardamom, coriander, dill, poppy, and sesame.

Or they could be classified according to their *properties,* by arranging them in three groups: *stimulating condiments* such as black pepper, capsicum peppers, garlic, horseradish, and mustard; *aromatic spices* like anise, cardamom, cinnamon, cloves, and ginger; and *sweet herbs*, for example, basil, chervil, fennel, parsley, and sage.

Still another method of arranging the spices would be according to the *families* to which the plants belong. This plan would be of interest primarily to the botanist but perhaps confusing to others: the *Umbelliferae* would include anise, caraway, celery seed, chervil, coriander, cumin, dill, fennel, and parsley; the *Labiatae,* basil, marjoram, mint, oregano, rosemary, sage, savory, and thyme; the *Lauraceae,* bay leaves, cassia, and cinnamon; the *Zingiberaceae,* cardamom, ginger, and turmeric; and so forth.

To simplify the presentation of the descriptive material in this book, spices and herbs will be considered together under the broad general heading of "spices," and arranged in alphabetical order under their English names.

Before we examine the individual spices and herbs, however, let us take a brief look at their fascinating history, which may be said to have commenced during the third millennium B.C.

A BRIEF HISTORY
OF SPICES

Ancient Egyptian and Arabian beginnings
(from about 2600 B.C.)

THE first authentic, if fragmentary, records of the use of spices and herbs may date from the Pyramid Age in Egypt, approximately 2600 to 2100 B.C. Onions and garlic were fed to the one hundred thousand laborers who toiled in the construction of the Great Pyramid of Cheops, as medicinal herbs to preserve their health.

A monument dedicated to the Egyptian pharaoh Sahure, dating from the twenty-fifth century B.C., records the receipt of a great quantity of ebony, gold, and silver and eighty thousand measures of myrrh from the "land of Punt."

Later, when they became essential ingredients in the embalming process, cassia and cinnamon were imported to Egypt from China and Southeast Asia. To appease the gods of death, the bodies of important personages were preserved against decay by embalming, which involved cleansing the interior of the abdomen and rinsing it with fragrant spices, including cumin, anise, marjoram, cassia, and cinnamon.

The origin of perfumery is shrouded in obscurity, but the word perfume (*per,* through, and *fumum,* smoke) suggests that it was first obtained by burning aromatic gums and hardened oozings from resinous woods such as bdellium, balsam, myrrh, and frankincense. These shrublike, thorny perennial desert trees and bushes grew for the most part in hot, dry regions stretching from western India to central Africa. As unpleasant odors were associated with evil, so were sweet clean scents linked with purity and goodness. Thus a demand was created for the fragrant gums collected from these shrubs for use in embalming, perfumes, medicine, and anointing oils and as incense offerings in fumigation, to please the ancient gods, and to banish evil spirits, insects, pests, and serpents.

The upper classes in Egypt also fumigated their homes with incense to ward off the foul odors of the crowded lower classes. Since it has been proved in recent years that the burning of incense produces phenol, or carbolic acid, an antiseptic widely used during the nineteenth century, this custom may have had some merit.

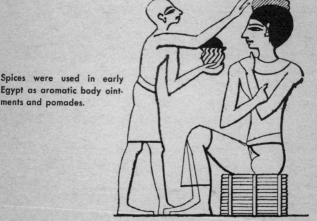

Spices were used in early Egypt as aromatic body ointments and pomades.

In ancient civilizations no sharp distinction was made between food plants used for flavoring, spice plants, medicinal plants, and sacrificial plants. If certain leaves, seeds, roots, and gums had a pleasant, pungent

PERFUMING THE EMBALMED BODY WITH FRAGRANT SPICES IN EARLY EGYPT

taste and an agreeable odor, an extensive demand gradually developed for them, culminating in their use as condiments.

The earliest mention in the Bible of an aromatic substance occurs in Genesis 2:12 in a reference to the land of Havilah: "And the gold of that land is good: there is bdellium and the onyx stone." Bdellium was a fragrant gum resin obtained from a shrublike tree, *Commiphora mukul,* growing in arid regions of western India. From incisions made in the bark oozed an odoriferous gum that hardened into small, transparent,

EGYPTIAN BEARERS WITH FRUITS, FLOWERS, AND HERBS
Onions (in the triangular rack) were an important health food, fed to the workers during the construction of the Great Pyramid of Cheops, about 2590-2568 B.C.

waxlike pellets resembling fragrant pearls, which early Egyptian women carried about in pouches as perfume. Bdellium was often sold as a cheap aromatic substitute for myrrh.

Pleasant odors were highly valued in biblical days, as noted in II Chronicles 16:14, in the burial arrangements, including the burning of spices, made for King Asa.

A wealth of information concerning ancient herbs and spices was discovered by the German Egyptologist Georg Ebers in a remarkable medical document dated about 1550 B.C. This comprehensive roll, reported by him in 1874 and now known as the Ebers Papyrus, is some sixty-five feet in length and contains extensive information about surgery and internal medicine, as well as listing some eight hundred medicinal drugs. These include many of the herbs and spices we use today as condiments: anise, caraway, cassia, coriander, fennel, cardamom, onions, garlic, thyme, mustard, sesame, fenugreek, saffron, and poppy seed. The Egyptians employed these aromatic spices in medicine, cosmetic ointments, perfumes, aromatic oils, cooking, fumigation, and notably embalming.

During the second and first millennia B.C. Arabia Felix, "Fortunate Arabia," prospered almost beyond belief as the great monopolistic carrier of goods between East and West. Profits from incense production were added to revenues from other merchandise. Frankincense, a resin derived from several species of stout-trunked, shrubby trees of the genus *Boswellia,* was Arabia's most valuable natural product and was produced extensively in the valleys of Hadramut and Dhofar. This translucent amber-colored gum, which ignites easily, yields a pleasant odor when burned and was in great demand as an incense. It was carried northward along the "Incense Route" to the markets of Egypt and Syria.

COLLECTION OF FRANKINCENSE
This sixteenth-century illustration portrays the collection of the amber-colored gum as it oozed from the bark of the frankincense trees in southern Arabia.

At first primitive donkey caravans transported the merchandise, which included not only locally produced balm and frankincense, but also goods en route from other lands: pearls and precious stones from India, cinnamon from the Far East, and ivory and myrrh from the nearby East African coast. Then about 1000 B.C. a significant revolution took place in Arabian trade, when the undemanding single-humped Arabian dromedary camel, *Camelus dromedarius,* was first used for local and long-distance land transportation. This long-suffering, patient beast, plodding along at two miles an hour and carrying burdens of up to five hundred pounds, could cover twenty-five miles a day, required very little food and water, and thus (since larger loads were possible) cut down the costs of the caravan.

Myrrh was another aromatic substance scripturally famous. It is still used today, to a limited extent, as a basic ingredient of incense in Catholic churches, and as the basis of some mouthwashes—it is reputed to have styptic properties useful in checking bleeding of the gums. In Matthew 2:11 it is related that myrrh was one of the precious gifts offered to the infant Jesus by the Magi. Consisting of rounded brownish aromatic lumps or fused tears of dull-surfaced gum resin, myrrh was obtained for the most part from *Commiphora myrrha*, a small, scrubby, thorny tree indigenous to southern Arabia, Abyssinia, and the land of Punt (a region in East Africa at the south end of the Red Sea, opposite the modern Arabian port of Aden and extending southward along the Somali coast). It was especially coveted by ancient Egyptian rulers for fumigation in their temples and for embalming purposes.

As the myrrh tree itself was not grown in Egypt, the

EGYPTIAN SHIPS
Ships of this type were dispatched from Egypt about 1485 B.C. by Queen Hatshepsut to the land of Punt to bring back frankincense, cinnamon, baboons, dogs, and myrrh trees.

pharaoh, Queen Hatshepsut, decided in 1485 B.C. that several should be obtained and planted in front of a steep rock wall west of Thebes, near the temple of Deir-el-Bahri, to establish a splendid terraced myrrh garden in homage to the god Amon.

An expedition consisting of five sailing vessels departed from Thebes and traveled down the Nile to the delta, through a channel into the Red Sea, then south along the East African coast until it reached Punt. When the ships returned with thirty-one cherished myrrh trees, they are reported to have been heavily laden also with such precious commodities as ivory, ebony, gold, silver, cinnamon, eye cosmetic, panther skins, monkeys, baboons, dogs, and great quantities of myrrh resin. In return for these trees and goods, the Egyptians had traded the natives of Punt an abundance of cheap, flashy beads, necklaces, and other bagatelles. Queen Hatshepsut's commercial venture was a great success, for the court reporters boasted that no king had ever been presented with such opulent possessions.

It should be noted that Queen Hatshepsut's fleet had brought back cinnamon, among other valuable commodities. The exact origin of this ancient spice is uncertain, since cinnamon trees are not indigenous to Somaliland or indeed to any part of Africa. According to the historian J. I. Miller there are indications that as early as the second millennium B.C. cassia and cinnamon from China and Southeast Asia may have been brought from Indonesia to Madagascar in primitive outrigger canoes, along an archaic connection by water known as the "Cinnamon Route." These aromatic barks were then transported northward along the East African coast to the Nile Valley and the land of Punt.

The Arabian traders who supplied cassia and cinnamon protected their business interests by deliberately

TRANSPORTING A MYRRH TREE (QUEEN HATSHEPSUT'S PUNT EXPEDITION)

shrouding the sources of their products in mystery. Consequently, the ancient Greeks and Romans held the most preposterous ideas concerning the origin of these Eastern spices. Herodotus, the noted Greek historian of the fifth century B.C., passing on information he had presumably received from the Arabs, stated that cassia grew in shallow swamps, the borders of which were protected by ferocious winged animals resembling powerful bats, which uttered piercing cries.

A PRIMITIVE INCENSE OFFERING

Herodotus gave an even more extraordinary account of the harvest of cinnamon on the mountain peaks somewhere in the neighborhood of Arabia. Large birds were said to carry the cinnamon twigs to their nests, which were attached with mud to steep cliffs, inaccessible to man. To harvest the cinnamon, the legend continued, large pieces of fresh donkey meat were placed near the precipitous haunts of these huge creatures, which seized the heavy chunks of carcass with avidity and carried them up to their nests. These lofty perches, not having been built to support such a weight, would collapse to the ground. The natives would then hurriedly collect the cinnamon and take it to the trading centers where, due to its scarcity and alleged dangers of harvest, it was sold at a very high price.

For many centuries the deceitful Arab merchants maintained a strict monopoly in Oriental spices by pretending that cassia and cinnamon came from Africa and deliberately discouraging the Mediterranean importers from making direct contact with the lands that really produced these lucrative commodities— China, India, and Southeast Asia. By reporting harrowing tales to demoralize competition and keeping

MEASURING HEAPS OF INCENSE
In the twelfth century B.C. King Rameses III had a special building constructed near Thebes to store incense for the worship of Amon.

Camel, 1477

consumers and producers apart, they were able to perpetuate probably the best-kept trade secret of all time. The geographical location of the Arabs made them natural middlemen, and it is understandable that they were reluctant to see the profitable spice trade slip from their grasp. It was not until the first century A.D. that the great Roman scholar Pliny pointed out that the Arabian yarns had been fabricated to inflate the prices of these exotic Eastern commodities.

In ancient times spices were very valuable articles of exchange and trade, like precious metals, pearls, and jewels, as confirmed by a number of passages in the Bible. For example, consider the story of Joseph and his brothers in Genesis 37:25. The young Joseph was his father's favorite. Jealousy turned into hate, and the brothers decided to kill him, but: "they sat down to eat bread: and they lifted up their eyes and looked, and, behold, a company of Ishmeelites came from Gilead with their camels bearing spicery and balm and myrrh, going to carry it down to Egypt." Joseph was sold for twenty pieces of silver to these spice traders from Gilead, beyond Jordan, who were traveling to the court of the pharaoh to sell their wares. Another important reference to the use of spices in the Bible is found in II Chronicles 9:1 in a mention of a journey the Queen of Sheba made to King Solomon in Jerusalem (about 950 B.C.) to develop and maintain trade relations. She was concerned with the menacing competition of a joint trade alliance between Kings Solomon of Israel and Hiram of Tyre that permitted Phoenician ships built of cedar from Lebanon to trade along the Red Sea shores and in the Indian Ocean, a development that threatened the queen's maritime and entrepôt trade.

Early Chinese influence (from about 2700 B.C.?)

Turning to another part of the world, we find that spices and herbs were used at a very early date in China, although ancient reports in available records are shrouded in mythology and superstition.

According to time-honored legends Shen Nung, the "Divine Cultivator," first tiller of the soil, and founder of Chinese medicine, is said to have discovered the curative virtues of herbs and established the practice of holding markets for the exchange of various commodities. About 2700 B.C. (?), according to ancient myths, he is alleged to have written the *Pen Ts'ao Ching*, or *The Classic Herbal*, the earliest treatise on medicine, which mentioned more than a hundred medicinal plants, among them the spice cassia under the name of *kwei*. It is related in Chinese folk tradition that Shen Nung used to pound plants, grasses, and barks with a red stick, then test their properties on himself, sometimes taking as many as twelve poisons a day during this experimentation. It should be noted, however, that modern scholars, such as F. N. L Poynter and H. L. Li, tell us there is no evidence whatsoever to justify the old-fashioned ideas concerning the tremendous antiquity of Chinese medicine; they hold the opinion that the *Pen Ts'ao Ching*, although containing much herbal lore going back several centuries B.C.,

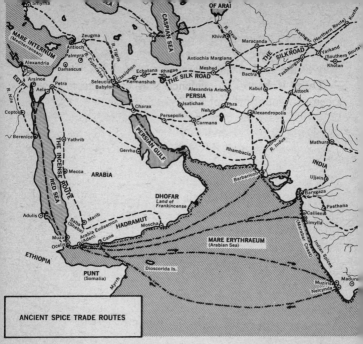

ANCIENT SPICE TRADE ROUTES

was compiled by some unknown authors in the late Han dynasty, about the first century A.D.; furthermore, that the legendary figure Shen Nung could not have written anything, as there was no written language in his day. The most comprehensive and celebrated Chinese herbal, entitled *Pen Ts'ao Kang Mu,* was compiled by Li Shih Chen and first published in A.D. 1596.

The first authentic record of the use of cassia (*kwei*) in China may be found in the *Ch'u Ssu* (*Elegies of Ch'u*), written in the fourth century B.C. *Ginger (chiang)* was mentioned even earlier by the philosopher Confucius (551–479 B.C.) in his *Analects*.

Despite the lack of clearness concerning the ancient use of spices in China, it is known that cassia was utilized at a very early date in Egyptian embalming. Since it did not grow in Egypt or Arabia, it seems logical that this aromatic bark must have been used even earlier in China, where it was native and was cultivated probably centuries before it ever found its way to the land of the pharaohs.

There is historical evidence that cassia must have been an important spice in south China as early as 216 B.C., when the province "Kweilin," meaning "Cassia Forest," was founded. The name Kwei River, in this same province of south China, becomes Cassia River when translated.

Seasonings from India and nutmeg and cloves native to the Moluccas (Spice Islands) were introduced into China at a very early date. A reliable tradition holds that Chinese courtiers in the third century B.C. were required to carry cloves in their mouths to sweeten their breath when addressing the emperor.

During the fifth century A.D. ginger plants were grown in pots and carried aboard Oriental vessels on long sea voyages between China and Southeast Asia to provide fresh food and prevent scurvy.

Mesopotamian contributions (during the first millennium B.C.)

Ancient cuneiform records concerning spices have been found in Mesopotamia in the fertile Tigris and

HINDU PERFUMER
MIXING SPICES

Euphrates valleys, where many aromatic plants were known. Sumerian clay tablets of medical literature dating from the third millennium B.C. mention various odoriferous plants, including thyme.

The increased use in medicine of drugs of vegetable origin (from herbs) instead of surgery may have been encouraged in ancient Mesopotamia by the very drastic decrees threatening unsuccessful surgeons if an operation failed. The Code of Hammurabi, of about 1700 B.C., stipulated that if a surgeon should be found responsible for a patient's death, the surgeon's hands were to be amputated.

A scroll of cuneiform writing from the great library in Nineveh, established by King Ashurbanipal of Assyria (668–633 B.C.), records a long list of aromatic plants, among them thyme, sesame, cardamom, turmeric, saffron, poppy, garlic, cumin, anise, coriander, silphium, dill, and myrrh. The Assyrians utilized sesame at a very early date as a vegetable oil.

The luxurious and refined habits of royalty in Assyria traditionally involved the use of large quantities of perfume and aromatics. The immoral and effeminate monarch Sardanapalus (identified by some as Ashurbanipal) is reputed to have allowed his passion for cosmetics free rein, thereby emphasizing his penchant to dress and paint himself like a woman; when threatened by the rapid advance of a ruthless enemy, he is said to have ordered a pile of aromatic woods to be lighted and to have placed himself upon it with his concubines and treasures, to be suffocated by the fragrant smoke.

Neighboring Babylonia was ruled by King Merodach-baladan II (721–710 B.C.). The peaceful hobby of this fierce soldier was horticulture, and in his royal gardens he cultivated sixty-four different species of plants. He wrote what may have been the world's first treatise on vegetable gardens, with precise instructions concerning the cultivation of a long list of plants including such spices and herbs as cardamom, coriander, garlic, thyme, saffron, and turmeric.

Babylonia had become the center of a religious cult of systematized sorcery, based on cosmic magic, revering the deity Sin, the ancient medical god of the moon, who was believed to control the growth of medicinal plants. The alleged medically potent parts of such herbs, therefore, were never allowed to be exposed to the rays of the sun but were harvested instead by moonlight, when magic healing potions were prepared.

By the sixth century B.C. onions, garlic, and shallots had become popular condiments in Persia, even among the poorer classes. During the early part of the reign of King Cyrus (559–529 B.C.) there is a record of a wholesale purchase by a grocer of 395,000 bunches of garlic.

As a consequence of their conquest and occupation of Egypt, the Persians became familiar with onions and garlic, long prized by the Egyptians, and had learned to produce essential oils from roses, lilies, coriander, and saffron.

Sesame seed, however, was too expensive for the average Persian laborer, since two months of his pay were required to purchase one bushel of the seed. Oil of sesame was used by the rich as a food, ointment, and medicine and in the ceremonial lamps in the temples. Because most regions of Persia were too hot for the cultivation of olive trees, sesame seed oil was the only available substitute for animal fats.

During the fifth century B.C. King Darius I of Persia received an annual tribute of over sixty thousand pounds of frankincense from the Arabs.

India, a center of spice origins (during the first millennium B.C.)

Some of the spices grown in India today—long

pepper, black pepper, cinnamon, tumeric, and cardamom—have been known there for thousands of years.
Excavations in the Indus Valley reveal that herbs and
spices had been used even before about 1000 B.C.,
when the sacred Ayurvedic texts, or lore of prayer and
sacrificial formulas of the Brahmanical system of religious belief, were formulated. The medical writings of
both Charaka (first century A.D.) and Susruta II
(second century A.D.) make frequent references to
uses of herbs and spices covering the period back to
about 500 B.C. Susruta II enumerated over seven
hundred drugs of plant origin, including cinnamon,
cardamom, ginger, turmeric, and various kinds of pepper.

Susruta the older (fourth century B.C.?) was famous
primarily as a surgeon. He recommended that the bed
sheets of a patient, as well as the sickroom where an
operation was to be performed, be fumigated with
the pungent vapors of white mustard, bdellium, and
other aromatic plants to ward off malignant spirits;
after the operation he recommended that a sesame
poultice be applied to the wound—recommendations
that may have foreshadowed the antiseptic theories of
modern times.

Various spices such as cardamom, ginger, black
pepper, cumin, and mustard seed were included in the
ancient Susruta *mushkakadigana,* or herbal medicines,
prescribed to remove fat and to cure urinary complaints,
piles, and jaundice.

In the Ayurvedic system of medicine, based on the
earliest Brahmanic texts, certain spices such as cloves
and cardamom were to be wrapped in betel-nut leaves
and chewed after meals to increase the flow of saliva
and aid digestion. All fetid odors were then supposed to
disappear as the breath became fragrant. It was suggested that one lie down for a while on the left side after
chewing the spices.

Since the spices cardamom and turmeric, indigenous to India, were cultivated as early as the eighth century B.C. in the gardens of Babylon, the propagating material or seeds of these spices must have been introduced to Babylonia from India far back in time.

Increased use of spices in Greece and Rome (331 B.C. to A.D. 641)

Alexander extended Greek influence throughout the lands that had been the Persian Empire, including Egypt. Starting in 331 B.C., his conquests extended through Turkistan, Afghanistan, Pakistan, and northwestern India, including the valley of the Indus. Greek settlements and commercial posts were founded between the Mediterranean and India along the western section of the trade route which was to become known during the first century A.D. as the "Silk Road."

With his conquest of Egypt Alexander the Great founded the port of Alexandria, destined to become

The campaign of Alexander the Great in northern India in 326 B.C. led to increased botanical knowledge concerning spices and herbs.

GRECIAN PRIESTESS MAKING AROMATIC OFFERINGS

the most important trading center between the Mediterranean and the Indian Ocean, the gateway to the East, and a meeting place for commercial travelers of three continents.

The ancient Greeks imported Eastern spices like pepper, cassia, cinnamon, and ginger to the Mediterranean area, but they also consumed many herbs produced in neighboring countries. Anise, for example, was used in the kitchen, caraway and poppy seeds in the preparation of bread, fennel for seasoning vinegar sauces, coriander as a condiment in food and wine, mint as a flavoring in meat sauces, and inexpensive garlic was widely used by the rustic country people in much of their cooking. Because parsley and marjoram could prevent drunkenness, according to the Greeks, they were woven into the wreaths that decorated the drinkers' heads at their feasts.

Spices and herbs played an important role in ancient Greek medical science. Hippocrates (460–377 B.C.), known as the "Father of Medicine" and the framer of a code of medical ethics that he imposed on his followers (the Hippocratic oath), wrote many treatises or medicinal plants, including saffron, cinnamon, thyme, coriander, mint, and marjoram. He stressed that great care should be given to the preparation of herbs for medical use. Some should be gathered early, some late; some should be dried; some should be crushed. Of the four hundred simples, or herbal remedies, utilized by Hippocrates, at least half are in use today.

The noted Greek philosopher and scientist Theophrastus (372–287 B.C.), sometimes called the "Father of Botany," had been a fellow pupil with Alexander the Great under Aristotle, and later utilized botanical information that was gathered during Alexander's India campaign. He wrote two books, *On Odors* and *An Enquiry into Plants,* that summarized the knowledge of his time concerning spices and herbs. In the latter,

Theophrastus made the important, fundamental obser-
vation that the flower must always precede the fruit,
that is, that a fruit is the product of a flower. He also
wrote treatises dealing with aromas, weariness, swoon-
ing, paralysis, weather, and theriaca (these were antidotes to the bites of poisonous animals and were
composed of numerous peculiar ingredients such as
opium, the flesh of vipers, aromatic gums, and spices).
He pointed out that most fragrant spice plants came
from those hot regions in Asia that were abundantly exposed to the sun.

The outstanding Greek author on botany and medicine of the period, however, was Dioscorides, the
leading Greek physician of the first century A.D. and
author of *De Materia Medica,* which for fifteen hundred years was to be the standard work on botany and
medicine in both the East and the West. The original
manuscript of this herbal was not illustrated. A magnificent transcription of it, the "Vienna Dioscorides"
or Codex dedicated to the Princess Anicia Juliana at
Byzantium about A.D. 512—now preserved in the Aus-
trian National Library in Vienna—contains numerous
illuminated illustrations, mainly of medicinal plants

though also of animals, copied from Arabic, Turkish, and Hebrew sources dating back as far as the first century B.C.

Dioscorides' careful and sober judgments concerning medicinal remedies, in which he mentioned all the herbs and spices known at the time of Christ, were based more on systematic analysis than were the works of his predecessors, whose writings were founded largely on magic and superstition.

Silphium was the most famous drug of the ancient Mediterranean world. The plant of the same name, from which the drug was obtained, grew chiefly in the hills near Cyrene (Libya), in North Africa, where it flourished between the seventh and second centuries B.C. Large quantities were exported from Cyrene to Greece, and often it was sold by weight at the same rate as silver. By the first century A.D., however, the plant had virtually become extinct, possibly due to overgrazing, since it was important as cattle fodder.

The botanical identification of ancient silphium is not clear. It is generally believed to have been *Ferula tingitana*, a sweet-smelling umbelliferous plant with thick stalks and roots that grows today as a rarity in Cyrenaica. The juice of this plant was known as "laserwort juice."

The name silphium has also been applied, perhaps erroneously, to a foul-smelling Persian plant of the carrot family (genus *Ferula*), whose roots and rhizomes are the source of the medicinal gum resin asafetida. It was carried westward by Alexander the Great during the fourth century B.C. and is known as "stink-finger" in Afghanistan. As the silphium of Cyrene became extinct, asafetida may have gradually replaced it as a drug.

The genus *Silphium,* a name given by Linnaeus in 1737 to a group of hardy North American herbs of the family *Compositae,* occurs today in the Mississippi Valley and eastward, but these plants are not related to the silphium of the Greeks.

An extremely versatile herb, silphium was in great demand by the Greeks for use as a condiment, food preservative, gum resin, edible vegetable, and in medicine. As a condiment silphium was grated over meats and cabbage, as cheese is today. The stalk was considered an appetizing vegetable delicacy. As a drug the plant was an all-inclusive therapeutic agent, prescribed for fevers, coughs, lumbago, mange, and diseases of the eye; it was applied to remove corns and ingested to cure toothache, promote menstruation, dissolve blood clots, and eliminate worms. It was also employed as an antidote for scorpion bites.

The residents of Cyrene advertised and promoted silphium to such an extent that visitors occasionally tired of hearing about it. Antiphanes, an Athenian poet who visited Cyrene during the fourth century B.C., wrote: "I will not sail back to the place [Cyrene] from which we were carried away, for I want to say goodbye to all horses, silphium, chariots, silphium stalks, steeplechasers, silphium leaves, fevers, and silphium juice."

The economic importance of silphium in ancient Cyrene, a Spartan colony, is recorded on the inside of a Laconian *kylix* (cup), probably made by Cyrenaic potters in the sixth century B.C., now in the Bibliothèque Nationale in Paris. It is believed to show King Arcesilas II of Cyrene himself supervising the weighing and loading of a ship with this renowned bygone herb.

Several ancient trade routes were used to transport spices and other luxury goods from India to the Western world, some by land, some by sea, some by a combination of the two. Among the oldest was the south-north sea route from the main ports on the west coast of India, including Muziris, Barygaza, and Barbaricon, through the Persian Gulf to Charax; then along the Arabian coast to Arabia Eudaemon (Aden) and up through the Red Sea to Egypt. From Charax alternate routes ran up the Euphrates and Tigris valleys to Seleucia, and from there to Antioch on the Mediterranean (see map page **34**).

From Barbaricon a land route led northward through the Indus Valley to Attock, thence up the Kabul River and over the Hindu Kush Mountains to Bactra. At this junction with the "Silk Road," the goods were transported westward through the city of Rhagae (Rayy, near modern Teheran) to Seleucia, thence north by the Euphrates River to Antioch, or south to the Persian Gulf and then on Arab ships around Arabia up the Red Sea to Petra. A similar land route to the Indus Valley ran from Barygaza, north through Mathura to the Kabul River, and so to Bactra.

The "Silk Road," initially used during the first century A.D., began in China and passed westward either through Khotan on the southern route or Kucha on the northern route, both joining at Kashgar to proceed over the Pamir Mountains to Bactra and thence to Seleucia and the Mediterranean. From Bactra another important route ran northwest, by the Oxus River, through Khiva, just south of the Sea of Aral; thence westward by land to the Caspian Sea, across that sea, and then by land to the Black Sea and eventually to Byzantium. The object of this northern route was to avoid passage through Persia during periods of war with Rome.

The "Incense Route" used at an earlier period, ran from Hadramut in South Arabia northward to Petra, thence to the markets of Syria and Egypt.

Finally, as a result of the discovery in the first cen-

CASSIA IN CHINA From an illustration of 1671. The bark of this tree, *Cinnamomum cassia*, is one of the oldest known spices.

tury A.D. of the monsoons and their importance to ships under sail, there followed establishment of the direct sea route from ports in Roman Egypt—Berenice was one—to the pepper markets of the Malabar Coast of India.

Some early written reports about pepper appear in Pliny (first century A.D.), who thought that prices were much too high for this spice. For example, long pepper cost 15 denarii, white pepper, 7 denarii, and black pepper, 4 denarii a pound. One denarius was worth approximately sixteen U.S. cents.

During Pliny's time Rome developed an active spice trade with South Arabia and Somaliland and, by direct route, with India. In the Roman Empire the consumption of spices as food condiments soared. Critical observers blamed the constant drain of gold to the East on the high prices paid for silk, gems and pearls, ebony and sandalwood, balms and spices, and especially on the exorbitant cost of pepper. Pliny complained that by the time they reached Rome, spices were sold at one hundred times their original cost. Small in bulk, high in price, and in a steady demand, spices were especially desirable articles of commerce.

The balance of trade with India became very unfavorable to Rome, amounting to some twenty million denarii a year (roughly $3,200,000 U.S.), since large amounts of gold and silver were shipped to the East to pay for the costly imported commodities. This exchange situation has been confirmed by the numerous ancient gold and silver Roman coins of the first century A.D. that have recently been unearthed on the west coast of India. Red coral from the western Mediterranean, valued in India as a charm against disease and danger, was one of the few costly commodities exchanged by Rome for Oriental goods.

The prices of these imported luxuries had gradually become exorbitant owing to losses by shipwrecks, storms, robberies, and the insatiable greed of the Arabian middlemen. In 24 B.C. an effort was made to incorporate the South Arabian spice kingdoms into the Roman Empire of Augustus, and Aelius Gallus, prefect of Egypt, was appointed to lead an Arabian campaign. It was a disaster. From the beginning, everything went wrong. While crossing the Red Sea, many ships ran aground and sank. The fleet landed too far north, and long distances had to be covered by foot. Then instead of following the well-established "Incense Route," about 120 miles inland, the Roman troops confined their trek to the coastal area. Six months later they had not yet reached the region of present-day Aden, heat stroke was prevalent, and a retreat was ordered. The geographer and historian Strabo pointed out that this defeat was due not to the enemy but to sickness, fatigue, hunger, and bad roads. Thus for the time being South Arabia remained undefeated.

At one time, several centuries B.C., spices were actually grown in the kingdom of Sheba in south-. western Arabia Felix, including some exotics imported from the Orient. This was made possible through irrigation from the dam at Marib that burst (or was destroyed as a result of wars) during the sixth century A.D., following which event the surrounding area now known as the Yemen became the desert it is today.

During the age of the Roman emperor Claudius, in about A.D. 40, a Greek merchant named Hippalus discovered the full power of the vast wind systems of the Indian Ocean, the monsoons, observing that they reversed their direction twice a year. The southwest monsoon prevailed between April and October, favorable for the trip from Egypt to India, and the northeast monsoon, between October and April, favoring the return voyage from the Orient. The word monsoon is derived from the Arabic *mawsim,* meaning season. It may be that for many centuries the variations of the

MONSOON WINDS PROMOTED THE SPICE TRADE
Seasonal monsoon winds, which affected historic sailing routes in the Indian Ocean, were discovered by Hippalus about A.D. 40. The prevailing winds blow from the southwest from April to October and from the northeast from October to April.

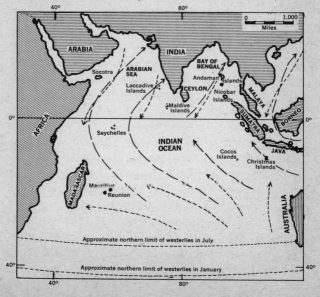

monsoons had been both capitalized on by the Arabs and carefully concealed by them from other nations. By taking advantage of these winds, Hippalus showed that it was possible to make the round trip between Berenice, on the Egyptian coast of the Red Sea, and the pepper-producing Malabar Coast of India in less than a year, a voyage that had previously taken at least two years. The discovery of the monsoons was destined to reduce the importance of Arabia's overland spice routes and contribute to the financial ruin of her once-opulent cities. Until the era of steamships, the monsoons were to dominate European trade with the Orient.

Having learned the fundamental secrets of the monsoons, the Romans built ships on a vastly increased scale and eventually broke the Arab monopoly of the Indian trade. Toward the end of the first century, their increased commerce with India resulted in an even greater indulgence in spices and further culinary excesses on the part of the Romans. Apicius, a well-known gourmet and epicure of the time who is reputed to have spent vast sums to satisfy his craving for exotic foods, wrote ten books on the art of cooking. His culinary experiences were compiled several centuries later in a work entitled *De Re Coquinaria*. His recipes included numerous spices intended to preserve food, aid the digestion, and improve the flavor of the dull Roman fare. One of Apicius' favorite desserts included poppy seed and honey. He featured not only such imported spices as pepper, turmeric, and ginger in his recipes, but also various temperate herbs then cultivated in the Roman Empire: anise, basil, caraway, coriander, fennel, garlic, bay leaves, cumin, dill, parsley, marjoram, and poppy seed.

The Romans were the most extravagant users of aromatics in history. Lavish use of spices was not confined to the kitchen but extended to fumigation and cosmetics. Huge supplies of aromatic spices, for example, were strewn along the path behind the funeral urn bearing the ashes of the commander Germanicus during the first century A.D. It was quite customary for men to be heavily perfumed and even the legionaries reeked of the fragrances of the East.

Spice-flavored wines were in demand, for spices were supposed to add "heat" to the bouquet. Spice-scented balms and oils were popular for use after the bath. The addition of spices to these unguents thickened them and rendered them more fragrant. Even lamp oil was enhanced by pungent aromatics, apparently to keep harmful vapors away. After a feast many Romans would sleep on costly saffron-filled pillows in the belief that they would avoid a hangover. Since spices were considered to have medicinal properties, they were utilized also in poultices and healing plasters.

During the rule of Domitian, an emperor whose torment of the Christians culminated in a reign of terror and horror, John, a prophet of Ephesus, mentioned

MUCH CINNAMON AND FRANKINCENSE LOST IN THE FALL OF BABYLON

In Revelations 18:11-13, written about A.D. 90, the prophet John symbolically predicted the coming downfall of sinful Rome. To avoid persecution by the emperor Domitian, he substituted the name of ancient Babylon for that of Rome, as he obscurely described how the merchants of the earth would mourn over their losses of merchandise, including cinnamon and frankincense, upon the destruction of the city.

spices in his prediction of the downfall of Rome (Revelations 18:11–13, written about A.D. 90). For reasons of security, knowing that only thus could he avoid persecution for his references to the Romans' luxuries and ungodliness, he deliberately wrote obscurely and metaphorically, pretending that he was describing ancient Babylon instead of Rome.

The discovery of the monsoons had led to a sharp decline in the prices of aromatics, owing to the increased supplies of these products. Mark 14:3–6 tells of a woman's anointing Jesus with spikenard, a fragrant ointment extracted from the stems and roots of a small herbaceous plant, *Nardostachys jatamansi*, from northern India. Some of those present were indignant at this waste—the spikenard could have been sold for more than three hundred pence (about $48 U.S.) to be given to the poor. Pliny's remark, some sixty years later, that the cost of spikenard had decreased from 300 denarii to about 100 denarii a pound gives a good indication of how the value of this exquisite perfume was affected by the Greek discovery of the monsoons.

The increase in direct commerce between Rome and India brought a halt to the long-standing subterfuge of Arab traders. In the past no accurate information concerning the sources of cloth, precious stones, timbers, and spices had been allowed to reach the merchants in Egypt, but now the veil of secrecy was lifted. A fascinating description of trade and travel in the Indian Ocean and Arabian Sea was written about A.D. 90 by an unknown Greek sea captain, who recorded objectively and vividly (in a treatise known as *The Periplus of the Erythraean Sea* [*Sailing around the Indian Ocean*]) the local conditions, imports, and exports of the East African, Arabian, and Indian ports. The safest harbors were described in detail, full instructions were given as to where to anchor, how to

CONSTANTINOPLE
Official capital of the Eastern Roman, or Byzantine, Empire from A.D. 395 to 1453, Constantinople was for many centuries a focal point of spice trade routes between East and West.

avoid storms, and how the monsoons could be used advantageously. This vital information, which guided the traveler down the Red Sea, along the southern coasts of Arabia to northern India, and south to the pepper ports of the Malabar Coast, served to stimulate trade between the Mediterranean region and the East.

The extension of the Roman Empire to the northern side of the Alps brought the Goths, Vandals, and Huns of those regions into contact for the first time with pepper and other spices from the East. Many barbarians, Goths in particular, served in the Roman armies or sought asylum in the empire. These barbarians already were familiar with a few temperate herbs like caraway, onions, rosemary, and thyme. They gradually were attracted by the luxuries of Rome's higher standard of living and learned to appreciate such sophisticated material refinements as Oriental spices. When Alaric, the Gothic king and conqueror, appeared with his uncivilized hordes before the walls of Rome in September 408, he was well aware of the value of pepper, then worth its weight in silver. As tribute to prevent the sacking of the city, he demanded 5,000 pounds of gold, 30,000 pounds of silver, 4,000 silk tunics, 3,000 valuable skins, and 3,000 pounds of pepper. During this first siege, the beleaguered Roman citizens managed to meet Alaric's exorbitant demands, thus temporarily postponing the inevitable; but Rome fell to the invading Goths during Alaric's third siege, on August 24, 410, an event that initiated the collapse of the Western Roman Empire.

In 330 the emperor Constantine founded the city of Constantinople, built on the site of ancient Byzantium, which was destined to become the new capital of the Eastern Roman or Byzantine Empire. Caravan and sea routes began to develop around this rising metropolis. During this period two spices, cloves and nutmegs, grown on the distant Moluccas became known for the first time in the West. Indonesian sailors had brought these precious condiments to eastern India, China, and Ceylon, whence they found their way into Arabian and Roman trade routes.

One of the first westerners to visit the East was the sixth-century merchant and traveler Cosmas Indicopleustes from Alexandria, who visited India and Ceylon. He later became a monk and in about 548 wrote a book entitled *Topographia Christiana,* in which he described the importance of the spice trade in Ceylon, a prominent trading center for the silk, cloves, sweet aloes, and many valuable commodities imported from China and other Far Eastern regions. He also stopped at Malabar in India and in his book described accurately how pepper was harvested in the hill country, including the manner in which this pungent spice was dried and prepared for the market.

Arab domination: The Muslim Curtain
(A.D. 641 to 1096)

The Roman spice trade was vitally affected by the fall of the empire, which may be said to have culminated in the occupation of Alexandria by the Arabs in 641. The well-organized trading in commodities between India and Rome, which had been skillfully initiated by the emperor Augustus during the end of the first century B.C., was brought to an end by the irresistible onslaught of Islam.

Time-honored trade routes were interrupted as the swiftness of the Arab conquest shattered Mediterranean unity and brought confusion, despair, and stagnation to its commerce. Gold, now controlled by the Arabs, became extremely scarce. Not until the twelfth century did it resume its important role in the European monetary system, and then only after the Mediterranean was reopened to commerce and spices again became available.

Mohammed (A.D. 570–632), who established the principles of Islam in the Koran, was not only a great prophet, legislator, and founder of the religion that bears his name, but was also an experienced spice merchant. As a youth he worked with Meccan tradesmen who dealt in spices with Syria and South Arabia. Subsequently he became a camel driver and caravan leader for a widow of means named Khadija, fifteen years his senior, whom he married in 595. For several years, before he claimed direct divine revelation and began his prophetic career, he was a partner in a shop in Mecca that traded in such agricultural commodities as myrrh, frankincense, and Oriental spices.

By the middle of the eighth century the great empire founded by Mohammed extended some seven thousand miles—from Spain in the west to the borders

of China in the east. Muslim influence was spread to Ceylon and Java, for the most part by a roving Arab trading population. Having won religious victories in India by the sword, Mohammedan missionaries settled on the Malabar Coast and became spice traders.

The important city of Basra was founded at the head of the Persian Gulf in 635, at the point where the Tigris and Euphrates rivers meet. This thriving port, celebrated in *The Arabian Nights*, was destined to serve as a trading center for commodities from India, Arabia, Turkey, and Persia.

During the four centuries following the death of Mohammed, his worshipers developed a flourishing civilization. The Mohammedans were not only skillful in trade and commerce, but were also outstanding scientists for their time; they perfected, for example, the ancient method of extraction of flower scents from blossoms and herbs by means of cold fat (enfleurage), as well as several techniques of distillation of essential oils from aromatic plants. The English word alembic is derived from the Arabic *al-anbiq,* meaning "a still."

Avicenna (980–1037), the Arab physician and philosopher who wrote *The Canon,* a system of medicine long regarded in the Orient and Occident as a medical textbook of the highest authority, is also said to have founded the Graeco-Arabic school of medicine. Avicenna's medical writings were considered authoritative and were used in European universities up to the seventeenth century.

Rhazes (850–925), who became chief of the great hospital in Baghdad, was another famous Mohammedan physician and the prolific author of a voluminous encyclopedia of medicine and therapeutic knowledge. The Latin translations of the works of both Rhazes and Avicenna exerted a profound influence on European medicine long after Mohammedan military power had waned. Rhazes was also noted for his resourcefulness. Tradition has it that he selected the site for the hospital in Baghdad by hanging pieces of meat in the four corners of the city to find where putrefaction was the slowest—thereby recognizing a connection between putrefaction and disease.

By the ninth century sugar was being produced in Persia and utilized by Arab physicians to formulate aromatic syrups, flavoring extracts, and other palatable elixirs, many of which included spices (our English word julep comes from the Arabic *julāb*). Perfume-saturated waters such as rose water were produced on a commercial scale at Shiraz in Persia as crude distillation methods were improved. The nocturnal journey to the celestial spheres ascribed to the Prophet Mohammed gave rise to a cycle of fanciful anecdotes that became highly popular. According to one of these epic legends, emphasizing the significance attached to fragrant odors, the Prophet is supposed to have stated: "When I was taken up to heaven some of my sweat fell to earth and from it sprang the rose; who smells the scent of the rose smells Mohammed."

Following the example of the Arabs, especially after the period of the Crusades, the European spicers and apothecaries of the Middle Ages prepared their spiced drinks and other semipharmaceutical preparations by mixing sweet syrups of violets and roses with spices such as ginger, pepper, nutmegs, cinnamon, saffron, cardamom, and herbs from monastic gardens.

The increasing invasions from the north by the Lombards and Goths and the resulting disruption of the Roman economy in Italy caused Constantinople, or "the new Rome," to become the eastern capital of the Roman world from the time of its foundation, about 330, until 1453, when it was captured by the Turks. From the seventh to the eleventh centuries a new trade route was developed northward from Constantinople, for the former channels had been cut off by the Moslems and barbarians. Following the development of commerce with the Hanseatic League in northern and central Europe, goods were transported on the Russian rivers Don, Dnieper, and Volga, by way of Kiev and Nizhni Novgorod, to the Baltic Sea. Some early but limited Baltic trade in such spices as pepper, cinnamon, and ginger was carried on with England in exchange for wool. By the end of the seventh century, an English pepper tax had been imposed.

Herb plantings fostered by Charlemagne (A.D. 812) and sustained by medieval monasteries

Although small physic (medicinal-plant) gardens had been known in Europe for several centuries before his time, Charlemagne (742–814), king of the Franks and emperor of the West, was an important figure in the development of herbs. A patron of literature, art, and science, he organized for the first time in his realm larger systematic plantings of temperate condimental plants. In 812 Charlemagne ordered a number of useful plants, among them anise, fennel, fenugreek, and flax, to be grown on the imperial farms in Germany.

Information concerning spices in Europe during the so-called Dark Ages (from 641, the fall of Alexandria, to 1096, the First Crusade) is rather scarce. The use of Oriental spices was drastically curtailed in the normal diet of Europeans north of the Alps. Only small lots could be obtained by ecclesiastical groups and a few merchants; for example, in 716 Chilperic II, king of the Franks, authorized the delivery to the monastery of Corbie, in Normandy, of merchandise from Fos that included one pound of cinnamon, two pounds of cloves, and thirty pounds of pepper. In 745 Gemmulus, a Roman deacon, sent a gift of pepper and cinnamon to Boniface, the Archbishop of Mainz. During the ninth century aromatic condiments, including pepper and cloves, were used to season fish in the Benedictine monastery at St. Gall in Switzerland.

In England the Statutes of Ethelred, at the end of the tenth century, required Easterlings (East Germans from the Baltic and Hanseatic towns) to pay tribute that included ten pounds of pepper for the privilege of trading with London merchants. Some authorities suggest that the word sterling (English currency) is derived from "Easterlings," the early German spice traders in England who sold goods from the East. The sterling silver penny of medieval England is thought to have been coined by these Hanse merchants.

Even apart from their use by church officials, there must have been a limited consumption of Oriental spices in Europe during the tenth century, for the Moorish physician and merchant Ibrahim Ibn Yaacub, following his visit to Mainz in 973, reported that such Eastern condiments as pepper, ginger, and cloves could be purchased in this remote corner of the Western world. These costly Eastern commodities may have been brought to Mainz by Jewish traveling merchants known as "Radanites," who, to a limited extent, kept international trade channels open between East and West during the eighth, ninth, and tenth centuries. Although ordinary trade between the Is-

AN EARLY EUROPEAN HERB GARDEN

lamic world and Christian Europe was blocked, the Radanite traders, tolerated by both Mohammedans and Christians, enjoyed freedom of movement. These Jewish intermediaries transported woolen cloth, furs, Frankish swords, eunuchs, and white female slaves from Europe to the Orient; on the return trip they took back to Spain and France such Oriental luxuries as musk, aloes, pearls, precious stones, and various spices, including cinnamon, cloves, and pepper.

Throughout the Dark Ages the cultivation of herbs and spices in Europe was taken care of by the Church, for the most part in Benedictine monastery gardens. Early medieval botanical knowledge was recorded by St. Hildegard (1098–1179), a German nun famed for her visions and prophesies, who founded the convent of Rupertsberg and wrote the Latin treatise *Physica*. Herbs—sage and thyme, for instance—were locally grown in western Europe, as were such aromatic and medicinal plants as anise, fennel, parsley, and coriander, introduced from the Italian Benedictine garden at Monte Cassino. Spiced drinks formed an important part of monastic medicine.

Religious herb and spice feasts formerly celebrated by the Goths were later modified by the Christian Church. Many of the primitive superstitions stemming from early Teutonic times were thus continued, like tying bundles of herbs to stable doors to keep the witches out and wearing amulets of wolf dung to ward off disease.

During the Middle Ages the ancient lore of herbal remedies was perpetuated by sorcery-practicing herb women, whose pagan techniques displeased the Church. The mixtures prepared by these witchlike quacks, mingling hocus-pocus with scraps of common sense, ranged from harmless folk remedies to venomous abortives, injurious love potions, disgusting elixirs, and outright poisons.

With the advent of Arabian travelers and geographers more information became available concerning the areas where spices were produced. Ali al-Masudi, a tenth-century historian, described in his *Meadows of Gold* the vast cultivated plantings of the *maharaj,* or king of the East Indian Archipelago, whose produce included cloves, nutmegs, mace, cardamom, sweet aloes, and camphor.

WITCHES, HERBS, AND MAGIC POTIONS
In the Middle Ages, European superstition linked witches and herb women with magic potions, which allegedly included snakes, chickens, and herbs such as anise.

GENOA
Toward the end of the thirteenth century Genoa enjoyed a great boom in trade, of which spices formed an important part.

Eastern trade reopened by the Crusades (eleventh, twelfth, and thirteenth centuries)

The First Crusade took place in 1096 and in 1099 Jerusalem was conquered. Until then the West had relied on scattered reports from occasional travelers for information concerning the Near East. Now thousands of pilgrims described the mode of living in Syria and Palestine. Many Westerners developed a taste for Eastern luxuries.

Apart from the religious aspects of the Crusades, interest was stimulated in their economic benefits. Shippers in Venice and Genoa in Italy were promised landing facilities to establish trading centers on the shores of the Holy Land, provided these landing points could be captured and secured. This was the beginning of a trade through which food, clothing, wool, and metal for the crusading soldiers were exchanged for such goods as fruit, jewelry, and spices, which were brought back to Italy.

The high point of Venice's enrichment came during the Fourth Crusade, in 1204, when having transported Crusaders and pilgrims to Constantinople, Venetian shippers participated in the barbaric plundering of that city. Priceless booty of the dismembered Greek Empire contributed to the wealth and commercial importance of Venice.

The efficiency of the trading merchants led to basic changes in European eating and cooking habits. These were not restricted to the upper classes but slowly made their way down through the middle class, owing to the unprecedented availability of imports from the Holy Land—dates, figs, raisins, almonds, lemons, oranges, sugar, rice, and various Oriental spices including pepper, nutmeg, cloves, and cardamom. The great economic growth and wealth in such Italian ports as Genoa, Pisa, and Venice were largely due to changes in commerce brought about by the Crusades.

Spices played an important role in this commercial prosperity that not only brought East and West together, but culminated eventually in the Renaissance. Thus pepper, cloves, cinnamon, and cardamom can be said to have contributed indirectly to the works of Michelangelo, Titian, Raphael, and Leonardo da Vinci.

By the time the stream of pilgrims waned, the standard of living in Europe had improved immensely and what had previously been considered luxuries from the East were regarded as necessities. The economic gains of the Italian shipowners soon developed into a European trade monopoly that included merchants of Nuremberg, Augsburg, Bordeaux, and Toulouse, as well as of cities farther to the north, such as Antwerp and Bruges, which for a time became the most important commercial center for northwestern Europe.

During the reign of Henry II (in 1180) a pepperers' guild of wholesale merchants was established in London; it was subsequently incorporated into a spicers' guild, succeeded in 1429 by the present Grocers' Company. This guild was granted a charter by Henry VI to sell wholesale—*vendre en gros* (hence our word grocer)—and to manage the trade in spices, drugs, and dyestuffs. This organization was given the exclusive power to "garble," that is, to cleanse, separate, and select spices and medicinal products. St. Anthony was the patron saint of the spicers, pepperers, and grocers.

The original spicers and pepperers were the forerunners of the apothecaries, who in turn were destined to become general medical practitioners. This sequence emphasizes the vital role that spices formerly played in Occidental medicine. For many centuries (from the fourth century B.C. to at least the seventeenth century A.D.) spices were among the most important ingredients of the *materia medica,* used as correctives of hot or cold "humors," at a time when an imbalance of these "humors" was thought to be the cause of all disease.

In the thirteenth century a pound of pepper cost the equivalent of 60 U.S. cents in Marseilles but over $1 in England. Peppercorns, counted out one by one, were accepted as currency to pay taxes, tolls, and rents, partly because of a shortage of gold and silver coins. Many European towns kept their accounts in pepper. Fortunate brides received pepper as a dowry.

By the late Middle Ages Oriental spices were valued roughly as follows: A pound of saffron cost the same as a horse; a pound of ginger, as much as a sheep; two pounds of mace would buy a cow. A German price table of 1393 lists a pound of nutmeg as worth seven fat oxen.

Despite the world inflation of recent years, spices five hundred years ago were relatively more expensive than today. However, when one considers the

Spices were in demand in medieval Europe to mask the unpleasant odor and taste of decomposing food.

wretched victuals of fifteenth-century Europe, it is easy to understand the extraordinary value placed on spices. Food was neither wholesome nor palatable. Cattle, slaughtered in October, were salted and kept until the following spring. Spices were believed to have a beneficial preservative action in meat. Potatoes were unknown and very few other vegetables could be obtained, either in or out of season. There were few lemons to flavor beverages, no sugar to sweeten them. Neither tea nor coffee nor chocolate was available. Spices, however, such as pepper, cinnamon, ginger, and cardamom, when mixed with the coarsest, dullest, even the most repulsive fare, could make it more palatable. Spices were used to camouflage bad flavors and odors, and it was also believed that their consumption would prevent illness. Spiced wines were popular; in fact, the more spices in the wine, the more delectable it was thought to be. But as sugar, coffee, tea, cocoa, and tobacco became available in the succeeding centuries, the demand for spices gradually decreased.

By the end of the thirteenth century unparalleled wealth had accumulated in Genoa and Venice. Merchandise arrived from northern Europe, the Mediterranean area, the Far East, and Africa, and these Italian ports made a profit on every transaction. Thanks partly to their favorable geographical location, partly to their increasing wealth and willingness to undertake great risks, the Venetians in particular enjoyed an unprecedented boom in trade, as an inexhaustible stream of merchandise—sacks of spices, pearls, precious stones, carpets, and other valuable goods—passed through their canals and customs houses en route from Asia to central Europe.

In the declining years of the Roman Empire, epidemics had been spreading, culminating in the dreadful plague during Justinian's reign (541), when it is said that from five to ten thousand deaths occurred daily over a period of several weeks in Constantinople alone. Although Europe had been in close contact with the Holy Land during the Crusades, no further serious outbreak of the plague took place until the fourteenth century, when the Black Death appeared in Italy, having

GARDENER HARVESTING HERBS, 1477

already devastated Asia and northern Africa. This ravaging disease killed approximately twenty-five million Europeans between 1347 and 1350, roughly one-fourth of the continent's entire population. Ships bringing precious luxuries such as spices from the East also introduced the dread bacillus of the plague, spread by inconspicuous but deadly rat fleas.

During the next four hundred years physicians treating the plague tried every imaginable means of self-protection against infection. Among the popular devices was an extraordinary, allegedly prophylactic costume consisting of a long, black leather gown, leather gloves, leather mask with glass-covered eyeholes, and long beak filled with spices or other aromatic materials to mask the odors and filter the malignant vapors. The pest-doctor carried a wand to feel the victim's pulse. Sponges were soaked with extracts of cinnamon and cloves and placed beneath the noses of the sick or dying. Rooms were fumigated with sage smoke. Saffron, garlic soup, and juniper wine were prescribed as medicines.

The search for spice routes and the age of discovery (fifteenth and sixteenth centuries)

About 1260 the brothers Nicolo and Maffeo Polo left Venice to visit business connections in the Crimea and to learn more of the sources of the precious stones and spices then arriving by caravan from the Far East. Their travels eventually took them to the court of Kublai Khan of Mongolia. The great khan gave them golden tablets and his complete protection and informed them magnanimously that he wished to enter into trade relations with Venice on terms very favorable to the Italians. In 1269 the Polos returned to Venice and two years later set out again for Asia, taking with them Nicolo's young son, Marco (1254–1324). Twenty-six years later, in 1297, three ragged

PLAGUE-DOCTOR'S COSTUME WITH SPICE-FILLED BEAK
Med-seventeenth century European costume worn by physicians attending plague patients. The gown, shirt, breeches, boots, and gloves were all made of leather. The long beaklike nose piece was filled with aromatic spices and the eyeholes were covered with glass.

figures turned up at the Polos' residence in Venice bringing with them, in the seams of their tattered clothing, pearls, diamonds, sapphires, rubies, and emeralds. They related many fantastic, unbelievable tales of the fabulous wealth of China and of the magnificence of Zaytun (Tsinkiang or Chuanchow in southeast China), an immense port that exported damask silk, satin fabrics, and many spices.

In 1298, during a war between Genoa and Venice, Marco Polo was captured in battle and imprisoned in Genoa for about a year. While in confinement he dictated the story of his travels to a fellow prisoner. In those memoirs Polo made frequent mention of spices. He reported that for every shipload of pepper that went to Alexandria, a hundred arrived in Zaytun. He described the pleasing flavor of the sesame oil of Afghanistan and the plants of ginger and cassia of Kain-du (the city of Peking), capital of Kublai Khan, where people drank a flavorful wine of rice and spices. He reported that the rich in Karazan ate meat pickled in salt and flavored with spices, while the poor had to be content with hash steeped in garlic; that in Hangchow an officer of the great khan had informed him that ten thousand pounds of pepper were brought into that heavily populated city every day. Remarkably observant, Polo described in realistic detail vast plantings of pepper, nutmegs, cloves, and other valuable spices he had seen growing in Java and in the islands of the China Sea, and the abundance of cinnamon, pepper, and ginger on the Malabar Coast of India. He mentioned many unusual Chinese achievements—elaborate buildings, huge cities, marble palaces, block printing, paper money, the mining of pit coal; told of fountains of liquid (petroleum) that burned miraculously; and described four-masted sailing vessels each carrying up to six thousand baskets of pepper.

After Marco Polo's release from captivity and return to Venice, he was frequently called on to repeat his accounts of the magnificence of the great khan, whose revenues consistently amounted to many millions in gold; in fact, Polo used the term millions so much in speaking of great wealth that he was given the nickname of "Marco Millioni."

At first only a few people believed his stories, but gradually European merchants realized that these faraway exotic and productive regions could be reached by ship. Marco Polo's vivid description of his extensive wanderings in effect raised the "Muslim Curtain" that had fallen between Asia and Europe for six centuries. He bridged the gap between East and West and stimulated the great Age of Exploration. While later explorers such as Columbus and Cook merely touched the coastal regions of the lands they discovered, Polo accurately described the inland continent of Asia and its people.

After the fall of Constantinople to the Turks in 1453, the need for a sea route to the Orient became more urgent than ever. The spread of the Ottoman Empire made old land routes to the sources of silk and spices unsafe; transiting caravans were paralyzed. The most punitive of all duties imposed by the Muslim rulers were reserved for the flourishing spice trade—the sultan of Egypt, for example, took as tariff one-third of the value of every cargo that entered his domain. European traders were bled white.

Prince Henry of Portugal, who in 1418 had established a naval college at Sagres, gave the greatest impetus to exploration for new routes to new lands. Believing that the economic future of his country depended on expansion of commerce, he called to his service the leading navigators, geographers, and astronomers of the day and inspired and equipped expeditions to find the Orient by sea. As all available knowledge of geography and navigation was accumulated and compiled, a vast improvement took place in their charts. With the aid of the mariner's compass, then coming into general use, the Portuguese mariners

MARCO POLO DICTATING HIS MEMOIRS FROM A PRISON CELL IN GENOA, 1298

His accounts of the spices and riches of the Orient stimulated the great age of exploration.

worked their way down the western coast of Africa, sailing farther and farther south in hopes of finding an all-sea route to India. The Madeira Islands were reached in 1420 and the Cape Verde group in 1445.

In 1460, the year of Prince Henry's death, a Portuguese squadron returned from the west coast of tropical Africa with a rich cargo of slaves and "grains of paradise," aromatic seeds also known as "Melegueta peppers" (*Amomum melegueta*). Although related to ginger and not pepper, the sudden abundance of this competitive flavoring caused an abrupt decline in the Lisbon price of black pepper and led to the financial ruin of many spice merchants. The "Pepper Coast" of Guinea is said to owe its name to these "grains of paradise."

By 1471 Portuguese ships had dared to cross the Equator, thereby confounding geographers who had claimed that the area was a flamingly hot and uninhabitable zone. Bartholomew Díaz discovered and doubled the Cape of Good Hope in 1486, confirming Prince Henry's belief that the Indian Ocean could be reached by sea. On June 7, 1494, the two major colonial powers, Spain and Portugal, signed the Treaty of Tordesillas, under which the line of demarcation, or *raya*, between their discoveries in the New World was

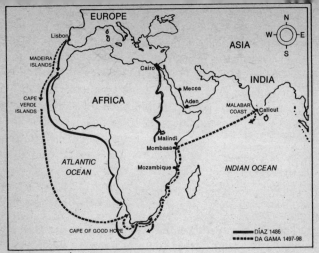

VOYAGES OF DÍAZ AND DA GAMA

established on the meridian 370 leagues west of the
Cape Verde Islands (approximately 46 degrees west).
It provided that all land discovered on the western
side of this line belonged to Spain and all land discovered on the eastern side belonged to Portugal, thus
giving Portugal title to Brazil.

Although he was called "the Navigator," Prince
Henry never navigated, but in his quest for geographical knowledge he designed, prepared, and financed
many exploratory voyages out of Lisbon. Through his
conscientious efforts he planted the seeds of the fruitful harvests to be gathered by Díaz, Columbus, da
Gama, Cabral, and Magellan.

Christopher Columbus (1451–1506), son of a
Genoese weaver, acquired much seafaring knowledge
and experience in the service of the Portuguese. From
these he concluded that there was undiscovered fertile,
inhabited land in the western part of the ocean. However, he was rebuffed as a poor geographer and a
vain boaster when he approached the *Junta dos Mathe-
maticos* in 1485 and asked the Portuguese crown for a

fleet to reach India in the east by sailing west. His project was flatly rejected. Columbus then went to Spain, where after many refusals King Ferdinand and Queen Isabella finally agreed to his requests. By May 1492 the Spanish monarchs confirmed the fateful contracts by which Columbus was appointed "Admiral of the Ocean Sea" and viceroy and governor-general of all the lands and islands he should discover; he was given as well a tax-free share of 10 percent of all the pearls, precious stones, gold, silver, and spices that he might bring back to Spain. The Spanish sovereigns gave him a letter of introduction to the "great khan," the supposed title of the emperor of China.

The admiral set out from Palos in August 1492 with his three tiny but seaworthy ships, the *Santa Maria,* the *Pinta* and the *Niña,* and a crew of ninety men and boys. Despite bad food, maggoty water, and near-mutiny for two months, the great objective of land in the west was reached on October 12, 1492; the coral reefs of San Salvador (one of the Bahama Islands) were sighted, tallying exactly with the way Columbus had envisaged the approaches to the shores of India. He discovered Cuba, which he thought was part of the territory of the great khan, and then Santo Domingo.

One day in early November 1492, following a reconnaissance of the northern coast of Cuba, Martin Alonso Pinzón, the captain of the *Pinta,* brought Columbus two pieces of bark, claiming he had found cinnamon plantings. But upon inspection of the trees the admiral found that they were not cinnamon. Pinzón also reported that an Indian had been seen carrying some bright red objects that looked like nuts; these were probably native chili peppers, a species of *Capsicum.*

Two envoys sent inland on a journey of several days were unsuccessful in their effort to find the great

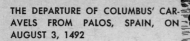

THE DEPARTURE OF COLUMBUS' CARAVELS FROM PALOS, SPAIN, ON AUGUST 3, 1492

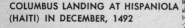

COLUMBUS LANDING AT HISPANIOLA (HAITI) IN DECEMBER, 1492

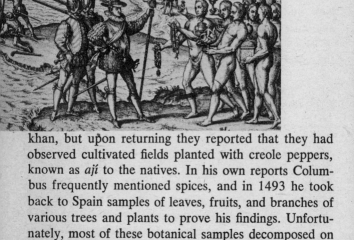

khan, but upon returning they reported that they had observed cultivated fields planted with creole peppers, known as *ají* to the natives. In his own reports Columbus frequently mentioned spices, and in 1493 he took back to Spain samples of leaves, fruits, and branches of various trees and plants to prove his findings. Unfortunately, most of these botanical samples decomposed on the return voyage and were thrown overboard.

Amazingly competent as a dead-reckoning navigator, Columbus managed to return to Spain in March 1493, after weathering two rough winter storms. He was given a magnificent reception, followed by many feasts and banquets. The nagging thought remained, however, that he had not found Zipangu (Japan) or any valuable Oriental spices, such as cinnamon or cloves; nor had he been able to deliver his letter of introduction to the great khan. On the other hand, he had found yams, kidney beans, maize, the fleshy edible cassava roots, tobacco, many new kinds of fruits and nuts, rare birds of gorgeous plumage, and native cotton; moreover he had "discovered" the hammock used by the island natives and soon to be imitated and adopted by European seamen.

Instead of the magnificent Chinese Empire, however, with its marble bridges and mighty palaces, roofed with the finest gold, with floors paved with golden plates two fingers thick, as had been described by Marco Polo, the admiral had encountered a few miserable villages with palm-thatched huts, inhabited by naked savages he called "Indians," who possessed only limited amounts of gold.

In September 1493 Columbus started out on his second voyage with a fleet of seventeen caravels and

INDIANS FLEE IN FEAR OF COLUMBUS

1,500 men to establish Spanish power in the New World and continue the search for gold and spices. On this trip the admiral took with him the Spanish physician Diego Chanca, who described in vivid detail the flora and fauna of the New World. Thanks to Dr. Chanca, we are reliably informed concerning the pungent *ají* fruits utilized by the natives in Hispaniola to season their yams, meat, and fish. Because of its great "heat" this new spice, called "red pepper" by the Spaniards, caused blisters on the tongue. Presumably it was of the same species of *Capsicum* as the red pepper fruits reported from northern Cuba during the first voyage. Later this condiment became popular in Hungary as "paprika pepper," even though it was in no way related to the *Piper nigrum,* or black pepper, of antiquity.

Dr. Chanca reported examining a medium-sized evergreen tree, with a smooth gray trunk, whose aromatic fruits were characterized by a flavor resembling a combination of cinnamon, nutmeg, and cloves—the allspice or pimento tree, indigenous to the West Indies and Latin America. Columbus and his men were not aware of the importance of these pungent allspice berries, and it was not until many years after the death of the admiral that this new spice became popular in Europe. Since the allspice berries resemble peppercorns in shape they were called *pimienta,* the Spanish word for pepper. The high value placed on the true black pepper of India undoubtedly explains why various aromatic and pungent plants found by the early explorers of the Western Hemisphere were called "peppers."

A number of minor spices locally used in the New World were never adopted outside their immediate native locale. One of the most interesting and unusual of these is *Quararibea funebris* (Llave) Vischer, a small tree (silk-cotton family) indigenous to the warm, dry regions of southern Mexico, the dried flowers of which provide a highly pungent spice rather suggestive of fenugreek in odor. Since they used them to flavor their chocolate drinks, the Aztecs called these peppery, sticky flowers *cacaoxochitl*. Today the flowers, known in modern Mexico as *flor de cacao,* are still in demand in the market place of Oaxaca for flavoring *pozonque,* a thick, frothy, aromatic beverage made with chocolate, finely ground corn meal, and water. Although allspice and eventually vanilla were accepted in Europe in the sixteenth and seventeenth centuries as desirable and appetizing spices from the New World, the even more piquant *cacaoxochitl,* rivaling the biting chili peppers in pungency, never became a popular spice outside of Mexico. Yet, according to R. E. Schultes, the odor of this little-known spice is so persistent that botanical specimens of *Quararibea funebris* collected in Mexico in 1841 were still highly aromatic over a century later.

On his fourth and last voyage westward, in 1502, Columbus sought a water passage to the opulent and more civilized parts of the Indies, where spices and other resources were abundant, but he was blocked by the Isthmus of Panama. No longer a hero, he died in relative obscurity in 1506, convinced to the end that he had reached the fringes of the fabulous East.

In 1497 and 1498 England took up the search for a direct sea route to Asia. By order of Henry VII the Italian navigator Giovanni Caboto (John Cabot) undertook two voyages for the purpose of discovery. Although he failed to find spices, his explorations of Newfoundland, the Gulf of St. Lawrence, and the coastal regions of Greenland and Labrador enlarged the sphere of influence of the British crown.

Henry the Navigator had searched in vain for the source of the "Western Nile" in an effort to locate the

Quararibea funebris, AN OB-
SCURE SPICE
Long before the arrival of
the Spanish in Mexico, the
Aztecs used these highly
pungent flowers, known as
cacaoxochitl, to flavor their
chocolate drinks.

legendary and supposedly powerful Christian emperor named Presbyter Johannes, or Prester John, who was reported to have broken the power of the Muslims in bloody fighting. Rumors circulated throughout much of Europe of the existence of this magnificent ruler and his vast domain on the far side of the great desert that formed the boundary of the Old World known to civilization. Prince Henry hoped that the combined forces of Portugal and Prester John could outflank Islam, destroy Mohammedanism, and achieve for Por-

SIXTEENTH-CENTURY CARAVELS
Ships such as these played an important role in the spice trade.

tugal the greatest possible commercial advantages. Even though they never found the realm of Prester John—the myth was eventually exploded through the increase of geographical knowledge—the fifteenth-century Portuguese navigators, in part because of their efforts to open communications with this monarch, had discovered the Cape of Good Hope and gradually prepared the way for the exploratory achievements of Vasco da Gama.

In 1497 King Manuel I of Portugal ordered da Gama to search for a sea route to India. On July 8 of that year a flotilla of four ships, under the command of da Gama in the flagship *Saõ Raphael,* sailed from Lisbon taking with them stores for three years and the best nautical equipment available at the time—charts, astrolabes, compasses, hourglasses, quadrants, and sounding leads. After passing the Cape of Good Hope, discovered by Díaz eleven years earlier, da Gama charted and explored some one thousand miles of undiscovered coast before reaching Mozambique, the southernmost of the East African ports under Arab control. The flotilla continued up the coast to Mombasa and Malindi, and on April 24, 1498, set sail from the latter port on an east-northeast course across the

Arabian Sea. Taking advantage of the monsoon winds, da Gama arrived at Calicut on the west coast of India on May 20, 1498, thus completing the first voyage from western Europe around Africa to the East—the most significant feat in the history of the spice trade.

After a stay of nearly six months in Calicut, at that time the greatest commercial port on the Malabar Coast, da Gama started on his homeward voyage. Despite appalling hardships and the loss of two-thirds of his crew because of scurvy, he finally reached Lisbon in August of 1499 with a valuable cargo of precious stones and spices and the glad tidings that the Hindu king, the zamorin of Calicut, and various Indian merchants were willing to enter into direct trade with King Manuel I of Portugal. A logbook kept by an unidentified sailor with da Gama's fleet records that the zamorin sent a message to King Manuel, written with an iron pen on a palm leaf, the tenor of which was: "Vasco da Gama, a gentleman of your household, came to my country, whereat I was much pleased. My country is rich in cinnamon, cloves, ginger, pepper, and precious stones. That which I ask of you in exchange is gold, silver, corals, and scarlet cloth."

King Manuel, seeing at once the opportunity to add new colonies to his kingdom and to make Lisbon the Venice and the Genoa of the West, was understandably eager to develop trade relations with the zamorin. Hurriedly he fitted out a fleet of thirteen caravels and on March 9, 1500, sent it on Portugal's first merchant voyage to India, under the command of Pedro Alvarez Cabral (1460–1526). For some unknown reason, Cabral sailed westward, out across the South Atlantic, and upon landing in South America, took official possession of Brazil in the name of Portugal. Resuming his voyage to the Orient, he lost four ships in a storm off the Cape of Good Hope but the re-

VASCO DA GAMA (1469-1524)

mainder of his fleet reached Calicut, India, in September 1500.

Cabral managed to establish two Portuguese trading posts on the Malabar Coast, in Calicut and Cochin. He did so despite an attack by irate Mohammedan merchants, who massacred over fifty of his garrison. Returning to Portugal in 1501 he brought to his king full evidence that a new trade route had been opened; on the docks of Lisbon he displayed his rich cargo of spices, with sack after sack of cinnamon, cassia, gin-

SIXTEENTH-CENTURY EUROPEAN CARGO BOATS TRANSPORTING SPICES AND OTHE PRODUCE

BARTERING FOR SPICES IN THE MARKET PLACE OF A GERMAN CITY IN THE SIXTEENTH CENTURY

ger, pepper, nutmegs, mace, and cloves. His valuable shipload also contained some small, carefully guarded chests of diamonds and pearls.

News of the triumphant voyages of da Gama and Cabral reached Venice, shocking to numbness its bankers and merchants, who realized at once that their spice-trade monopoly was broken. Pepper in Venice was now five times as expensive as in Lisbon. The sultan of Egypt was equally disturbed, for no longer could he count on the exorbitant revenues received through taxes on spices passing through his realm. The centers of commerce suddenly shifted from the Italian and Egyptian ports to the harbors of Portugal and Spain. The duty-free sea route to India, despite the cost in money and human lives, was far cheaper than the harassing overland route with its middlemen and their outrageous taxes, tariffs, and duties. The Venetian spice trade, which had been supplying Europe with about 1½ million pounds of pepper annually in addition to other spices, was temporarily disrupted.

For the Portuguese, however, this encouraging new trade advantage was not an unmixed blessing. Portugal at the time had only a million inhabitants and was a country of limited resources. The sudden abundance of spices triggered a temporary decline in the price of these commodities, and a number of Lisbon's merchants went bankrupt in those early years of the sixteenth century.

King Manuel sent trade missions to develop new markets for his spices, particularly to the leading German trading firms, among them the affluent Fuggers and Welsers in Augsburg. From the Augsburg financiers he obtained much-needed capital to finance future exploration, including Magellan's circumnavigation of the globe (1519–1522). As the wealth of the Orient poured into Europe through Lisbon, the Portuguese crown monopolized the lucrative but risky pepper trade. Cargoes of East Indian vessels still at sea were sold at high prices by the king of Portugal to the large European syndicates, many of which were located at Antwerp. To meet these inflated prices and still make a

EUROPEAN SPICE MERCHANTS
In the sixteenth century, the Fugger firm of Augsburg traded in spices over the new sea route to India and acted as papal bankers.

GERMAN SPICE
WAREHOUSE OF
THREE HUNDRED
YEARS AGO

profit, the syndicates charged even higher prices to the wholesalers and retailers, who in turn raised the costs to the European public. From time to time, the smaller participating firms would be wiped out when something went wrong in their speculations. On the other hand, when the pepper speculations were successful, immense profits resulted. The price of pepper in Antwerp by the mid-sixteenth century served as a barometer for European business in general.

By 1560 overland trade to the Orient was reestablished. Substantial quantities of spices, including as much as a million pounds of pepper, were being shipped again through the traditional Levantine trade routes via Alexandria, but even so this was perhaps no more than one-fifth of the volume of spices that reached Europe through Portuguese and Spanish ports. The discovery of the direct sea passage to India led to a marked increase in the consumption of spices throughout Europe.

On September 20, 1519, the Portuguese navigator Ferdinand Magellan, with the approval of King Charles V, left Spain with a fleet of five vessels to visit the Spice Islands by following the western route. In 1520 he sailed through the straits of Patagonia that were later named for him, and discovered the Philippines a year later after a long, tedious, difficult voyage. Dismaying losses from scurvy, hunger, and thirst led to outbreaks of mutiny. Magellan himself was killed in April 1521 on the island of Mactan, in the Philippines, as the result of the treachery of a native sovereign.

Survivors of the expedition eventually managed to reach the Spice Islands, but only one ship, the *Victoria,* returned home to Sanlúcar (September 1522). Eighteen men of an original crew of 230 had survived the first westward circumnavigation of the globe. In spite of the overwhelming human losses, the expedition was a financial success—the twenty-six tons of cloves, scores of sacks of nutmegs, mace, and cinnamon, and deckload of fragrant sandalwood brought back to Spain more than covered the cost of the entire expedition. The captain of the *Victoria,* Sebastián del Cano, was rewarded with a substantial pension and a coat of arms that included two cinnamon sticks, three nutmegs, and twelve cloves.

In 1519 the Spanish conquistador Hernán Cortés was given command of an expedition that culminated in the conquest of Mexico. His soldiers also made a great contribution to the history of spices while on military reconnaissance in the moist, shady coastal rain

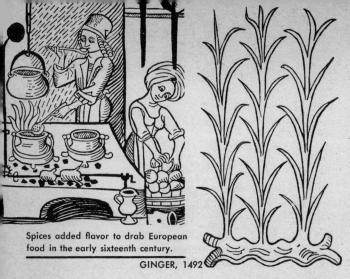

Spices added flavor to drab European food in the early sixteenth century.

GINGER, 1492

forests of southeastern Mexico. They found vanilla. This youngest and newest of the tropical spices was being used by the Aztecs as a delicate flavoring to season their chocolate beverages.

During the sixteenth and seventeenth centuries ginger plantings were successfully established in the West Indies with propagating material brought from the East Indies. Since ginger was probably the easiest of the Oriental tropical spices to grow, its simple cultivation requirements soon led to its being produced on a large scale in Santo Domingo, Jamaica, and Barbados. Early Jamaican records report that in 1547 one thousand tons of ginger were exported from the West Indies to Spain.

***Portugal, Holland, and England
struggle for control of the Far Eastern
spice-producing regions (sixteenth, seventeenth,
and eighteenth centuries); the United States
enters the pepper trade (1795)***

The Portuguese under Albuquerque had won several decisive naval battles over the Muslims by 1511, thereby gaining control of many ancient Oriental spice-producing areas—the Malabar Coast of India, Ceylon, Java, Sumatra, and the great Malayan spice trading center of Malacca. By 1514 they dominated Ternate and the other Spice Islands.

The Portuguese imperial taxes in Ceylon (1612) included a land tax, based on twelve percent of gross produce, to be paid one-third in pepper and two-thirds in currency. Thus the custom of paying taxes in pepper was not limited to the West.

As Portugal grew rich directly from the spice trade, the Dutch prospered indirectly, for they provided ships and crews to carry goods northward from Lisbon to Antwerp and Amsterdam. Profiting also from commerce in grain, herring, and salt, the Hollanders gradually acquired sufficient capital to expand their trade to the Far East. Drake's successful voyage around the world in 1577–1580 and the destruction of the Spanish Armada in 1588 ensured England's place as a great naval power. By the end of the sixteenth century neither Holland nor England was content to abide by the Treaty of Tordesillas, under which Spain and Portugal had divided the world between themselves a century earlier.

The British founded their East India Company in 1600, incorporated as "The Governor and Company of Merchants of London Trading into the East Indies." Two years later the United (Dutch) East India Company was formed with a capital of about 6½ million *guilders*. This corporation, financed by many share-holding individuals, provided sufficient funds to undertake an ambitious venture, the development of a Dutch empire in Asia. Although in the early seventeenth century the British were as strong as the Dutch, the Hollanders were far more willing to take the tremendous risks involved to achieve imperial supremacy in the East. The arrival of the Dutch in the Indian

Ocean with their well-trained troops and more powerful fighting ships was destined to be disastrous for Portugal.

The Portuguese, meanwhile, had consolidated their own eastern empire in a most brutal fashion and with great loss in good willl that could have stood to their advantage. Their regime in the Spice Islands was noteworthy for its violence, plunder, and oppression of the natives, including the poisoning of the king of Tidore in 1524. In Ceylon, settled by the Portuguese in 1505, the cinnamon forests were ruthlessly exploited, a system of slavery was established, and a cinnamon monopoly for the benefit of Lisbon was secured by the end of the sixteenth century.

Between 1605 and 1621 the Dutch managed to drive the Portuguese out of the Spice Islands, giving

CLOVES, 1487

the Netherlands a virtual monopoly of the trade in nutmeg and cloves. They concentrated their cultivation of nutmeg trees on the islands of Banda and Amboina, and of cloves on Amboina; a scheme was conceived in 1651 to uproot all nutmeg and clove trees on the remaining islands so that the monopoly would be complete and easier to maintain. The penalty of death for possessing, selling, or secretly cultivating cloves or nutmegs forced the natives of the Spice Islands to accept this plan. By 1681 approximately three-fourths of the nutmeg and clove trees of the Moluccas had been destroyed, thus creating an artificial scarcity of these spices in Europe, and driving prices up for the benefit of the Dutch East India Company.

The story of spices in the East Indies in the seventeenth and eighteenth centuries was written in blood. The Dutch occupied Ceylon in 1636, and were as cruel to the cinnamon slaves as the Portuguese had been. Villages were forced to supply a stipulated quota of cinnamon bark, and when in default the men were tortured or killed, while the women were severely whipped.

By the end of the seventeenth century the enterprising Dutch colonizers had crushed the Portuguese, virtually driven the British out of the East Indies, and thereby gained complete control of the lucrative spice trade—there was a Dutch monopoly not only in nutmegs, mace, and cloves but also in Ceylonese cinnamon, Indian pepper, ginger, and turmeric.

Occasional overproduction drove the Hollanders to destroy excess spice stocks. For example, in the year 1760 such large quantities of cinnamon and nutmegs were burned in Amsterdam that spectators could wade in nutmeg butter.

But the days of this stranglehold were numbered. Between 1770 and 1772 Pierre Poivre, the French administrator of the island of Mauritius, managed to

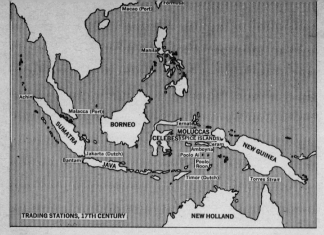

TRADING STATIONS FOR SPICES IN THE EAST INDIES IN THE SEVEN-TEENTH CENTURY

smuggle clove, nutmeg, and cinnamon plants out of the Dutch-controlled Spice Islands. New spice plantings were established in Réunion, the Seychelles, and other French colonies. The blockade of Dutch East Indian ports by British ships in 1780 barred the export of spices to Holland.

No monopoly can last forever. In 1799 the Dutch East India Company, its profits having become smaller and its administrative expenses increasing, went bankrupt. The empire-building firm was dissolved, as Holland's greatest period of trading affluence came to an end. Losses from piracy and smuggling combined to bring about an economic collapse, and despite strict controls spices were introduced and cultivated in other tropical areas that had freed themselves of Dutch influence or that had never been under its heel.

The Dutch ports of India's Malabar Coast were conquered and taken over by England as the Netherlands lost its leadership in European commerce. In 1795 the British planted clove trees in Penang, an island near the west coast of the Malay Peninsula. By 1796 England had taken over all Dutch possessions in the East Indies except Java. Even Java was temporarily occupied by them from 1811 to 1816 under Sir Stamford Raffles.

Many decades of constant fighting finally drove the Dutch and English to define their respective rights in a treaty signed in 1824, nine years after the Vienna Congress. By its terms the Dutch received all the islands of the Malay Archipelago except the northern half of Borneo; it remained British, as did India, Ceylon, Singapore, and the Malay mainland to the borders of Siam.

The relative calm of the mid-nineteenth century marked a temporary respite in the intense and prolonged struggle for supremacy in Far Eastern trade, especially in silks and spices, a military-economic competition that had been dominated successively by the Romans, Arabs, Venetians, Portuguese, Dutch, and English.

Toward the end of the eighteenth century the United States, having achieved stature as a national power, for the first time plunged into the world spice trade. The British taxes and trade restrictions of colonial days no longer obstructed American commerce. Well-built New England privateers, dependable and seaworthy vessels that had been tested and proved during the Revolution, became available for peacetime assignments. The stage was set and the timing right for the rapid development of the budding Yankee merchant marine. Schooners, sloops, brigs, and fast clippers set sail from such ports as Salem, Boston, Portsmouth, Bath, and New London, bound for the Orient. They traded American salmon, codfish, tobacco, snuff, flour, soap, candles, butter, cheese, beef, and barrel staves for such Eastern commodities as tea, coffee, textiles, indigo, and spices (pepper, cassia, cloves, cinnamon, and ginger). En route, there was bartering for sugar and rum in the West Indies. The most remunerative trade, however, was in spices, and especially in pepper.

These long voyages were fraught with danger. Added to the hazards of storms at sea, shipwrecks, and assaults from Barbary, Arabian, and Malay pirates were repeated seizures by French privateers. Trade was so imperiled that in 1798 the United States authorized the arming of American merchant vessels to fight off such attacks.

Between 1800 and 1811 Salem enjoyed a virtual monopoly of the Sumatra pepper trade, because of its aggressive shippers, swift vessels, and capable mariners. Salem, then the sixth largest city in the United States, for several years paid an average of 5 percent of the nation's total import duties, of which pepper formed an important part.

The first successful commercial pepper voyage from Salem was completed by the schooner *Rajah*, of 120 tons, which left Salem on "a secret voyage for ports unknown" in November 1795, returning eighteen months later to New York with a full cargo of bulk pepper taken on at Benkoelen in southwestern Sumatra. On this one voyage the ship's owners, Peele and Beckford, made a profit of seven hundred percent, thanks largely to the skill and cunning of the shipmaster, Captain Jonathan Carnes, on the dangerous 26,000-mile round trip. He was able to buy a large amount of pepper cheaply from the native rulers on the coastal areas of Sumatra and avoid the higher prices charged by Dutch merchants in Batavia, Java, for limited quantities of the spice.

The success of the *Rajah* stimulated other Salem merchants, notably the Crowninshields, to plunge into the pepper trade. In 1799 two Crowninshield ships, the *America* and the *Belisarius*, brought back to Salem sizable cargoes of pepper from the Coromandel Coast of southeastern India. The region most favorable for buying up large quantities of pepper, however, was Achin, on Sumatra's northern coast. By 1805 the *Rajah* and the *America* had each completed five trips to Sumatra, bringing back over twelve hundred tons of pepper on which duties of some $175,000 were paid to the United States Government.

Most of the enormous quantities of pepper imported by this small New England port of Salem had to be re-exported directly to such European ports as Stockholm, Gothenburg, Hamburg, Copenhagen, and Antwerp or were transshipped to Philadelphia, Boston, and Baltimore for processing and distribution by other American merchants and exporters. The largest single cargo on record for one of the Salem pepper fleet was of just over one million pounds (five hundred tons) of pepper, brought from Sumatra to Salem in 1806 by the *Eliza,* a sailing ship of 512 tons.

Except for three years when the British blockaded American ports during the War of 1812, the Salem pepper trade flourished from 1797 to 1846, reaching its peak in 1810. After 1846 an overproduction of spices brought a gradual decline in its economic importance until the final demise of the Salem pepper trade following the outbreak of the Civil War in 1861.

In its half century of supremacy Salem is reputed to have produced some of America's first millionaires, one being the shipping entrepreneur Elias Derby, who made his fortune in the lucrative India and Far Eastern trade although he himself never went to sea.

Modern spice trade (nineteenth and twentieth centuries)

Compared with tea, sugar, and other tropical products, the spice trade played a minor role in the economy of the British Empire. The Dutch retained their position as the leading spice producers of the nineteenth and early twentieth centuries. To do this their imperialistic system in the Dutch East Indies had to be tempered. A more benign form of government was instituted following the publication in 1860 of a novel entitled *Max Havelaar,* by E. Douwes Dekker, a former Dutch colonial officer in Java. In this book, written under the pen name "Multatuli," meaning "I have endured much," Dekker disclosed the brutal and inhuman treatment of the native laborers and peasants in the Dutch East Indian colonies. This powerful exposé had a profound effect on public opinion in Holland, which in turn forced government reforms.

The important spice-producing regions of Java and Sumatra, which were scientifically developed, were destined to remain under Dutch control until World War II. Through their efficient administration and new advances in tropical agricultural techniques, spice production so increased that by 1938, for example, over 55,000 tons of Indonesian black and white pepper were exported, while in that same year India exported only 700 tons of pepper. Today, with the Dutch forced out of Indonesia, the situation has changed: India has joined Indonesia as the world's leading pepper producer—each country now exports between 20,000 and 30,000 tons of pepper annually.

Nor does Indonesia still supply the world's markets with large quantities of cloves, as it did during past centuries when the Spice Islands were at their zenith. In fact, the republic finds it necessary to import cloves today from China, Zanzibar, and the Malagasy Republic to supply flavoring for the popular Indonesian *kretek* cigarettes, which contain about one-third ground cloves and two-thirds tobacco.

Although Columbus never reached the glittering palace of the great khan or inhaled in his travels the true aroma of cinnamon bark or clove buds, he did succeed in opening up the Western Hemisphere to world commerce and presenting three new spices to the Old World. The pungent, inexpensive, and useful capsicum peppers were soon introduced to Europe, Africa, and Asia, where they could be grown as well as enjoyed by the common man; allspice and eventually vanilla became important flavoring condiments exported from the West Indies and Latin America to Europe.

Substantial spice plantations have now been established in the Americas. The best quality cardamom comes from Guatemala, the finest nutmegs and mace from Grenada, select black pepper from Brazil, and substantial quantities of sesame seed from Mexico and Nicaragua. Although in the sixteenth century the spice trade was almost exclusively centered on India, Ceylon, Java, China, and the Moluccas, by 1973 the pendulum has started to swing, at least to some extent, toward significant spice-producing regions in the Western Hemisphere.

Unlike the sixteenth and seventeenth centuries, when monopolies dominated the spice trade, commerce in spices is relatively decentralized at the present time. The most important trading center for spices in the West may be said to be New York, followed by Hamburg and London; in the East, Singapore remains the principal entrepôt.

An unusual culinary development occurred early in the twentieth century—onions and garlic were successfully dehydrated for the first time *on a commercial basis*, following many years of experimentation. As early as 1780 a British patent with the title "Drying Vegetables" had been issued, and by 1845 a patent had been issued in the United States on a process for drying potatoes. The Pajaro Valley Evaporating Company of Watsonville, California, produced dehydrated onions on a small scale in 1889. (In 1950 several tins of this product, dehydrated in Watsonville sixty-one years before and protected by oiled paper around the threads of the screw caps, were found in Skagway, Alaska—and the onions were still pungent and edible.) Further work on the dehydration of onions and garlic in powdered and granular form was carried out during World War I. The dehydration of onions and garlic on a large scale in Egypt, Eastern Europe, and the United States, starting in the nineteen–thirties, was a most significant technological change in the processing of spices and herbs.

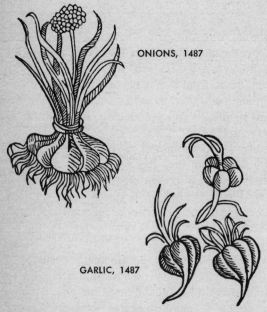

ONIONS, 1487

GARLIC, 1487

Another important development in modern spice processing has been the increased commercial use of *oleoresins* in the industrial market for spices. The oleoresins of a spice, consisting of natural resins and volatile essential oils, contain the constituents of flavor, odor and pungency of the spice in concentrated form. Oleoresins are products obtained by extraction of the spice by solvents, with subsequent removal of the solvent. Spices may contain from 3 to 30 percent by weight of oleoresin, with an average of about 10 percent. Spices produced under primitive tropical conditions may become contaminated by molds and bacteria. While these products should not be used as condiments in this condition, they can be successfully extracted to give a noncontaminated oleoresin. The use of oleoresins allows for a more uniform flavor level adjustment in a finished food product.

Since the introduction of ginger oleoresin in 1899, there have been differences of opinion within the food industry as to the value of oleoresins in comparison with dried natural spices: In baking, dried spices are generally preferred, since to a large degree the traditional appearance of the natural spice is desired—as in the case of cinnamon buns, for example; while in the canning and frozen-food industries, oleoresins of spices are more widely used. Often here, the particulate matter of the spices is objectionable. At the present time, oleoresins represent approximately one-sixth of the total dollar volume of the spice business in the United States.

The dramatic advance of chemical technology in recent years poses a dangerous threat to the spice trade, and could eventually cause serious economic damage to the spice-producing underdeveloped countries of the world. Even today, it is a comparatively simple matter for chemists to synthesize spice essences and flavors from cheaper and more abundant raw materials such as wood pulp and coal tar, a development which, if carried to extremes, could portend disaster in the long run for the world's plantations of tropical spices. For example, a single chemical plant in Wisconsin is now capable of producing from wood pulp enough imitation vanilla flavor to supply the total United States requirements of this flavoring.

As we look back across some five thousand years of recorded history we begin to grasp the pivotal part that spices have played in the development of modern civilization. In an epoch when Europe knew nothing of sugar, tea, coffee, chocolate, potatoes, citrus fruits, or tobacco, to say nothing of plumbing or refrigeration, Oriental spices supplied flavor and piquancy for food and drink and fragrant aromas to mask a multitude of unpleasant odors. So useful, indeed indispensable, were spices, both politically and economically, that kings sent expeditions in search of them, merchants risked life and fortune to trade in them, wars were fought over them, whole populations were enslaved, the globe was explored, and such far-reaching changes as the Renaissance were brought about by the restless, ruthless competition.

Today, happily, we no longer are dependent upon spices to protect our noses, but we have discovered in them an almost infinite variety of new pleasures and experiences with which to delight our palates. They have become, in short, less a necessity and more a treasured enhancement of the art of living.

Part II
THE SPICES

ALLSPICE

Pimenta dioica L.
(formerly *Pimenta officinalis* Lindl.)

A. Flowering branch
1. Bud
2. Flower
3. Vertical section of bud
4. Calyx and pistil (gynoecium)
5. Stamens, side and front views
6. Transverse section of ovary showing two cells
7. Cluster of fruit (berries)
8. Seed, side and front views
9. Vertical section of seed showing curved embryo

ALLSPICE (PIMENTO)

Family: Myrtaceae

LATIN	• <u>Pimenta dioica</u> L.
SPANISH	• Pimienta gorda
FRENCH	• Piment
GERMAN	• Piment
SWEDISH	• Kryddpeppar
DUTCH	• Piment
ITALIAN	• Pepe Di Giamaica
PORTUGUESE	• Pimenta-Da-Jamaica
RUSSIAN	• Yamayski Pyerets
ARABIC	• Bahar
JAPANESE	• Ôrusupaisu

ALLSPICE *(Pimento)*

ALLSPICE, usually known as pimento outside the
United States, is the dried, unripe berry of the tree
Pimenta dioica (formerly called *Pimenta officinalis*)
and is a native of the West Indies and Latin America.
It is the only major spice grown, on a commercial
basis, exclusively in the Western Hemisphere.

The name allspice is due to its flavor, which resembles a combination of cinnamon, nutmeg, and
cloves. The allspice tree, important for its fruits,
should not be confused with another closely related
member of the myrtle family indigenous to the West
Indies, *Pimenta acris* Kostel., the leaves of which are
distilled to produce an oil that, combined with alcohol and water, forms the cosmetic lotion bay rum.

Allspice, the capsicum peppers, and vanilla are the
only important tropical spices indigenous to the Western Hemisphere, the allspice tree having been discovered
in the Caribbean Islands by the early Spanish explorers in the sixteenth century. Most allspice is grown
on the island of Jamaica, but it is also produced in
Guatemala, Honduras, Mexico, Brazil, and the Leeward Islands. In efforts to introduce allspice to other

parts of the world—Java, Sumatra, and elsewhere in the Far East—the trees failed to produce fruit, and the attempts to establish it in the Orient have now been virtually abandoned. Thus pimento has remained a Western Hemisphere product.

Allspice is a medium-sized evergreen tree, 25 to 40 feet tall, with a slender, upright trunk and smooth grayish bark. It is grown principally in limestone hills in the southwestern part of the island of Jamaica at elevations of less than 1,500 feet. Allspice trees are also native to the rain forests of southeastern Mexico, Guatemala, and Honduras, where they sometimes attain heights of 100 feet or more.

The allspice or pimento berries of commerce are the dried, unripe, but full-grown aromatic fruits, which are harvested three to four months after flowering. They are nearly round, range in size up to ¼ inch in diameter (about the size of a pea), and are reddish-brown in color.

Long before the Spaniards arrived in Central America, the Mayan Indians had for centuries used allspice berries to embalm and help preserve the bodies of important leaders.

With the high value placed on the spices of India and the Spice Islands, it is no wonder that aromatic and pungent plants were much sought for by the early explorers of the New World. Francisco Hernandez, traveling through Mexico between 1571 and 1577 for King Philip II, first came upon the allspice tree in the Tabasco region and named it *piper Tabasci*. Because the allspice berries bear some resemblance in shape and flavor to peppercorns (from which black and white pepper are ground), the name *pimienta* (pepper) was given them by the Spaniards, a name later corrupted and anglicized to pimento. In the seventeenth century allspice was known also as *pimienta de Chiapas*, for it was found in that southeastern department of Mexico near the Guatemalan border.

From the seventeenth through the nineteenth centuries allspice berries were commonly used aboard ship to preserve meat during long voyages—a custom that still exists in Scandinavia, where the berries are used to preserve fish in barrels en route from the outlying fishing areas to the coastal markets of Norway, Finland, and Sweden.

The great demand for umbrella sticks made of pimento, stylish at the end of the nineteenth century in Britain and the United States, led to wanton cutting of the saplings. Only the strict controls legislated in 1882 and equally strict enforcement of them saved the young allspice trees in Jamaica from this passing vogue.

"Pimento walks" were popular in Jamaica in the last century. Where thick natural growths of allspice existed, owing to the scattering of pimento seeds by birds, the weeds, underbrush, and less developed seedlings were thinned out. The more vigorous pimento trees, left at about 25-foot intervals, formed the picturesque "pimento walks."

Pimento is usually grown from seed, preferably from fresh ripe fruit selected from well-developed clusters of regularly fruiting trees. The seeds are extracted by squeezing them with the fingers from their pulpy covering before planting. They must then be planted immediately to obtain a high percentage of germination, which commences in about two weeks and continues for several months. The seedlings may be transplanted to plastic pots and grown in humid, shady situations. About one year after germination the seedlings should be 10 to 18 inches high and ready for planting in the field.

In a mature grove there are two kinds of fruiting pimento trees: those commonly called "female"; and nonfruiting or barren trees, generally designated as "male." Evidence about this association of sex with fruiting is conflicting; the so-called male trees occasionally bear small quantities of fruit (some of the flowers of such trees are structurally hermaphroditic, and by botanists the species is said to be polygamo-dioecious). The fruitful and unfruitful pimento trees are so similar in appearance that which trees are fertile usually cannot be determined until after flowering—sometimes only after five or six years in the field.

Progress has been made in recent years in vegetative propagation of pimento in Jamaica employing various techniques including budding, approach grafting, and "bottle grafting." The selected scion or budwood is put in a bottle of moist fertile soil, then taken to the nursery, where it is placed in close proximity to a young seedling plant to which it will be grafted. The wood and cambium of both cuts are brought together, and the union is taped. The soil in the bottle is kept moist to keep the scion alive. If a swelling appears at the taped part after ten weeks or so, it means that the graft has been successful. The portion of the scion below the union (which goes into the bottle) is then removed, and a new budded plant is the result. Such vegetative propagation enables the planter partially to overcome the handicap of too large a percentage of barren trees—possibly up to 50 percent in a given planting.

Initially, young pimento seedlings are planted in stands of three plants each, with 20 feet between the stands. Only temporary shade is recommended. When bearing commences, in the sixth year, many "male" or nonbearing trees are removed and the most promising "female" ones retained, a ratio of one barren tree to every ten "females" being recommended to assure adequate pollination. In Jamaica the final spacing between the pimento trees in a plantation is usually about 20 feet, because closer planting would encourage growth of a tall timber tree instead of one with fruiting branches close to the ground.

Under favorable conditions the allspice tree begins to bear at the age of seven or eight years but is not in full bearing until the fifteenth year. It may then bear for one hundred years or more. Jamaican production statistics for trees of all ages indicate an average yield of approximately 2½ pounds of dried pimento berries per tree. A large allspice tree under the most favorable conditions may yield up to 100 pounds of dried pimento berries in one year.

The leaves of the allspice tree contain about 2 percent of an essential oil, pimento leaf oil. When essential oil production rather than berries is desired, the pimento orchard is planted at a much closer spacing; by cutting the new growth the plants can be kept "headed back" to form small bushes, which facilitates harvest of the leaves.

The berries also contain an essential oil, oil of pimento, ranging in content from about 4 to 4.5 percent for the Jamaican pimento, about 2.5 percent for the Mexican and Guatemalan, and 2 percent for the Honduran pimento. The custom of boiling the Central American and Mexican pimento berries may somewhat reduce the essential oil content. In Jamaica the berries are not boiled.

Most Jamaican allspice berries, which are smaller than the Central American or Mexican, are harvested from cultivated trees or natural escapes from cultivated stock; the harvest of allspice in Central America and Mexico is almost entirely from wild sources, which are gradually being depleted. In remote and virtually inaccessible regions of Central America and southeastern Mexico, chicle- (shewing gum) collecting laborers also harvest allspice berries from the natural virgin rain forests during June, July, and August of each year. This harvest is carried out under very primitive conditions. Branches of large wild pimento trees are chopped off and the berries then picked off the ground. Only too frequently, however, the entire bearing (female) trees, some of them up to 100 feet in height, are chopped down just to gather the fruits—especially when it is considered too much trouble or too dangerous to climb them. The non-producing (male) trees, of course, are spared. A clearing is made in the jungle to dry the allspice berries for a few days in the sun on straw mats before they are taken to larger collection centers, where they are boiled to combat mold and dried again before being packed for export.

In Jamaica, on the other hand, strict supervision is given to the harvesting. To avoid loss of aroma, the pimento berries are hand-picked before they are fully ripe (a practice also followed with cloves and black pepper in other parts of the world). After being dried in the sun for seven to ten days on concrete patios and given a preliminary cleaning by the growers, the berries are shipped to the Government Pimento Clearing House for a final cleaning before being packed in bags for export.

Copper fungicidal sprays are used from time to time in Jamaica to check a leaf disease known as "Pimento Rust" (*Puccinia psidii Wint.*). Spraying is supposed to be discontinued, however, at least two months before the harvest begins.

The price of the pimento (allspice) is determined not only by its appearance but also by its essential oil content. The Jamaican pimento, for example, was quoted by the *Chemical Marketing Reporter* on March 5, 1973, at $1.06 per pound f.o.b. New York (in large lots); on the same date the Guatemalan pimento was quoted at 95 cents per pound, and the Mexican at 89 cents per pound. The annual export of pimento (allspice) from Jamaica is usually about 4,500,000 pounds, a quantity that represents approximately two-thirds of total world production of the spice.

Allspice is one of the very few commodities today that is virtually controlled by monopolistic practices. Since Jamaica produces most of the world crop of allspice, its government in recent years has set the market price for each year's coming crop. The smaller producers—Guatemala, Mexico, and Honduras—have had to fall in line, for their production has been much smaller and not so high in quality (up to the present time, at least) as the Jamaican product. Likewise, the spice buyers in New York, London, Hamburg, and Stockholm have been obliged to accept the Jamaican pimento price.

Allspice berries are sold both whole and ground. Whole berries are used in meat broths, gravies, and pickling liquids. Ground allspice is delicious in desserts such as "Pineapple Treasure," fruitcakes, pies, relishes, sausages, and preserves. Its use is also suggested with sweet yellow vegetables. Allspice is usually a component of mixed pickling spice and is an important ingredient of Benedictine and chartreuse liqueurs.

Spiced Figs With Custard

1 pound dried figs	2 whole allspice berries
6 whole cloves	¼ cup sherry
2 sticks cinnamon, 2 inches each	Custard
	Ground nutmeg

In deep saucepan, place figs with cold water to cover, cloves, cinnamon, and *allspice*. Bring to a boil, reduce heat, cover, and simmer about 45 minutes or until figs are tender. Cool. Remove whole spices and stems from figs. Cut in quarters and purée until smooth in electric blender or put through food grinder. Stir in sherry. Spoon spiced figs into 8 sherbert glasses; top with custard. Refrigerate. Before serving, sprinkle with ground nutmeg.

CUSTARD

⅔ cup light brown sugar, firmly packed
2 teaspoons flour
1 teaspoon ground cinnamon
½ teaspoon ground allspice

½ teaspoon salt
2 eggs, lightly beaten
3 cups milk
1½ teaspoons pure vanilla extract

Combine brown sugar, flour, cinnamon, *allspice,* and salt in heavy saucepan or top of double boiler. Blend in eggs. Add milk and cook over low heat or hot water, stirring constantly, until mixture coats a metal spoon. Remove from heat and stir in vanilla.

Yield: 8 servings

Pineapple Treasure

3 very small fresh pineapples
1 pint vanilla ice cream
1 cup heavy cream, whipped
3 tablespoons light rum
¾ teaspoon ground allspice
½ cup chopped fresh pineapple

½ cup diced orange sections
½ cup sliced bananas
¼ cup diced maraschino cherries
Pineapple wedges
¼ cup grated coconut

Prepare this dessert the day before serving. Slice pineapples lengthwise, including the leaves. Cut meat out of the pineapple, leaving ½-inch wall. (Save the scooped-out portion to use in the ice cream mixture or in fruit cups and salads.) Place shells in freezer to chill while preparing ice cream mixture. Soften ice cream and fold in whipped cream, rum, *allspice,* and fruit. Spoon into pineapple shells. Wrap in foil and freeze until desired firmness. This dessert may be frozen firm or soft (like custard). If frozen hard, remove from freezer 30 minutes before serving. Serve with fresh pineapple wedges and grated coconut.

Yield: 6 servings

Plum Chutney

¾ cup cider vinegar
¾ cup water
1 cup sugar
½ teaspoon salt
3 sticks cinnamon
1 whole piece ginger,
   1½ inches
½ teaspoon whole allspice
   berries

½ teaspoon whole cloves
3 pounds Italian prune
   plums
1½ cups diced peeled
   apples
1 cup seedless raisins
¼ cup instant minced onion

Combine vinegar, water, sugar, salt, and cinnamon in saucepan. Tie ginger, *allspice,* and cloves in bag and add. Bring to boiling point and boil 2 minutes. Wash, pit, and quarter plums. (Measure; there should be 8 to 9 cups.) Stir plums, apples, raisins, and onions into syrup. Cook over medium heat 30 to 40 minutes cr until mixture thickens, stirring frequently. Pour into hot sterilized jars. Seal at once. Store at least 6 weeks before serving. Serve with meats or poultry.

Yield: 8 jars, ½ pint each

Spiced Tomato Marmalade

3 pounds ripe tomatoes,
   peeled
3 pounds sugar
2 lemons

1 orange
½ teaspoon salt
½ teaspoon ground ginger
½ teaspoon ground allspice

Cut tomatoes into quarters. (There should be 7½ cups.) Place in 3-quart saucepan. Add sugar and let stand while preparing lemons and orange. Peel lemons and orange, cut fruit into small pieces; add to tomatoes. Cut peels into thin, fine slivers. Cover with water and cook 10 minutes. Drain and discard water. Add peels to tomatoes along with salt and ginger. Bring to boiling point and cook about 35 minutes, uncovered, over medium-low heat until mixture is thick and the peels are transparent, stirring occasionally. (This marmalade will be a little thin.) Add *allspice* and cook 5 minutes longer. Ladle into hot sterilized jars. Seal airtight.

Yield: 2 jars, ½ pint each

Bananas Bonanza

3 bananas
¼ cup lemon juice
¼ cup bread crumbs

1 tablespoon sugar
½ teaspoon ground allspice

Peel and cut bananas into 2-inch pieces. Brush with lemon juice. Roll in mixture of bread crumbs, sugar, and *allspice*. Place each piece on skewer. Toast over hot coals.

Yield: 12 2-inch pieces

Burgers on the Stick

1 pound ground beef
1 egg, slightly beaten
1 tablespoon instant minced
  onion

1 teaspoon salt
½ teaspoon ground allspice
⅛ teaspoon ground black
  pepper

Combine all ingredients in mixing bowl. Shape into patties around stick. Cook over hot coals until done as desired.

Yield: 6 patties

Vegetable Kebabs

1 fresh zucchini
1 tomato
6 medium-sized fresh
  mushrooms

2 tablespoons butter or
  margarine, melted
2 teaspoons lemon juice
⅛ teaspoon ground allspice
⅛ teaspoon salt

Cut zucchini into ½-inch pieces and tomato into wedges. Arrange zucchini, tomato wedges, and mushrooms on skewer. Combine butter, lemon juice, *allspice,* and salt. Brush vegetables with sauce. Cook over hot coals 4 to 6 minutes or until tender.

Yield: 4 servings

Hot Dog Twists

2 cups biscuit mix
1 teaspoon ground allspice

⅔ cup milk
24 frankfurters

Combine biscuit mix, *allspice,* and milk. Stir with fork to form a soft dough; then beat vigorously until stiff. Knead 8 to 10 times on lightly floured board. Roll a 9 by 16-inch rectangle that is ¼ inch thick. Cut into ¾ by 8-inch strips. Wrap each strip around a frankfurter, then place on stick. Cook over hot coals for 10 minutes, or until done.

Yield: 24 servings

ANISE SEED

Pimpinella anisum L.

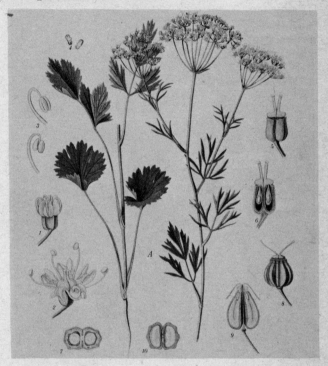

A. Vegetative and flowering portions of plant
1. Bud
2. Open flower
3. Stamens, front and side views
4. Pollen grains
5. Pistil, showing inferior ovary
6. Vertical section of ovary
7. Transverse section of ovary
8. Fruit (schizocarp)
9. Vertical section of fruit showing resin canals
10. Transverse section of fruit

ANISE SEED

Family: Umbelliferae

LATIN	• <u>Pimpinella anisum L.</u>
SPANISH	• Anís
FRENCH	• Anis
GERMAN	• Anis
SWEDISH	• Anis
ARABIC	• Yānîsūn
DUTCH	• Anijs
ITALIAN	• Anice
PORTUGUESE	• Erva-doce
RUSSIAN	• Anis
CHINESE	• Huei-Hsiang
JAPANESE	• Anisu

ANISE SEED

ANISE, *Pimpinella anisum,* is a graceful annual herb of the parsley family 2 to 3 feet high, with feathery leaves. Anise is indigenous to Asia Minor, the Greek islands, and Egypt and is the source of one of the oldest known aromatic seedlike fruits.

The bulk of the world's supply of anise, also known as aniseed, is produced in Mexico, Spain, Germany, Turkey, and Italy, but it is widely cultivated in most temperate and warm climates, including India and South and Central America.

The anise plant is slow-growing, normally requiring a frost-free growing season of about 120 days. A light, fertile, sandy loam with good drainage is recommended in warm and sunny situations with uniform, well-distributed rainfall. The seed should be planted in early spring directly in the field, for the taprooted seedlings are harmed by transplanting. Five to ten pounds of seed per acre may be planted in rows about 2 feet apart, with the seedlings thinned to 6-inch intervals.

Blossom clusters of white flowers appear about three

months after planting, and a month later the fruit may be sufficiently mature to harvest. The "seed" (actually a mericarp) is then threshed out and dried outdoors in light shade or artificially at a moderate temperature.

Under favorable conditions a yield of 500 to 800 pounds per acre of dried seeds, which are greenish-gray, light-colored, and crescent-shaped, may be expected. The seeds are hairy, about ⅕ inch long. There are approximately 100,000 in one pound. After being dried, they are usually stored in bags.

In first-century Rome anise was a flavoring in *mustaceus,* a popular spiced cake baked in bay leaves and eaten after a feast to prevent indigestion.

In 1305 anise was listed by King Edward I among the commodities liable to toll and was sufficiently popular that such fees helped produce the funds to repair London Bridge.

According to the Royal Wardrobe Accounts of the year 1480, the personal linen of King Edward IV was perfumed by means of "lytil bagges of fustian stuffed with ireos and anneys."

Through steam distillation, an essential oil may be recovered from crushed anise seeds, a process that gives an oil yield of 2 to 3 percent. Anethole is the principal constituent of this highly aromatic, pale yellow, syrupy, volatile oil.

Anise seed and anise oil are characterized by a very strong, licoricelike flavor and odor, although this umbelliferous herb anise is not related to *Glycyrrhiza glabra,* the perennial European plant of the pea family whose sweet roots are the source of true licorice. Anise oil, rather than the licorice root itself, is generally used to provide licorice flavoring.

Anise oil is widely used in beverages, baked goods, soups, confectionery, cough drops, and cordial liqueurs. It is the basis of the French cordial anisette and of the popular Turkish alcoholic beverage *raki.*

Throughout Latin America, anise-flavored *aguardiente* (distilled from sugar cane) is one of the most universally popular alcoholic drinks. Anise oil is utilized in medicine for its carminative and expectorant properties and as a masking agent for flavoring otherwise evil-smelling and bitter-tasting drugs; it has been used also as an antiseptic, as a flavoring in dentifrices, and as a sensitizer in bleaching colors in photography.

Anise seed is available as a spice either whole or ground. The whole seed may be used as a flavoring for soups and cakes. Anise leaves can be used as a seasoning or as a garnish for green salads.

In recent years anise odor has been used in England and the United States as an artificial scent for "drag hunting" with fox hounds—a sack saturated with oil of anise is dragged across the countryside as a lure for the hounds. Powdered anise seed is used to flavor horse and cattle feed. Oil of anise is supposed to be an excellent bait for mouse and rat traps, as well as an enticing fish lure.

The star anise (*Illicium verum* Hook f.), whose oil is also licoricelike in flavor and odor, is a small evergreen tree native to southwestern China. When ripe, the hard brown fruits of this tree open out in the form of a star, hence the name. The flowers are yellow and from a distance resemble the narcissus.

The star anise tree comes into production in the sixth year and may continue bearing for 100 years or more. A mature tree 25 years of age may produce 50 to 60 pounds of dried fruits, containing up to 2½ to 3 percent of essential oil. Although star anise, of the *Magnoliaceae,* is entirely different from anise botanically, the fruits of both contain essential oils of similar chemical composition and therefore they taste very much alike, although star anise is somewhat harsher in aroma.

Traditionally the Japanese have used ground star anise bark as incense. In the Orient the seeds are chewed after meals to promote digestion and sweeten the breath.

In 1971 the United States Government lifted the ban on the importation of spices from Mainland China. For the first time in over twenty years, the U.S. spice industry was able to import star anise seed. Initial acceptance of star anise has been slow, since its flavor was unfamiliar to an entire generation of Americans. However, dogs and cats are rapidly getting used to the taste of star anise, since it has become a popular flavoring in pet food.

The Florida anise tree (*Illicium floridanum* Ellis) is indigenous to the Gulf area of the United States from Florida to Louisiana. An evergreen shrub 6 to 10 feet in height, bearing purple flowers, it is grown in this country and in Europe primarily as an ornamental.

STAR ANISE
Illicium verum Hook f.

Anise Wafers

1½ teaspoons anise seed,
   crushed
2 tablespoons boiling water

⅓ cup butter or margarine
1 cup sifted all-purpose
   flour

Combine *anise seed* and boiling water in a custard cup.
Cover and steep 10 minutes. Remove from heat, cool,
and chill. Cut butter into flour with pastry blender or

2 knives until the mixture resembles coarse meal. Add *anise* water, discarding seeds. Toss the mixture lightly with a fork to form a dough. Shape dough into 1-inch balls. Place 2 inches apart on ungreased cookie sheets. Flatten to ⅛-inch thickness with a glass, covered with a damp cloth or waxed paper. Bake in a preheated hot oven (400°F.) 10 to 12 minutes or until edges have lightly browned. Cool on wire racks. Store airtight.

Yield: 2 dozen wafers

Anise Fruit Cup

¾ cup water
½ cup sugar
2 tablespoons lime juice
½ teaspoon anise seed, crushed
¹⁄₁₆ teaspoon salt

1 cup pineapple wedges
1 cup grapefruit sections
1 cup orange sections
2 cups diced unpeeled apples
1 cup diced pears

To make syrup, combine water, sugar, lime juice, *anise seed,* and salt in a small saucepan. Mix well. Bring to boiling point and boil 2 minutes. Cover and steep 10 minutes. Cool and chill. Place fruit in a mixing bowl. Strain syrup over fruit. Chill. Ladle fruit into sherbet glasses. Spoon about 2 tablespoons of the syrup over each serving. Garnish with mint leaves, if desired. Serve as a dessert.

Yield: 6–8 servings

Anise Lemonade

1 can (6 fl. oz.) frozen lemonade concentrate
1 teaspoon anise seed

1 can (8½ oz.) crushed pineapple

Prepare lemonade following directions on can. Drain pineapple, reserving liquid. In small saucepan mix *anise seed* with pineapple juice. Bring to boil; simmer 5 minutes. Add to lemonade. Divide drained crushed pineapple among 4 tall glasses. Pour in lemonade. Add ice and serve chilled. Garnish with maraschino cherry or a scoop of lemon sherbet, if desired.

Yield: 4 servings, 8 fluid ounces each

Fig Conserve

1 pound dried figs
1 teaspoon anise seed,
 crushed
2 cups water
1 cup sugar

4 teaspoons fresh lemon
 juice
¾ cup chopped walnuts or
 blanched, toasted
 almonds

Soak figs and *anise seed* in water 4 hours. Bring to boiling point. Add sugar and cook slowly, uncovered, 25 minutes or until syrup has thickened and figs are tender. Cool. Stir in lemon juice and walnuts or almonds. Serve as an accompaniment to meats.

Yield: 6 servings

Anise Fish Chowder With Pineapple

1½ pounds ready-to-cook
 fish (eel, pickerel, or
 carp)
9-ounce can mussels
 (optional)
4½-ounce can shrimp
1 bay leaf
1 strip orange peel, ¼ inch
 wide
⅛ teaspoon crushed red
 pepper
¾ teaspoon anise seed
4 cups water

¼ cup rice wine, brandy, or
 cooking sherry
3½ teaspoons salt
½ cup onion flakes
¼ teaspoon instant minced
 garlic
3 threads saffron
2 tablespoons hot water
½ cup pineapple tidbits
1 tablespoon cornstarch
2 tablespoons water
Soy sauce
Cooked rice

Cut fish into 1-inch pieces. Place in a 2-quart saucepan. Add next 11 ingredients. Cover and cook gently 15 minutes or until fish is flaky. Crumble saffron, mix with the hot water, and add, along with pineapple. Blend cornstarch with the 2 tablespoons of water and stir into the soup. Bring to boiling point, reduce heat, and cook 1 minute. Serve in soup bowls with 1 teaspoon soy sauce or soy sauce to taste. As an accompaniment, serve a small bowl of cooked rice with each serving.

Yield: 2 quarts

2 teaspoons anise seed
½ cup butter or margarine
¾ cup sugar
2 large eggs
¼ teaspoon salt

2 cups sifted all-purpose
 flour
1½ teaspoons double-acting
 baking powder

Crush *anise seed* and mix with shortening. Gradually blend in sugar. Beat in eggs. Sift flour with baking powder and salt. Gradually stir into the first mixture. Mix dough until ingredients are well blended and smooth. Shape into 1-inch balls. Place on a lightly greased cookie sheet, 2 inches apart. Bake in a preheated moderate oven (350°F.) 10 minutes or until light brown. Cool on wire cooling racks. Store airtight.

Yield: 4 dozen cookies

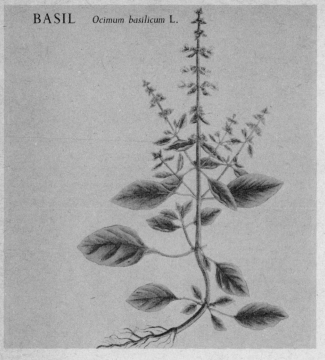

BASIL   *Ocimum basilicum* L.

BASIL

Family: Labiatae

LATIN	• <u>Ocimum basilicum L.</u>
SPANISH	• Albahaca
FRENCH	• Basilic
GERMAN	• Basilienkraut
SWEDISH	• Basilkört
ARABIC	• Raihān
DUTCH	• Basilicum
ITALIAN	• Basilico
PORTUGUESE	• Manjericão
RUSSIAN	• Bazilik
JAPANESE	• Bajiru
CHINESE	• Lo-le

BASIL, 1487

BASIL

BASIL, *Ocimum basilicum,* known also as sweet basil, is an annual spicy herb of the mint family said to be native to India, Africa, and Asia. It is now produced commercially in France, Hungary, Bulgaria, Yugoslavia, Italy, Morocco, and to some extent almost all other warm and temperate countries in the world including the United States, where California produces a superior quality.

It is a small bushy plant, profusely branched, which grows to a height of about 2 feet. Domestic yields are 8 to 10 tons of fresh herb per acre. The glossy leaves are grayish-green beneath, up to 2 inches long and ¾ inch wide. The flowers are small, greenish- or purplish-white in color.

The aromatic and sweet-smelling leaves of many plants belonging to the mint family have long been used for flavoring foods, and basil is one of the most important. Others utilized since ancient times include marjoram, peppermint, sage, savory, and thyme.

Basil is propagated by seed, which is sown at the rate of about 5 pounds per acre, usually in rows 30 inches apart; the seedlings are later thinned to about

6 inches within the rows. The seed can be drilled with an ordinary onion-seed drill. The distance between the rows is usually determined by tillage methods; mechanical harvesting requires a relatively wide spacing of approximately 30 inches. Germination requires from ten to fourteen days. Weed control is important, for any weeds included in the harvested crop might impair or ruin its flavor and quality. Well-drained soil is recommended, and if possible sunny, wind-sheltered spots should be selected.

Basil herbage (the young leafy stems) should be cut for drying on a dry day just before the flowers appear. In harvesting, the plants are cut back only part-way to the ground, so that under favorable circumstances additional crops may be obtained. In California three to four cuttings are made annually, utilizing modern farming techniques.

When the leaves are to be marketed, they are dried artificially to preserve the green color, at temperatures of less than 110°F. under cover.

An essential oil of basil, golden yellow in color, is produced through steam distillation of the fresh herb. A yield of about 0.15 percent may be expected, which is equivalent to about 24 to 30 pounds of oil of basil per acre. This essential oil is used in many perfumes.

Basil is one of the oldest herbs known to man. For many centuries it has been cultivated and revered in India as *tulsi,* a plant sacred to Vishnu in the Hindu religion. Even today it is commonly cultivated near the Hindu temples. When a Hindu dies, a basil leaf is often buried with him.

Some authorities state that the word basil comes from the Greek *basileus,* meaning king, because its smell was so superb that it was fit for a king's house. Another theory holds that the name is the shortened form of *basiliscus* ("little king"), or basilisk, a fabulous dragon so venomous that it could kill with a glance.

Basil was supposed to be an effective antidote to the poison of this serpentine lizard, so-called from the crown or coronet on its head.

Basil has many contradictory associations of good and evil. Although sacred in India, it frequently has been identified with hatred and death elsewhere. After her gruesome dance Salome is said to have concealed the head of John the Baptist in a pot of basil to give it loving care. This same morbid use of basil is mentioned by Keats in "Isabella, or the Pot of Basil"; Isabella hides the severed head of her lover, Lorenzo:

> She wrapp'd it up; and for its tomb did choose
> A garden-pot, wherein she laid it by.
> And cover'd it with mould, and o'er it set
> Sweet Basil, which her tears kept ever wet.

Dioscorides, the famous Greek physician and herbalist of the first century A.D., advised that too much basil was "hard of digestion" but suggested that a moderate amount when taken with wine was good for the eyes.

In the Middle Ages it was believed scorpions would breed under pots where basil was growing.

In the herbals basil was recommended for head colds and as a cure for warts and worms. Hilarius, an early French physician, claimed that a scorpion could be born in the brain if one merely smelled basil. The Arabian physicians of the Middle Ages strongly recommended basil for various ailments.

In more recent times basil has been used in the Far East as a cough medicine, for kidney trouble, and for diarrhea.

By long custom, even today an Italian suitor may signify his matrimonial intentions by appearing with a sprig of basil in his hair. In France and Italy window pots of basil are used to keep insects away.

Although basil is an important ingredient of the liqueur chartreuse, and snuff may be made from ground basil leaves, its most important use is as a culinary herb. Basil leaves, which rival oregano as a seasoning for pizza, may be used for flavoring stews, sauces, sausages, dressings, salads, and mock turtle soup. By custom, and no doubt by Italian association, it has a special affinity for tomatoes and tomato-base recipes.

A popular and relatively inexpensive herb, basil makes savory even such dull and unpretentious dishes as beef stew, to which its fragrant bouquet adds welcome zest and flavor. It is an important ingredient in the Italian specialty Chicken Cacciatore.

Its taste is reminiscent of cloves—warm, sweet, and highly aromatic.

During the past few years, basil has enjoyed an outstanding rate of growth in usage in the United States—its consumption having increased at the rate of 10 to 20 percent per year as compared to 5 to 10 percent for most herbs.

Chicken Cacciatore

1 (2½-lb.) chicken, cut into 8 pieces	1½ teaspoons salt
½ cup olive oil	⅛ teaspoon ground black pepper
1 large onion, finely chopped	1 tablespoon parsley flakes
1 clove garlic, minced	1½ teaspoons basil leaves, crumbled
½ cup celery, diced	⅛ teaspoon oregano leaves
2 green peppers, chopped	¼ cup white wine
1 can (1 lb. 12 oz.) tomatoes	1 cup sliced fresh mushrooms

In large saucepan or Dutch oven brown chicken on all sides in hot oil about 10 minutes. Remove from pan; set aside. In same saucepan sauté onion and garlic for 1 minute. Add celery and green peppers and sauté for 3 to 5 minutes. Stir occasionally. Mash tomatoes with fork and add. Return chicken to pan. Season with salt and pepper. Cover pan and simmer 30 minutes, stirring occasionally. Add parsley, *basil,* oregano, wine, and mushrooms. Continue to cook 15 minutes longer or until chicken is tender. Serve with spaghetti, if desired.

Yield: 4 servings

Fish Marinara

2 tablespoons salad or olive
   oil
⅓ cup chopped celery
¼ teaspoon instant garlic
   powder
1 tablespoon salt
1 tablespoon dried parsley
   flakes
1¼ teaspoons crumbled
   oregano leaves

¾ teaspoon crumbled basil
   leaves
⅛ teaspoon cayenne
1 teaspoon sugar
1 tablespoon instant minced
   onion
4½ cups canned tomatoes
1 pound frozen perch fillets,
   thawed
Hot cooked rice

Heat salad oil in saucepan. Add celery and cook 5 minutes or until tender. Add seasonings, onion, and tomatoes. Cook over low heat 30 minutes or until slightly thick. Add defrosted fish 5 minutes before cooking time is up. Serve over hot cooked rice.

Yield: 6 servings

Spinach With Rice

1 cup uncooked long-
   grained rice
¾ teaspon salt
1 teaspoon lemon juice
¼ pound fresh spinach,
   chopped
1 tablespoon butter or
   margarine

½ teaspoon crumbled basil
   leaves
⅛ teaspoon instant garlic
   powder
1/16 teaspoon ground black
   pepper

In covered saucepan cook rice in 1½ cups boiling water with salt and lemon juice. Just before rice is tender, add chopped spinach. Cook until tender, about 5 minutes. Add remaining ingredients. Mix well.

Yield: 3–4 servings

Sicilian Tomato Salad

1 quart (about 30) cherry
  tomatoes
¼ cup olive or salad oil
1 teaspoon paprika
½ teaspoon salt

½ teaspoon basil leaves
½ teaspoon ground black
  pepper
Dash of instant garlic
  powder

Wash tomatoes and cut in half. Combine remaining
ingredients and pour over tomatoes. Chill about 15
minutes. Serve on salad greens.

Yield: 4–6 servings

Fish Rolls Deluxe

2 packages (12 oz. each)
  frozen fillets of sole,
  thawed
2 tablespoons olive or
  salad oil
¼ cup flour
1 tablespoon paprika
⅛ teaspoon ground black
  pepper
¼ teaspoon instant minced
  garlic
1 teaspoon water

¼ cup olive or salad oil
1 can (10½ oz.) cream of
  mushroom soup
1 can (7½ oz.) minced
  clams, drained
1 can (4½ oz.) shrimp,
  drained and chopped
½ teaspoon basil leaves,
  crushed
⅛ teaspoon ground black
  pepper

Brush fish fillets with the 2 tablespoons of olive or salad
oil. Combine next 4 ingredients and sprinkle over fish.
Roll each fillet in jelly-roll fashion and place on broiler
rack. Broil under medium heat about 6 inches from
heat source, turning once, until done (about 12 minutes). In the meantime add minced garlic to the 1
teaspoon of water and set aside for 10 minutes. Heat
the ¼ cup of olive or salad oil, add softened garlic
and sauté 5 minutes. Blend in remaining ingredients
and simmer 1 minute or until sauce is thoroughly
heated. Place fish rolls on a warm platter and spoon
sauce over all.

Yield: 6 servings

Eggplant With Basil Casserole

3 tablespoons sweet pepper
   flakes
2 tablespoons celery flakes
1½ tablespoons instant
   minced onion
⅛ teaspoon instant minced
   garlic
⅓ cup water
6 slices bacon
1 pound ground chuck
1 can (16 oz.) whole
   tomatoes
1 can (6 oz.) tomato paste

½ teaspoon basil leaves
½ teaspoon salt
¼ teaspoon ground red
   pepper
⅛ teaspoon ground black
   pepper
1 bay leaf
2 medium-sized eggplants,
   1 pound each
Boiling water
1 teaspoon salt
1½ cups grated sharp
   American cheese

Combine first 5 ingredients; let stand 5 minutes for vegetables to soften. In the meantime, in a large skillet cook bacon until partially cooked. Remove to absorbent paper. Add softened vegetables to bacon fat and cook over low heat, stirring frequently, until onion is lightly browned. Add ground chuck and cook, stirring frequently, until brown. In a large bowl combine tomatoes, tomato paste, *basil leaves,* the ½ teaspoon of salt, red pepper, black pepper, and bay leaf. Add to beef mixture. Cook, uncovered, over low heat, stirring frequently until thickened, 30 to 45 minutes. Meanwhile, slice unpeeled eggplants crosswise in ½-inch slices. Place in large amount of boiling water to which the 1 teaspoon of salt has been added. Return to boil and cook 5 minutes. Drain on absorbent paper. In a buttered 2-quart casserole place a layer of eggplant; top with tomato sauce and cheese. Repeat until all ingredients have been used. Cover and bake in a preheated moderate oven (350°F.) 30 minutes. Remove cover, top with reserved bacon and bake another 10 minutes or until bacon is crisp.

Yield: 6 servings

BAY (LAUREL) LEAVES

Laurus nobilis L.

A. Flowering branch	9. Sterile stamen (staminodium)
1. Cluster of flowers	10. Pistil
2. Male flower	11. Transverse section of ovary
3. Vertical section of male flower	12. Fruit (drupe)
4. Corolla	13. Transverse section of fruit
5. Stamens, mature and immature	14. Vertical section of fruit
6. Pollen grains	
7. Female flower	
8. Vertical section of female flower	

BAY (LAUREL) LEAVES

Family: *Lauraceae*

LATIN	• Laurus nobilis L.
SPANISH	• Laurel
FRENCH	• Laurier
GERMAN	• Lorbeer
SWEDISH	• Lager
ARABIC	• Ghār
DUTCH	• Laurier
ITALIAN	• Alloro
PORTUGUESE	• Loureiro
RUSSIAN	• Lavr
JAPANESE	• Gekkeiju
CHINESE	• Yueh-kuei

BAY *(Laurel)* LEAVES

THE bay tree, *Laurus nobilis,* also known as sweet bay and laurel, is an evergreen member of the laurel family native to the Mediterranean region and Asia Minor. It grows to a height of 50 to 60 feet and is often shaped by gardeners to a pyramidal form. The smooth bark is olive green or reddish. The highly aromatic leaves are thick, dark green, and glossy on the upper surface but pale green beneath. The elliptical leaf is 1 to 3 inches long by ½ to 1 inch wide, stiff, almost brittle, in texture, and wavy along the edges. The bay tree is polygamous—it may have male flowers, female flowers, and hermaphroditic flowers all at the same time. The flower, which is small and yellow or greenish-white, is followed by a dark purple one-seeded berry about the size of a small grape.

Laurus nobilis, source of the bay leaves used for culinary purposes, should not be confused with the West Indian bay tree *Pimenta acris,* whose leaves are distilled to produce bay rum; or with the cherry laurel, *Prunus laurocerasus,* whose leaves contain prussic acid and under certain conditions (wilted) are poisonous.

The bay or laurel tree grows well in the subtropics and is cultivated today as a spice or an ornamental in the Far East, the Mediterranean area, the Canary Islands, Greece, Turkey, Mexico, France, Belgium, Central America, and the milder climates of North America. It can be propagated by cuttings from half-ripened shoots, which root in six to nine months. The trees grow best in a rich, well-drained soil. In many regions of commercial culture where such soils do not occur naturally, it is necessary to set each young plant in a large hole 2½ feet across by 2 feet deep, filled with compost and sand. Although tolerant of several degrees of frost when mature, the young bay tree is susceptible to any frost and requires seasonal protection.

Bay leaves are harvested by manual picking, early in the day. To retain the natural green color of the leaves, they are dried in thin layers in trays kept in a moderately warm, sheltered place. When drying, the leaves may be pressed lightly under boards to avoid a tendency to curl. Bay leaves should not be dried in the sun, for this would cause the leaves to turn brown and lose much of the essential oil. After about fifteen days of drying, the leaves are packed in sealed containers.

In the remote mists of mythology Apollo, the sun god, incessantly pursued the reluctant nymph Daphne, until the gods mercifully turned her into a laurel tree; the plant is still known in Greece as the Daphne tree.

In ancient Greece and Rome laurel leaves and branchlets were used as wreaths to crown their victors. At the Olympic games, founded in 776 B.C., the champions wore garlands of laurel. Our word baccalaureate means "laurel berries" and signifies the successful completion of one's studies, for it alludes to the bay wreaths worn by poets and scholars when they received academic honors in ancient Greece.

In Palestine and the Middle East the bay tree was well known in biblical times. In Psalms 37:35 we find this simile: "I have seen the wicked in great power, and spreading himself like a green bay tree." The image is an apt and dramatic one, for the handsome, luxuriant evergreen growth of the bay tree must have been very striking in an arid, barren land where so many of the trees were miserable, thorny, stumpy, and weather-beaten.

In Rome the bay tree was not only a symbol of glory, but was also reputed to provide effective protection against thunder and lightning. The emperor Tiberius (42 B.C.–A.D. 37) is said to have had such faith in this belief that during electrical storms he would place a laurel wreath on his head and hide under his bed.

The emperor Nero (A.D. 37–68) is reported to have fled to Laurentium during an outbreak of the plague so that he might conserve his health by breathing air purified by bay trees.

Victorious Roman legionnaires would wipe the blood off their swords and lances with bay leaves as a gesture of atonement.

Although the bay tree was regarded as a protection and as a harbinger of good luck in Italy, there was a superstition that when these trees died a great disaster would follow. Small wonder that the people of Padua long held to this belief, for in 1629 a pestilence broke out there immediately after the bay trees in the city fell sick and perished. Shakespeare, in *Richard II*, Act II, Scene IV, referred to this superstition:

Captain: 'Tis thought the King is dead; we will not stay.
The bay trees in our country are all wither'd.

During the Middle Ages bay berries were believed to stimulate women's periods and hence were used in heavy doses to promote abortion.

In the *Grete Herbal*, printed in England in 1526 by Peter Treveris, a paste of powdered bay berries mixed with honey was recommended "against the evil color of the face and against a manner of red things that come in young folks' faces."

Culpepper, in his *Complete Herbal*, written about the middle of the seventeenth century, recommended oil of bay berries:

> The oil made of the berries is very comfortable in all cold griefs of the joints, nerves, arteries, stomach, belly, or womb; and helpeth palsies, convulsions, cramps, aches, trembling, and numbness in any part, weariness also, and pains that come by sore travailing. All griefs and pains proceeding from wind, either in the head, stomach, back, belly, or womb, by anointing the parts affected therewith; and pains of the ears are also cured by dropping in some of the oil, or by receiving into the ears the fume of the decoction of the berries through a funnel. The oil takes away the marks of the skin and flesh by bruises, falls, &c. and dissolveth the congealed blood in them. It helpeth also the itch, scabs, and weals in the skin.

The bayberry of coastal American dunes *(Myrica pensylvanica)* is wholly unrelated to the bay berry of literature and world commerce alluded to in the passages above. Confusion frequently results when the same name is used in different countries for different plants.

At the present time bay leaves are used mostly for nonmedicinal purposes and are among the most important herbs in the spice trade. The dried leaves contain from 1 to 3 percent of a highly aromatic volatile oil, which can be isolated by steam distillation.

Oil of bay and oil of bay leaves are used in the preparation of pickling spice and in the flavoring of vinegar.

Bay leaves, bitter, spicy, and pungent in taste, are

popular in French cuisine for flavoring bouillabaisse, bouillons, meats, fish, poultry, vegetables, and stews, and they add zest to "Hearty Bean Soup."

Bouillabaisse

1 cup diced onions
½ cup sliced carrots
4 cloves crushed garlic
2 tablespoons chopped
  parsley
2 small bay leaves
4 teaspoons salt
½ teaspoon saffron
¼ teaspoon thyme leaves
¼ teaspoon fennel seed
¼ teaspoon ground black
  pepper
½ cup olive or salad oil

1 pound striped bass or
  sea bass
1 pound codfish
1 pound red snapper
¾ pound mackerel
1 cup white wine
1½ pounds tomatoes,
  quartered
2½ pounds lobster
1 dozen cherrystone clams
1 dozen mussels
¾ pound peeled and
  deveined shrimp

Sauté onions, carrots, garlic, spices, and herbs in oil, about 5 minutes. Add bass, codfish, red snapper, mackerel, and wine. Cook 5 minutes over high heat. Add tomatoes and remaining seafood. Add water to cover (about 1 quart). Continue to boil vigorously for 20 minutes.

Yield: 8–10 servings

Hearty Bean Soup

2 cups diced potatoes
1 cup sliced carrots
2 cans (1 lb. 4 oz. each)
  chick-peas
1 can (1 lb.) lima beans
1 can (1 lb.) tomatoes
4 whole cloves

3 bay leaves
2 teaspoons instant minced
  onion
1 teaspoon parsley flakes
1 teaspoon salt
⅛ teaspoon ground black
  pepper

Cook potatoes and carrots in 1½ quarts boiling water about 20 minutes until tender. Remove vegetables from water; set aside. Reserve water. Purée 1 can chick-peas and add to water with remaining ingredients. Simmer

25 to 30 minutes. Remove *bay leaves* and cloves. Add reserved cooked vegetables. Serve as main dish soup with cooked sausage.

Yield: 6–8 servings

Barbecued Ribs

1 tablespoon instant minced
  onion
1 tablespoon ground
  cinnamon
1 teaspoon ground black
  pepper
1 teaspoon salt
½ teaspoon instant minced
  garlic

1 bay leaf, *crumbled*
2 tablespoons soy sauce
3 pounds lean pork
  spareribs
2 teaspoons light brown
  sugar
¼ cup water

Combine minced onion, cinnamon, black pepper, salt, minced garlic, *bay leaf,* and soy sauce. Prick spareribs with fork and rub in soy sauce mixture. Marinate overnight or 12 hours. Cook meat over slow-burning fire 1 hour, turning often. Brush meat while cooking with brown sugar mixed with water as often as meat looks dry. Cut into serving pieces.

Yield: 4–6 servings

Codfish Chowder
(Party size)

2 pounds codfish
4 cups water
2 teaspoons salt
¼ cup diced salt pork
4 cups diced potatoes
⅓ cup onion flakes
¼ teaspoon instant minced
  garlic

1 tablespoon salt
1 bay leaf
½ teaspoon ground black
  pepper
3 cups milk
2 tablespoons butter or
  margarine
Paprika

Wash codfish and place in a saucepan. Add water and salt. Slowly bring to boiling point and simmer 10 minutes or until fish is flaky. Lift fish from the stock, reserving the stock. Remove and discard skin and bones from the fish and set fish aside. Fry pork until crisp. Remove pork from fat, drain on paper towel, and set aside. Add pork fat to the fish stock along with potatoes, onion flakes, minced garlic, salt, and *bay leaf.* Cover, bring to boiling point, and cook 20 minutes or until potatoes are tender. Add fish, black pepper, milk, and butter or margarine. Cover and simmer 5 minutes. Add crisp pork and serve hot garnished with paprika.

Yield: 1 gallon

Quick Curry of Lamb

2 tablespoons instant
  minced onion
2 pounds lean lamb, cut in
  1-inch pieces
2 tablespoons shortening
1 tablespoon curry powder
1 apple, peeled, cored, and
  cut in pieces

1 can (12 oz.) tomatoes
¼ teaspoon instant garlic
  powder
1 teaspoon salt
⅛ teaspoon ground black
  pepper
1 bay leaf
3 tablespoons flour

Mix instant onion and 2 tablespoons water; let stand 8 minutes for onion to soften. Brown lamb lightly in shortening with softened onion and curry powder. Add apple, tomatoes, and garlic powder. Stir in 2 cups water or stock, salt, pepper, and *bay leaf;* mix well. Simmer, covered, until lamb is tender, 1 to 1½ hours. Mix flour with ¼ cup cold water until smooth; add and cook until thickened, stirring. Serve with boiled rice or rice pilaf.

Yield: 4 servings

Carmelite Soup

2 cups diced potatoes
1 cup sliced carrots
2 cans (1 lb. 4 oz. each)
  chick-peas
4 whole cloves
3 bay leaves
2 teaspoons instant minced
  onion

1 teaspoon parsley flakes
1 teaspoon salt
⅛ teaspoon ground black
  pepper
1 pound Italian sausage,
  cooked and sliced
3 hard-boiled egg yolks

Cook potatoes and carrots in 1½ quarts of boiling water, about 20 minutes or until tender. Remove vegetables from water; set aside. Reserve water. Purée chick-peas and add to water with remaining ingredients. Simmer 25 to 30 minutes. Remove *bay leaves* and cloves. Add reserved cooked vegetables and sausage. Serve as main dish soup. Garnish with chopped egg yolks.

Yield: 6–8 servings

CAPSICUM PEPPERS

Capsicum annuum L.

A. Flowering branch	**7.** Transverse section of ovary
1. Vertical section of flower	**8.** Fruit (berry)
2. Throat of corolla showing attachments of stamens	**9.** Transverse section of fruit
3. Anthers	**10.** Seed
4. Pollen grains	**11.** Vertical section of seed showing curved embryo
5. Pistil	**12.** Transverse section of seed
6. Style and flattened stigma	

CAPSICUM PEPPERS

Family: **Solanaceae**

	Paprika	Cayenne Pepper
LATIN	• Capsicum annuum L.	Capsicum frutescens L.
SPANISH	• Pimentón	Pimentón
FRENCH	• Poivre de Guinée	Poivre rouge
GERMAN	• Paprika	Cayennepfeffer
SWEDISH	• Spansk Peppar	Kajennpeppar
DUTCH	• Spaanse Peper	Cayennepeper
ITALIAN	• Peperone	Pepe di Caienna
PORTUGUESE	• Pimentão	Pimentão-de-Caiena
RUSSIAN	• Struchkovy Pyerets	Kayenski Pyerets
JAPANESE	• Papurika	Keien peppâ
CHINESE	• Hsiung-ya-li-Chiao	La-Chiao
ARABIC	• Filfil Ahmar	Filfil Ahmar

	Chili Pepper
LATIN	Capsicum frutescens L.
SPANISH	Chile
FRENCH	Piment enragé
GERMAN	Beissbeere
SWEDISH	Spansk Peppar
DUTCH	Spaanse Peper
ITALIAN	Peperone
PORTUGUESE	Pimentão picante
RUSSIAN	Struchkovy Pyerets
JAPANESE	Tôgarashi
CHINESE	Hung-Fan-Chiao
ARABIC	Filfil

CAPSICUM PEPPERS

PAPRIKA, red pepper, and cayenne pepper are ground condiments made from the juiceless ripe, dried pods of plants of the genus *Capsicum*, commonly known as "chili peppers" or "chilies." They are members of the Solanaceae (nightshade family) indigenous to Mexico, Central America, the West Indies, and much of South America.

The Spaniards came to the New World looking for the black pepper of Asian origin that they had known

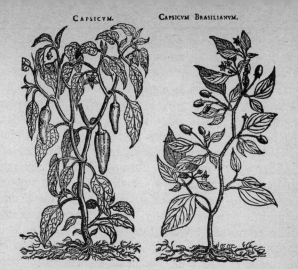

SOUTH AMERICAN CAPSICUMS (CHILIES)
Woodcut from Clusius, *Exoticorum libri* (1605). Left: probably C. *annuum;* right: possibly C. *chinense.*

in Europe. Instead, they accidentally came upon an even more piquant spice in the multicolored, variformed pods of the capsicum peppers, already cultivated for many centuries by the native Indians in tropical America.

Peter Martyr reported in September 1493 that Columbus had brought back to Spain "peppers more pungent than that from Caucasus," peppers of many kinds and colors. In the middle of the sixteenth century C. de Leon, a Spanish traveler in Peru, noted that the favorite condiment of the Peruvian Indians, called *uchu,* came from the pods of a pepperlike plant. Long before the arrival of the Spaniards, the Mayan Indians of northern Guatemala used the capsicum peppers medicinally, calling them *lc,* and taking them internally to cure cramps and diarrhea.

By 1650 the cultivation and use of the capsicum peppers as a condiment had spread throughout Europe, as well as to the Asian and African tropics. In other parts of the world, in different soils and climates, the capsicum fruits took on modified characteristics—probably through selection by man. In Hungary the peppers that evolved, known as *paprika,* were much milder than their American ancestors. In Spain, where the returning conquistadores first introduced the seeds to European soil, successive generations of the capsicums became larger in size but their pungency gradually disappeared.

After a long period of cultivation in many different environments, much hybridization has taken place. Considerable variation exists among the *Capsicums* in growth habit, size, color, shape, flavor, pungency, and even in their botanical classification. Carolus Linnaeus (1707–1778), Swedish botanist and founder of the modern system of botanical nomenclature, described two species of *Capsicum* in 1753, and in 1767 he added two more. By 1832 the German botanist A. Fingerhuth had described twenty-five different species of *Capsicum.* Some confusion exists today as to exactly how many species are involved—over ninety species have been described—but recent authorities, including C. B. Heiser, Jr., recognize five main cultivated species of *Capsicum: C. annuum, C. frutescens, C. chinense, C. pendulum*, and *C. pubescens.*

Commercially, *C. annuum* is the most widely cultivated species throughout the world, and almost all the varieties cultivated in the United States and Europe belong to it. It includes nearly all the sweet peppers, as well as a large number of pungent, strong-flavored forms. It is an annual herbaceous plant that normally is 1 to 3 feet high, though some varieties are taller. It is distinguished by white flowers that are solitary (one per node). Its fruits are extremely diversified; they may vary in length from ½ inch to 11 inches and in mature color from yellow to brown or purple to bright brick red. The glossy ripe pods contain a spongy central column bearing numerous rows of flat, kidney-shaped seeds. Some fruits are long and thin, some small and round, others large, fleshy, and conical.

A variety of *C. annuum (C. annuum* var. *minimum)*, often called "bird pepper" or *chilitepin,* grows naturally in northern South America and throughout much of Central America and Mexico and is found in a few of our southern states. Bird pepper may be similar to the wild progenitor of the cultivated varieties of chilies.

In colder climates the large, sweet, thick-skinned, fleshy pods of such mild-tasting varieties of *C. annuum* as the bell peppers Ruby King and California Wonder are eaten as vegetables, either green or ripe, cooked or raw. They may be included in salads, cooked as stuffed peppers, or utilized in pickling. Even in Mexico among the many types of *C. annuum* peppers there are some so mild that they are sold in the markets as sweets, like candied ginger.

In addition to the mild varieties of *C. annuum,* there are many pungent, strong-flavored types. In general, however, the fruits of *C. frutescens*—the well-known Tabasco variety is one—are smaller and more burningly pungent than those of *C. annuum.* Both species provide the chilies of commerce.

The plants of *C. frutescens* are perennial and taller than those of *C. annuum,* ranging up to 6 feet in height, with prominently angled branches and clusters of greenish-white flowers in the leaf axils, usually two flowers or more per node. The *C. frutescens* stems become woody and much thicker than those of *C. annuum.*

C. frutescens is cultivated mainly in the tropics and in the warmer regions of the United States, since the growing seasons in the northern temperate zones are too short for full fruit maturity. The fiery elongated pods, varying in color from red to orange to yellow, rarely exceed 4 inches in length. Usually the fruits are only 1 to 1½ inches long, and ¼ to ¾ inch in diameter. Because of their high cost of production, the smallest, hottest varieties are gradually disappearing and are being replaced by types with larger pods. Through selection and plant breeding, varieties that combine the desired features of large pod, maximum pungency, and a high number of pods per plant are being developed.

Other species of chilies of lesser economic importance are grown in the Western Hemisphere. *C. chinense* Jacq., closely related to *C. frutescens,* is cultivated throughout tropical South America, the Caribbean region, and southern Central America, usually in lowland areas. The fruits of this extremely variable species are generally round and highly pungent; the plants are usually characterized by large leaves and three to five flowers at each node.

C. pendulum Willd., grown for the most part in Ecuador, Peru, and Bolivia, is distinguished by the yellow- or brown-spotted corollas of its flowers and its conical pungent fruits.

A fifth cultivated species, the small and hairy *C. pubescens* Ruiz & Pavon, grows at higher elevations than the other chilies. It is largely confined to Andean South America but may occasionally be found in the highlands of Central America and Mexico. Its flowers are bluish or purple, its pungent fruits small, handsome, and oblong, with black seeds. As in most chilies, the most common colors of the ripe fruits are red and orange.

The well-known bland seasoning paprika may be obtained from any one of many varieties of *C. annuum.* Even in the dried pods from which brilliant red paprika powder is made there is a wide range of pungencies, shapes, and appearances. In Spain and Morocco the peppers grown for paprika are round, about the size of an apricot; while in the Balkan countries and in California the paprika is produced from longer, more conical and pointed varieties. Usually the peppers grown for paprika are medium-sized, mild, and quite fleshy.

Through careful breeding and selection, paprika pepper varieties are chosen to meet standards of color, flavor, and number of pods per plant. The plants are propagated by seed, sown as early in the spring as possible for this long-season annual crop. Seed may also be sown in hothouses and the seedlings transplanted later to the field. Warm, well-drained sandy loam or clay loam soils are recommended. The final field spacing is about 3 feet between the rows and 15 inches between plants. Thorough weeding and frequent cultivation are required. Flowering commences about three months after sowing and continues for another three months.

The harvest may extend over several months during the summer and fall ripening period; hot, dry weather is desirable during the harvest. Only fully mature fruits are picked, and five or six pickings may be required.

Although in the United States the paprika pods are not generally cured before drying, in most European paprika-producing countries the pods are cured for from three to twenty-five days before the final drying. Curing involves either hanging the pods in long strands or piling them in windows in sheltered locations.

Various methods of artificial drying are employed. At moderate temperatures two to three days may be needed in a heated building to remove about 85 percent of the moisture; in California, by a current of forced hot air in tunnels or by stainless steel belt driers, the drying may be completed in thirty hours. In Mexico, Morocco, and some European countries, the paprika pods are dried in the sun for five to fifteen days.

Under favorable conditions, a yield per acre of about 2,500 pounds of dried paprika may be obtained. Formerly the United States requirements of paprika were imported mostly from Spain, Hungary, Yugoslavia, Morocco, and Bulgaria. American paprika, grown and produced in southern California, has become more important in recent years and now supplies more than any individual foreign country, although less than the total imports from all countries. California produces both sweet and mildly pungent varieties. The American paprika, being mechanically dried under controlled conditions, makes possible year-round shipments of standardized color and uniform pungency.

Most paprika sold in the United States is the "sweet," nonpungent type, with a brilliant red color. Its effect is most striking on light-colored foods—used liberally as a garnish spice, it gives a blush for eye appeal and adds flavor to a wide variety of such colorless foods as cheese, eggs, potatoes, and light-hued sauces. Commercially, large quantities of paprika are used in the manufacture of sausages and other meat products. Famous European dishes featuring paprika include *Rosenpaprika* and Hungarian goulash. A Hungarian proverb maintains: "One man may yearn for fame, another for wealth, but everyone yearns for paprika goulash."

Paprika owes its vivid natural color to several carotenoids in the pod itself. These red and yellow pigments include carotene (the coloring matter of the carrot) and capsanthin. Paprika is used for extractable as well as surface color.

An unusual asset of paprika is that pound for pound it is higher in vitamin C (ascorbic acid) content than the citrus fruits. Dr. Szent-Györgyi, a Hungarian scientist, was awarded a Nobel Prize in 1937 for isolating vitamin C in paprika and for his discovery that paprika pods were one of the richest available sources of this requisite vitamin.

Oleoresin of paprika, obtained through solvent extraction of the ground paprika pods, is a natural vegetable coloring agent that is extensively produced in Europe, Morocco, and California. It is utilized in the manufacture of meat and sausage products, salad dressings, and other processed foods where a bright, natural, red color is desired in a highly concentrated form.

The pungency of the capsicum pods is due to a crystalline substance known as capsaicin. In the milder types of *C. annuum* the capsaicin content is very low, but in the hotter varieties of *C. frutescens* the fruits may contain from 0.2 to 1 percent of this highly pungent ingredient, concentrated mainly in the thin tissues of the placental region where the seeds are attached to the spongy central portion. In general, the small, thin-skinned peppers of *C. frutescens*—such as the tiny "birdseye" or "devil" peppers, which are as "hot" as live coals—have the highest capsaicin content and consequently are the most pungent.

During the preparation of paprika a mild product is obtained if the central "cores" with their placental region are removed. Spanish paprika, for example, calls for the complete removal of the seeds and the central placental section, thus reducing the yield and the pungency but increasing the mildness, cost of production, and price.

Medicinally, capsicum peppers have been used internally in the past as stomachics, carminatives, stimulants, aids to digestion, and as a cure for various ailments including dropsy, colic, diarrhea, toothache, black vomit, and gout. Externally they have been employed as a counterirritant to cure rheumatism.

In the West Indies a stomachic preparation called *mandram* is still used today. It is prepared by adding cucumbers, shallots, lime juice, and Madeira wine to mashed pods of small, acrid bird peppers.

Modern usage of the pungent capsicums, however, is mainly limited to the field of seasoning. *C. frutescens* plants are grown on a large scale in India, Thailand, Mexico, Japan, Turkey, Uganda, Nigeria, Ethiopia, and Tanzania. Under favorable conditions, these perennial plantings may remain in production for three or four years. India is the world's largest exporter of chilies.

Unlike allspice, *Pimenta dioica* (sometimes known as Jamaican pepper or pimento), which is an evergreen tree indigenous to the Western Hemisphere that never prospered in the tropics of the Orient, chili peppers have been cultivated so successfully during the past four hundred years that they now grow as escapes from cultivation in warm regions throughout the world. In almost every tropical country they have become the most popular condiment for local consumption, being employed as daily additives to native foods. Some exotic yet widely used seasonings based on the pungency of capsicum pods are Indian curry, North African *felfel,* and the fiery West Indian pepper sauces.

One of the reasons for this far-reaching popularity of the chilies in tropical climates may be their ability to raise the body temperature, producing perspiration and thereby causing the surrounding oppressive air to seem cool by comparison. Likewise, by stimulating the flow of saliva and the gastric juices they may overcome loss of appetite and aid weak digestions. Another reason may be found in the monotony of the diet in countries where the chilies have become extremely popular: Rice in India, corn and beans in Mexico and Central America, and cassava from the tapioca plant in the Amazon are all extremely bland foods that may be varied by strong and cheap seasoning.

COMMON TYPES OF CAPSICUM (CHILI) PEPPERS
Left: the mild Anaheim for paprika; upper right: the bland Ancho for chili powder; lower right: the hot, biting Santaka for cayenne or crushed red pepper. The Anaheim and Ancho chilies are grown in southern California and northern Mexico; the Santakas are imported from Japan.

Just as black pepper was exclusively the spice of the wealthy in the Middle Ages, chilies (including *C. annuum* and *C. frutescens*) have become the common spice of the world's underprivileged masses in the twentieth century. In fact, more chili peppers are produced and consumed than any other spice in the world.

Dried ripe pods of many different varieties of *C. annuum* and *C. frutescens* are utilized to prepare the packaged or processed condiments known as cayenne pepper, ground red pepper, crushed red pepper, chili powder, whole chili peppers, chili pequins, chili con carne seasoning, barbecue sauce, *chilitepines,* and small hot chilies.

Some of the better-known varieties of pungent peppers are: Cayenne, Birdseye, Chili Pequin, Tabasco, Japanese Santaka, Japanese Hontaka, Ancho, Du Chili, Coral Gem, Devil, Louisiana Sport, Chilitepines, Jalapeño, and Bombay Cherries.

These capsicums vary widely in size, shape, color, flavor, and pungency. Some Japanese, Mexican, African, and Louisiana varieties are very small (less than 1 inch in length) and highly pungent. Other larger red peppers and chili peppers from California are over 6 inches in length, redder in color, and not as "hot."

Cayenne pepper, always a ground product, is made from the smaller, more pungent capsicums grown in India, Africa, Mexico, Mainland China, Japan, Louisiana, and other areas—but not in Cayenne, French Guiana. It varies in color from orange-red to deep dark red. This biting condiment should be used with restraint, for a small amount will add considerable zest and flavor to dull dishes. To simplify consumer identification, some manufacturers have eliminated the word "cayenne" and labeled their pungent produce "red pepper."

Red pepper may sometimes refer to cayenne pepper, but it usually designates a ground red pepper that is milder than cayenne. It is prepared from larger, less pungent red peppers from the Carolinas, California, Louisiana, and Turkey. Ground red pepper adds color and flavor to Mexican-style dishes, spaghetti, soups, and stews.

Crushed red pepper, also known as "peperone rosso" and "pizza pepper," has increased in popularity in recent years for use in Italian and Mexican foods. Many hot varieties of *C. annuum* and *C. frutescens* are crushed and mixed to produce this pungent seasoning used in sausages, meats, spaghetti, and pizza.

Chili powder is a blend of spices that includes ground chilies, ground oregano, ground cumin, garlic powder, and other ground spices. A combination of chili peppers and other herbs was used by the Aztec Indians in Mexico prior to 1500, a forerunner of our chili powder. Today this popular condiment is the basic ingredient of most Mexican-type dishes, like chili con carne and hot tamales, and is in demand as a general seasoning for eggs, shellfish, vegetables, gravies, and stews. Canners and food processors use large amounts of chili powder in chili con carne, chili with beans, Mexican-type foods, sausage products, pork and beans, and other processed foods. Contrary to popular belief, chili powder is not always "hot"—it may include also some of the less pungent capsicums.

Whole chili peppers and *chilitepines,* available in whole form, are especially popular in the southwestern part of the United States. The former usually consist of the long, dried red chilies, while the latter include smaller, more acrid, fiery orange-red capsicums, mostly of Mexican origin. These whole pungent capsicums are so irritating to the skin that it is advisable to wear gloves when preparing them for table use to avoid "burning" the fingers. The whole chilies may be utilized to prepare chili vinegar, mixed with other spices to prepare pickles, or cut up to add pungency to sauces and gravies.

Capsaicin, the pungent principle of the capsicum pods, is utilized in the manufacture of ginger ale and ginger beer.

A dark red, extremely acrid and pungent liquid, oleoresin of capsicum, can be extracted from the pods with alcohol or ethyl ether. The pungency of this extract can be controlled and standardized for use in seasoning instead of the ground capsicum product.

Oleoresin of capsicum is used in the food and pharmaceutical industries where a highly concentrated pungency is required. Oleoresin of paprika, on the other hand, is utilized for its concentrated color, not its pungency.

On steam distillation, the dried, crushed capsicum fruits yield little or no essential oil, but the content of fixed oil in the whole dried pods may vary from 10 to 13 per cent.

During recent years the growing American interest in outdoor barbecue cooking has greatly increased the demand for popular blended seasonings—chili con carne seasoning, barbecue sauce, Tabasco sauce, taco seasoning, enchilada seasoning, and barbecue spice—that include the ground pungent pods of varieties of *C. annuum* and *C. frutescens* as a basic ingredient.

Veal Paprikash With Spätzle

¼ cup salad or olive oil
½ cup chopped onions
¼ cup chopped green peppers
1 tablespoon paprika
2 pounds veal cubes
¼ cup flour
1 teaspoon salt
¼ teaspoon ground black pepper

1 tablespoon butter or margarine
1 tablespoon flour
½ teaspoon paprika
½ cup milk
1 cup sour cream
Spätzle

Heat oil in 10- or 12-inch skillet. Add onions, green peppers, and the 1 tablespoon of *paprika*. Cook slowly, stirring frequently, until onion is lightly browned. Dredge meat in a mixture of flour, salt, and pepper. Add meat to skillet and brown slowly on all sides. Add ⅓ cup water; cover and simmer, stirring occasionally. Add more water if needed. Cook 45 to 60 minutes or until tender. Meantime, while meat is cooking prepare and set aside *spätzle*. Just before veal is tender, melt butter in small saucepan over low heat. Blend in flour and the ½ teaspoon of *paprika* until smooth, stirring constantly and until mixture bubbles. Remove from heat and gradually add milk. Return to heat and bring rapidly to a boil, stirring constantly; cook 1 to 2 minutes. Remove from heat and add sour cream slowly, beating vigorously. When veal is tender pour sauce into skillet. Cook mixture over low heat, stirring constantly, 3 to 5 minutes or until heated; do not boil. Serve with *spätzle*.

SPÄTZLE

3 teaspoons salt
2⅓ cups sifted all-purpose flour

1 egg, slightly beaten

Bring 2 quarts water and 2 teaspoons of the salt to boil in a 4-quart saucepan. Sift flour with the remaining 1 teaspoon of salt. Combine egg with 1 cup water. Gradually add flour mixture to egg mixture, stirring until smooth. Spoon ½ teaspoon batter into boiling salted water, dipping spoon into water each time. Remove *spätzle* from water when they rise to surface. Add melted butter, if desired.

Yield: 4–6 servings

Hungarian Goulash

2 pounds boneless beef stew meat
1 tablespoon shortening or beef suet
2 cups thinly sliced onions
1 can (1 lb. 11 oz.) sauerkraut
1 cup canned tomatoes

1 tablespoon paprika
1 teaspoon caraway seeds
⅛ teaspoon cayenne
Salt to taste
½ cup chopped green peppers
1 cup sour cream

Cut beef into 1-inch cubes. Melt shortening in Dutch oven and brown meat on all sides. Add onions and sauté until golden brown. Add sauerkraut, tomatoes, ½ cup water, *paprika,* caraway seeds, cayenne, and salt. Cook, covered, over low heat about 1 hour. Add green peppers. Cook until tender, about 10 to 15 minutes. Remove 1 cup liquid from pan. Gradually add sour cream, stirring so it will not curdle. Pour mixture back into pan. Serve with cooked noodles.

Yield: 4–6 servings

Hungarian Beef Casserole

⅓ cup onion flakes
2 tablespoons olive oil
2 tablespoons paprika
2 teaspoons salt
2 teaspoons caraway seed
1 teaspoon marjoram leaves
½ teaspoon instant garlic
    powder
¼ teaspoon ground black
    pepper

½ cup catsup
1½ cups beef broth
3 tablespoons olive oil
3 pounds lean chuck, cut in
    1½-inch pieces
¼ cup flour
1 cup sour cream
Cooked broad noodles

Combine onion flakes and ⅓ cup water; let stand 10 minutes for onions to soften. Heat the 2 tablespoons oil in a skillet; add softened onions and cook over low heat until lightly browned. Blend in *paprika,* salt, caraway seed, marjoram leaves, garlic powder, and black pepper. Stir in catsup and beef broth. Heat to boiling; remove from heat and reserve. In the meantime, heat the 3 tablespoons of oil in a deep saucepan. Dredge the meat in the flour and cook, a few pieces at a time, until browned on all sides. Add the broth mixture. Bring to a boil, reduce heat, and simmer slowly 2½ hours or until tender. Stir in sour cream just before serving. Serve over broad noodles.

Yield: 6 servings

Fresh Cauliflower Antipasto

1 small head cauliflower
1 green pepper, cut into
    strips ½ inch wide
½ cup carrots, cut into
    ½-inch pieces
½ cup sliced mushrooms
½ cup sliced celery
½ cup sliced stuffed green
    olives

½ cup wine vinegar
½ cup olive oil
¼ cup lemon juice
2 tablespoons sugar
2 teaspoons crushed red
    pepper
1 teaspoon salt
½ teaspoon basil leaves,
    crumbled

Break cauliflower into flowerets. Add with remaining ingredients and ¼ cup water to large skillet and bring to boil. Reduce heat and simmer, covered, 5 minutes. Cool and refrigerate overnight. Drain before serving.

Yield: 6 antipasto servings

Tomato Relish

12 medium-sized (6 lbs.) ripe tomatoes
4 medium-sized onions
2 sweet red peppers
1 cup cider vinegar
⅓ cup light brown sugar, packed
2 tablespoons salt
1 tablespoon celery seed

2 sticks cinnamon, 2 inches long
½ teaspoon crushed red pepper
½ teaspoon cumin seed
½ teaspoon instant minced garlic
½ teaspoon whole allspice
½ teaspoon whole cloves

Peel tomatoes and onions and put through a food chopper with red peppers, using medium blade. Place in preserving kettle. Add vinegar, brown sugar, salt, celery seed, cinnamon, *red pepper,* cumin seed, and garlic. Tie allspice and cloves in a bag and add. Stir and cook slowly 1½ hours or until thickened. Remove cinnamon and spice bag. Ladle into hot sterilized jars. Seal at once.

Yield: 7 jars, ½ pint each

Corned Beef, Cabbage, and Tomato Hero Sandwich

3 cups finely shredded raw cabbage
½ cup finely chopped celery
1 tablespoon finely chopped onion
¼ cup mayonnaise
1 teaspoon salt or salt to taste

¼ teaspoon crushed red pepper
4 Italian hero rolls
Butter or margarine
½ pound corned beef, sliced
Tomato slices, cut ¼ inch thick
Outside leaves of lettuce or watercress

Mix cabbage, celery, onion, mayonnaise, salt, and *crushed red pepper.* Split rolls in half lengthwise and spread with softened butter or margarine. Place slices of cooked corned beef on bottom half of each roll.

Spread with cabbage mixture. Top with tomato slices, sprinkled with additional salt and *crushed red pepper*. Top with lettuce or watercress.

Yield: 4 sandwiches

French Fried Deviled Eggs

6 large hard-cooked eggs
1 teaspoon powdered
    mustard
1 tablespoon cold water
½ teaspoon salt
½ teaspoon ground black
    pepper

Dash red pepper
1 tablespoon pickle relish
1 tablespoon mayonnaise
2 large egg yolks, beaten
Fine dry bread crumbs

Peel eggs and cut into lengthwise halves. Remove yolks and mash or put through a sieve. Mix mustard with water and let stand 10 minutes for flavor to develop. Add to egg yolks along with next 5 ingredients. Mix well. Spoon into cavities of egg whites. Put 2 halves together. Hold in place with toothpicks. Dip eggs into beaten egg yolks and then into fine dry bread crumbs. Fry until golden brown in deep fat preheated to 370°F.

Yield: 6 servings

Exotic Quick Spinach

3 packages (10 oz. each)
    frozen chopped spinach
1½ tablespoons butter or
    margarine
1½ tablespoons flour
1 teaspoon curry powder
¼ teaspoon salt
⅛ teaspoon crushed red
    pepper

$\frac{1}{16}$ teaspoon ground black
    pepper
½ cup heavy cream
¼ cup milk
½ teaspoon lemon juice
2 hard-cooked egg whites,
    coarsely chopped
2 hard-cooked egg yolks,
    sieved

Cook spinach according to package directions. Drain and reserve ¼ cup of the liquid. Keep spinach hot until serving time. In a small saucepan melt butter or margarine. Blend in flour, curry powder, salt, *crushed red pepper,* and black pepper. Combine the ¼ cup of spinach liquid, cream, and milk. Add to flour mixture. Cook over low heat, stirring constantly, until thickened and smooth. Stir in lemon juice. Serve spinach topped with curry sauce. Garnish with hard-cooked egg whites and yolks.

Yield: 6 servings

Cheese and Sausage Quiche

2 tablespoons onion flakes
2 tablespoons water
¼ pound hard sweet Italian sausage, coarsely chopped
4 large eggs, lightly beaten
1 cup heavy cream
¾ cup milk
1 tablespoon parsley flakes

¼ teaspoon ground red pepper
⅛ teaspoon ground nutmeg
⅛ teaspoon ground black pepper
¼ pound Muenster cheese, shredded
1 9-inch unbaked pastry shell

Combine onion flakes and water; let stand 5 minutes for onion to soften. In the meantime cook sausage in a skillet, tossing frequently, until browned on all sides. Remove from pan and reserve. Add softened onion flakes to skillet and cook over low heat until golden. In a large bowl combine beaten eggs, cream, milk, parsley flakes, *ground red pepper,* nutmeg, black pepper, and onion flakes. Sprinkle shredded cheese over bottom of pastry shell. Top with sausage. Pour egg mixture over all. Bake on the lowest shelf in a pre-heated hot oven (425°F.) 15 minutes. Reduce heat to 300°F. and bake 40 minutes longer or until custard is set. Serve hot.

Yield: One 9-inch quiche

CARAWAY SEED

Carum carvi L.

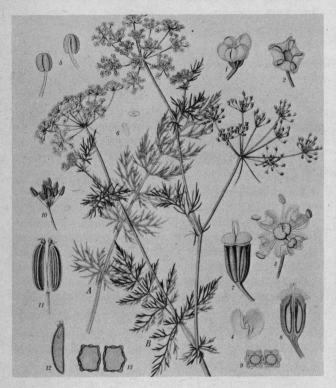

A. Lower leaf
B. Flowering and fruiting branch
1. Bud, side view
2. Bud, front view
3. Open flower
4. Single petal
5. Stamen, front and side views
6. Pollen grains
7. Pistil, side view
8. Vertical section of pistil
9. Transverse section of ovary
10. Cluster (umbel) of fruit
11. Fruit (schizocarp)
12. Vertical section of half of fruit (mericarp)
13. Transverse section of fruit

CARAWAY SEED

Family: Umbelliferae

LATIN	• <u>Carum carvi L.</u>
SPANISH	• Alcaravea
FRENCH	• Carvi
GERMAN	• Kümmel
SWEDISH	• Kummin
ARABIC	• Karauya
DUTCH	• Karwij
ITALIAN	• Carvi
PORTUGUESE	• Alcaravia
RUSSIAN	• Tmin
CHINESE	• Yuan-Sui
JAPANESE	• Karuwai

CARAWAY SEED

CARAWAY or caraway seed is the fruit of an erect hardy biennial herb similar to a carrot (and like it, a member of the parsley family) and is known botanically as *Carum carvi*. It is native to Europe, Asia, and North Africa.

Although it is widely cultivated today in many parts of the temperate zones, including northern Europe, Russia, and the United States, for many years Holland has been the world's most important commercial source of caraway.

Caraway, grown in the northern and northwestern part of the United States, has gradually escaped from cultivation and is now a widely naturalized species.

Caraway, like all biennials, requires a second growing season to mature. Seed planted in March of one year germinates in about two weeks and ripens in the summer of the second year. It grows best in a moderately light clay soil that is rich in humus and well tilled. Caraway seed is usually sown in rows about 14 inches apart, at the rate of about 6 to 8 pounds per acre. Thorough weed control is required.

A cover crop that matures in the first season—mustard, poppy, beans, or white clover—is often sown simultaneously; coriander is also useful for this purpose. The cover crop matures more quickly and is harvested before the caraway sends up its flowering stem.

The smooth flowering stems grow 1½ to 3 feet high, bear finely cut leaves, and produce rounded clusters of white flowers that commence to flower in May of the second year, ripening two months later.

When the oldest fruits have turned brown, the harvesting must be done with care. It is better to harvest early, rather than late; otherwise the fruiting cluster may be shattered and the seeds lost.

Harvesting often is done early in the morning while the dew is still on the plants, for then the seeds fall less readily than in the hottest part of the day. After being cut, the seed stalks are stacked in piles for about ten days to complete the ripening and drying before threshing.

The "seeds" (each is a split half of a fruit) are about ⅕ inch long, are curved and tapered at each end, have five pale ridges, and are somewhat horny and translucent.

Seed yields vary from 1,000 to 2,000 pounds per acre. The "straw," amounting to another 2,000 pounds per acre, is used as cattle feed.

Caraway is believed to have been cultivated and consumed longer in Europe than any other condiment. The seeds have been found in the debris of the lake dwellings in Switzerland, irrefutable evidence of the antiquity of the plant in Europe.

Caraway is known in the Orient by such names as "Roman cumin," "foreign cumin," "Persian" or "Andalusian" caraway, another indication that this spice is not a product of the Far East. It was known to the Arabs as early as the twelfth century as *karauya*, from which our word caraway is derived.

It has been cultivated in Europe, from Sicily to northern Scandinavia, since the Middle Ages. German medical books of the twelfth century mention the word *Cumich* or *Kümmich,* a term still used in southern Germany for caraway.

Caraway was known in England in the fourteenth century, for along with coriander, garlic, and pepper it is mentioned in the *Form of Cury,* a record of ancient English cookery compiled by the master cooks of King Richard II about 1390. In the sixteenth century caraway was popular in England and was more freely used than today. Shakespeare mentions it in *Henry IV, Part 2*, Act V, Scene III:

> *Shallow:* Nay, you shall see my orchard where, in an arbour, we will eat a last year's pippin of mine own grafting, with a dish of caraways, and so forth. . . .

The essential oil content of caraway seeds may average about 3 to 5 percent. Oil of caraway was recommended by Dioscorides, the renowned Greek physician and herbalist of the first century A.D., as a tonic for pale girls. Caraway seed oil is used today to flavor sausages, meats, canned goods, perfume, mouthwash, and gargle preparations. It is an essential ingredient of the liqueur kümmel. In India it is used for flavoring soaps, as it is believed to have antibacterial properties. Because carvone, the principal constituent of the essential oil, can be produced synthetically, the demand for oil of caraway has been decreasing in recent years.

Caraway seeds are a favorite flavoring for many kinds of rye bread (the seeds usually found in rye bread are caraway seeds, not rye seeds). Caraway seeds, which taste warm, sweet, biting, acrid but pleasant, are also widely used to flavor cakes, biscuits, cheese, applesauce, and cookies. Caraway Sauerkraut with Knockwurst is a traditional German favorite.

The young leaves of the caraway plant may be used in soups. The thick, fleshy roots may be eaten as a vegetable.

Caraway seed is a mild stomachic and may be utilized as a carminative in order to expel gas from the alimentary canal.

The price of caraway seed—most used in the United States is imported from Holland and Poland—has shown wide swings through the years, reflecting the vagaries of supply and demand.

Caraway Potato Dumplings

6 medium-sized potatoes, cooked
1½ slices white bread
2 tablespoons butter or margarine
2 eggs, well beaten
1 tablespoon caraway seed
1 tablespoon parsley, finely chopped
1½ teaspoons salt
½ teaspoon ground nutmeg
⅔ cup sifted all-purpose flour
¼ cup cornstarch

Mash potatoes; refrigerate, uncovered, overnight or 5 to 6 hours. Cut bread slices into ½-inch cubes; sauté in butter until golden. Set aside. Stir eggs, *caraway seed,* parsley, salt, and nutmeg into potatoes. Add flour and cornstarch; mix well. Shape into 2-inch balls. Poke 2 bread cubes into center of each ball; reshape. Drop dumplings into boiling salted water (1 teaspoon salt to 1 quart water). Do not crowd dumplings. Cook, uncovered, 8 to 10 minutes. Remove dumplings from water with perforated spoon. Drain well. Serve with Caraway Sauerkraut with Knockwurst.

Yield: 12 dumplings

Caraway Blue Cheese Wafers

1¼ cups sifted all-purpose flour
1¼ cups butter or margarine
⅓ cup (2 oz.) blue cheese, crumbled
1 tablespoon caraway seed
Caraway seeds *for topping*

Combine flour, butter, blue cheese, and *caraway seed.*

Blend until mixture resembles coarse crumbs. Stir in 5 teaspoons water. Form into roll 1½ inches in diameter; wrap in foil. Chill overnight or several hours until firm enough to slice. Cut into slices ⅛ inch thick and place on cookie sheets. Sprinkle additional *caraway seeds* over tops. Bake in preheated hot oven (400°F.) 10 minutes or until lightly browned around edges.

Yield: 3 dozen wafers

Caraway Potatoes

¼ cup bacon fat
4 cups cubed potatoes (6 or
   7 medium-sized potatoes)
1 teaspoon salt

1 teaspoon caraway seed
4 teaspoons paprika
Dash cayenne
½ cup hot water

Heat bacon fat in a heavy 9-inch skillet. Add potatoes and the next 4 ingredients. Cook a few minutes, uncovered, stirring to spread the seasonings. Add hot water. Cover and simmer 30 minutes or until potatoes are almost tender. Remove cover and cook *only* to evaporate water. Do not fry the potatoes at any time.

Yield: 6 servings

Fresh Pepper Celery Chowchow

4 cups coarsely chopped
   celery
1 cup chopped green
   peppers
1 cup chopped red peppers
½ cup chopped onions

½ cup wine vinegar
1 tablespoon mixed
   pickling spice
⅓ cup sugar
1 tablespoon salt
1 teaspoon caraway seed

Chop vegetables coarsely, using blender or coarse knife of food grinder. Place in bowl and set aside. Combine vinegar and mixed pickling spice in saucepan. Boil for 5 minutes. Strain and add remaining ingredients. Pour over vegetables. Cover and refrigerate 24 hours. Store in refrigerator.

Yield: 4½ cups

Caraway Pork Loin With Sauerkraut

1 teaspoon salt
½ teaspoon onion salt
¼ teaspoon ground black
    pepper
2 tablespoons caraway seed

4 pounds pork loin
1 tablespoon currant jelly
1 can (1 lb. 11 oz.)
    sauerkraut, drained

Combine salt, onion salt, black pepper, and 1 tablespoon of the *caraway seed*. Rub into meat on all sides. Place pork, fat side up, on rack in an uncovered roasting pan. Roast in preheated slow oven (325°F.) about 2 hours. Pour off fat in roasting pan. Spread currant jelly over pork. Place sauerkraut around pork in roasting pan. Sprinkle with remaining 1 tablespoon *caraway seed*. Roast ½ to ¾ hour longer or until done.

Yield: 6–8 servings

Caraway Sauerkraut With Knockwurst

2 pounds knockwurst
1 bay leaf
¼ teaspoon whole black
    pepper
1 can (1 lb. 11 oz.)
    sauerkraut

2 tablespoons caraway seed
½ cup brown sugar
2 cups diced tart apples

Place knockwurst in a saucepan with 2 inches boiling water, bay leaf, and whole black pepper. Cover and cook 12 to 15 minutes. Remove knockwurst from water and place in warm place, reserving water. Add sauerkraut and *caraway seed* to the cooking water. Stir in brown sugar and apples. Cover and cook 15 minutes. Serve hot with Caraway Potato Dumplings.

Yield: 6–8 servings

CARDAMOM

Elettaria cardamomum Maton

A. Leaf	6. Transverse section of ovary
1. Flower	7, 8, 9. Various views of ovary
2. Vertical section of flower	10. Transverse section of fruit
3. Stamens, front and side views	11, 12, 13. Seeds
4. Pistil with opened portion of corolla attached	14. Vertical section of seed
5. Vertical section of ovary	15. Transverse section of seed

CARDAMOM

Family: Zingiberaceae

LATIN	• **Elettaria cardamomum** Maton
SPANISH	• Cardamomo
FRENCH	• Cardamome
GERMAN	• Kardamom
SWEDISH	• Kardemumma
ARABIC	• Hāl
DUTCH	• Kardemom
ITALIAN	• Cardamomo
PORTUGUESE	• Cardamomo
RUSSIAN	• Kardamon
JAPANESE	• Karudamon
CHINESE	• Pai-tou-k'ou

CARDAMOM

CARDAMOM (*Elettaria cardamomum*) is a tall herbaceous perennial, with branching subterranean rootstock, belonging to the ginger family. It is indigenous to South India and Ceylon, where it grows in moist evergreen forests at altitudes of between 2,500 and 5,000 feet. The plant throws up leafy shoots 6 to 18 feet tall, which bear at their base one or more flowering stems 2 to 4 feet high. The flowers are small, about 1 to 1½ inches long, and are white or pale green in color with a violet central lip. The fruit, a small ovoid green capsule ½ to ¾ inch long, contains 15 to 20 hard brownish-black angular seeds that are characterized by a powerful aromatic odor and flavor. The spice may consist of the whole fruits or the hulled seeds.

The earliest reports of Ayurvedic medicine in India, dating back to the fourth century B.C., mention cardamom as an aromatic medicinal spice prescribed to cure urinary complaints and remove fat.

Cardamom was an article of Greek trade during the fourth century B.C. The inferior grades were known as *amōmon;* the superior, more aromatic, as *kardamōmon.*

By the first century A.D. Rome was importing substantial quantities of cardamom from India. Recommended by Apicius as an aid to digestion for those who indulged in gastronomic excesses, it was one of the most popular Oriental spices in the Roman cuisine. Cardamom was listed among the Indian spices liable to duty at Alexandria in A.D. 176.

Cardamom is strictly a tropical crop that requires a moderately warm climate with a mean annual temperature of about 72°F. and 100 to 160 inches of rainfall. A rich and moist loam with a good proportion of humus and excellent drainage is recommended. Until about 1800, cardamom was not grown on plantations but was obtained from wild plants in southern India and Ceylon. The customary system of production was to cut down trees and brushwood in selected forest areas and allow the cardamom seedlings to spring up. When the plants became exhausted, after several years of production, these patches of land were abandoned and new clearings were made.

Propagation is carried out today by seed or by planting sections of the rhizomes of a mature plant. In plantation culture a spacing about 9 by 12 feet under light shade is suggested. The plants commence bearing in the fourth year and continue to produce for ten to fifteen years before requiring replacement. A plantation is in production during eight or nine months of the year.

The capsules are harvested when they are about three-quarters ripe, but still green, full, and firm. To avoid collecting pods that are immature or too ripe, the same area in a plantation is harvested five or six times each year. Under good conditions, an average annual yield per acre will be 100 to 200 pounds of dried capsules. The capsules should be washed free from dirt and then dried—either in the sun for three to four days or in artificially heated rooms for 18 to 20 hours. Ten pounds of dried cardamom capsules produce about 6 pounds of decorticated seeds after the pods are hulled. There are about 50,000 decorticated cardamom seeds in one pound.

About 80 per cent of the world's supply of cardamom is produced in India, for the most part in the states of Kerala, Mysore, and Madras. In normal years, India ships overseas about 2,500 tons of cardamom and consumes internally at least as much as she exports. Recently Guatemala has become an important producer and exporter of cardamom, although the spice is seldom used in Central America. Ceylon, Tanzania, Malaysia, and Cambodia also export cardamom. Cheap substitutes or "false cardamoms," known as "Nepal," "Bengal," and "Bastard," of local importance only, are produced in Nepal, Sikkim, and Thailand from several species of *Amomum.*

Two main cultivated varieties of *Elettaria cardamomum* provide the true cardamom of commerce: the Malabar, cultivated mostly in India in the states of Coorg and Mysore, which has trailing racemes that grow horizontally along the ground; and the Mysore, distinguished by erect, arching flower stems and larger fruits than the Malabar. Most planters in Madras and Travancore-Cochin in India prefer the Mysore type, since the fruits are less likely to become damaged or spoiled than is the case in the trailing variety; furthermore, in the export market the larger pods are more desirable. About 1920 cardamom seeds (of the Mysore type, to all appearances) were introduced to the department of Alta Verapaz in central Guatemala; subsequently plantations have been developed in the southwestern Guatemalan departments of Suchitépequez, Sololá, and Quezaltenango.

Today the most important grades of cardamom in the trade are:

"Greens" (green pods, artificially dried in kilns or hot-rooms)

Sun-dried pods (light-colored, dried in the sun)

Decorticated (hulled seeds)

Bleached (pods that have been chemically bleached by fuming with burning sulfur or by hydrogen peroxide. This type has become less important in recent years.)

Greens and sun-dried pods account for about 85 percent of the world export market in cardamom, seeds for about 10 percent, and bleached for the balance.

The trade no longer refers to the most popular grades of cardamom as "longs" or "shorts" or "short-longs" or "rounds." The bulk of the green cardamoms are called "F.A.Q." (Fair Average Quality) and include such grades as "Alleppey [Indian] F.A.Q.," "Ceylon Greens," "Clipped Coorg," "Mixed [Guatemalan] Greens," and "Sundried." These fair to average qualities are imported mostly by Sweden, Pakistan, Finland, Norway, Denmark, West Germany, the United States, and England. Substantial quantities of F.A.Q. cardamom greens are also exported to the Soviet Union by India on a barter basis. The best clean, unbroken green pods, free of dirt and insect damage and weighing at least 420 grams per liter, known as "Guatemalan Best Quality Greens" or "Indian Bold Mota Greens," are in demand in the Middle East. The best quality seeds are known as "prime seeds"; bleached grades include the "Bleached," the Mangalore [Indian] "Half-Bleached A," and "Half-Bleached B."

In the United States the spice is usually referred to as *cardamom*, sometimes as *cardamon*. In England, the Middle East, and the Far East the plural form *cardamoms* is generally used.

Cardamom is the third most costly spice, topped only by saffron and vanilla. The U. S. Department of Agriculture reports that the average price for cardamom seed imported into the United States during 1971 was $2.73 per pound in the country of origin; that for vanilla, $4.46 per pound. Although no official U.S.D.A. statistics are available for saffron, its average price that year was about $100 per pound.

Throughout the Arab countries, particularly in Saudi Arabia, cardamom is by far the most popular spice. Cardamom coffee, commonly known as *gahwa*, is a symbol of Arab hospitality, as well as a habitual beverage. The pouring of this cardamom coffee is a ceremonial ritual. The host moves among the guests serving them, according to their rank or status, from a brass pot with an elongated curved spout stuffed with fiber for straining. It is good form to accept up to three cups and to make an audible slurping noise—this tells the host how much one is enjoying himself and the coffee.

The preparation of cardamom coffee commences with the roasting of green coffee beans, which are then crushed with a brass mortar and pestle, producing a familiar and resonant clinking sound in Bedouin camps and villages. Subsequently, green cardamom pods are broken with the fingers and with their seeds are dropped into a pot of hot water, with a touch of saffron or ground cloves, some sugar, and the ground roasted coffee; after boiling for two to three minutes and a preliminary straining, the mixture is ready to be consumed. An extraordinarily large proportion of cardamom is generally utilized. As much as two teaspoons of cardamom pods and seeds are needed for each medium-small cup of coffee. The resulting brew is so highly aromatic that the taste of the coffee is overwhelmed by the powerful, spicy flavor of the cardamom. Several cardamom-with-coffee recipes that are milder and probably more appropriate for most American coffee drinkers are given at the end of this chapter.

It is said that a poor man in Saudi Arabia would rather forgo his rice than give up his cardamom. This unique popularity is rather difficult to explain, but there are several possible reasons. One is the belief that cardamom has a cooling effect on the body, especially important during the extreme heat of the summer months, when the temperature may reach 125°F. Second, it is supposed to be good for the digestion. Third, many Arabs have a traditional, deep-rooted confidence in cardamom's great power as an aphrodisiac.

In Scandinavia cardamom is used not in coffee but in baking. The ground cardamom is worked into flour to flavor pastries, buns, and other baked goods—it adds an exotic taste to apple pie. In Sweden, where it is very popular, the per capita consumption of cardamom is sixty times greater than in the United States. Cardamom is practically unknown to the American housewife, but in Sweden it is much more widely used than cinnamon.

In Norway ground cardamom frequently adds flavor to hamburgers and meat loaf. Either the cardamom greens or the cardamom seeds are ground up fine, like pepper, and worked into the meat before it is cooked.

Cardamom is sweet, pungent, and highly aromatic. In Scandinavia a man who has been drinking liquor will frequently chew cardamom seeds so that on returning home his wife will not smell alcohol on his breath. In India whole cardamom pods are chewed after meals in the belief that they aid digestion. Cardamom is an essential ingredient of genuine East Indian curry.

Both the seeds and pods of cardamom contain an essential oil, obtained through steam distillation. The whole fruits (including the seeds), when crushed, will yield 3.5 to 7 per cent essential oil; the husks alone yield .5 to 1 per cent essential oil. Traditionally oil of cardamom has been used in medicine as a carminative and as a flavoring to disguise the odor of foul-smelling drugs. This expensive essential oil (about $35 to $70 a pound) is used sparingly today by the perfume trade, by a few cigarette manufacturers to flavor tobacco, and by some meat packers to add flavor to sausages.

Cardamom is available in the pod (green or bleached), as decorticated seeds (the outer shell having been removed), or ground.

Cardamom Hamburgers

1 pound ground beef
2 tablespoons sweet pickle
  relish
1 tablespoon instant minced
  onion

1 teaspoon salt
½ teaspoon ground
  cardamom seed

Combine all ingredients and shape into 4 hamburgers. Grill over charcoal or pan broil until done as desired.

Yield: 4 servings

Cardamom Apple Pie

Unbaked pastry for 9-inch
  two-crust pie
5 cups sliced tart applies
¼ cup brown sugar
2 tablespoons butter or
  margarine

1 teaspoon ground
  cardamom seed
¾ teaspoon pure vanilla
  extract

Line 9-inch pie plate with half of pastry; arrange apple slices in pastry, sprinkling brown sugar between apple layers. Dot with butter. Add *cardamom* and vanilla. Roll remaining pastry in circle; place pastry circle over apples; seal and flute edges. Make slits in top of pastry. Bake in preheated hot oven (400°F.) 10 minutes; reduce oven temperature to 350°F. and continue baking for 30 to 35 minutes or until crust is lightly browned.

Yield: One 9-inch pie

Cardamom Sweet Potato Casserole

1 can (17 oz.) vacuum-packed sweet potatoes
4 tablespoons sugar
1 teaspoon pure vanilla extract
¼ teaspoon salt
¼ teaspoon ground nutmeg
¼ teaspoon ground cardamom seed
¼ cup milk
4 tablespoons butter or margarine

Mash sweet potatoes. Add 3 tablespoons of the sugar, vanilla, salt, nutmeg, and *cardamom;* mix well. Stir in milk. Melt 3 tablespoons of the butter and add. Turn into a buttered 1-quart casserole. Dot with remaining 1 tablespoon butter and sprinkle with the remaining 1 tablespoon sugar. Bake in preheated moderate oven (350°F.) 30 minutes or until brown.

Yield: 6 servings

Exotic Indian Chicken

½ teaspoon powdered mustard
1 teaspoon water
½ teaspoon crushed red pepper
½ teaspoon ground black pepper
½ teaspoon ground cardamom seed
½ teaspoon ground ginger
½ teaspoon ground cumin seed
1 teaspoon curry powder
¼ teaspoon instant garlic powder
1 tablespoon salt
⅓ cup cider vinegar
2 tablespoons lemon juice
1 pint yogurt
2 (3 lbs. each) ready-to-cook chickens, cut in serving pieces
⅓ cup salad or olive oil

In a small bowl combine powdered mustard and water; let stand 10 minutes for flavor to develop. Add next 10 ingredients and mix well. Blend in yogurt. Place chicken in a large bowl; pour seasoned yogurt mixture over chicken, turning pieces to coat evenly. Cover and refrigerate 12 hours or overnight. Heat oil in a large skillet; add chicken pieces and cook until lightly browned on all sides; add more oil if necessary. Place chicken in a shallow baking dish or casserole and top with reserved yogurt mixture. Bake, uncovered, in a pre-heated slow oven (325°F.) about 1½ hours or until chicken is tender. Baste frequently and if necessary brush with additional oil. Serve hot with rice.

Yield: 6–8 servings

Cardamom Meat Loaf

1 pound ground veal
1 pound ground pork
1 pound ground beef
1 cup soft bread crumbs
½ cup milk
2 tablespoons instant
  minced onion

2 tablespoons parsley flakes
3 teaspoons salt
1 teaspoon ground
  cardamom seed
1 teaspoon celery seed
3 slices bacon

Place veal, pork, and beef in bowl and blend together thoroughly. Soak bread crumbs in milk 10 minutes; mix thoroughly with fork. Add to meat with remaining ingredients except bacon. Place in a greased 9- by 5- by 3-inch pan. Top with bacon slices. Bake in preheated moderate oven (325°F.) 1½ hours.

Yield: 12 servings

Cardamom Coffee Variations
Cardamom Espresso

Combine 1 teaspoon *ground cardamom* with 4 table-spoons espresso coffee in the basket of an espresso cof-feemaker. Brew following manufacturer's directions using 1⅓ cups water. Serve in demitasse cups. Sweeten with sugar to taste.

Yield: 4 servings

Cardamom Instant Espresso

In a small coffee server pour ¾ cup boiling water over 1 tablespoon instant espresso coffee mixed with ¼ tea-spoon *ground cardamom*. Let stand 3 minutes. Serve in demitasse cups. Sweeten with sugar to taste.

Yield: 2 servings

Cardamom Instant Decaffeinated Coffee

In a small coffee server pour ¾ cup boiling water over 1 tablespoon instant decaffeinated coffee mixed with ⅛ teaspoon *ground cardamom*. Let stand 3 minutes. Serve in demitasse cups. Sweeten with sugar to taste.

Yield: 2 servings

Steeped Cardamom Coffee

In a small saucepan combine ½ cup cold water with 1 teaspoon shelled *cardamom seeds*. Bring to rolling boil and boil for 2 minutes. Strain seeds. Blend liquid with one of the following:

¾ cup hot double strength coffee or
¾ cup regular strength coffee mixed with 1 teaspoon instant coffee or

¾ cup boiling water mixed with 1 tablespoon instant espresso or 2 teaspoons decaffeinated coffee

Serve in demitasse cups. Sweeten with sugar to taste.

Yield: 2 servings

CELERY SEED

Apium graveolens L.

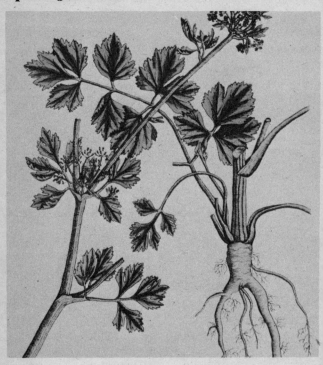

CELERY SEED

Family: *Umbelliferae*

LATIN	• <u>**Apium graveolens**</u> L.
SPANISH	• **Apio**
FRENCH	• **Céleri**
GERMAN	• **Sellerie**
SWEDISH	• **Selleri**
ARABIC	• **Karafs**
DUTCH	• **Selderij**
ITALIAN	• **Sedano**
PORTUGUESE	• **Aipo**
RUSSIAN	• **Syel'derey**
JAPANESE	• **Serorî**
CHINESE	• **Ch'in**

CELERY, 1492

CELERY SEED

CELERY "seed" is the dried fruit of a biennial (sometimes annual) herb of the parsley family, *Apium graveolens*, native to southern Europe. The seed used as a condiment is produced for the most part from a variety of wild celery commonly known in Europe as "small-age," while the plant grown as a vegetable or for salads is any one of a number of other varieties of the same species.

Celeriac, a wholly different group of varieties of the celery species, produces an edible turnip-shaped root, popular as a vegetable in Europe but relatively unknown in the United States.

Wild celery has been found woven into garlands in Egyptian tombs of the twentieth dynasty.

The Romans and Greeks grew celery for its medicinal qualities, rather than as a food. At that time it was also associated with funerals and considered by the ancients to be an omen of bad luck.

By the seventeenth century celery had been introduced to Europe as a food plant and was known in France as *ache*.

Celery is an erect herb 2 to 3 feet high with tapered stems, well-developed leaves, and flat-topped clusters of small white flowers. The seeds are generally produced in the second year and are very small (about $\frac{1}{20}$ inch in length), ovoid, light brown, aromatic; they have a characteristic warm and slightly bitter celery taste, combined with a suggestion of parsley-nutmeg flavor. These seeds are minute: Approximately 750,-000 weigh one pound.

Celery seed is used extensively as a condiment and for bird seed. In medicine it was once prescribed as a carminative, diuretic, and aphrodisiac.

By steam distillation the seeds yield about 2 percent of a thin and pale yellow essential oil, celery seed oil, used to flavor food products and in liqueurs, perfumes, and soaps. It was used in England in the nineteenth century as a cure for rheumatism and is utilized in India today as a tonic and nerve stimulant.

In California the celery seedlings usually are started in the summer and transplanted in the fall to the field in rows about 3 feet apart. The plants are then well mulched with straw as protection against severe freezing. The following August the seed may be harvested. The stalks are cut, and after a preliminary drying in the field the seed is threshed and thoroughly dried. A good per-acre yield of celery seed would be about 500 pounds.

Celery grows best in cool weather, and since it has shallow roots it requires considerable moisture. A sandy loam soil well supplied with organic matter is preferred. Adequate weed control is essential.

Celery is grown for seed extensively in France, India, and the United States. Our own production of celery seed is wholly inadequate for domestic needs and much is imported into this country from France and India. Most of the celery grown in the United States is produced for the vegetable market.

Celery salt, a combination of ground celery seed and fine table salt, has many seasoning applications —it is excellent, for example, with fish, eggs, soups, tomato juice, and croquettes.

Celery seed itself is a pleasant flavoring for tomato juice, sauces, soups, pickles, pastries, salads, and other savory dishes. It is usually available only in whole form.

Calico Salad

¼ medium head lettuce
¼ medium head romaine
2 cups diced unpeeled red apples
2 cups finely shredded green cabbage
1 cup finely shredded red cabbage

1½ teaspoons instant minced onion
½ teaspoon celery seed
1 teaspoon salt
1/16 teaspoon instant garlic powder
¼ cup salad oil
1 tablespoon cider vinegar

Wash salad greens and dry thoroughly. Place in a salad bowl. Arrange apples, green cabbage, and red cabbage in rows over the salad greens. Combine minced onion, *celery seed*, salt, garlic powder, oil, and vinegar. Beat with a rotary beater and pour over the salad just as it is being served. Toss lightly. Serve at once.

Yield: 6 servings

Carrot Relish

6 cups grated carrots
2 cups ground green peppers
2 cups ground red sweet peppers
2 cups ground cabbage
3 cups ground onions
4 cups cider vinegar

1½ cups brown sugar
3 tablespoons salt
4 teaspoons powdered mustard
1 tablespoon celery seed
1 large sweet red pepper, diced

Use coarse knife of food chopper for grinding vegetables. Combine ground carrots, green and red peppers, cabbage, and onions and set aside for later use. Bring vinegar, brown sugar, salt, powdered mustard, and *celery seed* to boiling point in an 8-quart kettle. Add ground vegetables. Cook 15 minutes or until thickened, stirring frequently. Add diced red pepper and cook 5 minutes longer. Seal airtight in hot sterilized jars. Store in a cool place.

Yield: 6 pints

Celery Seed Sour Cream Dressing

1 cup sour cream
2 tablespoons wine vinegar
1 tablespoon sugar
1 tablespoon water

1 teaspoon salt
½ teaspoon celery seed
¼ teaspoon ground black
   pepper

Combine all ingredients. Mix well. Refrigerate. Serve over salad greens.

Yield: Approximately 1¼ cups

Pickled Fresh Beets

24 medium beets, cooked
½ cup sugar
½ cup water
1½ cups cider vinegar
½ teaspoon instant garlic
   powder
1 teaspoon salt

1 tablespoon whole mustard
   seed
1 teaspoon whole celery
   seed
1 teaspoon whole black
   pepper
½ teaspoon whole allspice
¼ teaspoon whole cloves

Remove skins from beets and cut into crosswise slices ¼ inch thick. Set aside. Combine sugar, water, vinegar, garlic powder, salt, mustard seed, and *celery seed* in saucepan. Tie pepper, allspice, and cloves in a cheesecloth bag and add. Bring to boiling point and boil one minute. Add beets and bring to boiling point. Remove spice bag. Pack in hot sterilized jars. Seal at once.

Yield: 3 pints

Spring Cabbage Slaw

3 cups finely shredded
  cabbage
½ cup diced green pepper
3 scallions with tops, sliced
½ cup sliced radish
½ cup diced celery

½ teaspoon celery seed
½ teaspoon salt
⅛ teaspoon ground black
  pepper
2 tablespoons mayonnaise
1 tablespoon lemon juice

Combine cabbage, green pepper, scallions, radish, celery, *celery seed,* salt, and black pepper in a salad bowl. Mix mayonnaise with lemon juice and add. Toss only enough to blend ingredients with dressing.

Yield: 6 servings

CHERVIL

Anthriscus cerefolium Hoffm.

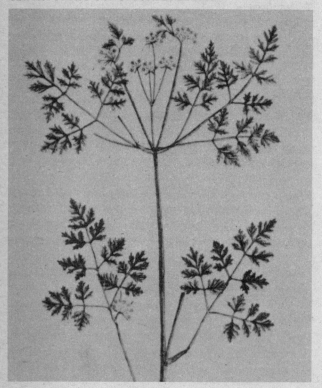

CHERVIL

Family: Umbelliferae

LATIN	• **Anthriscus cerefolium Hoffm.**
SPANISH	• **Cerafolio**
FRENCH	• **Cerfeuil**
GERMAN	• **Kerbel**
SWEDISH	• **Körvel**
ARABIC	• **Maqdunis Afranji**
DUTCH	• **Kervel**
ITALIAN	• **Cerfoglio**
PORTUGUESE	• **Cerefolho**
RUSSIAN	• **Kervel'**
CHINESE	• **San-lo-po**
JAPANESE	• **Châbiru**

CHERVIL

CHERVIL, *Anthriscus cerefolium,* is a small, low-growing annual of the parsley family. Distinguished by the bright, light-green color of its lacy and fernlike foliage, it is quite similar in appearance to parsley, although more delicate. The leaves are used for seasoning.

Chervil, a native of southern Russia and western Asia, was introduced to France and England by the Romans. By 1647 it was cultivated in Brazil, but only recently has it been grown commerically in the United States, principally in California. It is produced extensively in France but can be grown at higher elevations in the tropics.

Pliny, in the first century A.D., wrote of chervil as a seasoning and recommended its use as a cure for hiccoughs, mentioning also that it had been used by the Syrians as a food.

The chervil plant grows 8 to 16 inches high and resembles parsley in habit of growth. Its flowers are small and white. Tuberous-rooted varieties of chervil may be grown and eaten as a vegetable, like carrots.

The slender, black, needlelike seeds may be sown during March and April in moist, fertile, well-drained soil. When grown commercially, as it is in the Sacramento Valley, California, the crop is field sown with a row spacing of approximately 30 inches, and 6 inches between the chervil plants within the rows. Frequent watering is advisable, for the plant cannot tolerate hot, dry conditions. Transplanting is not recommended, as the root system is very delicate. Leaves may be harvested about ninety days after sowing, and the outside leaves should be picked first (this is also true of parsley). Chervil must be harvested frequently enough to avoid flowering, thus encouraging a new leaf crop. In harvesting, the plant is cut almost to ground level. To retain the desired green color, the leaves are dried at a moderate temperature of about 90°F.

Sweeter and more aromatic than parsley, chervil has been called the "gourmet's parsley." It has a delightful aniselike fragrance, with a slight hint of pepper flavor.

Chervil is usually included in the combination of three or more herbs—ground fine and carefully blended —known as *fines herbes* in the French cuisine (other herbs that may be used in *fines herbes* are parsley, tarragon, chives, sage, savory, and basil). Chervil is mixed with tarragon and chives to make ravigote, a savory sauce. Its tendency to bring out the flavor of other herbs makes chervil especially prized as an aromatic seasoning and supplement.

Mushroom Soup a la Budapest

2 tablespoons butter or margarine
3¾ cups coarsely chopped fresh mushrooms
1 tablespoon finely chopped onion
2 teaspoons salt

1 teaspoon paprika
¼ cup all-purpose flour
½ teaspoon chervil leaves
3 cans (13¾ oz. each) chicken broth
1 egg, slightly beaten
½ cup dairy sour cream

In a medium saucepan heat butter. Add mushrooms, onion, salt, and paprika. Blend in flour and *chervil*. Add broth and mix well. Stir and cook until soup has slightly thickened. Blend egg with sour cream. Stir some of the hot soup into egg mixture; return to soup. Heat and serve immediately.

Yield: 8 servings

Chervil Baked Chicken Breasts

¾ cup butter or margarine	1½ teaspoons chervil
¼ cup flour	⅛ teaspoon salt
½ cup dry white wine	4 chicken breasts, split
1 tablespoon dried chives	

In a small saucepan melt butter. Add flour and stir until smooth. Cook over low heat for 3 minutes. Add wine, chives, *chervil,* and salt. Cook another 3 minutes, stirring constantly (sauce will be thick). Brush both sides of chicken with sauce. Arrange in an ovenproof baking dish. Bake in a preheated moderate oven (350°F.) one hour or until chicken is tender.

Yield: 8 servings

CINNAMON (true)

Cinnamomum zeylanicum
Nees in Wall.

A. Flowering branch	4, 5. Various views of stamens
1. Flower	
2. Vertical section of flower	6. Pollen grain
3. Perfect stamen and two nonfunctional stamens	7. Pistil

CINNAMON AND CASSIA

Family: *Lauraceae*

	Cinnamon	Cassia
LATIN	Cinnamomum zeylanicum Nees in Wall.	Cinnamomum cassia Blume
SPANISH	Canela	Canela de la China
FRENCH	Cannelle	Cannelle de Cochinchine
GERMAN	Zimt	Zimtkassie
SWEDISH	Kanel	Kassia
ARABIC	Qurfa	Darasini
DUTCH	Kaneel	Kassia
ITALIAN	Cannella	Cassia
PORTUGUESE	Canela	[None known]
RUSSIAN	Koritsa	[None known]
JAPANESE	Seiron-Nikkei	Kashia keihi
CHINESE	Jou-kuei (or Jou-kwei)	Kuei (or Kwei)

CINNAMON AND CASSIA

CINNAMON (*Cinnamomum zeylanicum*) and cassia (*Cinnamomum cassia*) are two of the oldest spices known to man. Both condiments were probably known to the ancients at a very early period in history, for they are mentioned frequently in the Bible.

In Exodus 30:23–25 it is recorded that the Lord spoke to Moses and told him to use cinnamon and cassia, among other substances, to anoint the tabernacle of the congregation of the children of Israel: "Take thou also unto thee principal spices, of pure myrrh five hundred shekels, and of sweet cinnamon half so much, even two hundred and fifty shekels, and of sweet calamus two hundred and fifty shekels, And of cassia five hundred shekels, after the shekel of the sanctuary, and of oil olive an hin: And thou shalt make it an oil of holy ointment, an ointment compound after the art of the apothecary: it shall be an holy anointing oil."

Cassia—presumably brought from distant China to

GATHERING CINNAMON IN THE SIXTEENTH CENTURY

be exported to Tyre—is noted in Ezekiel 27:19: "Dan also and Javan going to and fro occupied in thy fairs: bright iron, cassia, and calamus, were in thy market."

Cinnamon, or the "sweet wood," has been prized for many centuries in the Orient for use in temples, to counteract the stench following offerings of burnt flesh.

There has been a confusion between cinnamon and cassia—this misunderstanding goes back for over 4,000 years—that exists even today in the United States. When we order cinnamon toast we should, to be correct, ask for "cassia toast," since cassia has almost entirely replaced cinnamon as a spice in this country.

Galen, one of the best-known Greek physician-authors of the second century A.D., pointed out that "the finest cassia differs so little from the lowest quality cinnamon that the first may be substituted for the second, provided a double weight of it be used."

Galen's opinion is still shared in the European and Mexican spice markets, but not in the United States. Roughly six times more cassia is used today in this country than the more delicately flavored cinnamon. Much of the true cinnamon imported into the United States is re-exported to Mexico.

In Great Britain "cinnamon" applies only to *Cinnamomum zeylanicum* and "cassia" to *C. cassia*. But in the United States the Food, Drug and Cosmetic Act of 1938 officially permits the term cinnamon to be used for both *C. zeylanicum* and *C. cassia,* as well as other species of cassia.

CINNAMON

As a measure of his grief, the emperor Nero is said to have burned a year's supply of Rome's cinnamon at his wife's funeral rites (A.D. 66).

Chilperic II, king of the Franks in A.D. 716, included 5 pounds of cinnamon in a list of spices and groceries supplied to a monastery in Normandy. In the ninth century cooks at the monastery of St. Gall in Switzerland used cinnamon, pepper, and cloves to season fish.

Cinnamon was the first spice to be sought after in most fifteenth- and sixteenth-century explorations, and thus it not only played a vital role in bringing Ceylon into contact with Europe but also led indirectly to the discovery of America.

When the Portuguese seized Ceylon in 1505 they ruthlessly forced its rulers to pay as tribute large quantities of bark collected from wild cinnamon trees.

In the middle of the seventeenth century, the Dutch took Ceylon from the Portuguese and in 1656 commenced strictly controlled, monopolistic cultivation of cinnamon.

The British, through their East India Company, broke this monopoly by force in 1796, only to have their own monopoly destroyed in 1833—an event that initiated considerable new plantings of cinnamon. By 1850 about 40,000 acres of cinnamon were under cultivation in Ceylon.

By 1973 Ceylonese cinnamon plantings had been reduced to about 34,000 acres, mostly grown in small plots of 10 to 20 acres. Even so, Ceylon today is the principal country producing high quality cinnamon (other important cinnamon-producing countries include the Seychelles and the Malagasy Republic). These acreage figures suggest the gradual downtrend that has occurred in some of the world spice trade during the past two centuries.

Cinnamomum zeylanicum is a moderate-sized bushy evergreen tree of the laurel family whose dried inner bark is the "true" cinnamon of commerce. In southern India and Ceylon, where it is native, this tree may reach a height of 30 to 40 feet, but in cultivation is grown as a "coppiced," or cut back, bush. Its highly aromatic leaves are 5 to 7 inches in length, bluntly pointed, dark glossy green above and lighter beneath. The flowers are small, yellow, and inconspicuous. The berries—about ½ to 1 inch long—are dark purple, ovoid, and one-seeded.

In southern Ceylon cinnamon thrives in deep sandy soil mixed with humus. It grows in sheltered situations up to altitudes of 2,000 feet, where the average rainfall is 80 to 100 inches and the average temperature is about 80°F. The most desirable Ceylonese varieties are known as "sweet cinnamon" and "honey cinnamon."

The seeds are planted, usually *in situ* (the final field position), in circular clusters in groups of four or five, with about 10 feet between the clusters. Germination occurs in about three weeks. Cinnamon is also propagated by cuttings.

Two to three years after planting the young trees are cut back to induce the formation of lateral shoots, which are pruned to leave six to eight per bush. The first harvest takes place during the rainy season some two years later when these shoots, having reached a height of 6 to 8 feet, are cut back close to the ground. Each such coppicing produces new shoots, which should themselves be ready for cutting in three years' time.

With curved knives the bark is peeled off the coppiced shoots in strips and left to ferment in bundles for twenty-four hours. The corky outer layer of the bark is then carefully scraped off, leaving the clean, light-colored bark which curls as it dries, assuming the appearance of a quill. Drying—first in the shade, then in the sun—may require three or four days. Good quills should be about ½ inch wide by $\frac{1}{16}$ inch thick. During drying the smaller quills are inserted into the larger quills, forming smooth, pale brown, canelike bundles or compound quills about 3 feet long that are known as "pipes." These quills are then selected for export, the cork-free ones of finest, smoothest quality being graded "00000," the coarsest graded "0," and the "chips," "pieces," "quillings" (broken pieces), "fourths," etc. graded accordingly.

The outer bark has a slightly acid flavor, and its removal tends to enhance the delicate aroma of true Ceylonese cinnamon. A yield of about 150 pounds of dried cinnamon quills per acre may be obtained, under favorable conditions, after about seven years.

CASSIA

Cassia, *Cinnamomum cassia,* is an evergreen of the

CINNAMON STICK AND LEAF

laurel family native to Vietnam and the eastern Himalayas. It is a taller tree, with thicker bark, larger leaves, and smaller flowers and fruits than true cinnamon. The spice named cassia should not be confused with the large genus *Cassia* in the *Leguminosae* or pea family from which senna leaves are obtained.

Known sometimes as "cassia lignea," "Chinese cassia," "false cinnamon," or "bastard cinnamon," cassia is one of the oldest known aromatic vegetable products used to flavor food; it is mentioned in the *Ch'u Ssu (Elegies of Ch'u)* written in the fourth century B.C.

In 1264 cassia sold in London for 10 shillings a pound, while sugar at the same time sold for 12 shillings, ginger for 18 shillings, and cumin for 2 shillings.

In the *Boke of Nurture*, written in fifteenth-century England by John Russell, cassia is described as similar to cinnamon but cheaper and commoner. "Synamome," he wrote, was "for lordes," but "canelle" (cassia) was for "commyn people." This contemptuous evaluation of cassia is no longer entirely valid. In fact, cassia is preferred to cinnamon in the United States.

Like cinnamon, cassia is cut back in cultivation to form a coppiced bush, and in general cassia is prepared for the market in much the same way as cinnamon except that the outer cassia bark is not removed by fermentation.

One other difference is that in preparing cassia, branch bark as well as stem bark is utilized. A longer period—ten to fifteen years—may be required for the first crops or coppicings of cassia, followed by a waiting period of ten years or so before each subsequent coppicing harvest.

CASSIA

Cinnamomum cassia Blume

A. Flowering branch
1. Flower
2. Vertical section of flower
3. Various views of stamens
4. Pistil
5. Fruit (berry)
6. Vertical section of fruit
7. Transverse section of fruit

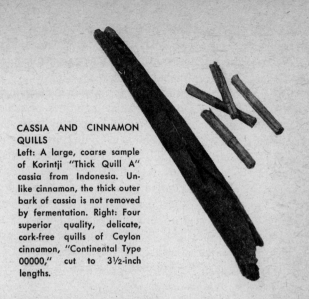

CASSIA AND CINNAMON QUILLS
Left: A large, coarse sample of Korintji "Thick Quill A" cassia from Indonesia. Unlike cinnamon, the thick outer bark of cassia is not removed by fermentation. Right: Four superior quality, delicate, cork-free quills of Ceylon cinnamon, "Continental Type 00000," cut to 3½-inch lengths.

Cassia bark resembles true cinnamon bark but is coarser and thicker, has a more intense aroma, has a higher essential oil content, and is not so delicately flavored as cinnamon. Cassia powder is reddish-brown, while cinnamon powder is tan in color.

The United States market is supplied with cassia cinnamon from four primary sources today: Padang "thin quill" (also known as "cassia vera") and Korintji "thick quill" cassia, *C. burmanii* Blume, of Indonesian origin and grown mainly in Sumatra; "cassia lignea" from Mainland China, a source that has become more important since the lifting of the trade ban in 1971; Saigon cassia, *C. loureirii* Nees, a species indigenous to North and South Vietnam; and *C. sintok* Blume, of minor commercial importance, native to Malaysia and still produced in that region.

The finest quality is the Saigon "thin quill," since it has the highest essential oil content; next in quality is the "cassia lignea" from Mainland China.

Both cassia bark and cinnamon bark contain essential oils. Cassia may yield 1 to about 4.5 percent, cinnamon 0.5 to 1.5 percent. The chief constituent of both essential oils is cinnamic aldehyde.

During the first century A.D., as noted in *The Periplus of the Erythraean Sea,* substantial quantities of malabathrum, or cinnamon leaf, were exported from the Malabar Coast of India. These leaves, used in the preparation of ointments by the Greeks and Romans, were probably collected from trees of *Cinnamomum tamala* Nees or from other Indian species of *Cinnamomum.* Later known as *Folia malabathri,* they were employed as a drug in Europe. Although obsolete today in Western medicine, these leaves, known as *tejpat,* are still used in India as a cure for colic and diarrhea, as well as a spice in Indian cookery, either in curries or as a garnish.

Cinnamon-leaf oil, containing a high content of eugenol, is used in perfumery in the United States at the present time, and may also be utilized as a starting material in the production of vanillin.

The dried unripe fruits of cassia are called "cassia buds." Highly aromatic, they resemble little cloves, are popular in confections, and may be used to add cinnamon flavor to sweet pickles. Cassia buds, produced in Mainland China, are gradually finding their way back to the United States market.

For good luck a bride in Indonesia has traditionally been given a symbolic beverage containing a pair of cassia buds that had been growing side by side on the tree.

Both cassia and cinnamon are important baking spices today—in ground form they are used in cakes, breads, buns, cookies, and pies. Cassia's flavor may be said to be more appropriate for "cinnamon" toast than cinnamon itself.

Stick cinnamon, an important ingredient in pickling,

may be used to flavor stewed prunes, spiced peaches, and beverages. It is especially popular in Mexico for the brewing of hot chocolate.

Cinnamon Hermits

3½ cups sifted all-purpose
   flour
4½ teaspoons baking
   powder
1½ teaspoons salt
2 cups light brown sugar,
   packed
½ cup shortening
1½ teaspoons ground
   cinnamon
½ teaspoon ground cloves
3 eggs
2 tablespoons milk
2 cups raisins

Sift together flour, baking powder, and salt; set aside. Gradually add sugar to shortening and spices. Beat in eggs. Blend in milk and add raisins. Gradually stir in sifted flour mixture. Drop by teaspoonfuls onto lightly greased cookie sheet. Bake in preheated moderate oven (375°F.) 15 to 18 minutes.

Yield: 6 dozen cookies

Cinnamon Sour Cream Coffee Cake

½ cup soft butter or
   margarine
1 cup sugar
2 eggs
1 cup dairy sour cream
2 cups sifted all-purpose
   flour
1 teaspoon baking powder
½ teaspoon soda
1 teaspoon almond extract
¾ cup chopped almonds
1 teaspoon ground
   cinnamon
2 tablespoons dark brown
   sugar

Cream butter and sugar until light and fluffy. Add eggs, one at a time, beating well after each addition. Stir in sour cream. Sift together flour, baking powder, and soda; add to creamed mixture. Stir in almond extract. In separate bowl combine almonds, *cinnamon,* and brown sugar. Spoon half of batter into greased and lightly floured 8-inch tube pan. Sprinkle half of *cinnamon* mixture on top. Cover with remaining batter, then top with remaining *cinnamon* mixture. Bake in preheated moderate oven (350°F.) 1 hour or until cake tester inserted in the center comes out clean. Serve warm or cold.

Yield: One 8-inch tube cake

Cinnamon Spiced Peaches

4 cups sugar
2 cups cider vinegar
4 sticks cinnamon, 3 inches
   each

1 tablespoon whole allspice
1 tablespoon whole cloves
5 pounds firm ripe fresh
   peaches

Combine sugar, vinegar, 1 cup water, and cinnamon in large saucepan. Tie allspice in cheesecloth bag and add. Mix well, cover, and cook 5 minutes. Remove skins from peaches; leave whole or slice. Add to liquid and simmer 3 to 5 minutes or until peaches are tender. Transfer peaches to hot sterilized jars, packing a stick of *cinnamon* in each jar. Fill jars with boiling syrup. Seal at once. Let stand 6 to 8 weeks before using.

Yield: 2 quarts or 4 pints

Cinnamon Coffee Cake

1 package active dry yeast
½ cup butter or margarine
½ cup sugar
1 teaspoon salt
1 cup milk, scalded
2 eggs, slightly beaten
5½ to 6 cups sifted all-
   purpose flour
1 tablespoon butter or
   margarine, melted
¾ cup sugar

¼ cup finely chopped
   walnuts
¼ cup raisins
4 teaspoons ground
   cinnamon
1 cup confectioners' sugar
   (optional)
4 teaspoons cold water
   (optional)
Glacé fruits (optional)
Chopped walnuts (optional)

Sprinkle yeast into ¼ cup warm water; set aside. Add butter, sugar, and salt to hot milk; stir until dissolved. Cool to lukewarm. Stir in yeast and eggs. Add flour gradually. Turn onto lightly floured board and knead until dough is smooth and elastic. Place in a lightly greased bowl. Cover; let rise in a warm place until double in size, about 2 hours. Punch down dough and roll out on lightly floured board to ½-inch thickness. Brush surface with melted butter. Combine remaining ingredients. Sprinkle over dough. Roll tightly jelly-roll fashion. Place in well-greased bundt pan. Pinch together edges of dough. Cover; let rise in warm place until double in bulk (about 1 hour). Bake in a preheated moderate oven (350°F.) for 50 to 60 minutes or until done. If desired, glaze with confectioners' sugar icing, using 1 cup sifted confectioners' sugar and 4 teaspoons cold water. Sprinkle top with glacé fruits and chopped walnuts.

Yield: One coffee cake

Scotch Cinnamon Cake

1½ teaspoons ground
  cinnamon
½ cup soft butter or
  margarine
1 tablespoon unsulfured
  molasses
¾ cup sugar
¾ cup seedless raisins
⅓ cup diced glacé lemon
  peel

2 large eggs
1¾ cups sifted all-purpose
  flour
¼ teaspoon salt
2½ teaspoons double-acting
  baking powder
¼ cup milk

Blend *cinnamon* with butter or margarine. Gradually add molasses and sugar. Stir in raisins and glacé lemon peel. Beat in eggs, one at a time. Sift flour with salt and baking powder. Add to the mixture alternately with milk. Beat batter half a minute. Turn into a well-greased, lightly floured 9- by 5- by 3-inch loaf pan. Bake in a preheated moderate oven (350°F.) 1 hour 15 minutes or until a toothpick inserted in the center comes out clean. Cool in pan 10 minutes. Turn out onto a wire rack to finish cooling. Sift confectioners' sugar over the top if desired.

Yield: One 9-inch loaf

Quick Cinnamon Blueberry Pudding

3 tablespoons butter or
  margarine
⅓ cup light brown sugar,
  firmly packed
¼ teaspoon ground
  cinnamon

1 can (1 lb. 5 oz.) blueberry
  pie filling
½ teaspoon ground
  cinnamon
1 package (11¾ oz.)
  vanilla flavor cupcake mix

Melt butter or margarine in an 8- by 8- by 2-inch pan.
Add brown sugar and the ¼ teaspoon of *cinnamon*. Mix
well and spread uniformly over the bottom of pan. Add
blueberry pie filling, spreading to cover pan bottom.
Mix the ½ teaspoon of *cinnamon* with the dry cupcake
mix and prepare as directed on the package. Spoon batter over the blueberry pie filling. Spread to cover filling
uniformly. Bake in a preheated moderate oven
(350°F.) 1 hour 15 minutes or until a cake tester
inserted in the center comes out clean. Place pan on a
wire rack to cool 10 minutes. Cut into squares and
serve blueberry side up.

Yield: 6 servings

Spicy Banana Split Pie

½ cup butter or margarine
1½ cups sifted confec-
  tioners' sugar
2 eggs
½ teaspoon ground
  cinnamon
⅛ teaspoon ground cloves
3 medium-sized bananas

1 tablespoon lemon juice
1 square (1 oz.)
  unsweetened chocolate,
  grated
1 (9-inch) baked pie shell
Whipped cream
¼ cup chopped pecans

Cream butter and add sugar gradually, beating until
fluffy. Beat in eggs, one at a time, beating 3 minutes
after each addition. Blend in spices. Peel and slice
bananas, and mix with lemon juice. Fold into sugar-
butter mixture, with grated chocolate. Turn into baked
9-inch pie crust. Chill 3 to 4 hours. Just before serving,
spread thin layer of whipped cream over surface of
pie. Sprinkle with chopped nuts.

Yield: 6–8 servings

CLOVES

Syzygium aromaticum L.

A. Flowering branch	4. Pollen grain
1. (Bottom) Bud with petals removed	5. Transverse section of ovary
1. (Top) Cap of petals	6. Fruit (berry)
2. Vertical section of bud	7. Transverse section of fruit
3. Stamens, front and side views	8. Embryo
	9. Section of embryo showing root

CLOVES

Family: Myrtaceae

LATIN	Syzygium aromaticum L.
SPANISH	Clavo
FRENCH	Girofle
GERMAN	Gewürznelken
SWEDISH	Kryddnejlika
ARABIC	Qaranful
DUTCH	Kruidnagel
ITALIAN	Garofano
PORTUGUESE	Cravo
RUSSIAN	Gvozdika
JAPANESE	Chōji
CHINESE	Ting-Hsiang

CLOVES

THE clove, *Syzygium aromaticum* (also known as *Eugenia caryophyllata* Thunb.), of the myrtle family, is a small, straight-trunked, conical evergreen tree that grows 30 to 40 feet high. The bark is rough and gray. The narrowly elliptic leaves, which are pinkish when young, and dark green when mature, are numerous and stalked.

The word clove comes from the French *clou,* meaning nail. The clove of commerce is the dried, unexpanded, nail-shaped flower bud, which is picked just before the pinkish-green blossom opens out and turns a deep red. Of spices that may be classified as flower spices, the clove is by far the most important.

The clove tree, as well as the nutmeg tree, is believed to be indigenous to the Moluccas, or Spice Islands, a group of volcanic islands in the East Indian Archipelago (now eastern Indonesia) that include Ternate, Matir, Tidore, Makyan, and Bachan.

The first references to cloves are found in Oriental literature of the Han period in China (third century B.C.) under the name "chicken-tongue spice."

Customs records show that by A.D. 176 cloves were imported into Alexandria; by the fourth century they were well known in Europe. The emperor Constantine is said to have presented St. Silvester, Bishop of Rome, A.D. 314–335, with numerous vessels of gold and silver, incense, and spices, including 150 pounds of cloves.

From the eighth century on, cloves gradually became an important commodity—one of the principal Oriental spices in European commerce. In England in 1265 the Countess of Leicester had to pay, according to her household records, 10 to 12 shillings per pound for them.

The Portuguese controlled the lucrative clove trade of the Spice Islands for nearly a century, from 1514 until the Dutch expelled them in 1605. The Dutch then maintained an almost complete monopoly of the clove trade during the seventeenth and eighteenth centuries.

The Dutch government, through the Dutch East India Company, took exclusive possession of the Moluccas and by 1651 had adopted stern measures to maintain their clove and nutmeg spice monopolies. It was decreed that clove trees could be grown only on the island of Amboina and were to be destroyed systematically and exterminated everywhere else in the Moluccas. Any person illegally planting or trading cloves was put to death. Of course, these rigorous decrees did not endear the Dutch officials to the native population.

One quaint custom that was brutally trampled down by the Dutch edict was this: When a child was born in the Moluccas, the parents would plant a clove tree by which to keep a rough record of the child's age. If the tree was subsequently destroyed, the parents believed it portended doom for the child. Thus, one ruthless edict wrought sorrow in the hearts of an entire population.

The primitive inhabitants of the Moluccas could offer little resistance to the oppression by the Hollanders, and it was the French who decided to try to break the spice monopoly. Pierre Poivre, the intendant governor of Île de France (now Mauritius), managed in 1770 to elude the Dutch authorities and smuggle some clove seedlings from the Moluccas to the French islands of Bourbon and Mauritius.

By 1818 plantings of Mauritius clove seedlings had been established in Zanzibar, and the Dutch clove monopoly was broken. The islands of Zanzibar and Pemba (now part of Tanzania), situated in the Indian Ocean about 25 miles off the east coast of Africa, are today the world's largest producers of cloves. It is estimated that about 4,500,000 clove trees have been planted on some 80,000 acres in these islands.

The clove tree is propagated by seed, requiring four to six weeks to germinate. The slow-growing seedlings may be planted in the field when about two years of age and should be spaced 20 by 20 feet, approximately one hundred trees to the acre. The first crop may be expected when the trees are 6 to 8 years of age, and the yields increase until they are about 20 to 25 years of age, when an average of about 8 pounds of dried cloves per tree may be obtained. The yield per tree varies considerably, for the clove is a sporadic producer. Especially heavy crops are often followed by very light ones. Production will continue for many years—the clove tree may bear for one hundred years or more —but yields gradually decline.

The clove tree does best in a deep volcanic loamy soil on sloping, well-drained tropical land at elevations up to 2,500 feet. It needs a location that is sheltered from the wind, in clearings or in open shade, where the average annual rainfall is about 100 inches.

When the buds become pink and are about ¾ inch long, they are ready to be harvested. In Zanzibar the clove crop is picked twice a year by men, women, and children using hooked sticks to pull the budding branches to within reach. Cloves must be picked with care, since once the buds open they are no longer of value as a spice. Also, the branches must not be broken or the yield of succeeding crops will be reduced. (The ripened clove fruits, purple drupes about 1 inch in length and ½ inch in width, are known as "mother of clove" and are unimportant in the spice trade.)

The buds are separated from the stems skillfully and deftly by brushing the clusters against the palm of the hand. Collected in baskets or aprons, the buds are then spread in the open on grass mats or concrete platforms for several days to dry. When dry—that is, when the stems have turned to a dark brown color and the heads to a lighter shade of brown—the cloves weigh about one-third the weight of the freshly harvested buds. It takes between 5,000 and 7,000 dried cloves to make one pound of the spice. After further cleaning and grading, the cloves are packed in mats or jute bags for export.

Since 1894 the clove industry in Zanzibar has suffered acutely, if intermittently, from a mysterious epidemic disease known as "sudden death." Since it usually affects older trees only, constant replanting with younger clove trees has been necessary to maintain the plantings. Drought or poor drainage, or both, are believed to contribute to the ravages of "sudden death," but the primary cause is suspected to be a virus.

The clove tree is very rich in essential oils: The yield of oil, obtained through steam distillation, may be about 16 percent from clove buds, from 4 to 6 percent from clove stems, and about 2 percent from clove leaves. These essential oils are used in perfumes, to flavor soaps, as an ingredient of toothpastes and mouthwashes, in medicine, to aid digestion, for their antiseptic action, and to relieve toothache.

Clove oil, clove-stem oil, and clove-bud oil are important in that they contain from 80 to 92 percent eugenol, the initial substance in one of the methods of manufacturing synthetic vanillin or artificial vanilla, a vanilla substitute.

In the late nineteenth century smokers in central Java began to mix cloves with tobacco in their hand-rolled cigarettes, in a ratio of roughly one part ground cloves to two parts tobacco. This new product was called *kretek* because of the crackling noise it made as it burned. The current demand for *kretek* cigarettes, still produced for the most part on simple hand rollers, is so great as to require a labor force of about 70,000 workers in Indonesia. Approximately half the total world production of cloves goes to the *kretek* cigarette industry in Indonesia.

Cloves, characterized by their strong, pungent, sweet flavor, have diverse uses in different countries. Indonesians must have their *kretek* cigarettes; Indians use cloves to flavor the betel nut, chewed by millions; in England they are mixed with apples in apple tarts, and in France cloves and onions are basic ingredients for soup stock; in the United States cloves (available either whole or ground) are most frequently used whole for studding ham and pork. Whole cloves may also be added to pickled fruits, spicy sweet syrups, meat gravies, and cranberry punch.

Ground cloves are popular in chocolate puddings, such baked goods as fruitcake, and other desserts.

In recent years world trade in cloves has averaged about $17,000,000 per year. Tanzania (the islands of Zanzibar and Pemba) accounts for roughly one-half of the world output, followed by Indonesia, the Malagasy Republic, Ceylon, Brazil and Malaysia. Indonesia is by far the largest importer of cloves, while other importing countries include the United States, the Soviet Union, India and West Germany. Cloves are imported into the U.S.A. mostly from the Malagasy Republic.

The traditional demand for clove oil in medicine has been decreasing in recent years. Likewise, its use in the production of vanillin has been increasingly supplanted by a cheaper by-product of paper pulp manufacturing.

The average price for cloves imported into the United States during 1967 was 33 cents per pound. A short crop in Tanzania in 1968—because of adverse weather conditions—caused a sharp rise in the price of cloves. By 1972 this price had exceeded $2.25 per pound, demonstrating the violent changes that may suddenly occur in the prices of spices.

Holiday Fruitcake

1½ cups butter or
   margarine
1 cup sugar
1 teaspoon baking soda
1½ teaspoons salt
1½ teaspoons ground
   cinnamon
1 teaspoon ground ginger
1 teaspoon ground allspice
1 teaspoon ground cloves
1 teaspoon ground nutmeg

¾ cup light molasses
4 cups sifted all-purpose
   flour
5 eggs, unbeaten
4 cups mixed, diced glacé
   fruit
1 cup currants
1 cup raisins
1 cup slivered almonds
½ cup sliced pecans

Cream together butter, sugar, soda, salt, cinnamon, ginger, allspice, *cloves,* and nutmeg. Blend in molasses. Stir in 1 cup of the flour. Beat in eggs, one at a time. Gradually stir in remaining 3 cups flour, mixing well. Add glacé fruit, currants, raisins, and nuts; mix well. Pour batter into well-greased, lightly floured 10-inch tube cake pan or two 9- by 5- by 3-inch loaf pans. Bake tube cake 3 hours, or loaf cakes 2 hours, in preheated slow oven (300°F.). Keep a large shallow pan of hot water on rack underneath cakes while baking. Cool cakes in pan 30 minutes. Turn out on wire rack to finish cooling. Store in a tightly closed container.

Yield: 6 pounds

Spiced Holiday Fruit Punch

½ cup sugar
3 sticks (2 inches each)
 cinnamon
1 teaspoon whole cloves
1½ cups pineapple juice

2 cups bottled cranberry
 juice
½ cup lemon juice
1 quart ginger ale

In a medium saucepan combine sugar with 1 cup water, cinnamon, and *cloves.* Bring to boiling point; boil 5 minutes. Remove cinnamon and *cloves;* chill. Mix with cranberry, pineapple, and lemon juices. Just before serving pour over ice in a punch bowl. Add ginger ale. If desired, garnish with pineapple or lemon slices pierced with *whole cloves.*

Yield: About 2 quarts

Blackberry Clove Cake

½ cup butter or margarine
¾ cup sugar
½ teaspoon pure vanilla
 extract
2 large egg yolks
1 cup blackberry jam
3 tablespoons cold water
2 cups sifted all-purpose
 flour

1 teaspoon soda
¾ teaspoon ground
 cinnamon
½ teaspoon ground cloves
⅛ teaspoon salt
2 large egg whites, stiffly
 beaten
Whipped cream

Cream butter and sugar and vanilla until light and fluffy. Beat egg yolks, jam, and water until well mixed. Sift together flour, soda, cinnamon, *cloves,* and salt and add to butter mixture alternately with jam mixture. Fold in the beaten egg whites. Turn into a lightly greased and floured 9- by 5- by 3-inch loaf pan and bake in a preheated moderate oven (350°F.) for 1 hour 20 minutes or until toothpick inserted in the center comes out clean. Allow to cool in the pan 10 minutes, then turn onto a wire rack to cool. Serve warm or cool with whipped cream.(NOTE: The cake forms a slight indentation in the center but this is not harmful to the texture.)

Yield: One 9-inch loaf

How to Make a Pomander Ball

Orange, lemon, or lime
Whole cloves
Ground cinnamon

Orris root (which may be
purchased at a drugstore)

Wash orange, lemon, or lime and wipe dry. Insert *whole cloves* into skin so that the whole surface of the fruit is covered, using a skewer or bobby pin to start holes if you find skin difficult to pierce. (Try not to insert *cloves* in a straight line, for the skin is likely to split.) Mix equal parts of ground cinnamon and orris root and put a heaping teaspoon of mixture into a small bag along with *clove*-studded orange, lemon, or lime. Shake bag to coat well with the mixture. Wrap loosely or place in a foil-covered tray or basket. Store in a dry place until fruit shrinks and hardens, usually 3 to 4 weeks. Wrap pomander ball in net and tie with a colored ribbon. Hang in closet or place in bureau drawers for its pleasing aroma and as a moth repellent.

New Zealand Cold Chicken Pie

2½ pound broiler-fryer
   chicken
2 ribs celery
2 medium-sized onions
4 whole cloves
1 teaspoon salt
1 envelope unflavored
   gelatin
2½ cups hot chicken stock

2 teaspoons salt
1 teaspoon parsley flakes
½ teaspoon ground
   marjoram
½ teaspoon ground thyme
Dash instant garlic powder
4 hard-cooked eggs, sliced
Pastry for 1 9-inch crust

Cook chicken until tender with 2 cups water, celery, onions, *cloves,* and 1 teaspoon salt. Cool. Cut cooked chicken into chunks. Soften gelatin in ¼ cup cold water; add to chicken stock. Add chicken, salt, and spices. Arrange hard-cooked eggs over bottom of 10- by 6- by 2-inch baking pan; pour chicken mixture over eggs. Cover with pastry rolled to ⅛-inch thickness. Trim, turn under, and flute edge. Bake 30 minutes in a preheated hot oven (425°F.). Cool. Store in refrigerator until filling congeals. Slice and serve with a vegetable or fruit salad.

Yield: 10 servings

Spiced Beef Tongue

1 fresh beef tongue	6 large carrots, halved
Cold water to cover	6 stalks celery, cut into
1 tablespoon salt	2-inch pieces
3 bay leaves	6 small whole potatoes
6 whole cloves	4 medium tomatoes, peeled
4 black peppercorns	4 tablespoons flour

Place tongue in large pan and cover with cold water. Add salt, bay leaves, *whole cloves,* and peppercorns. Boil moderately about 2 hours. Remove from water, reserving the liquid. Skin tongue and place it in roaster. Strain liquid and pour over tongue to half cover it. Place carrots, celery, potatoes, and tomatoes around tongue. Cover and cook slowly in preheated moderate oven (350°F.) for 2 hours or until tender. Gravy may be thickened with flour, if desired.

Yield: 6 servings

Hasenpfeffer (Pickled Rabbit)

1 4- to 5-pound rabbit (fresh or frozen)	6 black peppercorns
	1½ bay leaves
1 cup vinegar or dry wine	6 whole cloves
1 cup water	3 tablespoons butter or
1 tablespoon instant minced onion	margarine
	¼ cup flour
1 teaspoon salt	1 cup sour cream

Skin and cut rabbit into serving pieces. Place in crock and cover with vinegar or dry wine and water. Add minced onion, salt, black peppercorns, bay leaves, and *cloves.* Marinate for at least 2 days. Remove meat, reserving liquid, and brown in butter or margarine, turning often. Gradually add marinade. Simmer until meat is tender. Stir in flour to make gravy. Cook 30 minutes more. Just before serving, stir in sour cream.

Yield: 4–6 servings

CORIANDER SEED

Coriandrum sativum L.

CORIANDER SEED

Family: *Umbelliferae*

LATIN	• <u>Coriandrum sativum</u> L.
SPANISH	• Culantro
FRENCH	• Coriandre
GERMAN	• Koriander
SWEDISH	• Koriander
ARABIC	• Kuzbara
DUTCH	• Koriander
ITALIAN	• Coriandolo
PORTUGUESE	• Coentro
RUSSIAN	• Koriandr
JAPANESE	• Koendoro
CHINESE	• Hu-Sui

CORIANDER SEED

CORIANDER, *Coriandrum sativum,* is an annual herb of the parsley family indigenous to southern Europe and the Mediterranean region. This green, shiny plant, which grows to a height of 2 to 3 feet, has a much-branched stem and finely divided leaves. Its small flowers are white or pinkish, and its dried ripe fruits are the spice known as coriander seed.

Coriandrum, the name used by Pliny, is derived from the Greek *koris,* meaning bedbug—the fetid, unpleasant "buggy" odor of the foliage and of the green, unripened fruit is responsible for the name. As the globular fruit ripens and dries, this disagreeable odor gradually fades away and is replaced by a fragrant spicy aroma.

Coriander is another of the ancient flavoring substances known to have been used since very remote times. It was familiar to the Egyptians and Israelites before the Exodus, as mentioned in the Bible in Exodus 16:31: "And the house of Israel called the name thereof Manna: and it was like coriander seed, white; and the taste of it was like wafers made with honey."

As early as 1550 B.C. it was used in Egypt for medicinal and culinary purposes, the Ebers Papyrus reports. Hippocrates (about 400 B.C.) and other Greek physicians of his era recommended coriander for its medicinal virtues. Cato, a Roman statesman and agriculturist of the third century B.C., favored it as a food seasoning. As civilization spread, coriander became a widely known commodity. In the first century A.D. its seeds were to be found in the shops of Pompeii.

In A.D. 812 Charlemagne ordered that coriander be grown on the imperial farms in central Europe. It was introduced to England prior to the Norman Conquest by the Romans. Coriander was used in love potions during the Middle Ages, and it was mentioned in *The Thousand and One Nights* as an aphrodisiac.

In early seventeenth-century Paris coriander was an ingredient of *eau de Carnes*, a liqueur that acquired fame for a dual role: It was consumed internally and was also recommended for external use as a fragrant toilet water.

Coriander was one of the first herbs grown in America by the colonists, having been introduced to Massachusetts before 1670.

Its cultivation spread also to warmer climates, especially India, where it was destined to be extensively grown, not only for its use as a condiment in curry powder, but also for medicinal use—as a tonic, cough medicine, stomachic, and flavoring agent to remedy and modify the disagreeable griping or nauseating qualities of other medicines.

Coriander grows under a wide range of conditions, but thrives on a medium to heavy soil in sunny locations with good drainage and well-distributed moisture.

Sown in early spring, the crop requires three and one-half to four months to mature. Seed is planted in rows 15 to 30 inches apart at the rate of about 15 pounds per acre. Frequent weeding is recommended. Harvesting occurs in July or August when the color of the seeds has changed from green to yellowish-brown. The seeds should be fully ripe when harvested to assure that the unpleasant odor of the unripe fruit has disappeared.

The plants are cut when there is dew—in early morning or late evening—to avoid shattering. After the stacked plants have ripened and dried in the field for several days, the seeds are threshed, dried, and stored in sacks or closed containers. Thorough drying is essential to produce the most fragrant aroma, which improves the longer the seeds are kept.

Under favorable conditions a yield of 1,000 to 1,500 pounds per acre of dried coriander seed may be obtained.

The coriander seed is globular, almost round, brown to yellowish-red, and about ⅕ inch in diameter, with alternating straight and wavy ridges.

Coriander seeds contain from ½ to 1 percent of a pale yellow essential oil that may be isolated from the dried fully ripe fruits by steam distillation. This is one of the older commercial essential oils, having been mentioned in Berlin price lists of 1574. It is used today for flavoring perfumes, candy, cocoa, chocolate, tobacco, meat products, baked goods, canned soups, liqueurs, and alcoholic beverages (especially gin) and to mask offensive odors in pharmaceutical preparations.

The exhausted seed material, or residue, is used locally as cattle feed.

Coriander seed is produced principally in the Soviet Union, India, Morocco, Poland, Romania, Yugoslavia, Argentina, and the United States. Some coriander is grown in Kentucky for the liquor industry, and a limited amount is grown as a winter crop in California and as a summer crop in the central states. The very large production in many foreign countries, where cheap labor is available, and the relatively low market price of coriander seed (about ten cents per pound) limit the commercial possibilities for this crop in the United States. Approximately 3 million pounds of coriander seed are imported annually into this country, mostly from Morocco and Romania.

Imported coriander seed is one of the spices that may require fumigation to eliminate any possible insect infestation. (Other imported spices that often need this treatment are cumin seed, capsicum peppers, ginger, and turmeric.) One leading spice importer in the United States regularly fumigates coriander seed received at the company's processing plant for about six hours with methyl bromide, a fumigant recognized and approved by the Food and Drug Administration.

Known in Spanish-speaking regions as *culantro* or *cilantro,* coriander seed has become a favorite flavoring and food additive in several Latin American countries, especially Peru. It has a warm, distinctive, fragrant odor and a pleasant taste, mild and sweet yet slightly pungent, reminiscent of a combination of sage and lemon. It is available whole or ground. The whole seed is used in mixed pickling spice, while in ground form it is often an ingredient of curry powder and spice mixtures and a flavoring for pastries, cookies, buns, sausages, and frankfurters.

Mulligatawny (Spiced Ceylon Soup)

1 to 1½ pounds chicken
   necks, backs, and wings
1 quart water
1 cup sliced tomatoes
¼ cup instant minced
   onion
4 cloves garlic
1½ tablespoons ground
   coriander seed

2 teaspoons salt
1 teaspoon fennel seed
10 whole black peppercorns
1 stick cinnamon (2 inches)
4 caradamom seeds
1 cup coconut milk or
   regular milk
Juice of 1 lemon

Slash chicken bones in several places and place in a

saucepan with remaining ingredients except milk and
lemon juice. Cover and simmer for 1 hour. Push mixture through a sieve, extracting as much liquid from
bones and vegetables as possible. Return soup to saucepan. Add milk and lemon juice and heat thoroughly.
Serve at once. (In Ceylon, a small dish of cooked rice
is passed with the soup.)

Yield: 6 servings

Kemroune
(Moroccan Shrimp)

1 pound fresh shrimp	1 teaspoon parsley flakes,
1/4 cup dried parsley flakes	crumbled
1 1/2 teaspoons salt	3/4 teaspoon ground
1/2 teaspoon whole black	coriander seed
pepper	1/2 teaspoon ground cumin
1 bay leaf	seed
Boling water to cover	1/2 teaspoon paprika
1/4 cup salad or olive oil	1/4 teaspoon instant garlic
1 tablespoon lemon juice	powder
3/4 teaspoon salt	

Place shrimp in saucepan with parsley flakes, salt, black
pepper, and bay leaf. Add enough boiling water to cover
shrimp. Cover and cook below boiling point 8 minutes
or until shrimp turn pink. Drain, remove shells, and devein. Chill. Combine remaining ingredients. Serve as the
dipping sauce for shrimp.

Yield: Hors d'oeuvres for 6–8 persons

Magic Fondant

2/3 cup sweetened condensed	1 teaspoon pure vanilla
milk	extract
1 1/2 teaspoons ground	4 3/4 cups sifted
coriander seed	confectioners' sugar

In a small bowl combine sweetened condensed milk,
coriander, and vanilla; mix well. Gradually add sugar,
stirring until mixture is smooth. Use as filling between
2 nut meat halves or form into small balls and roll in

colored crystals, chopped nuts, or grated semisweet chocolate.

Yield: 1¼ pounds of candy

Coriander Butter Wafers

2 cups sifted all-purpose
  flour
1 cup sugar
2 tablespoons ground
  coriander seed
¾ cup butter or margarine

1 egg, slightly beaten
1 teaspoon pure vanilla
  extract
1 tablespoon milk
Colored granulated sugar
  (optional)

Sift flour, sugar, and *coriander* into mixing bowl. Add butter or margarine and work in with pastry blender. Blend egg, vanilla, and milk. Stir into mixture to form dough. Shape into ½-inch balls. Place 2 inches apart on ungreased cookie sheet. Flatten with bottom of glass covered with damp cloth. Sprinkle with colored sugar, if desired. Bake in hot oven (400°F.) 6 to 8 minutes or until pale brown around edges. Cool on wire rack. Store airtight.

Yield: Approximately 6 dozen wafers

Chicken Vindaloo

3- to 4-pound ready-to-cook
  chicken
⅓ cup instant minced
  onion
½ teaspoon instant minced
  garlic
1⅓ cups water
2½ tablespoons ground
  coriander seed
1 tablespoon ground
  turmeric
2½ teaspoons ground
  cumin seed

1 teaspoon ground ginger
¾ teaspoon ground black
  pepper
¾ teaspoon ground red
  pepper
2 tablespoons cider vinegar
5 tablespoons salad or olive
  oil
2 bay leaves
1 stick cinnamon (2 inches)
2½ teaspoons salt

Wash chicken, cut into serving pieces, and prick skin with a fork. Soften minced onion and garlic in ⅓ cup of the water. Mix *coriander,* turmeric, cumin, ginger, black and red pepper into a paste with vinegar and 1 table-spoon of the oil; add onions and garlic. Rub paste into the chicken; let marinate in refrigerator overnight. Heat the remaining 4 tablespoons of oil in a heavy saucepan or Dutch oven. Add chicken pieces, bay leaves, cinnamon, and salt. Brown chicken on all sides. Add remaining 1 cup water; cover, and simmer until chicken is tender, about 45 minutes. Serve with boiled rice or rice pilaf, if desired.

Yield: 6 servings

CUMIN SEED
Cuminum cyminum L.

CUMIN SEED
Family: Umbelliferae

LATIN	• <u>Cuminum cyminum</u> L.
SPANISH	• Comino
FRENCH	• Cumin
GERMAN	• Römischer Kümmel
SWEDISH	• Spiskummin
ARABIC	• Kammūn
DUTCH	• Komijn
ITALIAN	• Comino
PORTUGUESE	• Cominho
RUSSIAN	• Kmin
CHINESE	• Ma-Ch'in
JAPANESE	• Kumin

CUMIN SEED

CUMIN, *Cuminum cyminum,* is a small annual herb of the parsley family, believed to be a native of upper Egypt, Turkistan, and the eastern Mediterranean region. It grows from 1 to 2 feet tall and produces a stem with many branches bearing long, finely divided, deep green leaves and small flowers that are white or rose-colored. The seedlike fruit, commonly termed "seed," is elongated, oval, approximately ¼ inch long, and yellowish-brown in color—somewhat similar in appearance to the caraway seed but longer.

The plant is grown extensively today in Iran, India, Morocco, China, southern Russia, Indonesia, Japan, and Turkey. It is not grown in the United States on a commercial scale.

Cumin was well known to ancient civilizations, for it has been cultivated since earliest times. It was included in the list of medicinal plants used in Egypt and recorded in the Ebers Papyrus (1550 B.C.).

It is referred to in the Bible, in both the Old and New Testaments; for example in Isaiah 28:27: "For the fitches are not threshed with a threshing instrument, neither is a cart wheel turned about upon the cummin; but the fitches are beaten out with a staff, and the cummin with a rod." Today the cumin is still threshed with a rod on many primitive farms of the eastern Mediterranean region.

In Matthew 23:23, Jesus reproved the scribes and Pharisees for tithing articles such as cumin so carefully —"for ye pay tithe of mint and anise and cummin"— while neglecting more basically important matters such as justice, mercy, and faith.

In the first century Pliny referred to cumin as the best appetizer of all the condiments.

During the Middle Ages in Europe cumin was a popular flavoring, one steeped in superstition. Cumin seed was believed to keep lovers from becoming fickle and poultry from straying from home. Records tell us that in A.D. 716 cumin was used in monasteries in Normandy. It has been utilized as a condiment in England since the thirteenth century, and by 1419 cumin was one of the taxable imports in London from which the crown received income. It is frequently mentioned in herbals of the sixteenth and seventeenth centuries. Since the Middle Ages, however, cumin has gradually been replaced as a condiment by the more popular caraway.

In India cumin is grown from seed, sown broadcast at the rate of about 30 to 35 pounds per acre. The plants require a mild, equable climate and a fairly long growing season of three or four months. A rich, well-drained, sandy loam soil and a sunny location are recommended. A tender annual, cumin cannot withstand severe dry heat during the growing season, and careful weeding is necessary.

The crop is ready for harvest when the plants begin to wither. In the eastern Mediterranean area the harvesting, drying, and threshing are carried out with hand labor. A yield per acre of about 400 to 500 pounds of dried cumin may be obtained under favorable conditions.

Iran is the major world exporter of the cumin seed known as "green cumin" and cultivated mainly in the Khurasan province in the northeastern part of that country. Annual cumin seed production in Iran averages about 8,000 tons, but in years when rainfall is favorable the output may jump to about 50,000 tons, thereby causing overproduction and a drop in prices. In 1971 the average price of cumin seed from Iran imported into the United States was 26 cents per pound; in 1966, however, it had been about 32 cents per pound; in 1900 the price was 5 cents per pound.

Another aromatic herb, known in Iran as "black cumin" (*Bunium persicum* B. Fedtsch.), the seeds of which are smaller but sweeter-smelling than those of *Cuminum cyminum,* grows wild in the Middle East, especially in the mountains of southeastern Iran, but is not important as an export crop.

Dried crushed cumin seed, distilled with steam, yields from 2 to 4 percent of an essential oil used in perfumery and for flavoring liqueurs.

In indigenous medicine in India, cumin seeds have traditionally been employed as a stimulant, carminative, and stomachic, useful in diarrhea and colic.

In Holland and Switzerland cumin is used to season some kinds of cheese, while in France and Germany it is used to flavor cakes and bread.

Cumin seed, with its strongly aromatic, hot, and bitter taste, is an essential ingredient of curry powder and chili powder; it is also used commercially in the preparation of meats, pickles, cheese, sausages, and chutney. Cumin makes an excellent seasoning for soups and stews, for which it is widely utilized throughout Latin

America. The growing popularity in recent years of Mexican-type foods in the United States has increased the demand for cumin seed; the annual importation of this seed—from Iran, Indonesia, India, Syria, and Turkey—has risen from less than 150,000 pounds in 1900 to about 5,000,000 pounds in 1971. It is available at the present time either whole or ground.

Colombian Tossed Vegetable Salad

½ head lettuce
1 cup shredded cabbage
½ cup thinly sliced carrots
½ cup sliced onion
½ cup sliced celery
¼ cup salad or olive oil
1 tablespoon lemon juice
1 tablespoon cider vinegar
1 teaspoon salt
½ teaspoon ground cumin seed

½ teaspoon sugar
⅛ teaspoon ground black pepper
⅛ teaspoon instant garlic powder
2 medium tomatoes, sliced
½ cup cooked beets, cut into julienne strips
2 hard-cooked eggs, sliced

Tear lettuce into bite-sized pieces. Place in a salad bowl. Add cabbage, carrots, onion, and celery. Combine oil, lemon juice, vinegar, and seasonings. Pour over salad. Toss lightly. Top with tomatoes and beets. Garnish with hard-cooked eggs.

Yield: 6 servings

Marinated Smothered Chicken

2½- to 3-pound ready-to-cook frying chicken
2 teaspoons salt
1 teaspoon sugar
½ teaspoon anise seed
¼ teaspoon ground ginger
2 medium bay leaves
2 tablespoons soy sauce

2 tablespoons salad oil
1 tablespoon cider vinegar
¾ cup flour
4 tablespoons shortening
1½ cups hot water
½ teaspoon ground cumin seed
4 cups hot cooked rice

Wash chicken and cut into serving pieces. Combine the next 8 ingredients, bring to boiling point, and pour over chicken. Cool. Cover and refrigerate overnight. When ready to cook, remove chicken from marinade, reserving the marinade. Roll chicken in flour. Brown over low heat in shortening, adding shortening as needed. Add water to marinade and pour over chicken. Cover and simmer 30 minutes. Add *cumin* 10 minutes before cooking time is up. Serve hot over rice.

Yield: 6 servings

Rancho Chili Con Carne

¾ teaspoon instant minced
   garlic
¾ teaspoon water
1 teaspoon olive or salad
   oil
2 pounds ground chuck
1 tablespoon salt
3 tablespoons chili powder
½ teaspoon cumin seed

4 cups (two 1-lb. cans)
   tomatoes
¼ cup tomato paste
½ teaspoon sugar
½ teaspoon ground black
   pepper
2 cups (1-lb. can) red
   kidney beans
Cooked hot rice

Soften instant minced garlic in the ¾ teaspoon water. Sauté in hot oil. Add meat, stir, and cook until meat is brown. Stir in salt, chili powder, *cumin seed,* and tomatoes. Cook 25 minutes. Add tomato paste, sugar, and pepper. Cook 15 minutes. Add kidney beans, heat, and serve with hot, fluffy rice.

Yield: 6 servings

Cumin Bean Beef Roll

2 slices smoked bacon
1 can (8 oz.) red kidney
   beans
1 tablespoon sweet pepper
   flakes
1 teaspoon onion salt
1 teaspoon chili powder
¼ teaspoon ground cumin
   seed
¼ teaspoon ground black
   pepper

⅛ teaspoon ground red
   pepper
1⁄16 teaspoon instant garlic
   powder
½ cup sour cream
6 cubed steaks, ¼ inch
   thick
2 tablespoons tomato paste
Olive or salad oil
¼ teaspoon onion salt

Cook bacon until crisp; drain on absorbent paper. Cool and crumble. Drain and mash kidney beans. Stir mashed beans and sweet pepper flakes into the hot bacon fat. Cook 10 minutes over low heat. Remove from heat and stir in the next 6 ingredients. Cool. Blend in sour cream and crumbled bacon. Spread each steak with equal amounts tomato paste and bean mixture. Roll and fasten with toothpicks. Brush with olive or salad oil. Broil, turning once. Remove from broiler; sprinkle top with onion salt before serving.

Yield: 6 servings

Texas Cheese Casserole

1½ pounds ground beef
1 tablespoon oil
1 tablespoon salt
½ teaspoon instant minced garlic
½ teaspoon ground cumin seed
1 can (No. 2½) tomatoes
½ teaspoon sugar

Dash ground black pepper
¼ cup instant minced onion
¼ cup water
1 can (1 lb.) kidney beans
3 tablespoons chili powder
3 cups corn chips
1 cup grated American cheese

Brown meat in oil, stirring frequently. Add salt, garlic, *cumin,* tomatoes, sugar, and pepper. Stir and cook until mixture has thickened, about 25 minutes. Meantime, in separate small bowl, combine onion and water and let stand 10 minutes to soften. Set aside to use in assembling casserole. Add kidney beans and chili powder to thickened mixture. Place 2 cups of corn chips in 2-quart baking dish. Sprinkle rehydrated chopped onion and half of grated cheese on top. Pour chili over onion and cheese. Top with remaining corn chips and grated cheese. Bake at 350°F. for 15 to 20 minutes.

Yield: 6–8 servings

DILL

Anethum graveolens L.

DILL

Family: Umbelliferae

LATIN	• Anethum graveolens L.
SPANISH	• Eneldo
FRENCH	• Aneth
GERMAN	• Dill
SWEDISH	• Dill
ARABIC	• Shibith
DUTCH	• Dille
ITALIAN	• Aneto
PORTUGUESE	• Endro
RUSSIAN	• Ukrop
CHINESE	• Shih Lo
JAPANESE	• Diru

DILL

DILL, *Anethum graveolens,* is an annual of the parsley family indigenous to the Mediterranean region and southern Russia. A medium-sized herb with small feathery leaves and yellow flowers, dill is related to anise, caraway, coriander, cumin, fennel, and parsley.

The plant is grown in the subtropical and temperate climates of India, England, the United States, parts of Scandinavia, and even near the Arctic Circle in northern Norway. In the United States it is cultivated mainly in the North Central States and the Pacific Northwest. It grows wild in Spain, Portugal, and Italy, where it is often a weed.

Dill is believed to have a soothing effect on the digestive tract as well as sedative qualities. Its name is derived from the Old Norse *dilla,* meaning to lull, a result this herb was reputed to have when given to crying babies. Dill was cultivated in Palestine and by the Greeks and Romans. It was often mentioned by medieval writers—one of them was Alfric, a tenth-century Archbishop of Canterbury—and the words *dill* and *till* were used in Germany and Switzerland when referring to dill as early as A.D. 1000. Because it was popularly supposed to have magical properties, dill was used as a weapon against witchcraft and as an important ingredient of exotic love potions and aphrodisiacs. Cultivated in England since 1570, it was not introduced commercially in the United States until the early part of the nineteenth century.

Most of the dill in this country is grown to produce dillweed oil, not dill "seed," although some dill is cultivated in California as a source of the herb dillweed, which in recent years has become increasingly popular in the United States. To obtain the highest quality dillweed, either for the herb or the essential oil, the dill plant should be cut before it flowers. To produce dill seed, however, the fruits should be allowed to mature on the plant before the harvest, as is done in Europe where dill seed is in demand.

The culture of dill requires a well-drained sandy soil and full exposure to the sunlight. About 7 pounds of dill seed are sown per acre; they germinate in fourteen to sixteen days. Transplanting is not recommended, since the seedlings have a central taproot that should not be disturbed. Commercially, the seed is sown in rows approximately 30 inches apart, with seedlings thinned to about 6-inch intervals. These plants grow to an average height of 3 to 4 feet and seldom have more than one upright stalk. Little care is needed other than weeding, although extreme heat may damage the crop. Fertilization may be required, for the crop is a heavy feeder and tends to exhaust the soil. For home use dill may be grown in a window box or in a vegetable garden, with a closer spacing between the plants.

Seed sown in early spring will produce a mature crop about mid-August, and if the seed is desired the plants should be harvested when the fruits commence to turn yellowish-brown. To minimize loss of seed because of shattering, cutting is done in early morning or late evening when the plants are moist with dew.

Dill seeds are dried on trays in the sun or artificially at moderate temperatures. Under normal conditions one acre should yield 500 to 700 pounds of dill fruits. The dill seeds, oval and about $\frac{3}{16}$ inch in length by $\frac{1}{10}$ inch wide, are tan in color and light in weight. One ounce contains more than 10,000 seeds. While a substantial amount of the world's dill is produced in India, production in the United States has risen steadily during the past few years.

The seeds yield between 2 and 4 percent of an essential oil of similar composition to oil of caraway, for both oils have a high content of carvone. Oil of dillweed is an important flavoring in the pickle industry.

Dill leaves, known also as dillweed, can be chopped finely, fresh or dried, and sprinkled on soups, salads, and such seafoods as lobster or crayfish.

Dill seed is used most frequently as a condiment, either whole or ground. It is utilized as a flavoring in pickling cucumbers, and in Scandinavia, where it is popular, used in bread, potatoes, and vegetables. In France the seeds are used extensively to flavor pastries, as well as sauces, while in India it is used for culinary, carminative, and medicinal purposes and as an ingredient of curry powder.

The reputed medicinal attributes of the pungent, aromatic dill include curing the hiccoughs, soothing stomach aches, easing digestion, relieving insomnia, and masking bad breath. In medieval times injured knights are said to have placed burned dill seeds on their open wounds to speed the healing process. Dill's pleasant flavoring is reputed to be beneficial for diabetic patients and for persons on a low-salt diet.

Dill vinegar is made by soaking the seeds or the dillweed in vinegar for several days.

Dill has a clean odor faintly reminiscent of caraway
—pungent and pleasantly aromatic.

Both dill seed and dillweed are usually sold in the
whole form.

Grilled Shrimp Kebabs

⅓ cup salad oil
2 tablespoons cider vinegar
1 tablespoon lemon juice
1 teaspoon dill seed
1 tablespoon salt
1 teaspoon dry mustard
¾ teaspoon garlic salt
½ teaspoon onion salt
⅛ teaspoon ground black
   pepper

1 pound raw peeled and
   deveined shrimp
Small whole fresh
   mushrooms
Green pepper, cut into
   1-inch squares
Onion slices, about ¼ inch
   thick

Combine first 9 ingredients. Mix well. Add shrimp. Marinate in refrigerator for several hours, turning occasionally. When ready to cook, string shrimp on long skewers,
alternating with mushrooms, green pepper, and onion
slices. Baste shrimp and vegetables with marinade. Place
skewers over a bed of slow-burning charcoal. Grill 15
to 20 minutes or until done, basting often with sauce
left in bowl. (Cooking time depends upon heat of fire.)
Serve in frankfurter rolls, if desired.

Yield: 4 servings

Cabbage Salad Dill-icious

4 cups finely shredded
   cabbage
1 cup diced celery
¼ cup chopped parsley
½ cup sour cream
1 tablespoon minced onion

1½ teaspoons dill seed
½ teaspoon salt
1/16 teaspoon ground
   black pepper
2 teaspoons lemon juice
Green pepper rings

Combine first 3 ingredients in a mixing bowl. Mix sour
cream with onion, *dill seed,* salt, black pepper, and

lemon juice. Add to salad. Toss lightly and serve. Garnish as desired with green pepper rings.

Yield: 6 servings

Beef in Dill Marinade

1 can (10½ oz.) beef broth
½ cup white vinegar
¼ cup salad oil
2 tablespoons dill seed
1 tablespoon instant minced
onion

2 teaspoons salt
¼ teaspoon coarsely ground
black pepper
3½- to 4-pound round or
shoulder steak, 2½ to
3 inches thick

Combine broth, vinegar, oil, *dill seed,* onion, salt, and black pepper in small saucepan. Bring to boiling point; reduce heat and simmer, uncovered, 5 minutes. Cool thoroughly. Place meat in a tight-fitting bowl or pan. Pour marinade over meat; cover container. Marinate in refrigerator at least 18 hours, turning meat occasionally. Broil 4 inches from source of heat or over hot charcoal fire about 25 minutes or until done as desired, turning and basting frequently with marinade.

Yield: 6–8 servings

Beef Balls in Dilly Cream

1 pound ground lean beef
1 teaspoon salt
¼ teaspoon ground black
pepper
½ cup fine dry bread
crumbs
1 tablespoon instant minced
onion
2 tablespoons water
2 tablespoons shortening
1 can (10½ oz.) cream of
mushroom soup

1 beef bouillon cube
½ cup boiling water
1 teaspoon dill seed
¼ teaspoon instant garlic
powder
1 tablespoon chili sauce
¾ cup sour cream
¼ teaspoon ground black
pepper
¼ teaspoon salt
Cooked rice

Combine first 6 ingredients. Shape into 1-inch balls. Brown in hot shortening. Add mushroom soup, beef bouillon cube, water, and *dill seed.* Cover and simmer

10 minutes. Add garlic powder and chili sauce. Cook 2 minutes. Stir in sour cream, black pepper, and salt. Heat *only* until hot. Serve over rice.

Yield: 36 1-inch balls

Quick Dilly Corn Muffins

¾ cup milk
1 tablespoon dill seed
1 egg, slightly beaten

1 package (*12 oz.*) corn
  muffin mix

Combine milk and *dill seed* in small saucepan. Scald milk; cool to lukewarm. Stir egg into milk mixture. Blend all into corn muffin mix; stir with fork until blended (batter will be slightly lumpy). Fill well-greased muffin tins half full with mixture. Bake in a preheated hot oven (400°F.) 15 minutes. Serve piping hot.

Yield: 12 muffins

Sweet and Sour Spiced Beef

3- to 4-pound fresh brisket
  of beef
1 cup boiling water
1 tablespoon salt
½ teaspoon ground black
  pepper
½ teaspoon dill seed

1½ tablespoons instant
  minced onion
½ bay leaf
5 whole cloves
4 tablespoons lemon juice
  or vinegar
3 tablespoons sugar

Place meat in stew pan with water, salt, pepper, *dill seed,* onion, bay leaf, and cloves. Cook over low heat for 2½ hours or until tender. Add lemon juice or vinegar and sugar. Serve meat hot or cold.

Yield: 6–8 servings

FENNEL

Foeniculum vulgare Mill.

A. Flowering and fruiting branch
1. Bud
2, 3. Views of open flower
4. Single petal
5. Stamens
6. Pollen grains
7. Pistil
8. Vertical section of pistil
9. Transverse section of ovary
10. Fruit Schizocarp
11. One half of fruit (mericarp)
12. Transverse of section of fruit

FENNEL SEED
Family Umbelliferae

LATIN	• <u>Foeniculum vulgare</u> Mill.
SPANISH	• Hinojo
FRENCH	• Fenouil
GERMAN	• Fenchel
SWEDISH	• Fänkål
ARABIC	• Shamār
DUTCH	• Venkel
ITALIAN	• Finocchio
PORTUGUESE	• Funcho
RUSSIAN	• Fyenkhel'
JAPANESE	• Uikyō
CHINESE	• Hui-Hsiang

FENNEL, 1492

FENNEL SEED

FENNEL, *Foeniculum vulgare,* is a tall, hardy, aromatic perennial of the parsley family native to southern Europe and the Mediterranean area, especially in the vicinity of the sea. It is distinguished by its finely divided, feathery green foliage and its golden-yellow flowers. The spice fennel "seed" is the dried fruit of the common fennel of commerce, also known sometimes as "garden fennel."

The name fennel is derived from the Roman *foeniculum,* a variety of fragrant hay. It has been known since antiquity and long been used as a condiment by the Chinese, Indians, and Egyptians. The Romans esteemed the young shoots as a vegetable, and the herb is still very popular in Italy. The ancient Chinese and Hindus employed fennel as a snake-bite remedy.

Fennel was a symbol of success in ancient Greece and was called *Marathon,* in reference to the famous battleground on which the Greeks gained a glorious victory over the Persians in 490 B.C.

Pliny, in the first century, mentioned that snakes casting off their skins ate fennel to restore their sight. He recommended it for its medicinal value, especially for the strengthening effect he thought it had on the eyesight—a belief that was later widely endorsed by fourteenth- to seventeenth-century herbalists.

In the Middle Ages fennel was hung over doors to ward off evil spirits. Cows' udders were smeared with a fennel paste so that their milk would not be bewitched.

Fennel has been in use in northern Europe for over 900 years, and there are references to it in Anglo-Saxon medical recipes of the eleventh century. It was formerly known as "wild fennel." The ancient Saxons believed that nine sacred herbs—fennel was one—had the power to combat the causes of disease, which were also supposed to be nine in number.

In past centuries fennel has been used in medicine as a carminative, stimulant, and stomachic and as a cure for earaches, toothaches, coughs, asthma, and rheumatism. It was one of the ingredients of "gripe water," given to babies having digestive troubles. A versatile herb, it was recommended by the herbalists to fat persons who wished to reduce their weight.

Milton, in *Paradise Lost* (1667), Book IX, referred to fennel's agreeable aroma:

> When from the boughs a savory odor blown,
> Grateful to appetite, more pleas'd my sense
> Than smell of sweetest fennel, or the teats
> Of ewe or goat, dropping with milk at even.

During the sixteenth century fennel was an emblem of flattery—an Italian expression of that period, *dare finocchio*, meant "to give fennel" or to flatter.

The Puritans apparently were quite fond of chewing the seed in church, calling it "the meetin' seed." Longfellow in *The Goblet of Life* (1841) praised the virtues of fennel for improving the eyesight and conferring strength and courage:

Above the lowly plants it towers,
The fennel, with its yellow flowers,
And in an earlier age than ours,
Was gifted with the wondrous powers,
    Lost vision to restore.

It gave new strength, and fearless mood;
And gladiators, fierce and rude,
Mingled it in their daily food;
And he who battled and subdued,
    A wreath of fennel wore.

Another variety of fennel, *Foeniculum vulgare* var. *dulce* Alef., is cultivated in France for its young stems, which are used in salads, and for its seeds. A third variety of fennel widely cultivated in Italy, the sturdy, low-growing annual *Foeniculum vulgare* var. *azoricum* (Mill.) Thal., known also as *finocchio* or "Florence fennel," produces thickened leaf stalks that are boiled and eaten as a sweet vegetable, somewhat similar in taste to celery.

The common fennel is a perennial that grows well in most mild climates, but thrives in sunny situations in limy, well-drained loams. Culture of the crop is not recommended for localities heavily infested with aphids and mildew, which may cause severe damage. It is grown readily from seed, sown (in early spring) in commercial plantings at the rate of 8 to 9 pounds per acre in drills 2 feet apart; when established, the plants are thinned to 12 inches apart.

Fennel is closely related to dill, and to avoid cross-pollination and hybridization the two herbs should not be planted close to one another—the resultant seed might have a muddled flavor. Fennel is more aromatic, sweeter-smelling, and less pungent than dill seed.

Fennel seeds are harvested when they develop a greenish-gray color and are sufficiently hard. The yield, low the first season, increases to 700 to 1000 pounds per acre by the third year. The seeds are dried indoors on a floor or on screens, or in the open where weather conditions are favorable.

The dried fennel seeds are oval, greenish- or yellow-ish-brown in color, about $4/10$ inch long by $1/10$ inch wide, and resemble tiny watermelons. They emit an agreeable, warm, sweet odor, somewhat similar to that of anise.

The demand for fennel in the United States is relatively small, and only limited quantities of the herb are produced commercially in this country. Most of the fennel seed used is imported from India, Argentina, and Bulgaria.

The seeds, available whole and ground, are used mainly to flavor bread, pastries, confectionery, soups, sweet pickles, and fish dishes (fennel is often called "the fish herb").

The fresh needle-shaped leaves are used to flavor fish sauces and to garnish mackerel or salmon, thus counteracting their oiliness.

Fennel seeds yield 4 to 5 percent of a volatile oil, the main constituent of which is anethole. This oil is an adaptable flavoring agent used in the manufacture of pickles, perfumes, soaps, liqueurs, cough drops, and licorice candy.

Rice With Fish and Fennel Seed

3 tablespoons instant
  minced onion
2 tablespoons butter,
  margarine, or olive oil
2 tablespoons tomato paste
1 cup regular-cooking rice

1 pound fish fillets
1 tablespoon parsley flakes
1 tablespoon fennel seed
2 teaspoons salt
¼ teaspoon ground black
  pepper

Soften onion in 3 tablespoons water. Sauté in butter for 3 minutes. Add ½ cup water and tomato paste; simmer 5 minutes. Add rice, 2 cups hot water, fish, parsley flakes, *fennel seed,* salt, and black pepper. Turn into a

1½-quart casserole. Cover and bake 1 hour in a pre-heated moderate oven (350°F.) or until rice is soft.

Yield: 6 servings

Fennel Seed Bread

2 envelopes active dry yeast
¼ cup sugar
1¼ cups scalded milk
½ cup shortening, melted
2 eggs, beaten
3½ teaspoons salt

6 to 7 cups sifted all-purpose flour
¼ cup instant minced onion
3 tablespoons fennel seed
Melted butter or margarine

Soften yeast in ½ cup warm water (110° to 115°F.) with 1 tablespoon of the sugar. Cool milk to lukewarm and mix with softened yeast, remaining sugar, shortening, eggs, salt, and 2 cups of the flour. Add minced onion and *fennel seed*. Mix well. Cover and let rise in a warm place (80° to 85°F.) 1 hour or until bubbly. Stir in enough of the remaining flour to make a stiff dough. Knead on a floured board until satiny and elastic. Cover bowl and place in a warm place (80° to 85°F.) until double in bulk. Punch down; let rest 10 minutes. Shape into 2 loaves and place each into a 9- by 5- by 3-inch loaf pan. Brush tops of loaves with butter. Let rise until double in bulk. Bake in a preheated moderate oven (375°F.) 40 to 50 minutes or until done.

Yield: 2 loaves

Broiled Lobster With Fennel

2 fresh lobsters (1½ lbs. each) or 4 frozen lobster tails
⅓ cup unsalted butter or margarine
½ teaspoon fennel seed, crushed

1 tablespoon fresh lemon juice
⅛ teaspoon tarragon leaves
⅛ teaspoon ground black pepper
½ teaspoon parsley flakes
Lemon slices

If fresh lobsters are used, split, remove and discard tail vein, stomach, and lung. Frozen tails may be split. With a sharp knife loosen meat from the body shell. Melt butter or margarine and stir in next 4 ingredients until well blended. Spoon 1 tablespoon seasoned butter or margarine over each lobster and place on broiler rack. Place in a preheated broiler (400°F.) 4 inches from heat. Broil 15 to 20 minutes, basting with additional butter. Serve garnished with parsley flakes and lemon slices. Pour extra melted butter in sauce dishes and use for dunking.

Yield: 2 servings

Turkish Lamb Stew

2 pounds boneless shoulder
  of lamb
2 bay leaves
2 cloves garlic
4 cups meat stock or broth
2 teaspoons salt
4 medium potatoes
½ teaspoon ground sage
½ teaspoon fennel seed
½ teaspoon dill seed
½ teaspoon ground black
  pepper
4 medium onions, sliced
1 medium green pepper,
  sliced
4 medium tomatoes,
  quartered
¼ cup flour

Trim excess fat from lamb and cut into 1½-inch pieces. Place in medium-sized saucepan with bay leaves, garlic, meat stock, and salt. Cover and cook slowly 1½ hours or until meat is almost tender. Peel potatoes and cut into quarters; add potatoes, sage, *fennel,* dill seed, and black pepper; cook 25 minutes or until potatoes are fork tender. Add onions and green pepper and cook 10 minutes. Add tomatoes. Cover and cook 5 to 6 minutes or until vegetables are tender. Blend flour with ½ cup water until smooth. Add to stew. Cook 1 to 2 minutes or until slightly thickened.

Yield: 6 servings

FENUGREEK

Trigonella foenum-graecum L.

FENUGREEK

Family: *Leguminosae*

LATIN	• Trigonella foenum-graecum L.
SPANISH	• Alholva
FRENCH	• Fenugrec
GERMAN	• Bockshornklee
SWEDISH	• Bockhornsklöver
ARABIC	• Hulba
DUTCH	• Fenegriek
ITALIAN	• Fieno Greco
PORTUGUESE	• Alforva
RUSSIAN	• Pazhitnik
JAPANESE	• Koroha
CHINESE	• K'u-Tou

FENUGREEK, 1492

FENUGREEK

FENUGREEK, *Trigonella foenum-graecum,* is an erect annual herb of the bean family indigenous to western Asia and southeastern Europe. It long has been cultivated in the Mediterranean area, in India, and in North Africa. The principal exporting countries today include India, France, Lebanon, Egypt, and Argentina.

The generic name *Trigonella* comes from the Latin meaning "little triangle," in reference to the triangular shape of the small yellowish-white flowers. The species epithet *foenum-graecum* means "Greek hay"—the Romans who got the plant from Greece, where it was a very common crop in ancient times, gave it this name. Fenugreek is also called "goat's horn" or "cow's horn" because of the horn-shaped seed pods.

The seed is produced as a spice, as a food for humans, as forage for cattle, and to a lesser extent for medicinal purposes.

This robust herb has light green leaves, is 1 to 2 feet tall, and produces slender, beaked pods 4 to 6 inches long. Each pod contains 10 to 20 small, hard yellowish-brown seeds, which are smooth and oblong, about ⅛ inch long; each is grooved across one corner, giving it a hooked appearance.

Fenugreek grows best in well-drained loams in mild climates, such as the eastern and southern Mediterranean regions, with a low annual rainfall of 20 to 60 inches. Being a leguminous crop it restores nitrogen fertility to the soil, and it is cultivated as a cover crop in citrus fruit groves.

It is grown commercially from seed, the plants being spaced about 3 by 18 inches apart. The crop matures about 3 to 4 months after sowing. The seed, planted at a rate of about 20 pounds per acre, produces yields of some 600 to 800 pounds per acre under favorable conditions.

After the seeds mature the plants are uprooted and dried, so that the seeds then can be threshed, winnowed, dried once more, and stored.

Fenugreek is one of the oldest cultivated plants. Medical papyri from ancient Egyptian tombs report that it was used to reduce fevers and as a food. In religious rites it was one of the numerous components of the celebrated *kuphi* ("holy smoke"), an Egyptian compound incense used in fumigation and embalming.

Porcius Cato, a Roman authority on animal husbandry in the second century B.C., ordered *foenum Graecum* to be sown as fodder for oxen.

Charlemagne encouraged its cultivation in central Europe in A.D. 812.

Fenugreek was widely cultivated as a drug plant *(Semen foenigraeci)* until the nineteenth century. The mucilaginous seeds, reputed to have many medicinal virtues, were used to cure mouth ulcers, chapped lips, and stomach ailments. An ointment prepared from these seeds that was used in earlier European folk medicine

Clockwise from
upper left corner:
Savory,
Cayenne Chilies,
Bay Leaves,
Dill, Ginger,
Cassia, Sage,
Poppy Seed,
Nutmegs,
Coriander

Clockwise from
upper left corner:
Fennel, Chervil,
Basil, Cinnamon,
Horseradish,
Black Pepper,
Anise,
Mint Leaves,
Cardamom,
Mace

Clockwise from upper left corner: Marjoram, Caraway, Tarragon, Fenugreek, Vanilla, Celery Seed, Cumin, Saffron, Oregano, Cloves

Clockwise from
upper left corner:
Mustard Seed,
Tumeric,
Rosemary,
Sesame, Allspice,
Chives, Thyme,
Instant Minced
Onion,
Paprika, Parsley

had so repugnant an odor it was called "Greek excrement."

Fenugreek is employed today in Indian and Ethiopian medicine as a carminative and tonic for gastric troubles. When soaked in water the seeds swell and produce a soothing mucilage said to aid digestion. Fenugreek seed is used also by Indian women for its alleged power to promote lactation. Ground fine and mixed with cotton seed, it is fed to cows to increase the flow of milk. Mildewed or "sour" hay is made palatable to cattle when fenugreek herbage is mixed with it.

It is used as a conditioning powder to produce a glossy coat on horses. Indeed, in the Middle Ages fenugreek was recommended as a cure for baldness in men, and in Java today it is used in hair tonic preparations and as a cosmetic.

The powder made from the seeds is used in the Far East as a yellowish dye. Harem women in North Africa and the Middle East eat roasted fenugreek seed to achieve a captivating, buxom plumpness.

As a spice fenugreek adds nutritive value to foods as well as flavoring. It is an important crop for those countries in the Middle and Far East where meatless diets are customary for cultural and religious reasons; rich in proteins, minerals, and vitamins, it can be used to supplement the diet and help prevent deficiencies.

The use of fenugreek in Europe has declined in recent years, but in less developed areas of the world it may have some growth prospects as a nourishing food and as a relatively inexpensive condiment. In Egypt and Ethiopia fenugreek is a popular ingredient of bread, known to the Arabs as *hulba*, and in Ethiopia going by the Amharic name of *abish*. In Greece the seeds, boiled or raw, are eaten with honey.

Although the use of most spices in medicine has declined substantially in recent years, fenugreek may be an important exception to the rule. Recent studies in England indicate that fenugreek seed contains the steroidal substance *diosgenin*. Diosgenin, at present obtained mainly from the tubers of certain species of *Dioscorea* (wild yams) in Mexico and Central America, is of importance to the pharmaceutical industry as a starting material in the partial synthesis of sex hormones and oral contraceptives. The cultivation of *Dioscorea* is costly and difficult, requiring several years before the tubers grow to an economically marketable size. On the other hand, fenugreek may be grown easily as an annual leguminous herb that produces seed three to four months after sowing. Experimental programs involving plant breeding are being carried out to develop varieties of fenugreek seed with a high content of diosgenin. If these technical efforts should prove to be successful, this little-known spice could make a twofold economic contribution to the world's population problems by assisting in birth control and at the same time providing additional food.

The fenugreek seeds contain about 5 percent of a bitter fixed oil that can be extracted by ether. This oil has an overpowering celery-like odor that is extremely tenacious and in recent years has attracted the interest of the perfume trade. Steam distillation of the seeds has been attempted, but the oil yields have been very low.

Fenugreek seed, available either whole or ground, has a bitter taste reminiscent of burnt sugar and maple. It is a prominent component of many curry powders. In the United States it is used in the manufacture of chutneys and in various spice blends, but its most important culinary use in this country is as the source of fenugreek extract, the principal flavoring ingredient of imitation maple syrup.

Hearty Vegetable Bean Soup

3 pounds beef shanks
1 tablespoon salt
2 tablespoons ground
  fenugreek
⅛ teaspoon ground black
  pepper
2 cups diced potatoes

1½ cups diced carrots
1 cup diced celery
¼ cup chopped celery
  leaves
1 tablespoon parsley flakes
1 can (1 lb. 4 oz.) red
  kidney beans

In large kettle, combine beef shanks, salt, and 2 quarts water. Bring to boiling point; skim surface. Add *fenugreek* and black pepper. Simmer, covered, 1½ hours or until beef is tender. Remove shanks and cut meat from bones into bite-sized pieces. Return meat to kettle. Add potatoes, carrots, celery, celery leaves, and parsley flakes. Bring to boiling point, reduce heat. Simmer, covered, 20 minutes or until vegetables are almost tender. Add beans; simmer, covered, 10 minutes.

Yield: 10 cups

Fenugreek Beef Stew

¼ cup onion flakes
2 pounds beef stew meat
¼ cup flour
3 tablespoons cooking oil
1 can (8 oz.) tomato sauce
1½ teaspoons ground
  fenugreek

1 teaspoon salt
⅛ teaspoon ground black
  pepper
2 cups sliced carrots
2 cups quartered potatoes

Mix onion flakes with 3 tablespoons water; let stand 10 minutes to soften. Trim and discard excess fat from meat; cut into 1½-inch cubes. Dredge meat with flour. Heat oil in a Dutch oven or heavy saucepan, then add beef cubes and brown well on all sides. Add softened onion; sauté 2 minutes longer. Add tomato sauce, 1½ cups water, *fenugreek,* salt, and black pepper. Simmer, covered, 1½ hours or until tender. Thirty minutes before cooking time is up add vegetables.

Yield: 4–6 servings

GINGER
Zingiber officinale Rosc.

GINGER

Family: *Zingiberaceae*

LATIN	• <u>Zingiber officinale</u> Rosc.
SPANISH	• Jengibre
FRENCH	• Gingembre
GERMAN	• Ingwer
SWEDISH	• Ingefära
ARABIC	• Zanjabîl
DUTCH	• Gember
ITALIAN	• Zenzero
PORTUGUESE	• Gengibre
RUSSIAN	• Imbir'
JAPANESE	• Shōga
CHINESE	• Chiang

GINGER

GINGER, *Zingiber officinale,* a member of the ginger family indigenous to southern Asia and now common in most tropical countries, is an erect perennial herb, 2 to 4 feet tall, that grows from thick, white tuberous underground stems or rhizomes (both the aerial stem and the roots grow from these pungent and aromatic rhizomes).

The spice is obtained from the whole or partially peeled rhizomes, referred to in the trade as "hands." Ginger is the most important spice obtained from the rhizomes of any plant.

Long cultivated by the ancient Chinese and Hindus, ginger (*chiang*) was mentioned by the Chinese philosopher Confucius (551–479 B.C.) in his *Analects.* It was one of the first Oriental spices known in Europe, having been obtained by the Greeks and Romans from Arab traders.

The Latin generic name *Zingiber* is derived from the Sanskrit *singabera* ("shaped like a horn"), so called because of the resemblance of the roots of the plant to a deer's antler.

The Greek physician and author Dioscorides frequently referred to ginger in *De Materia Medica,* and described its warming effect on the stomach and its efficacy as an aid to digestion and an antidote to poisons. But he suggested that one choose, if possible, those roots not gnawed by worms. In the second century A.D., ginger was included in the list of imports to Alexandria from the Red Sea that were subject to Roman customs taxes.

Ginger is mentioned in the Koran 76:15–17: "Round amongst them [the righteous in Paradise] are passed vessels of silver and goblets made of glass . . . a cup, the admixture of which is ginger."

The spice was well known in England before the Norman Conquest—it is referred to in eleventh-century Anglo-Saxon leech-books. During the fourteenth century it was, after pepper, the most common spice and is said to have cost about 1 shilling 7 pence a pound, just about the same price paid for a sheep.

During the Middle Ages ginger was usually delivered to Europe from the Far East in the form of living rhizomes, so it is logical that ginger was the first Oriental spice to be introduced from the East Indies to the New World. Ginger was successfully transplanted to the West Indies early in the sixteenth century by the Spaniard Francisco de Mendoza, and by 1547 Jamaica was already exporting to Europe sizable quantities of this piquant spice. In 1584 Santo Domingo also was exporting ginger, as was Barbados by 1654.

In the Middle Ages ginger was considered to be so important a spice that the street in Basel where Swiss traders sold spices was named Imbergasse, meaning "Ginger Alley."

In sixteenth-century England ginger was noted for its medicinal powers and was recommended by Henry VIII as a remedy against the plague. Some years later fancy gingerbread became popular and was a favorite confection of Queen Elizabeth I and her court. Cheaper gingerbread was also available to the common man in England during Shakespeare's time: in *Love's Labour's Lost*, Act V, Scene I, Costard informs Moth: "An I had but one penny in the world, thou shouldst have it to buy ginger-bread."

Toward the end of the nineteenth century English tavern keepers used to keep ground ginger in constant supply for thirsty customers to sprinkle on top of their beer or ale and then stir into the drink with a red-hot poker.

In its cultivation, the ginger plant requires a consistently warm and moist climate, brilliant sunshine, and heavy rainfall. It thrives at lower elevations up to about 2,500 feet in the tropics, in rich, well-tilled, sandy loam.

Fertile seed is rarely produced, and it is propagated commercially only by division of the rhizome. Small pieces of selected rhizomes, 1 to 2 inches long, are planted a few inches below the soil surface on ridges at intervals of 12 to 15 inches. The harvest begins nine months to a year after planting, when the stalks begin to wither. The rhizomes are twisted and dug up carefully with a hoe. These "hands" are then cleaned, washed, scraped, boiled, peeled carefully with specially designed knives, and dried in the sun for about eight days.

A yield of 1,000 to 1,800 pounds per acre of dried ginger may be obtained under favorable conditions. The dried ginger weighs about 25 percent of the raw rhizome's weight.

Ginger is a soil-exhausting crop, requiring heavy fertilization. Whenever possible it is grown in rotation with other crops.

The dried and cured ginger is graded according to quality and appearance—in the best grades each hand is plump, free from mildew, light buff in color, and weighs 6 to 8 ounces. The aroma should be spicy-sweet and pungent. The taste should be hot and clean.

The principal countries exporting dried ginger are India (the world's largest producer), Nigeria, Jamaica, Sierra Leone, Haiti, and Taiwan. Of the several types of export ginger, the finest quality is the Jamaican "peeled bold" grade, so clean it can be sold in the grocery trade unground. There is also a good demand for the "rough-peeled" lemon-scented Cochin and Calicut ginger from the Malabar Coast of India, while the cheaper "unpeeled" lower-grade gingers from the other producing countries are normally ground or distilled.

The annual world production of dried ginger averages about 20,000 tons, of which fifty percent or more is consumed within the producing countries, especially India. Ginger ranks fourth in terms of value among the spices exported from India, after pepper, cardamom, and chilies.

The leading importers of ginger are the United Kingdom, the Arab countries, and the United States—about 1,800 tons of dried ginger are imported into this country annually.

Candied ginger, crystallized ginger, and preserved ginger, all considered to be confections rather than spices, are prepared from fresh green rhizomes that have been cleaned, peeled, shaped, boiled, and preserved in sugar solutions of varying strength. Preserved ginger is produced on a large scale in Hong Kong and Australia.

Ginger contains from 1 to 3 percent of a pale yellow, spicy essential oil that is obtained by steam distillation. Ginger oil has only limited use in food flavoring and perfumery, but in recent years it has been increasingly used in men's toilet lotions.

Oleoresin of ginger is more important, since it is used to flavor soft drinks. Obtained by solvent extraction from ground ginger, it embodies in highly concentrated form the penetrating ginger flavor. Its manufacture—for use in ginger ale in the United States and ginger beer in England—requires the importation of a considerable tonnage of ground ginger annually.

Ginger is available ground, cracked (broken into bits), or whole. As a flavoring it has a wide range of uses: Ground ginger is used extensively in gingerbread, pies, cookies, pickles, puddings, and the preparation of Oriental meat dishes such as Hawaiian Gingered Pork. Cracked and whole ginger are used in making flavored syrups and pickling vinegar.

Hawaiian Gingered Pork

2 pounds boneless pork shoulder, cut into 1-inch pieces
1 tablespoon salad or olive oil
1 green pepper, cut in strips
1 cup diagonally sliced celery
1/3 cup onion, diced
1/2 cup drained pineapple syrup
1 chicken bouillon cube

2 teaspoons ground ginger
1 teaspoon salt
1/8 teaspoon ground black pepper
1/8 teaspoon instant minced garlic
2 tablespoons cornstarch
1 can (1 lb. 4 1/2 oz.) pineapple chunks, drained (reserve syrup)
1 can (4 oz.) pimiento, drained and cut in pieces

In heavy skillet brown meat in hot oil, stirring often. Add green pepper, celery, and onion; cook 2 minutes longer, continuing to stir. Add 1/2 cup water, 1/2 cup syrup drained from pineapple, bouillon cube, and seasonings. Bring to a boil; reduce heat to medium, cover, and cook 30 to 40 minutes or until meat is tender. Blend together cornstarch and 2 tablespoons water. Stir, all at once, into skillet and cook over high heat stirring constantly until thickened. Add drained pineapple chunks and pimiento. Serve over rice.

Yield: 6 servings

Ginger Orange Rice

2 tablespoons onion flakes
3 tablespoons butter or
  margarine
2 teaspoons grated orange
  peel
½ teaspoon ground ginger
⅛ teaspoon poultry
  seasoning

⅛ teaspoon ground black
  pepper
½ cup orange juice
2 cups chicken bouillon
1 tablespoon parsley flakes
1 cup long-grained rice

Combine onion flakes and 2 tablespoons water; let stand 10 minutes for onion to soften. In saucepan melt butter; add softened onion and cook over low heat until onions are golden. Blend in orange peel, *ginger,* poultry seasoning, and black pepper. Add orange juice and bouillon and bring to a boil. Add parsley flakes and rice. Stir once with fork. Cover tightly; simmer slowly over very low heat 25 minutes or until rice is tender and all liquid is absorbed. Stir again with a fork before serving. Serve with poultry, ham, or pork.

Yield: 6 servings

Hawaiian Gingerbread

1 cup shortening
½ cup sugar
2 eggs
1⅓ cups all-purpose flour
2 teaspoons ground ginger
1 teaspoon baking soda
¼ teaspoon salt

1 teaspoon ground
  cinnamon
½ cup molasses
½ cup cold water
1 can (4 oz.) flaked coconut
Confectioners' sugar

Cream shortening and sugar. Add eggs; blend well. Add molasses. Sift together dry ingredients. Add to the shortening mixture alternately with cold water. Add and stir in coconut. Pour into a well-greased 11½- by 7½- by 1½-inch pan. Bake in a preheated moderate oven (350°F.) 35 minutes or until done. Sprinkle with confectioners' sugar. Cut into 2-inch squares and serve.

Yield: One cake

Spiced Pumpkin Custard

⅔ cup canned pumpkin
¼ cup dark brown sugar,
   firmly packed
¾ teaspoon ground ginger
½ teaspoon ground
   cinnamon
⅛ teaspoon ground cloves

½ teaspoon salt
1 teaspoon pure vanilla
   extract
4 large eggs
1½ cups light cream
⅓ cup heavy cream,
   whipped

In a large bowl combine first 7 ingredients; blend well. Add eggs, one at a time, blending well after each addition. Add light cream and mix well. Turn into 6 buttered 5-oz. custard cups. Place in a shallow baking pan set on the middle rack of a preheated slow oven (300°F.). Fill pan with boiling water to a depth of 1¼ inches. Bake for 1 hour or until a knife inserted in the center comes out clean. Remove from pan to wire rack. Serve warm topped with whipped cream.

Yield: 6 servings

Gingered Carrot Soufflé

1 cup mashed cooked
   carrots
½ cup light brown sugar,
   firmly packed
¾ teaspoon ground ginger
¾ teaspoon ground
   cinnamon
¼ teaspoon ground mace

¼ teaspoon salt
1 teaspoon pure vanilla
   extract
3 tablespoons butter or
   margarine
3 tablespoons flour
¾ cup milk
4 large eggs, separated

In a large bowl combine first 7 ingredients; mix well. In a saucepan melt butter or margarine. Blend in flour. Add milk and cook over low heat, stirring constantly, until thick and smooth. Set aside to cool slightly. In a small bowl beat egg yolks. Add a small amount of the warm liquid to the beaten yolks; mix well. Then combine it with the remaining thick sauce mixture; blend well. Add to the seasoned carrots and mix well. Beat egg whites until they stand in soft, stiff peaks. Carefully fold into carrot mixture. Turn into a 1½-quart soufflé dish which has been buttered only on the bottom. Bake on a rack in the bottom third of a preheated moderate oven (375°F.) 45 minutes. Serve immediately.

Yield: 6 servings

Ginger Pickled Beets

10 to 15 cooked beets
3 cups vinegar
1 cup water
1 teaspoon ground mace
1 teaspoon ground ginger
½ teaspoon ground cloves
2 tablespoons prepared
  horseradish
2 tablespoons sugar

If beets are small, leave whole; if large, slice. Place in hot sterilized quart jar or 2 pint jars. Heat vinegar with remaining ingredients. Bring vinegar to boiling point and boil 2 minutes. Pour over beets. Let stand 24 hours before using.

Yield: 1 quart or 2 pints

Ginger Chicken With Oranges

⅛ teaspoon instant onion
  powder
1 teaspoon celery salt
⅛ teaspoon ground black
  pepper
1 teaspoon ground ginger
2 teaspoons brown sugar
1 tablespoon lemon juice
1 frying chicken (about 3
  lbs.), quartered
⅓ cup honey
¾ teaspoon ground ginger
2 tablespoons butter or
  margarine
3 large navel oranges,
  unpeeled, cut crosswise
  into ¼-inch slices

Combine first 6 ingredients. Mix well and rub over chicken pieces. Refrigerate, covered, 1 hour. To make honey glaze, place in small saucepan, over low heat, honey, the ¾ teaspoon of *ginger,* and butter or margarine. Stir until blended. In a preheated broiler place chicken, skin side up, in foil-lined broiling pan (no rack), about 6 to 8 inches from source of heat for 15 to 20 minutes, until lightly browned. Turn chicken pieces. Broil bone side up 20 to 30 minutes, or until tender. Brush with honey glaze and broil another 5 to 10 minutes. Turn skin side up again and brush with honey glaze. Arrange orange slices, brushed well with honey glaze, on broiling pan. Broil about 10 minutes or until glaze melts and orange slices brown slightly and chicken is nicely browned. Use oranges as garnish for broiled chicken platter.

Yield: 4 servings

Tomato Chutney

5 pounds (11 cups) peeled
   and diced ripe tomatoes
1½ cups sugar
1 cup cider vinegar
1 cup seedless raisins
2 teaspoons salt
2 teaspoons ground ginger

½ teaspoon instant garlic
   powder
¼ teaspoon crushed red
   pepper
4 cinnamon sticks, each 2
   inches long

Combine all ingredients in a 4-quart saucepan. Bring to boiling point over high heat. Reduce heat to low and cook slowly 2 hours or until very thick, stirring frequently. Ladle into hot sterilized ½-pint jars. Seal at once. After 5 or 6 weeks serve with meats, poultry, and curried dishes.

Yield: 5 jars, ½ pint each

HORSERADISH

Cochlearia armoracia L.

HORSERADISH

Family: Cruciferae

LATIN	• Cochlearia armoracia L.
SPANISH	• Rabano picante
GERMAN	• Meerrettich
FRENCH	• Raifort
SWEDISH	• Pepparrot
DUTCH	• Mierikwortel
ITALIAN	• Rafano
PORTUGUESE	• Rabano-picante
RUSSIAN	• Khren
JAPANESE	• Seiyô wasabi
CHINESE	• Lagen
ARABIC	• Fujl Hār

HORSERADISH

HORSERADISH, *Cochlearia armoracia* (known also as *Armoracia rusticana* Gilib., and *Armoracia lapathifolia* Gilib.), is a hardy perennial plant of the mustard family. It produces stout white fleshy, cylindrical roots, which, when scraped or bruised, emit their characteristic highly pungent, penetrating odor, plus volatile oils that may cause tears to flow. This sharp smell is due to the glycoside sinigrin, which, decomposing by enzymatic action, liberates an acrid volatile oil containing sulfur, similar to mustard oil in taste and properties. Unbroken roots have no odor.

The generic name *Cochlearia* is derived from the Latin *cochlea*, a snail with a spiral, spoonlike shell, for the leaves of many horseradish species are hollowed like the bowl of a spoon. The English name horseradish suggests a coarse or very strong radish, as distinguished from the edible radish, *Raphanus sativus*.

Horseradish, native to temperate eastern Europe from the region near the Caspian Sea through Russia and Poland to Finland, is a relatively recent addition to

POUNDING
HORSERAD-
ISH ROOTS, 1493

the list of condimental herbs. It cannot be positively identified with any plant of ancient Oriental civilizations, nor was it mentioned by Apicius, the Roman epicure of the first century A.D., although his lengthy treatises on cookery named many other herbs and condiments.

By the thirteenth century, horseradish had been propagated and naturalized in western Europe, where it was used in Germany and Denmark as a medicine and condiment. During the Middle Ages horseradish leaves were eaten in Germany as a vegetable, and even today the chopped tender, young leaves are recommended as a healthful, attractive addition to green salads during the summer months.

It was known in England by the middle of the sixteenth century as "red cole" and soon became naturalized. John Gerard referred to it in his *Herball* (1597) as a condiment eaten by the Germans with fish and meat. It was brought to America by early colonial settlers, and by 1806 was included by McMahon in his list of esculent American garden plants.

The horseradish plant grows to a height of 2 to 3 feet, with an erect stem that is branched toward the top. Its small white flowers, when produced, are numerous and aromatic. The fruit pods are short, oblong, and wrinkled; they frequently fail to mature or to contain viable seed.

The two varieties of horseradish best known in the United States are the "common" type, with broad, wrinkled leaves, which produces the highest quality roots; and the "Bohemian," having narrow, smooth leaves and roots of inferior quality. Mature horseradish leaves are large, up to 15 inches or more in length, glossy, and dark green in color.

In this country, it is frequently found growing wild, as a naturalized escape, in moist semishaded environments, especially in New York State and in southern New England, where it may be a noxious weed. Once established, its vigorous, deep roots are difficult to eradicate. Horseradish grows well in the northern sections of the United States but not in the South.

According to a recent U. S. Census of Agriculture, about 3,000 acres of horseradish are cultivated annually in this country. The largest commercial production is located near East St. Louis, Illinois; it is also grown commercially in New Jersey, Pennsylvania, Wisconsin, and California. The crop is produced widely in central and northern Europe, where it is also naturalized.

The crop may be grown successfully in deeply worked moist loams of medium texture with adequate organic matter. Commercial fertilizers rich in potash are generally recommended. The land should be kept clean and free of weeds. Shallow, poor, dry soils with hard subsoils are to be avoided, for such terrain does not permit satisfactory development of the massive taproot and its feeders.

Since horseradish rarely flowers or produces viable seed, commercial propagation must be by root cuttings 8 to 14 inches long, which are slender as a lead pencil, usually cut off square at the top and on a slant at the smaller end. These cuttings are made in the late fall at harvest time and then collected and stored in a cool, moist place for planting the following spring, as soon as the soil can be worked. Furrows 3 to 6 inches deep may be prepared in rows 2½ feet apart; the cuttings should then be planted in these furrows at 2-foot intervals. With this spacing about 8,700 cuttings are set per acre. Since the cuttings are planted in a sloping position at an angle of 30° to 45°, the lower end of each root cutting should be firmly covered with soil. These root cuttings increase in diameter, but not in length, to become the marketable product.

Horseradish roots make their maximum seasonal growth in the autumn and the flavor is supposed to be improved by cold weather; for this reason, the harvest is usually delayed until late October or November. Several days prior to the harvest, the leafy tops are cut to the ground. Lifting, or harvesting, is done on a large scale by plowing out the roots or, if the planting is small, by forking them out. The crowns and roots are shaken out and separated from the soil. The straight lateral roots, 8 to 14 inches in length, are selected and saved for planting material. Fresh plantings should be made in a new location each year.

Roots to be marketed are trimmed, washed, and packed in burlap-covered barrels of 100 pounds net. They are never exposed to light, for then they would turn green, which is undesirable. Yields vary, according to local conditions, from 1 to 4 tons of marketable roots per acre.

Horseradish has been recommended since medieval times as a medicinal plant, especially in Europe—as a stimulant, antiseptic, diuretic, aid to digestion, and remedy for worms. Its use as an antiscorbutic, to prevent scurvy, is an ancient but valid one, as has subsequently been proved by the high vitamin C content of the roots. A poultice of the grated roots may be used instead of a mustard plaster as a rubefacient. Horseradish syrup is still prescribed in England as an expectorant medicine to treat hoarseness and coughs following influenza.

By far the most important use of horseradish, however, is as the well-known piquant condiment. The freshly grated roots are especially popular as a table relish, for use with roast beef, raw oysters, fish, and smoked tongue; or they may be utilized in pickling; in the preparation of horseradish sauce, various cocktail sauces, and horseradish vinegar; or to flavor prepared mustards.

Dehydrated horseradish in granular form has gained in popularity in recent years. During dehydration about 94 percent of the moisture is removed; water must be added to "rehydrate" the product and release the pungent flavor. When the fresh roots are unavailable, these convenient dehydrated horseradish granules are a satisfactory substitute.

A small deciduous tree, *Moringa oleifera* Lam., indigenous to India and Arabia, is known as the "horseradish tree." Its thick roots and tender pods are often used as an inferior substitute for true horseradish in curries and other culinary preparations throughout the tropics of the Old and New Worlds. An oil (ben oil) extracted from the seeds of this tree is used in cosmetics and as a lubricant for fine instruments.

Hot Horseradish Sauce

2 tablespoons butter or
  margarine
2 tablespoons flour
½ teaspoon salt
1 cup milk

1 tablespoon prepared
  horseradish
Dash ground red pepper
1 teaspoon lemon juice

In a small saucepan melt butter. Remove from heat and
blend in flour and salt. Stir in milk. Place over medium
heat and bring to boiling point, stirring constantly. Cook,
stirring, until medium thick. Add *horseradish* and red
pepper. Stir in lemon juice just before serving. Serve
with boiled beef or tongue.

Yield: One cup

Glazed Chicken

1 tablespoon instant minced
  onion
½ teaspoon powdered
  mustard
1 tablespoon water
1 cup dark brown sugar,
  firmly packed
½ cup cider vinegar
1 cup drained crushed
  pineapple
2 tablespoons soy sauce
1/16 teaspoon instant garlic
  powder

2 teaspoons rosemary leaves,
  crushed
½ teaspoon prepared
  horseradish
⅛ teaspoon cayenne
¼ teaspoon salt
1/16 teaspoon ground black
  pepper
4 broiler chickens (2½ lbs.
  each)

Combine minced onion, powdered mustard, and water.
Let stand 10 minutes; stir occasionally. In a deep, heavy
saucepan combine next 10 ingredients. Add onion and
mustard. Blend well. Bring to a boil; reduce heat and
simmer, uncovered, 10 minutes. Stir occasionally. Quarter chicken and place, skin side up, under a preheated
broiler about 6 inches from heat source; brush with
pineapple sauce and cook slowly, turning and basting
with sauce, until tender and nicely browned, about 30
to 45 minutes. Extra sauce may be stored in a covered

jar in refrigerator. (This is a delicious sauce for barbecued chicken.)

Yield: 8 servings (½ chicken each)

Spicy Cocktail Meatballs

½ pound chuck or round
   beef, ground
1 large egg
½ cup day-old bread cubes
1 teaspoon instant minced
   onion
½ teaspoon salt
¼ teaspoon ground black
   pepper

¼ teaspoon prepared
   horseradish
⅛ teaspoon ground nutmeg
Dash cayenne pepper
3 tablespoons shortening or
   cooking oil
Grated parmesan or
   cheddar cheese

Combine first 9 ingredients and shape into ¾-inch balls. Sauté in hot shortening or cooking oil until golden brown on all sides. Serve on toothpicks and dunk in grated cheese.

Yield: Approximately 30 meatballs

MARJORAM

Majorana hortensis Moench.

MARJORAM

Family: Labiatae

LATIN	• <u>Majorana hortensis Moench</u>
SPANISH	• Amáraco
FRENCH	• Marjolaine
GERMAN	• Majoran
SWEDISH	• Mejram
ARABIC	• Marzanjüsh
DUTCH	• Marjolein
ITALIAN	• Maggiorana
PORTUGUESE	• Manjerona
RUSSIAN	• Mayoran
JAPANESE	• Mayorana
CHINESE	• Ma-Yueh-Lan-Hua

MARJORAM AND OREGANO

ON the spice shelf sweet marjoram, a relatively mild flavoring, and oregano, the piquant "pizza" herb, are two separate condiments, and one has only to taste them both to be quite aware of their dissimilarity. Botanically, however, considerable confusion has existed for hundreds of years—and still exists today—concerning their correct identity, since the authorities do not agree among themselves. For many years both marjoram and oregano were known as *Origanum majorana* L. Today, some botanists identify both marjoram and oregano as *Majorana hortensis*, but most agree that this name belongs to the "sweet" or "knotted" marjoram of the mint family, indigenous to the Mediterranean region.

Oregano, formerly known as "wild marjoram" and "organy," is now usually recognized to be of two main types, Mexican and European. The pungent Mexican oregano, indigenous to the warmer areas of the Western Hemisphere, is of the genus *Lippia*, for the most part *L. graveolens* HBK., or *L. berlandieri* Schauer, small aromatic shrubs of the verbena family. The milder Euro-

OREGANO, 1492

POT MARJORAM, 1493

pean oregano of the mint family, on the other hand, is one of several species of *Origanum* native to the Mediterranean region, principally *Origanum vulgare* L.

The perplexing confusion between marjoram and oregano, and between the two types of oregano, is not limited to botanists—during shortages of marjoram some producing countries market oregano as "marjoram" to get a better price for their exportable product; when oregano is in short supply, these same exporters may ship marjoram as "oregano." Thus price may determine the label name of the exportable herb from time to time. In the United States during 1971 there was a marked difference in the import prices of these herbs, depending on their origin: French marjoram averaged 41 cents a pound; Greek oregano, 35 cents; and Mexican oregano, 17 cents.

Sweet or knotted marjoram is a low, tender, bushy perennial 12 to 18 inches high, which (since it winterkills easily) is grown as an annual in the northern climates. Its downy, narrow leaves are light gray-green in color, about ½ inch long. The inconspicuous white or pinkish flowers develop in terminal clusters.

Organum vulgare is a hardy perennial, 2 to 3 feet high with erect branching stems, and is sturdier and somewhat taller than marjoram. Its hairy leaves are a darker green color, and broader than those of marjoram. The flowers are purplish. Oregano is hardier than marjoram and can tolerate colder weather.

Pot marjoram, *Majorana onites* Benth., a sturdy perennial, is a popular ornamental easier to grow than sweet marjoram but of less value as a condiment since its leaves are very mild in flavor.

Sweet marjoram has a delicate, pleasant, sweet flavor; oregano's aroma is much stronger, lustier, more piquant. Both herbs possess a pleasantly bitter, aromatic undertone.

Before 1940 there was little interest in oregano in the United States. It was referred to in American cookbooks simply as "wild marjoram." During World War II, however, many G.I.'s in Italy became fond of pizza, which depends on oregano for full flavor. When the soldiers returned home, they started the pizza craze in the United States, with the result that during the past twenty-five years the demand for oregano, the "pizza spice," has increased at least 6,000 per cent; during this period there has been scarcely more than a minor growth in the demand for marjoram.

Both marjoram and oregano, or closely related varieties, were well known in the Graeco-Roman era. Marjoram was looked upon as a symbol of happiness. The ancient Greeks believed that if marjoram grew on a grave, it was a sign the deceased would enjoy eternal bliss.

Oregano, whose name is derived from the Greek and means "joy of the mountain," was popular in ancient Egypt and Greece as a condimental flavoring for fish, meats, vegetables, and wine. In Rome the herb was frequently mentioned in the cookbook of the epicure Apicius as a tasty seasoning for sauces. The Romans extended the use of both marjoram and oregano throughout their empire. During the Middle Ages marjoram was employed as an air sweetener and magic charm against witchcraft.

Marjoram was a well-known condiment in England in Shakespeare's time, as indicated in *All's Well That Ends Well,* Act IV, Scene V:

> *Clown:* Indeed, sir, she was the
> sweet-marjoram of the sallet,
> or, rather, the herb of grace.

Since the classical era marjoram and oregano—the latter in particular—have been used by physicians as stimulants, carminatives, nerve tonics, and cures for asthma, coughs, indigestion, rheumatism, toothaches, headaches, spider bites, and coronary conditions. At present, however, the importance of these two herbs is limited to the culinary field.

Both marjoram and oregano may be grown from seed sown in the spring or propagated by cuttings. For marjoram a warm, sheltered situation in full sunlight is recommended, with a rich, light soil and good drainage. Marjoram is planted in rows and intervals of about 9 by 9 inches, oregano about 12 by 12 inches apart. Germination is slow, and careful weeding at the seedling stage is essential.

The first harvest of the leaves and tender tops of both herbs occurs just as flowering commences, usually during July or August. The plants are cut 2 to 3 inches from the ground, and with favorable conditions a second cutting may be made in October. The oregano planting may be productive for four to five years, but in the North marjoram is usually renewed annually.

After the harvest the leaves are thoroughly dried, carefully cleaned, and stored as soon as possible.

On steam distillation, the dried leaves and flowering tops of marjoram yield from 0.2 to about 0.8 percent of an essential oil known as sweet marjoram oil. This oil is produced in Europe but only on a limited scale.

Oregano or "wild marjoram" leaves are distilled in Spain, Russia, and Italy. The Spanish oil, known as Spanish wild marjoram oil, is utilized widely in the United States as a flavoring in the preparation of sauces and other foods. This yellowish-green, pleasantly aromatic, spicy oil is used also to a limited extent for scenting soap and as an ingredient in liqueurs.

In the United States both marjoram and oregano are grown commercially for the production of the dried herb. Marjoram is also produced in France, Romania, Lebanon, Mexico, and Chile. It grows well in temperate climates rather than in the tropics.

In both marjoram and oregano, the condiment consists of the dried herb and leaves, available either whole or ground. Fresh marjoram leaves make a pleasant garnish for salads. The dried herb has many appetizing uses as a flavoring for vegetables, meats, liverwurst, bologna, some cheeses, chicken and turkey stuffings, soups, and sauces.

Oregano is exported to the United States from Greece, Mexico, Turkey, the Dominican Republic, France, Italy, and Portugal. In recent years the mild Mediterranean type (*Origanum* spp.) from Greece, used in Italian dishes, has been more popular in this country than the more aromatic and pungent Mexican oregano (*Lippia* spp.) used in chili powder, chili con carne, and other Mexican dishes. This Mexican oregano is known by at least three different names in the spice trade: "Mexican oregano," "Mexican marjoram," and "Mexican wild sage."

Oregano, made famous by its use in pizza, is equally good with any tomato dish, such as spaghetti, pasta sauce, or tomato salad. It is also an excellent seasoning for omelets, tomato juice, gravies, beef stew, and lamb. Oregano has a special affinity for sweet basil, and these two herbs blend well together—especially in dishes that include tomato products.

OREGANO
Origanum Vulgare L.

Family: *Labiatae*

LATIN	• <u>Origanum vulgare L.</u>
SPANISH	• Orégano
FRENCH	• Origan
GERMAN	• Dost
SWEDISH	• Vild Mejram
ARABIC	• Anrār
DUTCH	• Wilde Marjolein
ITALIAN	• Regamo
PORTUGUESE	• Ourégão
RUSSIAN	• Dushitsa
JAPANESE	• Oregano

Spiced Lima Bean Purée

2 packages frozen lima
   beans
4 tablespoons butter or
   margarine
2 tablespoons cream

1 teaspoon ground
   marjoram
1 teaspoon salt
¼ teaspoon ground ginger
Paprika

Cook beans according to directions on package until tender. Drain. Put beans and next 5 ingredients into glass top of blender. Cover and place on low speed until beans are liquefied. Heat. Serve with sprinkle of paprika on top.

Yield: 6–8 servings

Marjoram Tuna Casserole

7-ounce can tuna fish
1-pound can mixed
   vegetables
2 teaspoons lemon juice
2 tablespoons instant
   minced onion
1 tablespoon parsley flakes
10½-ounce can condensed
   cream of celery soup

⅛ teaspoon ground black
   pepper
¼ teaspoon salt
½ teaspoon marjoram
   leaves
10-ounce package corn
   muffin mix

Combine tuna fish, undrained vegetables, lemon juice,

minced onion, parsley flakes, celery soup, black pepper, salt, and *marjoram*. Mix well and heat. Turn into an 8- by 8- by 2-inch baking pan. Mix corn bread as directed on package. Spoon over the tuna-vegetable mixture. With a spatula spread batter to cover uniformly. Bake in a preheated hot oven (400°F.) 20 minutes or until brown. Serve hot.

Yield: 6 servings

Marinated Green Beans

2 packages (9 oz. each)
  frozen cut green beans
6 tablespoons salad oil
2 tablespoons cider vinegar
2 teaspoons marjoram
  leaves, *crumbled*

1 teaspoon sugar
½ teaspoon salt
¼ teaspoon ground black
  pepper

Cook beans as directed on package until just crisp-tender; drain and cool. In small bowl combine oil, vinegar, *marjoram,* sugar, salt, and black pepper. Beat until blended. Pour dressing over green beans; cover and marinate in refrigerator 12 hours.

Yield: 6 servings

Marjoram Meat Loaf

2 pounds ground chuck
¾ cup fresh bread crumbs
1 tablespoon instant minced
  onion
1 tablespoon water
1 tablespoon butter
1 can (8 oz.) tomato sauce
1 tablespoon marjoram
  leaves, *crumbled*

2 teaspoons salt
2 teaspoons parsley flakes
¼ teaspoon ground black
  pepper
2 eggs, beaten
2 slices bacon, cut in
  half

In large bowl combine meat with bread crumbs. Mix onion with water; let stand 8 minutes for onion to soften. In small skillet, sauté softened onion in butter until golden, about 3 minutes. Add to meat along with tomato sauce, *marjoram,* salt, parsley flakes, black pepper, and eggs. Mix lightly but well. Place meat in a greased 9- by 5- by 3-inch loaf pan, then unmold onto shallow baking dish (molding the meat in loaf pan gives it better shape). Top with bacon. Bake in a preheated moderate oven (325°F.) for 1¼ hours. Serve hot or cold.

Yield: 6 servings

Marinated Zucchini and Macaroni

2 pounds small zucchini,
  unpeeled
Boiling water
½ cup water
⅓ cup onion flakes
¼ cup celery flakes
¼ cup salad oil
1 tablespoon marjoram
  leaves, *crumbled*
2 teaspoons salt
¾ teaspoon ground black
  pepper
¼ teaspoon instant garlic
  powder
¼ cup cider vinegar
¼ cup lemon juice
2 cups cooked elbow
  macaroni
2 medium tomatoes, sliced

Quarter zucchini lengthwise; cut into 3-inch lengths. Place in colander; set into boiling water in large kettle (water should cover ½ inch of bottom of colander). Cover and steam zucchini about 8 minutes, or until crisp-tender. Remove colander; drain zucchini. Cool zucchini in single layer on baking sheet or tray. Refrigerate. Mix the ½ cup of water, onion flakes, and celery flakes; let stand 8 minutes for vegetables to soften. Heat 1 tablespoon of the oil in small skillet. Add softened vegetables and sauté about 3 minutes. Cool. Add *marjoram,* salt, black pepper, and garlic powder. Mix in vinegar and lemon juice. Place macaroni and zucchini in 2-quart casserole, arranging a few pieces of zucchini over top. Pour over ¾ cup of marinade, reserving remainder for tomato slices. Cover; refrigerate 12 hours, basting occasionally. One hour before serving, place tomato slices in reserved marinade; refrigerate. Arrange around edge of casserole. Serve with hot or cold meats or fish.

Yield: 6 servings

Braised Lamb

2 pounds shoulder of lamb
1 tablespoon olive or salad
  oil
1 can (6 oz.) tomato paste
¼ cup onion flakes
1 tablespoon salt
1 tablespoon parsley flakes

1¼ teaspoons ground
  oregano
¼ teaspoon instant minced
  garlic
¼ teaspoon ground black
  pepper
Cooked rice or spaghetti

Cut lamb into 1-inch pieces; trim off excess fat. Brown meat in olive oil in heavy skillet. Add 2 cups of water and tomato paste. Cover and cook 1 to 1½ hours or until meat is tender. Add seasonings and continue cooking 10 minutes. Serve with rice or spaghetti.

Yield: 6 servings

Stuffed Mushrooms

1 pound large mushrooms
1 cup soft bread crumbs
½ cup chopped prosciutto
¾ cup canned Italian plum
  tomatoes, drained
1 tablespoon parsley flakes
¹⁄₁₆ teaspoon instant garlic
  powder
½ teaspoon oregano leaves

¼ teaspoon ground black
  pepper
2½ tablespoons grated
  Parmesan or Romano
  cheese
1 tablespoon olive oil
¼ cup fresh lemon juice
4 tablespoons olive oil
¼ cup water

Remove stems from mushrooms. Wash and dry caps and reserve. Combine next 9 ingredients. Blend well. Dip each mushroom cap in lemon juice, then fill with about 1 heaping teaspoonful of bread crumb mixture. Arrange stuffed mushrooms in shallow baking dish or pie plate. Sprinkle with olive oil. Pour water in bottom of pan to prevent mushrooms from becoming too dry. Bake in a preheated hot oven (400°F.) for 15 minutes or until mushrooms are browned and heated throughout. Serve immediately.

Yield: 6 servings

Pasta Con Broccoli

3 tablespoons olive oil
6 anchovy fillets, cut in
  small pieces
1 package (10 oz.) frozen
  broccoli flowerets
2 tablespoons pignolia nuts
½ cup seedless raisins
¾ teaspoon crushed
  oregano leaves

⅛ teaspoon ground black
  pepper
½ pound medium-sized
  macaroni shells
Boiling water
1 tablespoon salt
2 tablespoons lemon juice
Grated Romano cheese

Heat oil in saucepan or skillet. Add anchovies and cook, stirring, until anchovies break into very small pieces. Add next 5 ingredients. Cover, cook gently, stirring occasionally, until broccoli is tender. In the meantime, cook macaroni shells in boiling salted water according to package directions until tender. Drain. Toss shells with lemon juice. Add broccoli mixture and toss gently. Serve immediately with grated cheese.

Yield: 4 servings

Spaghetti With Meat Sauce

1½ pounds ground chuck
1 tablespoon olive or salad
  oil
3 cans (6 oz. each) tomato
  paste
1 bay leaf
2½ teaspoons salt
2 teaspoons fennel seed
3 tablespoons instant
  minced onion

2 teaspoons oregano leaves
2 teaspoons sugar
¼ teaspoon ground red
  pepper
¼ teaspoon instant minced
  garlic
1 pound spaghetti
½ cup grated Parmesan
  cheese

Brown meat in oil in a 10-inch skillet or saucepan. Add 3 cups hot water, tomato paste, bay leaf, salt, and fennel seed. Bring to boiling point. Reduce heat and simmer 20 minutes. Add remaining seasonings 10 minutes before cooking time is up. Cook spaghetti according to package directions. Drain and arrange on a platter. Cover with sauce. Sprinkle with grated Parmesan cheese.

Yield: 6 servings

Easy Pizza Pie

2 packages (8 oz. each)
  refrigerated biscuits
1 can (10¼ oz.) meatless
  marinara sauce
1 teaspoon oregano leaves
⅛ teaspoon instant minced
  garlic
¼ pound Italian sausage,
  cooked and sliced

¼ cup small shrimp
¼ cup sliced mushrooms
1 can (2 oz.) rolled fillets
  of anchovies
¼ cup sliced stuffed olives
¼ cup grated Parmesan
  cheese

Roll dough to fit 12-inch round pizza pan. Bake in
preheated oven (350°F.) 20 to 25 minutes or until
browned. Heat sauce to boiling. Add *oregano* and garlic;
simmer 5 minutes. Spread sauce over dough. Arrange
sausage, shrimp, mushrooms, anchovies, and olives over
sauce. Sprinkle with Parmesan cheese. Place under
broiler 3 to 5 minutes or until heated. Cut into 6 pieces.

Yield: 6 servings

Beef Stew, Mexican Style

2 pounds beef stew meat
½ teaspoon instant minced
  garlic
½ cup chopped onion
¾ cup chopped green
  pepper
1 cup tomato purée

2 teaspoons salt
1 teaspoon whole oregano
  leaves
½ teaspoon chili powder
¼ teaspoon ground black
  pepper
5 tablespoons flour

In a heavy saucepan place all ingredients except flour.
Cover. Cook over medium heat until meat is tender, 1
to 1½ hours. (If a pressure cooker is used, cook 30
minutes at 15 pounds pressure.) Mix flour with ⅓ cup
water and gradually add to the stew. Cook until thickened, 5 to 10 minutes.

Yield: 8 servings

MINT LEAVES

Mentha piperita L.

A. Flowering branch
1. Flower in bud
2. Flower partly open
3. Flower fully open
4. Vertical section of flower
5. Calyx flattened out
6. Stamen
7. Pollen grains
8. Pistil showing style
9. Style and forked stigma
10. Transverse section through 4 fruits (nutlets)

MINT LEAVES

Family: *Labiatae*

LATIN	• <u>**Mentha piperita L.**</u>
SPANISH	• **Menta**
FRENCH	• **Menthe**
GERMAN	• **Pfefferminze**
SWEDISH	• **Pepparmynta**
ARABIC	• **Na'nā'**
DUTCH	• **Pepermunt**
ITALIAN	• **Menta**
PORTUGUESE	• **Hortelã**
RUSSIAN	• **Myata**
JAPANESE	• **Seiyo-Hakka**
CHINESE	• **Yang-Po-Ho**

MINT LEAVES

OF THE many species of mint, peppermint, *Mentha piperita,* and spearmint, *Mentha spicata* L., are among the foremost flavorings for food. Both are hardy perennial herbs of the mint family, indigenous to Europe and the Mediterranean region but naturalized throughout much of the temperate world in both northern and southern hemispheres.

Historically, spearmint is much older than peppermint. The latter was virtually unheard of as a distinct species until 1696, when the great English naturalist John Ray recommended it as a remedy for diarrhea. By 1721 peppermint had been admitted into the London Pharmacopoeia.

Spearmint and horsemint (*Mentha spicata* var. *longifolia* L.), on the other hand, were well known as early as the Graeco-Roman era as flavoring herbs, culinary condiments, appetizers, perfumes, and bath scents. At that time the aroma of crushed mint leaves, rubbed on table tops, symbolized hospitality.

Hippocrates and Dioscorides frequently mentioned mint in their medical writings. Pliny recommended it as an ingredient in forty-one therapeutic potions, and in some it was specifically prescribed as a stomachic, restorative, and carminative.

The ancient Hebrews scattered mint leaves on the synagogue floor, so that each footstep would produce a fresh, fragrant whiff.

Mentha is named after Minthes, a charming nymph in classical mythology who was metamorphosed into the humble, down-trodden mint plant by Proserpina, the suspicious wife of Pluto, in a fit of jealousy.

Mint is mentioned in the New Testament in Luke 11:42: "But woe unto you, Pharisees! for ye tithe mint and rue and all manner of herbs, and pass over judgment and the love of God. . . ."

Roman soldiers disseminated the mint plants throughout the Roman Empire. It was grown in many convent gardens in Europe as early as the ninth century. During the Middle Ages, in addition to conventional culinary use powdered mint leaves were used to whiten the teeth, cure sores of the mouth, heal bites from mad dogs, relieve the pain of wasp stings, prevent milk from curdling, and repel rats and mice (these rodents recoil from the scent of mint).

The Pilgrim fathers introduced spearmint to New England in the seventeenth century. By 1816 it was grown commercially in Rochester, New York, and by 1840 commercial peppermint plantings were developed in Ohio and Michigan. Subsequently both spearmint and peppermint have become naturalized, especially in moist areas, in much of the northern United States.

Commercial mint culture is extensive today in California, Oregon, Washington, Michigan, Ohio, Wisconsin, New York, and Indiana. Other countries important in production of mint include Romania, England, France, Egypt, Argentina, Russia, Bulgaria, and Morocco.

A mint planting is productive for five or six years, hence its site should be selected carefully. It should be a rich, friable, well-drained loam with adequate moisture, in an open sunny situation.

The peppermint plant, somewhat taller and more reddish than spearmint, may grow to a height of 2 to 3 feet. Its leaves are brighter green in color, more clearly stalked, and more pungent in taste than spearmint. The flowers of both varieties are pale violet.

The distinction between the two species, peppermint and spearmint, may be clarified by the following memory aid: P stands for peppermint which has a petioled (stalked) leaf; while S is for spearmint, with a sessile (nonstalked) leaf.

Peppermint rarely produces viable seed under cultural conditions—it is propagated by runners or easily rooted cuttings of the parent plant. These are laid almost end to end in furrows about 2 feet apart and covered to a depth of 3 or 4 inches. Weeding is important. The first year the rows retain their identity, but subsequently the plants spread over the field and are treated as a field crop.

When a planting is made in March it should be ready to be cut in July or August, when the plants are in full bloom. If the essential oil is to be extracted, the herbage is partially dried in the field, then taken to the stills. Should the fungus disease called "mint rust" threaten, the harvest should begin at once even if the crop is short of its full growth.

Partially dried peppermint leaves yield, on steam distillation, from 0.1 to 0.8 percent of the essential oil, which is commercially more useful than the leaves. Peppermint oil, pale yellow in color, is used to flavor chewing gum, candy, toothpaste, gargles, soap, confectionery, perfumes, liqueurs, and pharmaceutical preparations. The flavor and taste of both the herb and the essential oil may be described as fresh, strong, sweet, and tangy, with a cool aftertaste. Peppermint oil has such a sharp, penetrating odor that it can be used to locate leaks in pipes.

In commercial operations on large acreages the harvest and distillation processes often continue uninterrupted day and night for three or four weeks, until the harvest is completed. Since the entire mint plant contains essential oil, the stems are cut as close to the ground as possible.

The oil yield varies under favorable conditions from 30 to 40 pounds per acre. More than 1,000,000 pounds of peppermint oil are produced annually in the United States, the far western states being the leading producers.

Japanese mint (so called because it is largely grown there), *Mentha arvensis* var. *piperascens* Malinvaud, another important variety widely cultivated in Japan, Taiwan, Brazil, Australia, and the United States, is the chief commercial source of menthol. Japanese peppermint oil, known also as *Mentha arvensis* oil, is cheaper in price and inferior in flavor to true peppermint oil but has a higher menthol content. Since menthol is one of the most universally used flavoring agents, the world-wide production of Japanese peppermint oil is enormous. In some countries it is used not only for menthol production, but also to adulterate the more expensive true peppermint oil.

Peppermint oil and peppermint tea have traditionally been used in medicine for their antispasmodic, antiseptic, stomachic, aromatic, and carminative qualities to provide relief to those suffering from cramps, headaches, nausea, diarrhea, indigestion, and the common cold, among other ailments. Of all the essential oils peppermint oil is the most widely used medicinally.

Mint leaves are produced extensively in North Africa,

where they are used in mint tea, a most popular Arab beverage.

The aromatic peppermint and spearmint leaves are found on the spice shelf whole, rubbed, pulverized, or in the form of mint flakes. Mint jelly and mint sauce are famous accompaniments for roast lamb. As a condiment, mint is a popular flavoring in many candies, sauces, desserts, salads, jellies, vinegars, teas, and other beverages, including the mint julep.

Minted Yogurt Soup

½ cup raw, regular-cooking rice
1 tablespoon flour
2 teaspoons mint flakes, crumbled
1½ teaspoons salt

1 egg, lightly beaten
2 cans (10½ oz. each) chicken broth
1 cup (8 oz.) plain yogurt or sour cream

Combine rice, flour, *mint flakes,* and salt in large saucepan. Mix in egg. Add broth, yogurt, and 1½ cups water. Bring mixture to boiling point, stirring constantly. Reduce heat and simmer until rice is cooked, 25 to 30 minutes, stirring occasionally. Soup may be served hot or cold, topped with a dollop of yogurt, if desired. If soup is too thick, thin with a small amount of water.

Yield: 4–5 portions

Minted Lamb Kebabs

2 pounds boned lean lamb
1 cup dry red wine
¼ cup olive oil
1 tablespoon instant minced onion
2 teaspoons mint flakes
1½ teaspoons salt
½ teaspoon oregano leaves

¼ teaspoon instant garlic powder
¼ teaspoon ground black pepper
4 whole allspice berries
1 small eggplant
6 cherry tomatoes

Cut lamb into 1-inch cubes. Place meat in a small bowl or plastic bag. Combine remaining ingredients except eggplant and tomatoes; mix well. Pour over lamb cubes. Refrigerate 12 to 18 hours, turning occasionally. Peel eggplant and cut into 1-inch cubes. Arrange lamb on skewers alternately with eggplant. Broil 4 inches from source of heat 15 to 18 minutes or until done, turning and brushing several times with marinade. Place a cherry tomato at end of each skewer. Return to broiler for 2 minutes to heat tomato.

Yield: 6 servings

Skillet Mushrooms, Italian Style

2 tablespoons olive oil	¼ teaspoon mint flakes
6 anchovies, diced	¼ teaspoon ground black
1 pound fresh mushrooms,	pepper
sliced	⅛ teaspoon instant garlic
⅓ cup tomato sauce	powder
½ teaspoon salt	4 slices toast, buttered

Heat oil in a 9-inch skillet. Add anchovies, mushrooms, tomato sauce, salt, *mint flakes,* black pepper, and garlic powder. Mix well. Cover and cook over moderate heat 10 to 12 minutes, stirring frequently. Serve on buttered toast.

Yield: 4 servings

Minted Pear Halves

1 can (*1 lb. 14 oz.*) pear	1 tablespoon mint flakes
halves	

Drain juice from pear halves into a small saucepan. Add *mint flakes* and bring to boiling point. Cover and simmer 10 minutes. Pour through a fine strainer over pear halves. Cool and refrigerate until ready to serve. Serve as a meat accompaniment or for dessert.

Yield: 6 servings

Tomato Mint Salad

3 tablespoons olive or salad
  oil
3 tablespoons lemon juice
1 teaspoon mint flakes,
  crumbled
1 teaspoon paprika
1 teaspoon instant minced
  onion

¾ teaspoon salt
¼ teaspoon instant minced
  garlic
¼ teaspoon ground black
  pepper
3 to 4 large tomatoes, sliced
Lettuce leaves

Combine oil, lemon juice, *mint flakes,* paprika, onion, salt, garlic, and black pepper in a small bowl. Blend with a rotary beater until well mixed. Refrigerate at least 30 minutes. Serve over sliced tomatoes on a lettuce-lined salad plate.

Yield: 6 servings

MUSTARD SEED

Sinapis alba **L.**

A. **Flowering branch**	**6.** **Fruit**
1. **Bud**	**7.** **Mature fruit**
2. **Flower**	**8.** **Seed**
3. **Stamen**	**9.** **Embryos**
4. **Anther**	**10.** **Transverse section**
5. **Pistil**	**of seed**

MUSTARD SEED

Family: Cruciferae

LATIN	• <u>Sinapis alba L.</u>
SPANISH	• Mostaza
FRENCH	• Moutarde
GERMAN	• Senfsaat
SWEDISH	• Senap
ARABIC	• Khardal
DUTCH	• Mosterd
ITALIAN	• Senape
PORTUGUESE	• Mostarda
RUSSIAN	• Gorchitsa
JAPANESE	• Karashi
CHINESE	• Chieh

MUSTARD SEED

OF the many varieties of mustard, the most prominent are the herbaceous annuals *Sinapis alba* L. (syn. *Brassica hirta* Moench.), known as white or yellow mustard; *Brassica nigra* (L.) Koch., black mustard; and *Brassica juncea* Coss. and Czern., brown mustard. All are members of the mustard family: The first two are probably indigenous to southern Europe and the Mediterranean region; *B. juncea* primarily is native to northern Himalaya.

The world demand for both white and brown mustard seed is great, amounting to over 600 million pounds annually. During the past 20 years brown mustard has almost entirely replaced black mustard in cultivation and use.

In the United States the present consumption of mustard is larger than that of every other spice except pepper.

The word mustard is derived from the Latin *mustum*, or *must*, the expressed juice of the grape or other fruit; in ancient Rome must was mixed with ground mustard seeds to form a paste known as *mustum ardens* (hot must).

From very early times mustard has been used as a medicine and a condiment. Pythagoras (about 530 B.C.) suggested it as an effective antidote for scorpion bites; Hippocrates (about 400 B.C.) recommended the seeds for medicinal use both internally and externally; Diocletian, the Roman emperor, mentioned mustard in an official price-fixing edict in A.D. 301, alluding to it as a condiment and food that was consumed in the eastern parts of his empire. In that remote period young mustard plants were eaten as spinach; the seeds were used as a spice.

In 334 B.C., Darius III of Persia is reported to have sent Alexander the Great a bag of sesame seed, symbolizing the vast number of his army—whereupon Alexander returned a sack of mustard seed, intended to signify not only the number but also the powerful energy of his soldiers.

In the New Testament there are several references to the small seeds, including Matthew 13:31–32:

> Another parable put he forth unto them, saying, The kingdom of heaven is like to a grain of mustard seed, which a man took, and sowed in his field: Which indeed is the least of all seeds: but when it is grown, it is the greatest among herbs, and becometh a tree, so that the birds of the air come and lodge in the branches thereof.

At the time of Christ mustard seed was one of the smallest of all known seeds. (Orchid seeds, as infinitesimal as fine dust, are today considered to be the smallest in the plant kingdom, but these were not familiar to Jesus' audience in Galilee.) Yet by autumn the mustard plant sometimes grew to a height of 10 feet or more to become one of the largest annual herbs.

In A.D. 800 mustard was grown on convent lands near Paris to provide revenue. Charlemagne decreed in 812 that the herb be grown on the imperial farms in central Europe. During the Middle Ages mustard be-

MUSTARD, 1493

came an esteemed seasoning to supplement the drab and monotonous winter diet of salted meat. Its cultivation was extended by the Arabs to Spain and during the twelfth century it was introduced to Germany and England, where it was known as *senapium*.

When Vasco da Gama sailed from Lisbon on July 8, 1497, on his first voyage to the East around the Cape of Good Hope, he carried mustard in his provisions.

In seventeenth-century England mustard usually was sold in the form of balls of mustard paste (prepared, among other places, at Tewkesbury). Shakespeare refers to this condiment in *Henry IV, Part 2,* Act II, Scene IV:

> *Doll*: They says Poins has a good wit.
> *Falstaff*: He a good wit! hang him, baboon!
> His wit's as thick as Tewksbury mustard. . . .

In 1720 a certain Mrs. Clements of Durham, England is reported to have made herself a fortune by inventing a dry, pale-yellow mustard flour known as "Durham mustard," which she produced by hulling, grinding, and sifting the seeds in a mill.

The French humorist Anatole France observed in *La Revolte des Anges* (1914) that "a tale without love is like beef without mustard: an insipid dish."

The condiment mustard seed is available today in three forms:

Powdered dry mustard, known also as "mustard flour" or "ground mustard," is made by grinding the brown and white seeds finely and then removing the hulls by means of a multiple milling, screening, and sifting operation. If a "hot" mustard is desired, the pungency is intensified by increasing the proportion of the brown flour.

Prepared mustard, also known as "mustard paste," is a mixture of ground mustard seed, salt, vinegar, and spices. This very popular preparation is used on hot dogs, sandwiches, cheeses, eggs, meats, and salad dressings. The brilliant yellow color of prepared mustard in the United States is due to the addition, during its manufacture, of ground Alleppey (Indian) turmeric to a paste of yellow mustard. This mustard is packed in glass jars, while in Europe it is frequently packaged in tubes like toothpaste.

French mustard paste is prepared from brown or black seeds ground in vinegar. The resultant color is brownish, specked with fragments of mustard seed.

The whole seeds may be used in pickling or be boiled with vegetables—cabbage and sauerkraut, for instance.

Unlike most other aromatic spices, powdered mustard has no aroma when dry. It must be moistened for about ten minutes to develop its sharp, hot, and tangy flavor. When the powder is mixed with warm water, enzyme activity develops the pungent principle. Once the moistened powdered mustard has developed its aroma, it should be used within an hour or the flavor will gradually be lost. The mustard served in Chinese restaurants is usually freshly prepared in this manner. If the mustard is to be kept for an extended period, it must be acidified (as with lemon juice, vinegar, or wine) to arrest enzymatic activity and the mixture refrigerated. Prepared mustard has been acidified with vinegar and thus retains its strength. Manufacturers frequently urge the refrigeration of mustard products.

When added to mayonnaise, curries, or salad dressings, mustard tends to act as a preservative by retarding decomposition brought about by bacteria.

Part of the chemical structure of a "tear gas" used in World War I is also a part of the structure of the glycoside sinigrin—found in black mustard seeds—that is exceedingly irritating to the mucous membranes, especially those of the eyes and nose. Excessive amounts caused inflammation to the respiratory passages of soldiers in the trenches in France, leading to severe lung damage and, on occasion, death. On the other hand, such substances, when used in minute and strictly controlled amounts as in condimental mustard, stimulate the appetite by increasing the ctivity of the salivary glands.

Mustard seed can be grown in most temperate climates and is widely cultivated today in Argentina, Australia, Canada, China, Denmark, England, Ethiopia, France, India, Italy, the Netherlands, Poland, and the western parts of the United States—Montana, California, Oregon, Washington, and North Dakota. Mustard seed imported into the United States is mostly from Canada and Denmark.

The plant is hardy and so readily reproduces and adapts itself that at times it becomes a noxious weed. It is said that when the Spanish *padres* established the Mission Trail in California, they scattered mustard seeds to mark the trails as they went from mission to mission. Like Hänsel and Gretel's, the well-marked paths were then easy to find at a later date—these mustard trails can still be found in the vicinity of some missions.

White and brown mustard are fast-growing and require only limited rainfall. It is important, however, that the pods mature during dry weather. White (yellow) mustard prefers heavy sandy loam, while the brown does better on a lighter sandy loam. The seeds are planted in the spring, the brown earlier than the white, at the rate of about 4 pounds per acre for the white and 3 pounds for the brown. Since the seed-pods of older varieties shatter severely when ripe, the harvest used to be carried out during the early morning hours before the fully developed pods opened. Modern varieties, however, are so indehiscent that they can be harvested and threshed in a single operation when fully mature.

Mustard has been grown successfully for seed production in the western United States, using the most modern mechanized techniques for planting, harvesting, and threshing. Brown mustard yields about 1,000 pounds of clean seed per acre; the yield for white or yellow mustard is somewhat less, approximately 800 pounds.

Both white and brown mustard produce bright yellow flowers, each with six stamens and four petals, which form the cross characteristic of the mustard family and the reason for its Latin name, *Cruciferae* ("cross-bearer"). The white, a relatively mild-flavored species, is an erect annual that grows to about 24 inches high. The pungent brown type, although having smaller flowers, is a larger plant that reaches 3 feet or more in height.

The white mustard pods are rough and hairy, containing small yellowish seeds about $1/12$ inch in diameter, and $1/10$ grain in weight; the dark reddish-brown seeds of brown mustard are even smaller, about $1/25$ inch in diameter and $1/50$ grain in weight, with narrow smooth pods.

White mustard seeds contain almost no volatile oil. Those of brown mustard may yield, on steam and water distillation, from 0.75 to 1.25 percent of the essential oil used in the food industry. The seeds of both species yield about 28 to 40 percent of fixed oils, obtained by expression in an oil press, or by solvent extraction. These fixed oils, by-products of the condiment industry in many countries, may be used in soapmaking, for burning in lamps, and as lubricants. In addition to being grown for its seed, white mustard may be grown as a salad plant, cover crop, and "green manure" (plowed in, when half grown, to add organic matter to the soil). Brown mustard is grown mostly for its seed.

B. juncea, known as *rai* in India, is cultivated on a large scale in Bengal and Bihar. The fixed oil is an important Indian culinary product and is also used as a liniment for massaging the body, as an illuminant, a hair oil, and a lubricant. This brown mustard is grown extensively in parts of Africa and China, as well as India, for use as a vegetable, cover crop, and medicinal plant.

The use of mustard as a medicine in Western countries has declined in recent years. It previously had been used for centuries as a stimulant, a diuretic, an emetic, a rubefacient, and an all-round remedy (in plaster form) to relieve rheumatism and arthritis.

The mustards are important honey crops in some western states—in the Lompoc Valley of California, for example, where crops of mustard seed are grown commercially. The mustard plants bloom during May and June, when bees are abundant and feed actively on the copious mustard nectar, producing a substantial quantity of mild-flavored, light-colored honey.

There has been a notable increase in the consumption of mustard seed in the United States during the past fifty years; in 1920, per capita consumption amounted to 0.15 pounds, as compared to 0.45 pounds in 1972. lishments has created a tremendous demand for (and often waste of) "mini-packets" of mustard.

Mustard Salmon Croquettes With Cheese Sauce

1 can (1 lb.) salmon
1 teaspoon powdered
mustard
1 teaspoon water
Butter or margarine
4 tablespoons all-purpose
flour
1 cup milk, scalded
2 teaspoons parsley flakes
¼ teaspoon instant onion
powder

⅛ teaspoon ground black
pepper
¹⁄₁₆ teaspoon cayenne
1 teaspoon fresh lemon juice
About ¼ cup dry bread
crumbs
4 tablespoons butter or
margarine, melted
Cheese Sauce

Drain oil from salmon into a measuring cup; reserve.
Place salmon in a large bowl; remove skin and bones
and break into small pieces with a fork. Combine *powdered mustard* and water; let stand 10 minutes for flavor
to develop. Measure oil drained from salmon and pour
in a saucepan. Add enough butter or margarine to make
4 tablespoons. Cook over low heat until butter is melted.
Remove from heat and blend in flour. Gradually add
scalded milk. Cook over low heat, stirring constantly,
until mixture is thick. Remove from heat, add *mustard*
and next 5 ingredients; blend well. Add *mustard* mixture
to salmon; blend well. Refrigerate 2 hours or longer.
Shape into patties, coat with dry bread crumbs and
cook slowly in melted butter or margarine until lightly
browned on both sides. If necessary, add more butter or
margarine to pan. Serve hot with Cheese Sauce.

CHEESE SAUCE

½ teaspoon powdered
mustard
½ teaspoon water
1 can (11 oz.) cheddar
cheese soup

½ teaspoon prepared
horseradish
½ teaspoon Worcestershire
sauce

Combine *powdered mustard* and water; let stand 10
minutes for flavor to develop. In a small saucepan combine soup, horseradish, Worcestershire sauce, and *mus-*

tard. Cook over low heat, stirring frequently, until blended and heated throughout.

Yield: 4 servings

Chicken Salad

¾ teaspoon powdered
  mustard
¾ teaspoon warm water
2 teaspoons paprika
1½ teaspoons instant
  minced onion
1 teaspoon sugar
1 teaspoon salt
1 teaspoon basil leaves
¼ teaspoon ground black
  pepper

¾ cup olive oil
1-pound head cauliflower
½ cup wine vinegar
6 cups cooked diced chicken
1 medium-sized cucumber,
  thinly sliced
½ cup sliced toasted
  almonds

Combine *powdered mustard* and water; let stand 10 minutes for flavor to develop. Add paprika, instant onion, sugar, salt, basil, black pepper, and oil. Let stand 1 hour. Meanwhile, break cauliflower into small flowerets; cut into ¼-inch slices. Set aside. Add vinegar to paprika mixture; beat well. Combine dressing with cauliflower, chicken, and cucumber. Toss gently to blend. Refrigerate at least 2 hours. Just before serving toss with almonds.

Yield: 8–10 servings

Hamburger Relish

5 cups green tomatoes
4 cups green sweet peppers
3 cups onions
2 cups raw cabbage
2 cups peeled cucumbers
¼ cup salt
3 cups cider vinegar
1 cup sugar

⅓ cup sifted all-purpose
  flour
4 teaspoons powdered
  mustard
1½ teaspoons ground
  turmeric
½ teaspoon ground cayenne
½ cup chopped pimiento

Grind all vegetables in a food chopper, using coarse blade. Place in an 8-quart kettle along with salt. Cook over low heat 5 minutes or until mixture makes its own juice. Bring to boiling point and cook 10 minutes longer. Mix remaining ingredients, except pimiento, in a saucepan. Stir and cook 10 minutes or until thickened. Add to cooked vegetables. Add pimiento and bring to boiling point, stirring constantly. Pack in hot sterilized jars. Seal at once. Store in a cool place.

Yield: 8 jars, 1 pint each

Bread and Butter Pickles

6 quarts thinly sliced
  cucumbers
1 quart thinly sliced onion
  rings
½ cup salt
2 cups cider vinegar

1½ cups sugar
2 teaspoons mustard seed
2 teaspoons celery seed
2 teaspoons ground turmeric
1 teaspoon whole black
  pepper

Combine cucumbers, onions, and salt. Let stand 10 to 12 hours. Drain and discard water. Wash to remove excess salt and set aside. Combine remaining ingredients. Boil 3 minutes. Add cucumber and onions. Cook until cucumbers are clear, about 6 to 8 minutes. Pack in hot sterilized jars. Seal. Store in a cool place.

Yield: 6 jars, 1 pint each

NUTMEG and MACE
Myristica fragrans Houtt.

A. **Flowering branch with male flowers**
1. **Column of stamens**
2. **Vertical section of column of stamens**
3. **Transverse section of column of stamens**
4. **Pollen grains**
5. **Vertical section of female flower**
6. **Vertical section of pistil**
7. **Fruit with fleshy covering partly opened**
8. **Vertical section fruit showing aril surrounding seed**
9. **Seed surrounded by aril (mace)**
10. **Seed without aril**
11. **Vertical section of seed**
12. **Embryo**

NUTMEG AND MACE

Family: *Myristicaceae*

LATIN	• Myristica fragrans Houtt.
SPANISH	• Nuez Moscada
FRENCH	• Muscade
GERMAN	• Muskatnuss
SWEDISH	• Muskot
ARABIC	• Basbāsa
DUTCH	• Notemuskaat
ITALIAN	• Noce Moscata
PORTUGUESE	• Noz-Moscada
RUSSIAN	• Oryekh Muskatny
JAPANESE	• Nikuzuku
CHINESE	• Jou-Tou-K'ou

NUTMEG AND MACE

THE nutmeg tree, *Myristica fragrans,* indigenous to the Moluccas and other islands of the East Indian Archipelago, is truly remarkable in that it produces two separate spices, nutmeg and mace. It is a handsome, densely foliaged evergreen tree of the nutmeg family, with spreading branches, dark gray bark, and small, pale yellow, bell-shaped flowers. Its glossy oblong-ovate leaves, which resemble those of rhododendron or mountain laurel, are about 4 inches long, dark green above, paler beneath. Under cultivation it grows to a height of 40 to 60 feet and thrives at low elevations, in the warm and rainy tropics of both hemispheres.

The fleshy fruit, resembling an apricot, is globose in form, lemon yellow to light brown in color. When ripe, it splits in half, exposing the beautiful brilliant scarlet, netlike membrane, or aril, known as the *mace*, which closely enwraps a lustrous dark brown, brittle shell, inside of which is the single glossy brown, oily seed—the *nutmeg* of commerce. The ovoid, fragrant

NUTMEGS
From a seventeeth-century Dutch print.

nutmeg seeds are about 1¼ inches long and ¾ inch wide. The strongly aromatic, fragile, netlike mace is about 1½ inches long and 1/16 inch thick; when dried it is yellowish-brown in color.

Probably neither nutmeg nor mace was known to the ancients, although it is possible Pliny described them in the first century A.D. when he wrote about *comacum,* a tree with a fragrant nut and a perfume of two kinds. During the sixth century A.D. these spices were imported by Arab traders from the East Indies to Constantinople. By the end of the twelfth century both spices were well known in Europe from Italy to Denmark. It is recorded that in 1191 the streets of Rome were fumigated with nutmegs and other aromatic spices prior to the coronation of Emperor Henry VI. By the fourteenth century mace was highly regarded in England, where one pound of this costly spice had a value equivalent to that of three sheep.

Chaucer in *The Canterbury Tales* mentioned the pungent fourteenth-century mixture of nutmeg and ale:

". . . gynebred that was so fyn and licorys, and eek comyn,
with sugre that is trye, also of nutemuge put in ale."

The Portuguese discovery in 1512 that nutmeg trees were indigenous to the island of Banda in the Moluccas enabled them to dominate the nutmeg and mace trade for almost a century—until they were driven out by the Dutch in 1602. For many years the Dutch then ruthlessly controlled the production and sale of these products. Nutmeg cultivation was restricted to the islands of Banda and Amboina—systematic attempts were made to destroy all nutmeg trees growing elsewhere. The Dutch were thwarted in these monopolistic efforts, however, by fruit pigeons that swallowed fresh nutmeg seeds and voided them on nearby islands; and later by the French who, in 1770, introduced smuggled nutmeg plants into Mauritius.

An amusing incident concerning Dutch colonial administration during this period has been reported: Since prices for mace were higher than those for nutmeg, an Amsterdam official, unaware that both spices came from the same tree, is said to have sent strict orders to the Moluccas to reduce the number of nutmeg trees and plant more mace trees.

The British occupied the Moluccas from 1796 to 1802, and during that period introduced nutmeg cultivation first to Penang, later to Singapore—thus contributing to the collapse of the Dutch monopoly and helping to bring down the prices of nutmeg and mace.

Nutmeg culture was introduced to St. Vincent in the British West Indies in 1802. Experimental work started in Trinidad in 1806, followed by the development (commencing in 1843) of what were to be the most successful nutmeg plantations in the Western Hemisphere, on Grenada.

Connecticut is known popularly as "The Nutmeg State," owing to the tradition that slick Yankee peddlers of the early nineteenth century were wont to sell as the genuine spice whittled wooden imitation "nutmegs" to unsuspecting housewives.

The most important nutmeg-producing regions today are Indonesia, including Banda and other islands in the Moluccas where the spice originated; Grenada, in the West Indies; and Ceylon. Hurricane "Janet" destroyed about 90 percent of Grenada's nutmeg trees in 1955. New trees planted subsequently are now coming into bearing and Grenada is, after Indonesia, the main world supplier of nutmeg and mace. Annual world production amounts to about 7,000 tons of nutmeg and 1,000 tons of mace, 60 percent of which comes from Indonesia. The principal importing countries are the United States, West Germany, the Netherlands, and the United Kingdom.

The nutmeg tree thrives in sheltered valleys, on hot, moist tropical islands where it can "smell" the sea, at elevations from sea level to 1,500 feet. Friable, well-drained, sandy soils rich in humus are recommended, in addition to a well-distributed annual rainfall of 80 to 100 inches.

Propagation is usually carried out by planting fresh, selected seed in a well-watered nursery. Germination may require about six weeks. Young plants are transplanted to final field position when about six months old, spaced about 28 by 28 feet, in light shade.

The nutmeg tree is slow-growing, and the first small

crop may not be obtained until the seventh year. The yield increases with age, the most productive period being between the fifteenth and thirtieth years. Some trees may still be in production at the age of ninety. In full production, a good average annual yield per acre is about 500 pounds of dried shelled nutmeg and 75 pounds of dried mace. This comes out to about 10 pounds of dried shelled nutmeg and 1½ pounds of dried mace per tree.

The nutmeg tree is usually dioecious—that is, the male flowers are borne on one tree and the female flowers on another. Even though some so-called males may bear some fruit, the trees with only female flowers are the main crop producers. For efficient pollination and fertilization the male trees should be planted on the windward side of the plantation, and the traditional ratio of about one male to supply pollen for every ten females is still considered optimum on a nutmeg plantation. The natural excess of males causes an economic problem to the planter, for he cannot determine until about the sixth year which trees are male and which are female. To bring the proportion down to only 10 percent males, many male trees are either destroyed or are grafted with selected female scions.

The fruit ripens about six months after flowering, and the harvest continues throughout most of the year. In the East Indies some nuts are collected after they fall to the ground; others are harvested when the fruits burst open on the trees. Tree harvesting is accomplished by means of a long pole to which a basket, or *gai gai,* and prongs are attached; these disengage the fruit, allowing it to fall into the basket. In Grenada, however, fully ripened fruits that have fallen to the ground are harvested.

The collected fruits are brought back to the central drying area, where they are spread out to avoid fermentation. The nuts, including the mace, are carefully removed from the husks. The mace is detached from the seed shell by hand or with a knife and flattened out to dry slowly in the sun for ten days to two weeks. Sometimes the mace is dried by artificial heat. During drying the mace gradually becomes brittle and horny, turning from scarlet to orange to yellowish-brown. It is during this curing that it acquires its characteristic pungent aroma.

Following the removal of the mace, the unshelled nutmeg seeds are dried separately for four to eight weeks, either in the sun or over smoldering fires, until the kernel rattles in the shell. The shell is then broken with a wooden mallet or in a specially constructed cracking machine, and the nutmegs are removed. To avoid damage by insects, shelled nutmegs are often treated with lime; similarly dried mace may be fumigated with carbon bisulfide or methyl bromide.

The two basic types of nutmegs in the spice trade are the East Indian and the West Indian. Whole nutmegs from the East Indies are graded according to size—"80's," "110's," and "130's" to the pound, for example. There is also a grade known as "ABCD" (mixed sizes) and one called "Shrivels" (wrinkled nutmegs). The West Indian nutmegs come in one size: "Unassorted" (all sizes).

The average price for nutmegs imported into the United States during 1971 was 40 cents per pound; for mace, it was 56 cents per pound.

The East Indian nutmegs, on steam distillation, yield a higher essential oil content and are more piquant in flavor than the milder West Indian. Most of the nutmegs used for oil distillation are processed from an East Indian grade designated in the trade as "B.W.P.'s," which stands for "Broken, wormy, and punks." Distillers of nutmegs prefer this grade not only because of its lower price, but also because the worm-eaten nutmegs generally give a higher yield of essential oil—the worms having eaten the starchy whitish parts, leaving behind the darker portions that are rich in essential oil.

Depending on their origin and condition nutmegs, on steam distillation, may yield from 5 to 15 percent of the essential oil. The yield of essential oil of mace may vary from 7 to 14 percent. These essential oils of nutmeg and mace are very similar in their chemical composition and aroma. They are used to flavor baked goods, table sauces, confectionery, dentifrices, perfumes, and cosmetics. Medicinally they are utilized as carminatives.

The East Indian mace is more brilliant orange in color than the pale yellow West Indian, and likewise has a higher essential oil content and richer flavor on steam distillation. Mace is generally graded as "No. 1 Whole," "No. 1 Broken," "No. 2 Whole," and "No. 2 Siftings."

The essential oils of nutmeg and mace contain about 4 per cent of a highly toxic substance, myristicin, which, taken in excessive amounts, can cause a fatty degeneration of the liver cells. For this reason the oils are used in very small amounts, with great caution. Large doses of nutmeg spice are said to have a powerful narcotic effect and to be stupor-inducing. In an attempt to escape from reality at "nutmeg parties," beatniks and hippies sometimes eat two or three tablespoonfuls of powdered nutmeg as a hallucinogenic drug for "kicks." Its narcotic use is said to be frequent among prison inmates. Following these nutmeg "jags," serious hangovers, headaches, nausea, dizziness, and other toxic side effects have been reported by the nutmeg-eaters.

Nutmegs, frequently referred to in the ancient sacred Vedic literature of India, have been prescribed since early times by Hindu physicians as a cure for headaches, fevers, bad breath, and intestinal disorders. Since the ninth century this spice has been recommended in Arabian medical writings as a carminative, aphrodisiac, and for treatment of various ailments of the kidneys and stomach. During the sixteenth and seventeenth centuries European physicians and herbalists praised nutmeg as a virtual therapeutic cure-all. Today, however, although an important spice and condiment, nutmeg plays a very minor role in Western medicine.

Nutmegs contain from 25 to 35 percent of fixed or fatty oils sometimes known as "nutmeg butter," or "banda soap," obtained by subjecting the nuts to hydraulic pressure under heat. The West Indian nutmegs have a higher fixed oil content than the East Indian. Fixed oil of nutmeg is used in the manufacture of soap and perfumes.

The flavor of both nutmeg and mace is sweet, warm, and highly spicy. Nutmeg in general tends to be sweeter and more delicate in aroma than mace, since the essential oils of the two spices are found in two different structures in the same fruit and thus have slightly different chemical compositions.

Nutmeg is available whole or ground. Whole mace, known as "blades of mace," is not usually found in retail stores, but ground mace is readily available. Ground nutmeg is tan in color, as compared to the orange hue of ground mace.

Because both blend well with such sweet foods as cakes and cookies, nutmegs and mace are used mainly as mild baking spices. They are also used to flavor frankfurters, sausages, various other meat products, soups, prepared sauces, and preserves. Nutmeg is a popular condiment in such dairy products as eggnog, junkets, puddings, and fruit pies, including Lemon Nutmeg Bavarian Pie. Mace is favored for flavoring pound cakes, fish sauces, meat stuffings, and oyster stew. Mace makes doughnuts taste like doughnuts.

Lemon Nutmeg Bavarian Pie

1 package unflavored
    gelatin
4 eggs, separated
1 cup sugar
½ cup lemon juice
½ teaspoon salt
1 teaspoon grated lemon
    peel

½ teaspoon ground nutmeg
⅓ cup heavy cream,
    whipped
1 9-inch baked pie shell
Lemon slices
Ground nutmeg *for garnish*

Sprinkle gelatin over ¼ cup cold water; set aside. Beat egg yolks until thick and lemon-colored. Gradually beat in ½ cup of the sugar, lemon juice, and salt. Cook over hot water until custard coats a metal spoon, about 10 minutes, stirring constantly. Remove from heat and stir in softened gelatin, mixing until gelatin has dissolved. Blend in lemon peel and *nutmeg*. Chill until mixture is as thick as unbeaten egg whites. Beat egg whites until they stand in soft peaks; gradually beat in the remaining ½ cup of sugar. Fold into gelatin mixture. Fold in the whipped cream. Pour into baked 9-inch pie crust. Chill until firm and ready to serve. Garnish with whipped cream, if desired, lemon slices, and *ground nutmeg*.

Yield: One 9-inch pie

Pears With Lemon Pudding Sauce

1 package (3 oz.) lemon
    pudding
3 cups milk
½ teaspoon ground nutmeg
1½ teaspoons pure vanilla
    extract

6 cooked pear halves
Ground nutmeg *and shaved
    semisweet chocolate for
    garnish*

Make lemon pudding according to package directions, using the 3 cups of milk. Add *nutmeg* and vanilla and chill. Just before serving, drain pear halves and place one half in each of 6 dessert dishes, rounded side up. Pour lemon pudding sauce over each serving. Garnish with *ground nutmeg* and shaved semisweet chocolate.

Yield: 6 servings

Spiced Pineapple Mousse

1 can (6 oz.) frozen
   pineapple drink
½ teaspoon ground nutmeg
1 teaspoon pure vanilla
   extract

½ cup sugar
1 cup heavy cream, whipped
2 egg whites
Ground nutmeg

Let pineapple drink stand at room temperature to soften enough to stir. Open can and pour into a mixing bowl. Add *nutmeg,* vanilla, and sugar. Mix well. Fold in whipped cream. Beat egg whites until they stand in soft, stiff peaks and fold into pineapple mixture. Pile into punch cups, individual soufflé dishes, or sherbet glasses. Freeze until firm and ready to serve. Garnish with *ground nutmeg* and a mint leaf.

Yield: 6 servings

Oyster Stew

2 packages (12 oz. each)
   frozen oysters
¼ cup butter or margarine
1 teaspoon salt
½ teaspoon celery salt
¼ teaspoon ground mace

¼ teaspoon ground black
   pepper
¼ teaspoon instant onion
   powder
4½ cups milk

Defrost oysters. In saucepan, heat butter; add oysters with liquid, salt, celery salt, *ground mace,* black pepper, and onion powder and heat only until oysters curl slightly. Add milk, heat but do not boil. Pour in bowls and serve hot with crackers, if desired.

Yield: 8 servings

Mace Pineapple Rice Pudding

¾ cup precooked rice
1 package (3 oz.) vanilla
   pudding
1 cup evaporated milk
½ teaspoon pure vanilla
   extract

1 teaspoon ground mace
1 can (8 oz.) crushed
   pineapple, drained
Ground mace *for garnish*

Cook rice according to directions on package. Prepare vanilla pudding according to package directions, using evaporated milk and 1 cup water. Add vanilla, *mace,* and pineapple. Stir in rice. Garnish with a sprinkling of *mace* before serving.

Yield: 5–6 servings

Spiced Dream Hearts

1 cup shortening
1 package (3 oz.) cream cheese
½ teaspoon salt
½ teaspoon ground mace

½ teaspoon pure vanilla extract
1 egg yolk
1 cup sugar
2 cups sifted all-purpose flour

Blend together shortening, cream cheese, salt, *mace,* vanilla, and egg yolk. Gradually add sugar. Stir in flour, a little at a time. Fill a cookie press with dough. Form into heart-shaped cookies on ungreased cookie sheets 2 inches apart. Sprinkle tops with red-colored sugar, if desired. Bake in a preheated moderate oven (350°F.) 15 minutes or until lightly browned around the edge.

Yield: Approximately 6 dozen cookies

Golden Mace Cake

2 cups sifted all-purpose flour
1¾ cups sugar
3 teaspoons baking powder
¾ teaspoon salt
¾ teaspoon ground mace

⅔ cup butter or margarine
1 cup milk
6 egg yolks
1 teaspoon pure vanilla extract

Sift together flour, sugar, baking powder, salt, and *mace* into mixing bowl. Add butter, milk, egg yolks, and vanilla. Beat 2 minutes with electric mixer set at medium speed. Pour batter into a well-greased, lightly floured 8-by 2¾-inch tube pan. Bake in preheated moderate oven (350°F.) 1¼ hours or until done. Cool in pan 10 minutes. Turn out onto wire rack to finish cooling. Frost, if desired, with a lemon frosting.

Yield: 8–10 servings

Nutmeg Cake

2 cups brown sugar
2 cups sifted flour
½ cup shortening
1 egg
1 teaspoon nutmeg

1 cup sour cream
1 teaspoon baking soda
½ cup chopped walnuts,
   pecans, or almonds

With the fingers, blend the sugar with flour and shortening until crumbs form. Place half the crumbs in a greased 9-inch square pan 1½ inches deep. Add the egg to the remaining crumbs along with the *nutmeg* and sour cream mixed with the soda. Pour this batter into the pan and sprinkle with nuts. Bake 35 to 40 minutes in a preheated moderate oven (350°F.). Serve hot or cold.

Yield: 10–12 servings

Chicken Pie, Georgia Style

2½-pound broiler-fryer
   chicken
1 teaspoon salt
¼ teaspoon ground mace
½ cup shell macaroni
¼ cup butter or margarine
3 tablespoons all-purpose
   flour

1 cup milk
1 teaspoon salt
½ teaspoon ground black
   pepper
Pastry using 1 cup flour

Place chicken in saucepan with 1 cup water and 1 teaspoon salt and *mace*. Cover. Cook over medium heat 15 minutes. Add macaroni and cook 15 to 20 minutes longer. Drain off stock and turn chicken and macaroni into an 8- by 8- by 2-inch baking dish. Melt butter in a saucepan. Blend in flour. Stir in chicken stock and milk. Cook until slightly thickened. Add remaining salt and pepper. Pour over chicken and macaroni. Cover with pastry rolled to ⅛-inch thickness. Trim, turn under, flute edge. Cut a gash in the top to allow steam to escape. Bake 30 minutes or until brown in a preheated hot oven (425°F.).

Yield: 6 servings

Spiced Orange Meringue Squares

1¾ cups cake flour, sifted	1¼ cups sugar
¾ teaspoon baking soda	2 eggs, separated
½ teaspoon salt	2 teaspoons orange peel or
¼ cup butter or margarine	bits
¾ teaspoon ground mace	⅔ cup orange juice, strained
¼ teaspoon ground nutmeg	¹⁄₁₆ teaspoon salt

Sift together flour, baking soda, and salt. In mixing bowl cream butter, *mace,* and ⅛ teaspoon of the nutmeg until light and fluffy. Gradually add ¾ cup of the sugar. Add egg yolks, one at a time, beating well after each addition. Add orange peel. Alternately add sifted dry ingredients and orange juice, beating until smooth after each addition. Turn into two greased 8- by 8-inch pans. In small bowl add salt to egg whites and beat until foamy. Gradually add remaining ½ cup sugar and remaining ⅛ teaspoon nutmeg and beat until stiff peaks are formed. Spread evenly over cake batter. Bake in preheated moderate oven (375°F.) for 25 minutes. Turn out on racks to cool. Cut into 2-inch squares.

Yield: 32 2-inch squares

Holiday Mace Cake

1 package (1 lb. 1 oz.)	1 teaspoon ground mace
pound cake mix	2½ cups mincemeat
¾ cup orange juice	2 tablespoons maple syrup
2 eggs	Canned ready-to-spread
1 teaspoon orange peel or	vanilla frosting
bits	

Prepare pound cake according to package directions, substituting orange juice for liquid and adding eggs, orange peel, and *mace* to batter. Bake as directed. Cool. Cut cake horizontally in thirds. Combine mincemeat with maple syrup. Spread onto two of cake layers. On third cake layer spread vanilla frosting.

Yield: One cake

Spiced Yankee Trifle

2 round 8-inch sponge cake
   layers
1 cup strawberry or
   raspberry jam
6 tablespoons cooking
   sherry
2 packages (3⅝ oz. each)
   vanilla pudding

½ teaspoon ground nutmeg
1 tablespoon sugar
¼ teaspoon pure vanilla
   extract
½ cup heavy cream
Ground nutmeg

Split cake layers to make 4 layers. Spread one side of each layer with jam and sprinkle each with 1½ teaspoons cooking sherry. Place cakes in layercake fashion in a 9-inch glass serving bowl. Make vanilla pudding as directed on the package, add *nutmeg,* and pour over cake. Chill until ready to serve. Just before serving, add sugar and vanilla to cream. Beat until cream stands in soft peaks. Spread over trifle. Garnish with *ground nutmeg*.

Yield: 12 servings

GARLIC
Allium sativum L.

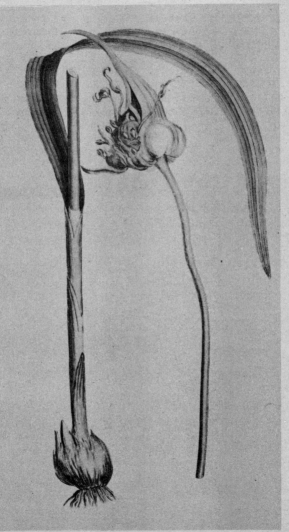

ONION PRODUCTS

Family: Liliaceae

	Onion	Garlic	Chives
LATIN	• Allium	Allium	Allium
	cepa L.	sativum L.	schoenoprasum L.
SPANISH	• Cebolla	Ajo	Cebolleta
FRENCH	• Oignon	Ail	Ciboulette
GERMAN	• Zwiebel	Knoblauch	Schnittlauch
SWEDISH	• Rödlök	Vitlök	Gräslök
ARABIC	• Basal	Thūm	Basal
DUTCH	• Ui	Knoflook	Bieslook
ITALIAN	• Cipolla	Aglio	Cipollina
PORTUGUESE	• Cebola	Alho	Cebolinha
RUSSIAN	• Luk	Chesnok	Luk-Rezanyets
JAPANESE	• Tamanegi	Ninniku	Asatsuki
CHINESE	• Yang-Ts'ung	Suan	Hsia-Ye-Ts'ung

ONIONS, GARLIC, AND CHIVES

THE common onion (*Allium cepa*), garlic (*Allium sativum*), and chives (*Allium schoenoprasum*) belong to the lily family. Onions are believed to be native to southwestern Asia, garlic to central Asia, and chives to northern Europe and Asia. These bulbous plants are characterized by their penetrating pungent aroma—strongest in garlic, not so strong in chives. They enjoy world-wide use as vegetable flavorings: the bulbs of onions and garlic, and the leaves of chives.

Onions and garlic are among the oldest known cultivated plants, and probably were cultivated in Egypt, China, and India before the beginning of recorded history. Egyptian priests placed onions and garlic as offerings on the altars of their gods. Several garlic bulbs were found in the tomb of Tutankhamen, dating from about 1358 B.C.

The Israelites in the wilderness, fleeing Egypt to the Promised Land, lamented the lack of these flavor-

CULTIVATING
GARLIC, 1493

ings in Numbers 11:5 —"We remember the fish,
which we did eat in Egypt freely; the cucumbers, and
the melons and the leeks, and the onions and the gar-
lick."

There is a Mohammedan tradition that when Satan
stepped out of the Garden of Eden after the fall of man,
garlic sprang up from the spot where he placed his left
foot and onions from where his right foot touched.

Garlic was a common food of the Roman laborer
and was given to the Roman soldier to make him more
courageous. The upper classes in Rome, however, dis-
dained it as a sign of vulgarity. Hippocrates, about 400
B.C., recognized the medicinal value of garlic, and
about five hundred years later Dioscorides recommended it as a cure for hemorrhoids and as a diuretic.

Onions and garlic, brought to England by the Romans, were well known during Shakespeare's time. He
mentions them in *A Midsummer-Night's Dream,* Act
IV, Scene II:

> *Bottom:* . . . And, most dear actors, eat no onions
> nor garlick, for we are to utter sweet breath. . . .

Since ancient times many extraordinary healing
powers have been attributed to garlic, for it has been

recommended as a stomachic; antiseptic; cure for asthma, bronchitis, and coughs; treatment for epilepsy, rheumatism, leprosy, and the common cold; and as a vermifuge, expectorant, and insect repellent. Some writers have gone as far as to assert that without the benefit of the alleged bactericidal properties of garlic, the Greek and Roman civilizations would have perished, although modern bacteriological evidence is not known to support such a contention. Garlic was an important constituent of the celebrated "Vinegar of the Four Thieves," used in Marseilles in 1722 for protection against the plague. As recently as 1916 (during World War I) the British army used garlic juice as an antiseptic for treatment of battle wounds.

It is believed that the onion was one of the crops brought to the New World by Columbus on his second voyage and planted in January 1494 at Isabela in the Dominican Republic. Onions were rapidly introduced into Mexico and Central and South America, and their use soon spread to the North American Indian.

Ambroise Paré, a sixteenth-century French surgeon, claimed that onions could be used to heal powder burns. The antiseptic qualities of onions were also appreciated by General Ulysses S. Grant, who is said to have advised the government in 1864: "I will not move my army without onions"—whereupon three carloads were shipped to him immediately.

Onion (Allium cepa)

The common onion, an herbaceous biennial plant, has a single large bulb from which arise one or more leafless stalks that may grow to about 2½ to 6 feet high (depending on the variety and growing conditions), with a terminal cluster of many small greenish-white flowers. Although the onion is hardy and may be grown under a wide range of conditions, it is a temperate climate crop and prefers relatively cool, moist, loamy, friable soil, rich in organic matter but moderately low in soil acidity.

The onion may be grown from its small black seed, from small bulbs called "sets," or from transplants; commercially, most onions are grown from seed. The bulb itself is used as a vegetable or as a seasoning, and the green parts of the plant may be mixed in a fresh salad.

The seed is planted in rows 12 to 16 inches apart or less, depending on conditions. In well-cultivated land, with effective weeding, herbicidal control, adequate irrigation, and fertilizer application, yields of 4 to 12 tons or more of fresh onion bulbs per acre may be obtained, depending on the weather, the fertility of the soil, and the variety of onion.

The development of the onion bulb is determined by the length of the day and the temperature. The longer and warmer the days are, the faster the bulb will grow. Although a biennial, the onion may complete its life cycle in one growing season if it is long enough, as in the tropics. In the United States, extended cool weather during the early part of the growing season favors premature seeding in the onion-growing districts of the West.

As the onion develops, the leaf bases begin to swell until a mature bulb is formed. This swollen ball of leaf bases forms the edible part of the onion bulb.

There are numerous cultivated varieties (or cultivars) of onions, and through careful selection and breeding many different sizes, colors, shapes, flavors, and degrees of firmness have been developed. Although onions are grown domestically in all the major farming regions of the United States, particular cultivars have been developed to meet the needs of each specific area; an onion cultivar adapted to central California, for example, usually will not produce mature bulbs properly in Louisiana.

Since 1935 in Egypt, Eastern Europe, and the United States dehydrated onions have become available as a condiment in the form of such dried onion products as *powdered, instant granulated, instant ground, instant minced, chopped, large chopped, sliced, large sliced,* and *onion salt.* All have full-strength onion flavor except onion salt, which is mixed with table salt.

Most United States processing plants for dried onion are in California, where optimum conditions of soil, climate, long growing season, and an available labor force exist, especially in the highly agricultural Imperial Valley, near the Mexican border, north through the San Joaquin Valley, and to the Oregon border. The staggered seed-sowing program permits a lengthy harvesting and processing season which may extend from May to November. The crop matures from the Imperial Valley northward.

Onions have been specially grown and developed for dehydration processing. Selections out of the cultivars such as the Southport White Globe, first developed a century ago in Southport, Connecticut, that combine the advantageous features of whiteness, large size, high solid content, superior flavor strength, and adequate seasoning power are used extensively. The White Creole is another variety of onion widely used in dehydration. Onion hybrids are beginning to be used and should become increasingly important.

Onion crops produced for dehydration are usually grown under irrigation from specially selected seed. The highly mechanized harvest follows about seven months after sowing. Prior to dehydration, the onions are inspected and graded, then peeled, derooted, topped, washed, and sliced to a uniform thickness so that drying will be even. Approximately 8 pounds of fresh onions produce 1 pound of the dehydrated product.

Dried onion (dehydrated onion) is produced by eliminating approximately 96 percent of the moisture through tunnel drying on trays, with circulating hot air; or drying by means of a continuous stainless steel belt upon which the sliced onion is fed and then passed through various chambers with varying degrees of heat. This low moisture content of about 4 percent is essential to avoid deterioration and maintain stability in the dried finished product. In both these drying methods the pieces of onion are neither cooked nor charred. The temperature is carefully controlled so that the onion solids will be dehydrated very slowly to avoid any discoloration that might cause damage to the flavor.

Dried onion, for use as a condiment rather than as a vegetable, is produced in many different particle sizes, all suitable for replacing raw onion. *Dried onion* is reconstituted in about thirty minutes and thus can be employed in its dry form if the food products to which it is to be added (sauces, gravies, soups, and the like) contain liquid. It should be noted, however, that larger-sized pieces, sold as *large sliced onion*, require a longer period of time for reconstitution.

One pound of *instant granulated onion* or *instant ground onion* added to 4 quarts of water is the flavor equivalent of 10 pounds of raw prepared onion. One pound of either *instant minced onion, chopped onion,* or *sliced onion,* added to 3 quarts of water, is the flavor equivalent of 8 pounds of raw prepared onion.

Food and spice manufacturers now pack these various types of dried onion products in cartons or glass containers, suitable for commercial use in many food products: dried soups, catsups, chili con carne, Chinese foods, gravies, dressings, omelets, vegetables, Spanish rice, salads, meats, onion salt and pickles, just to mention a few. Similarly packaged for the consumer, these convenient, uniformly flavored, easy-to-store dehydrated onion products are most satisfactory condiments for home use.

The United States is by far the largest producer of

dehydrated onions, followed by Egypt, Hungary, Bulgaria, and Israel. More than 70,000,000 pounds of dehydrated onions are produced annually in California.

Garlic (*Allium sativum*)

Garlic stands second to the common onion as the most extensively used member of the cultivated *Alliums*. Unlike the biennial onion, garlic is a hardy perennial with long, flattened, solid leaves. Its name is derived from the Anglo-Saxon *garleac* (*gar,* a spear; and *leac,* a plant), i.e., "spear-plant." The composite bulb consists of several small egg-shaped bulblets, termed "cloves," enclosed within a whitish membranous skin. The lavender or whitish flowers, which always abort, are produced at the end of a stalk that rises directly from the bulb. The roots, as in the onion, are fine and numerous.

Garlic is propagated by planting the cloves about 8 inches apart, with about 1 foot between the rows. Sunny locations and fertile sandy loam soils are desirable. Irrigation and weed control are important. The crop is harvested (usually mechanically) six to eight months after planting the cloves. Like that of the onion, bulb growth in the garlic is greatest when the growing season is long and the daytime temperatures are high, especially during the latter part of the growing season.

For every pound of garlic cloves planted, 5 to 7 pounds may be harvested at the end of the growing season. The average per-acre yield of garlic is from 10,000 to 12,000 pounds.

As a condiment, garlic has traditionally been more popular in southern Europe, the Mediterranean region, and Latin America than in England and Scandinavia.

The availability of dehydrated garlic has stimulated a tremendous growth in its popularity in the United States during the past decade—its use has increased about 1,000 percent. Much of the credit for this extraordinary development must be given to the convenience of the dehydrated products, such as *powdered garlic, instant granulated garlic, instant ground garlic, instant minced garlic, chopped garlic, sliced garlic,* and *garlic salt. Garlic salt* is dehydrated garlic combined with table salt, but the other forms consist of pure garlic.

When the moisture content is as low as it should be, there is very little aroma in either the *dried onion* or the *dried garlic.* The characteristic flavors develop when the dried products are rehydrated, allowing enzyme action to occur.

In the United States the modern dehydrated garlic industry, like the dehydrated onion industry, is centered in California.

Although the pungent odor of garlic is strongest in the bulb, it permeates the entire plant. Garlic owes its characteristic odor to the presence of the pale yellow, intensely obnoxious, volatile oil of garlic, which contains allyl propyl disulfide and diallyl disulfide. When extracted, it represents a yield of about 0.1 percent of the weight of the bulbs.

Less offensive and resembling more closely the true flavor of garlic, dehydrated garlic powder is in far more demand for flavoring than is oil of garlic, which is used mainly in pharmaceutical preparations.

The major dehydrated garlic-producing countries are the United States, Egypt, Bulgaria, Hungary, and Taiwan. Although the United States is by far the leading producer of dehydrated garlic products, it imports about 50 percent of its requirements of raw garlic to be eaten fresh.

Chives (Allium schoenoprasum)

The chive, a "little brother of the onion," is a small grasslike hardy perennial, normally 6 to 12 inches high, producing numerous stalks with globose heads of purple flowers amid an abundance of upright but flat, hollow leaves. The bulbs are much smaller and their flavor milder than those of the common onion.

Unlike onions and garlic, chives prefer the cooler climate of the Northern Hemisphere. When grown commercially they require an abundance of moisture and a light soil with adequate humus. They are grown more in Scandinavia, Germany, and England than in southern Europe or the Mediterranean region.

Chives may be grown from seed but are usually propagated by dividing the clumps in the spring or fall and planting the sets of tiny white bulbs, which will form new clumps, about 1 foot apart. Three or four times a year these clumps may be cut back to about 2 inches above ground. The first cutting and curing of the leaves takes place five or six weeks after spring planting, before flowering. Usually only the green tops or leaves of the chive are eaten, not the small, poorly developed bulbs.

The chive has traditionally been grown in many parts of the world in small home gardens, pots, or window boxes, rather than on a large commercial basis. The chive plants themselves form neat, attractive ornamental borders for herb gardens. The bright green leaves may be used in fresh salads or chopped and sprinkled on vegetables or potatoes. Chives may be included in many recipes calling for a mild, delicate onion flavor.

Commercial production of chives for quick-freezing and freeze-drying has been developed recently near San Francisco, California. This fresh-frozen product is used by dairies for flavoring and garnishing cottage cheese. The freeze-dried chives are available in packages for garnishing and culinary purposes. During the past five years, freeze-drying has substantially increased the demand in the United States for this previously little-known condiment.

Southern-Style Brunswick Stew

4-pound fricassee chicken
3 pounds beef shins
1 pound pork spareribs
5 tablespoons salt
¾ teaspoon whole black
    pepper
1 cup diced raw potatoes
1 package (10 oz.) frozen
    snap beans
1 package (10 oz.) frozen
    sliced okra
1 package (10 oz.) frozen
    corn

1 package (10 oz.) frozen
    lima beans
¾ cup onion flakes
3 cans (1 lb 12 oz. each)
    tomatoes
1 tablespoon sugar
1 teaspoon ground black
    pepper
¾ teaspoon instant garlic
    powder
½ teaspoon crushed red
    pepper

Cut up chicken and place in an 8-quart kettle with beef, spareribs, 2½ quarts water, 3 tablespoons of the salt, and whole black pepper. Cover and cook slowly 2 hours or until meat falls off the bones. Remove bones and discard. Cut chicken and meat into small pieces and return to stock. Add vegetables, remaining salt, and remaining ingredients. Cook gently, uncovered, 30 minutes. Freeze leftover stew for future use.

Yield: 6½ quarts

Onion Cheeseburgers

1 tablespoon instant minced
    onion
1 tablespoon water
1½ pounds ground lean
    beef

1½ teaspoons salt
¼ teaspoon ground black
    pepper
6 slices American cheese
Hamburger buns

Mix *onion* with water and let stand 3 to 5 minutes. Combine beef with *onion,* salt, and black pepper. Shape into 12 patties, each 4 inches in diameter and ¼ inch thick. Place slice of American cheese over 6 of patties. Cover with remaining meat. Press the edges together well to prevent cheese from oozing out while cooking. Brown on both sides in a hot, lightly greased skillet. Serve in warm split hamburger buns.

Yield: 6 servings

Onion Cheese Biscuit Squares

2 cups sifted all-purpose
  flour
2½ teaspoons double-acting
  baking powder
¾ teaspoon salt
About ¾ cup milk

3 tablespoons instant minced
  onion
¾ cup grated sharp
  cheddar cheese
¼ cup shortening

Sift together flour, baking powder, and salt. Add *onion,* cheese, and shortening. Blend with pastry blender, 2 knives, or a fork until the mixture resembles crumbs. Stir in enough milk to make a soft dough. Turn out onto a lightly floured pastry board. Knead about 20 seconds. Roll dough into a rectangle about ⅓ inch thick. Cut into 12 squares. Place on ungreased cookie sheets. Bake in a preheated very hot oven (450°F.) 10 to 12 minutes. Serve with bacon and eggs or as an accompaniment to vegetables, meat, or seafood salad.

Yield: 12 biscuits

Lobster Stew

1 lobster (1½ lbs.) or 1½
  pounds frozen lobster tails
¼ cup butter or margarine
1 quart milk
1 bay leaf
1 teaspoon instant minced
  onion

Dash instant garlic powder
1 teaspoon salt
¼ teaspoon ground black
  pepper
2 teaspoons fresh lemon
  juice
Paprika

If fresh lobster is used, plunge it, head first, in boiling water to cover. Cover and boil rapidly 5 to 7 minutes for each pound or until the lobster turns pink, counting time after water begins to boil again. If lobster tails are used, cook as directed on the package. Cut lobster meat into small pieces and sauté lightly in butter or margarine. Scald milk with bay leaf, *minced onion, garlic powder,* and salt. Add lobster meat, black pepper, and lemon juice. Heat half a minute. Serve hot garnished with paprika.

Yield: 3¾ cups

Spicy Sour Cream Dip

½ *teaspoon* instant minced onion
½ *cup sour cream*
¼ *cup mayonnaise*
¼ *teaspoon* instant garlic powder

¼ *teaspoon ground basil*
¼ *teaspoon salt*
Dash of ground black pepper
Dash of cayenne

Mix *onion* with ½ teaspoon water; let stand 3 to 5 minutes. Add to remaining ingredients and blend well. Place in the center of a large hors d'oeuvres plate.

Yield: About ⅔ cup

Shrimp Kebabs

½ *teaspoon powdered mustard*
½ *cup tomato sauce*
2 *tablespoons cider vinegar*
2 *tablespoons lemon juice*
1 *tablespoon brown sugar*
1 *tablespoon butter or margarine*
2 *teaspoons* instant minced onion
1 *teaspoon salt*

½ *teaspoon* onion salt
¹⁄₁₆ *teaspoon* instant garlic powder
¹⁄₁₆ *teaspoon cayenne*
1 *pound raw shrimp, peeled and deveined*
¾ *pound medium-sized whole mushrooms*
2 *green peppers, cut into 1-inch squares*
1 *box cherry tomatoes*

Mix mustard with 1 teaspoon warm water; let stand 10 minutes for flavor to develop. Prepare marinade sauce by combining in saucepan mustard with ¼ cup water, tomato sauce, vinegar, lemon juice, brown sugar, butter, *minced onion,* salt, *onion salt, garlic powder,* and cayenne. Cook slowly 5 minutes. Add shrimp. Marinate in refrigerator several hours or overnight. To cook, string shrimp on long skewers, alternating with mushrooms, green pepper, and cherry tomatoes. Baste shrimp and vegetables with marinade sauce. Place skewers over a bed of slow-burning charcoal or in broiler. Grill or broil 15 to 20 minutes, or until done, basting often with marinade.

Yield: 4 servings

Potato Pancakes

3 cups (3 large) finely
  shredded potatoes
½ cup milk
4 teaspons instant minced
  onion
1¼ teaspoons salt

⅛ teaspoon ground black
  pepper
1 large egg, beaten
2 tablespoons flour
Shortening for frying

Peel potatoes; shred on a fine shredder. Add milk immediately to prevent discoloration. Add *minced onion,* salt, black pepper, egg, and flour. Mix well. Drop by rounded tablespoonfuls onto a hot greased skillet or griddle. Brown on both sides.

Yield: 10 pancakes, 4½ inches each

Greek Stuffed Eggplant

3 small eggplants
1½ tablespoons lemon juice
½ cup onion flakes
1 teaspoon instant minced
  garlic
1 pound ground lamb
2 tablespoons olive or salad
  oil
½ cup bread crumbs

1 egg, beaten
2 tablespoons parsley flakes
½ teaspoon oregano leaves
½ teaspoon garlic salt
½ teaspoon salt
¼ teaspoon ground black
  pepper
1½ cups toasted bread
  cubes

Parboil eggplants 12 to 15 minutes in boiling water to cover. Remove from water; cut in half lengthwise and remove pulp to within ½ inch of skin. Chop pulp in small pieces; reserve. Brush cut surface of eggplants with lemon juice. Mix *onion flakes* and *minced garlic* in ¼ cup water; let stand 3 to 5 minutes. Add to ground lamb. In skillet sauté lamb in oil until pink color is gone. Add reserved eggplant pulp, bread crumbs, egg, parsley flakes, oregano, *garlic salt,* salt, and black pepper. Mix well. Fill shells with meat mixture. Top each with ¼ cup bread cubes. Place in greased baking pan. Bake in preheated moderate oven (350°F.) 30 minutes. Serve hot as main dish.

Yield: 6 servings

Grilled Lamb Chops

12 loin lamb chops (1 inch
  thick)
¼ cup butter or margarine,
  melted
½ teaspoon instant garlic
  powder

¼ teaspoon ground black
  pepper
1 tablespoon parsley flakes
1 teaspoon salt

Trim and discard excess fat from lamb chops. Combine butter or margarine, *garlic powder,* black pepper, parsley flakes, and salt; dip lamb chops into this mixture. Broil 25 minutes, turning to brown both sides.

Yield: 6 servings, 2 chops each

Italian Salad Dressing

6 tablespoons olive or salad
  oil
3 tablespoons wine vinegar
¼ teaspoon instant minced
  garlic

¼ teaspoon oregano leaves
¼ teaspoon basil leaves
¼ teaspoon salt
¼ teaspoon ground black
  pepper

Combine all ingredients. Let stand at least 1 hour. Beat with a rotary beater. Serve over mixed salad greens.

Yield: ½ cup

Zucchini Italian Style

2 pounds (6 cups) zucchini
  squash
2 pounds (4 medium)
  tomatoes
½ cup onion flakes
2 teaspoons salt
1 teaspoon crumbled
  oregano leaves

½ teaspoon ground black
  pepper
½ teaspoon instant garlic
  powder
2 tablespoons salad oil

Wash zucchini and slice crosswise ½ inch thick. Place layer in 10- by 6- by 2-inch casserole, using half the zucchini. Wash and cut tomatoes into slices ½ inch thick. Place a layer over zucchini, using half the tomatoes; add *onion flakes.* Combine seasonings and sprinkle half over the zucchini and tomatoes. Top with remaining zucchini. Sprinkle with half of remaining seasonings. Cover and bake in preheated moderate oven (375°F.) 30 minutes. Remove cover and arrange remaining tomato slices over top. Brush tomatoes with oil and sprinkle with remaining seasonings. Bake, uncovered, 30 minutes longer.

Yield: 8 servings

Baked Apple Rings

2 large baking apples,
    unpeeled
1 tablespoon sugar

1 tablespoon butter or
    margarine

Remove cores from apples and cut each into 3 rings. Place in baking pan. Combine sugar, 2 tablespoons hot water, and butter. Pour over apples. Cover and bake 20 minutes or until tender in a preheated slow oven (325°F.). Place under broiler 5 minutes to brown.

Yield: 6 servings

Chive Cheese Omelet

4 eggs, separated
½ teaspoon salt
⅛ teaspoon ground black
    pepper
¼ cup milk
1 tablespoon butter or
    margarine

1 teaspoon dried chives
½ teaspoon warm water
2 slices bacon, cooked and
    crumbled
½ cup shredded cheddar
    cheese

Beat egg yolks until thick and light. Add salt, pepper, and milk. Fold into stiffly beaten egg whites. Pour into hot buttered 9-inch skillet or omelet pan. Cook over low heat until omelet puffs up and is golden brown on bottom (about 3 to 5 minutes). Blend *dried chives* and warm water. Sprinkle *chives,* crumbled bacon, and cheese on omelet and quickly place in preheated moderate oven (350°F.) for 10 to 15 minutes longer or until top springs back when pressed with finger. Make

1-inch cuts at opposite sides and crease with back of knife. Fold on crease by slipping spatula or pancake turner under half the omelet. Slide onto platter. Serve immediately.

Yield: 4–5 servings

Eggs Benedict With Hollandaise Chive Sauce

4 English muffins
8 slices Canadian back
  bacon, broiled
8 eggs, poached

1 package hollandaise sauce
  mix
1 teaspoon dried chives

Split and toast English muffins, allowing two halves for each serving. Cover each muffin half with slice of broiled Canadian back bacon. Top each with poached egg. Prepare hollandaise sauce according to package directions. Stir in *chives*. Pour 1 to 1½ tablespoons sauce over each egg. Serve at once.

Yield: 4 servings

Pork Chops With Apple Rings

6 loin pork chops
¼ teaspoon instant garlic
  powder
2½ teaspoons salt
⅛ teaspoon ground black
  pepper

1 cup beef stock
2 teaspoons cider vinegar
1 small bay leaf
3 tablespoons flour

Trim excess fat from pork chops. Mix *garlic powder*, salt, and black pepper and rub on both sides of chops. Brown and place in a large baking dish. Mix beef stock and vinegar; pour over chops. Add bay leaf. Cover and bake in a preheated slow oven (325°F.) 1 hour or until chops are tender. Mix flour with ¼ cup water to a smooth paste and add to liquid in baking dish. Mix well. Cook, uncovered, 20 minutes. Serve hot with mashed potatoes and Baked Apple Rings.

Classic Chive Butter

1 tablespoon dried chives
1½ teaspoons warm water

¼ pound soft butter or
margarine

Moisten *chives* with warm water and add to soft butter. Blend well. Chill until firm. Serve with hot corn-on-the-cob, baked potato, ground beef, French bread, broiled meats, baked shrimp, cooked green beans, and other vegetables.

Yield: ½ cup

Garlic Barbecued Chicken

2 ready-to-cook frying
chickens, 2½ pounds
each
1 cup warm water

3 teaspoons salt
½ teaspoon garlic salt
¼ cup melted butter or
margarine

Cut chickens into quarters. Mix together water, salt, and ¼ teaspoon of the *garlic salt;* brush chicken quarters well with mixture. Place skin side up on grill. Turn every 10 minutes and grill slowly on both sides, basting often with salt water until almost tender, about 45 minutes. Combine remaining ¼ teaspoon *garlic salt* and butter; brush over chicken. Continue grilling and basting until tender, about 20 minutes.

Yield: 4 servings

Garlic Italian Bread

1 loaf Italian bread or
6 seeded rolls
½ cup soft sweet butter
½ teaspoon instant garlic
powder

3 tablespoons grated
Parmesan cheese

Cut loaf or rolls in diagonal slices, 1 inch apart, making sure not to cut through bottom crust. Combine remaining ingredients; mix until well blended. Spread mixture between slices. Place bread on an ungreased cookie sheet. Bake in a preheated moderate oven (350°F.)

10 minutes or until butter is melted and bread is hot. Serve immediately.

Yield: 6 servings

Chicken Chive Fricassee

3-pound broiler-fryer
  chicken
2 teaspoons salt
¼ teaspoon ground black
  pepper
4 tablespoons butter or
  margarine

2 tablespoons flour
1 chicken bouillon cube
1¼ cups hot water
⅛ teaspoon instant minced
  garlic
2 tablespoons dried chives
Cooked hot rice

Wash chicken and cut into serving pieces. Rub salt and pepper into chicken. Brown chicken in butter in Dutch oven. Blend flour with pan drippings. Stir in bouillon cube, water, and *minced garlic*. Cover and simmer 20 minutes or until chicken is tender. Add *chives* and cook 5 minutes. Serve hot with rice.

Yield: 6 servings

PARSLEY
Petroselinum crispum (Mill.) Nym.

PARSLEY

Family: Umbelliferae

LATIN	• **Petroselinum crispum** (Mill.) Nym.
SPANISH	• Perejíl
FRENCH	• Persil
GERMAN	• Petersilie
SWEDISH	• Persilja
ARABIC	• Baqdūnis
DUTCH	• Peterselie
ITALIAN	• Prezzemolo
PORTUGUESE	• Salsa
RUSSIAN	• Pyetrushka
JAPANESE	• Paseri
CHINESE	• Yang-Hu-Sui

PARSLEY

PARSLEY, *Petroselinum crispum,* is probably the best known and most extensively used of all culinary herbs in the United States. It is a hardy biennial that grows about 2 feet high and is native to the Mediterranean region. It has been produced so widely that in many cool, damp climates it has escaped from cultivation and may be found naturalized, even to the extent of being considered a weed.

There are numerous cultivated varieties of parsley including, among others, Curled Leaf, popular for flavoring and garnishing and also grown in California as the principal source of dehydrated parsley flakes; Hamburg, *Petroselinum sativum* L., with turniplike roots that are eaten as a vegetable in Europe; Neapolitan or Celery Leaf, grown for its leaf stalks which are eaten like celery; Dwarf, suitable for ornamental edging of a garden; and Plain-leaf or Italian, a less decorative but flavorful parsley that most closely resembles the original plants from southern Europe, the leaves of which were finely divided but not curled. The more popular curled varieties of the parsley family, such as *Petro-*

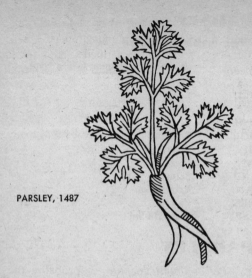

PARSLEY, 1487

selinum crispum, have been developed through many decades of continuous selection.

The name *Petroselinum* is derived from the Greek word *petros,* meaning "stone," for the plant was oftentimes found growing among rocks near the Mediterranean cliffs.

Parsley was not generally eaten by the ancient Greeks, but they used it to crown the victors at the Isthmian games. They also revered parsley as a symbol of death; it was a Greek custom to scatter it over the tombs of the dead—thus the phrase "to be in need only of parsley" referred to one who was moribund.

The Romans, on the other hand, ate parsley and enjoyed it. Galen, a Greek physician who settled in Rome in the second century A.D., observed that parsley was gratifying to the stomach and that it was a very common food, which was frequently eaten with lettuce.

At banquets both the Greeks and Romans put bunches of parsley on the tables, sometimes even wore them as wreaths around their necks, in the belief the wine fumes would be absorbed by the salubrious scent of the herb, thus preventing intoxication.

In medieval times the prescribed usages for parsley were deeply rooted in superstition. It was believed that the seed germinated slowly because it had to go down to the devil and come back up again seven times before it would begin to grow. Another belief was that to transplant parsley would bring bad luck—many gardeners refused to plant it at all, fearing the presence of danger. Black magic ritual recommended that if one wished to eliminate a bitter enemy it was only necessary to pluck a stem of parsley, muttering simultaneously that unfortunate's name. The designated victim was then supposed to die within forty-eight hours.

Parsley is said to have been introduced to England in 1548 from Sardinia. Some fifty years later Shakespeare mentioned it in *The Taming of the Shrew*, Act IV, Scene IV:

Biondello: . . . I knew a wench married in an afternoon as she went to the garden for parsley to stuff a rabbit. . . .

In the seventeenth century the colonists brought parsley to New England. Since then so much parsley has been grown in the United States that there is no need now to import the herb.

Although parsley is a biennial it is grown as an annual, since its foliage is the principal harvest. Propagation is by seed planted in beds in the early spring, with germination requiring about six weeks. The seedlings are transplanted in rows about 1 foot apart at 6-inch intervals. Six pounds of seed will plant about one acre. A moist, clay loam soil is recommended. Careful weeding is necessary, and in case of dry weather the parsley should be well watered. During the first year the dense foliage of dark green, finely divided leaves is produced. These may be cut at any time, collected, and dried. The plants bloom in the second year, producing flowering branches of small greenish-yellow flowers 6 to 12 inches above the leaves. When the seed is ripe, it should be collected and dried. Depending on the conditions, a yield of 500 to 1,000 pounds of parsley seed per acre may be obtained.

After seeding the usefulness of the plants is completed, and a fresh planting should be undertaken. In general, the demand is greater for the leaves than for the seed.

Parsley leaves for the most part are used in a fresh, green condition. Their characteristic flavor and green color can be retained if the leaves are dried rapidly.

Dehydrated parsley flakes are produced commercially in California; about 12 pounds of destemmed fresh parsley are required to produce 1 pound of the dehydrated product. When this type of parsley is processed, the stems, which represent 50 percent of the weight of the plants, are discarded before the main drying operation begins. There has been a marked growth in the use of the dehydrated parsley flakes in the United States during the past ten years—approximately $1\frac{1}{2}$ million pounds are now produced annually in this country. Since it is so convenient and so readily available during the entire year, this dehydrated product has brought about an increase in the over-all consumption of parsley and is gradually replacing fresh parsley leaves in many homes and restaurants. In addition to the United States, the countries that produce dehydrated parsley include West Germany, Belgium, Hungary, Canada, Spain, and France.

Both parsley leaves and seeds contain an essential oil, obtained by steam distillation, but the leaf oil must be used if the true odor and flavor of the leaves are required, for the flavor of the seed oil is bitter and not truly parsleylike. Unfortunately, the yield of essential oil in the leaves is so low—about $\frac{1}{15}$ to $\frac{1}{4}$ of 1 percent

—that expensive parsley-leaf oil is rarely used. There is a good demand for the lower-priced parsley-seed oil (the yield of which may vary between 3 and 6 percent) for flavoring food products and meat sauces and in perfumery.

Apiol, an oily compound obtained from bruised parsley seeds through solvent extraction, is used in medicine to treat kidney ailments and as an emmenagogue. Parsley tea is reputed to have carminative and diuretic properties and to aid digestion.

Healthful parsley leaves, with their familiar mild, agreeable flavor, are an excellent source of Vitamin C and iodine, as well as iron, and other minerals. Appealing to the eye, nose, and taste, parsley may be used both on and in most foods except sweets. It can be utilized as a seasoning and garnish in soups, salads, fish, meats, sauces, and vegetables and to add enticement to leftover dishes, even mashed potatoes.

Parsley, like cardamom, will sweeten the breath, as it tends to deodorize and freshen even the foulest garlic emanations.

Molded Turkey Loaf

2 envelopes unflavored
  gelatin
2½ cups cold turkey stock
1 tablespoon parsley flakes
1 tablespoon instant minced
  onion
1 teaspoon salt
½ teaspoon ground thyme
¼ teaspoon ground black
  pepper
1 tablespoon lemon juice
1 cup mayonnaise
3 cups cold turkey, diced
Parsley flakes *for garnish*

Soften gelatin in ½ cup of the turkey stock. Heat remaining stock and stir into gelatin. Add the 1 tablespoon of *parsley flakes,* minced onion, salt, thyme, black pepper, and lemon juice. Chill until the mixture begins to thicken. Fold in mayonnaise and turkey. Turn into an oiled 9- by 5- by 3-inch loaf pan. Chill until firm and ready to serve. Just before serving, turn out onto a serving platter. Garnish with *parsley flakes*. Serve cold in ½-inch crosswise slices.

Yield: 6 servings

Onion Corn Chowder

4 slices bacon, diced	¼ teaspoon ground black
4½ cups hot water	.... pepper
2 tablespoons instant	1-pound can whole kernel
minced onion	corn
2½-ounce package	6-ounce can evaporated
dehydrated potato soup	milk
1 teaspoon salt	Parsley flakes

Cook bacon in a large saucepan until crisp. Pour off excess fat. Add water, minced onion, potato soup, salt, black pepper, and corn. Cover. Bring to boiling point and boil 10 minutes. Add milk and cook 2 to 3 minutes. Serve hot, garnished with *parsley flakes*.

Yield: 4½ cups

Turkey Giblet Stuffing

½ cup celery flakes	3 tablespoons parsley flakes
½ cup instant minced	2½ teaspoons salt
onion	2 teaspoons poultry
1 cup water	seasoning
3 quarts toasted bread cubes	½ teaspoon ground black
(measure after toasting	pepper
cubes)	½ cup butter or margarine,
Chopped cooked turkey	melted
liver and gizzard	¾ to 1 cup giblet broth

Combine celery and onion in water; let stand 8 minutes for vegetables to soften. Blend with remaining ingredients. Spoon lightly into crop and body cavity of 12- to 15-pound turkey. Close openings with skewers and lacings.

Yield: Stuffing for 12- to 15-pound turkey

Green Rice With Egg Sauce

2 cups fluffy boiled rice
2 eggs, well beaten
⅔ cup milk
½ cup finely chopped raw
  spinach
3 tablespoons butter or
  margarine, melted
3 tablespoons sharp
  cheddar cheese

2 tablespoons parsley flakes
1 teaspoon instant minced
  onion
1 teaspoon salt
¾ teaspoon Worcestershire
  sauce
Creamed Egg Sauce

Combine all ingredients. Pour into a greased and lightly floured 1-quart casserole. Bake in a slow oven (325°F.) 45 to 50 minutes or until a knife inserted in center comes out clean. Serve hot with Creamed Egg Sauce.

CREAMED EGG SAUCE

1½ cups medium white
  sauce
⅓ cup shredded cheddar
  cheese
4 hard-cooked eggs,
  chopped

1 tablespoon lemon juice
1 teaspoon parsley flakes
½ teaspoon salt
⅛ teaspoon ground black
  pepper

Combine white sauce with cheese, eggs, lemon juice, *parsley flakes,* salt, and black pepper. Heat until hot. Serve over Green Rice.

Yield: 6 servings

Asparagus With Parsley Sauce

2 tablespoons butter or
  margarine
2 tablespoons flour
1 cup chicken stock
½ cup light cream
¾ teaspoon salt

⅛ teaspoon ground black
  pepper
2 large egg yolks
2 teaspoons parsley flakes
2 to 2½ pounds fresh
  asparagus, cooked

Melt butter or margarine in a saucepan. Remove from heat and blend in flour. Stir in chicken stock or 1 chicken bouillon cube dissolved in 1 cup boiling water and ¼ cup of the cream. Return to heat; stir and cook over low heat until the mixture begins to thicken (about 5 minutes). Add salt and ground black pepper. Beat egg yolks, mix with remaining cream, and stir into the sauce. Cook over low heat only until hot (about 2 minutes). Just before serving, add *parsley flakes*. Heat half a minute. Serve hot over hot cooked asparagus.

Yield: 6 servings

Clam Pantry Pasta

1 cup elbow or shell macaroni
1 cup green noodles
1½ quarts boiling water
1 teaspoon salt
2 cans (7½ oz. each) minced clams
¾ cup clam juice
1 tablespoon onion flakes
2 tablespoons butter or margarine

1 tablespoon flour
⅟₁₆ teaspoon instant garlic powder
⅟₁₆ teaspoon ground black pepper
⅓ cup milk
2 tablespoons parsley flakes
½ pint creamed cottage cheese
Grated Parmesan cheese

Cook macaroni and green noodles in boiling salted water for 10 minutes; rinse and drain. Set aside. Drain clams, reserving ¾ cup liquid. Soften onion flakes in 2 tablespoons of clam liquid; let stand 10 minutes. Cook softened onion in hot butter or margarine over low heat until golden. Remove from heat; stir in remainder of reserved clam liquid and next 4 ingredients. Stir constantly over low heat until smooth and slightly thickened. Stir in *parsley flakes*. In well-buttered, shallow, 1½-quart baking dish layer half of cooked pasta. Spread evenly with cheese and then drained minced clams. Cover clams with remaining pasta and pour clam sauce over all. Sprinkle top with Parmesan cheese. Cover with foil and bake in a preheated moderate oven (350°F.) 25 minutes or until hot and bubbly.

Yield: 4–6 servings

PEPPER

Piper nigrum L.

PEPPER

Family: Piperaceae

LATIN	• **Piper nigrum L.**
SPANISH	• **Pimienta**
FRENCH	• **Poivre**
GERMAN	• **Pfeffer**
SWEDISH	• **Peppar**
ARABIC	• **Filfil Aswad**
DUTCH	• **Peper**
ITALIAN	• **Pepe**
PORTUGUESE	• **Pimenta**
RUSSIAN	• **Pyerets**
JAPANESE	• **Koshō**
CHINESE	• **Hu-Chiao**

PEPPER

PEPPER, the world's most important spice, is prepared from the small, round berries of a woody perennial evergreen climbing vine, *Piper nigrum,* a species native to the damp jungles of the Malabar Coast of southwestern India but now widely cultivated in the tropics of both hemispheres. It belongs to the pepper family and is the true pepper, not to be confused with the three following wholly different spices often designated as peppers:

The capsicum group, including paprika, cayenne pepper, chili pepper, red pepper, bell pepper, and other podlike fruits of the nightshade family;

Jamaican pepper (also known as pimento or allspice), the berries of *Pimenta dioica,* an evergreen tree of the myrtle family; and

Melegueta pepper or "grains of paradise," the small, dark, aromatic seeds of *Amomum melegueta* Roscoe, an herbaceous, robust perennial plant of the ginger family that is indigenous to West Africa. Five centuries ago "grains of paradise" were popular in Europe as a substitute for true pepper, but today the demand for the seeds is limited almost entirely to Ghana and Nigeria, whose inhabitants use them as a seasoning. The section of West Africa once known as the "Grain Coast" owed its name to this spice.

Two other climbing vines, although species of the same genus as the true pepper, should be distinguished from it: *Piper longum* L., "Indian long pepper," and *Piper officinarum* L., "Javanese long pepper." These long peppers are still used in the Far East in curries and native medicines but have almost been forgotten in the Western world.

Over 3,000 years ago references to pepper were made in India, in ancient Sanskrit medical literature. Most European names for pepper are derived from the Sanskrit *pippali*, a word used to describe long pepper.

During the fourth century B.C. the philosopher-botanist Theophrastus described two kinds of pepper, the long and the black. Pliny in the first century A.D. reported that long pepper was worth 15 denarii, while black pepper cost 4 denarii. Long pepper (from northern India) was known before black pepper (from southern India) in the Graeco-Roman era, and for several centuries was regarded as being of superior quality to black pepper.

Colonists from India are believed to have introduced pepper cultivation to Indonesia about 100 B.C.

Pepper was one of the earliest articles of commerce between the Orient and Europe. Under Emperor Marcus Aurelius this trade had increased to such a degree that in A.D. 176 the Romans imposed a customs duty in Alexandria on long pepper and white pepper. Black pepper, which was cheaper, appears to have been excluded from taxation (presumably for political reasons, to please the masses).

Following the conquest of Caesarea in Palestine in A.D. 1101, each victorious Genoese soldier received two pounds of pepper as part of his spoils.

In the Middle Ages rents, dowries, and taxes were frequently paid in pepper, and some European landlords preferred to receive their rental payments in the form of scarce, high-priced peppercorns rather than money. Today the term "peppercorn rent" means something nominal or trivial, but in medieval times peppercorns were choice legal tender, eagerly sought after by the wealthier classes, since supplies were not always available.

Evidence of pepper's importance in the spice trade during the Middle Ages is to be found in the vernacular names given the spice merchants: In England, they were called "pepperers"; in France, *poivriers;* and in Germany, *Pfeffersäcke*.

By Shakespeare's time the pungency of pepper was well known in England, as this mention of it in *Twelfth Night*, Act III, Scene IV, testifies:

> *Aguecheek:* Here's the challenge; read it: I warrant there's vinegar and pepper in't.

It is difficult for us to realize today the profound effect pepper and other Oriental spices had on European commerce in the Middle Ages. The cities of Alexandria, Genoa, and Venice owed their economic prosperity to the brisk trade in these expensive commodities.

The basic need for spices, especially pepper, in greater quantity led to Vasco da Gama's search for and discovery of a sea route to the spice-producing Malabar Coast of India in 1498, a feat that enabled Portugal to secure a monopoly of the spice trade and contributed to the economic ruin of Alexandria, Genoa, and Venice. During the sixteenth century Lisbon became the most important trading center for Oriental spices and the richest European port; but in the seventeenth century the monopoly shifted from Portugal to Holland following the successful voyages to Indonesia by de Houtman in 1595 and van Neck in 1598. By 1605 the Dutch had driven the Portuguese out of the Moluccas, and gradually the Hollanders acquired control of the pepper-producing areas near Bantam in Java and Lampong in southern Sumatra, regions in which pepper is still grown today. As early as 1650, however, pepper cultivation had spread to the Malay Archipelago, outside the area of Dutch control, so that the Dutch were never able to maintain the same complete monopoly of pepper production and sales that they did for nutmegs and cloves.

By the time London became the world's spice center in the nineteenth century, increased production had brought the price of spices down, thus increasing consumption. Pepper was no longer exclusively a treat for the wealthy.

The collapse of the Dutch East India Company coincided with the entrance of the United States into the Far Eastern spice trade. In 1797 Captain Jonathan Carnes of Salem, Massachusetts, sailed the schooner *Rajah* into the harbor of New York with more than $100,000 worth of pepper from Sumatra. During the next fifty years ships from Salem and Boston played an important role in the world pepper trade. The daring Yankee captains of these trading vessels were the founders of our merchant marine.

Both black and white pepper are obtained from the berries that grow in clusters on the pepper vine. The berries are ready to be harvested about nine months after flowering. For *black pepper* they are picked while green (not yet fully ripe) and left in heaps for a few days to ferment. The berries are then spread on mats or on concrete floors to dry in full sunlight for about twenty hours, until they shrivel and turn dark brown or black. Thus the entire peppercorn, including the dark outer hull, forms the spice known as black pepper. When ground, the powdered black pepper consists of dark particles from the outer hull and light-colored bits of the core.

White pepper is produced from fully ripened berries, which are greenish-yellow and at the point of turning red. After being picked the berries are packed in sacks and soaked in slow-flowing water for about eight days. These softened berries are then trampled on or otherwise macerated to rub off the outer hull. The gray inner peppercorns are washed and dried in the sun for several days on mats or on concrete floors until they turn creamy white in color, to become the white pepper of commerce.

The pepper vine thrives in a moist, hot climate, from sea level up to about 1,500 feet of elevation in the tropics, with an evenly distributed annual rainfall of about 100 inches, producing best growth on fertile, flat or gently sloping land that is rich in humus and has good drainage and light shade.

Propagation is usually carried out by cuttings, selected from the upper portions of young, vigorous, high-yielding, healthy vines. These are grown in nurseries that are shaded, well watered, and heavily fertilized.

This woody climber grows to 30 feet or more in length, with a grayish stem that may attain a diameter of about $\frac{1}{2}$ inch. From its swollen nodes numerous rootlets are produced, which enable the plant to attach itself to a tree or other support.

The ovate, glossy, acutely tipped leaves are dark green above, pale green underneath, and 5 to 10 inches long. The minute white flowers are borne on slender, elongated spikes or catkins, 4 to 5 inches long, produced from the nodes opposite the leaves. Since a catkin is always opposite a leaf, profuse leaf development is essential for high yields. Each spike may produce 50 to 60 single-seeded berries.

Young living trees or sturdy 12-foot-high timber posts, established on low mounds prepared at a spacing of about 8 by 8 feet in the field planting site, serve as supports for the vines. These supports, or at least temporary stakes, are set out at the time of initial field planting, enabling the young pepper vines to start climbing immediately. Two or three cuttings may be planted adjacent to each support. The vines must be pruned from time to time to keep them to the height of the support, for if allowed to grow without restraint they would become too tall and their branching habit would be too irregular, thus obstructing the harvest. Pruning, commenced by cutting back the tips when the plants are about 2 feet high, encourages lateral branching and produces a vine that is cylindrical in shape, with dense foliage and a maximum number of fruiting branches.

A small crop may be harvested during the third year after planting, but full production is not attained until the seventh or eighth year. Under favorable conditions, the vines bear productively for fifteen or twenty years.

Maximum yields per acre are achieved only through the maintenance of highest cultural practices: Weeding must be carried out regularly; the young vines must constantly be tied in to the supports; rotted supports should be replaced; mulching and systematic applications of both organic and inorganic fertilizers are essential; pruning must be consistent; the shade must be controlled, depending on the locality (in Indonesia pepper is generally grown without shade, while in India some shade is deemed necessary). In areas where the vines are planted on mounds, new soil or compost should be added to the mounds from time to time to maintain maximum root development and to offset soil erosion. Root diseases must be checked, and insect pests controlled.

A full-grown, well-developed mature vine will yield approximately 4 to 5 pounds of dried berries, and a satisfactory yield per acre in full production would be approximately 10,000 pounds of green berries—that is, 2,800 pounds of dried white pepper (conversion factor, 28 percent from green to white), or about 3,500 pounds of black pepper (conversion factor, 35 percent from green to black). There are about 8,000 dried black or 11,000 dried white peppercorns in one pound.

Many types or grades of both black pepper and white pepper are recognized in the spice trade. These are usually identified by the ports from which the goods are exported or the region where the pepper is grown. The very important pungent grade of black pepper known as *Lampong,* for example, is produced in the Lampong district of southern Sumatra and other regions in Indonesia. Another leading black pepper is the *Malabar*, a highly aromatic type from southwestern India, including the Alleppey district and the southern Malabar Coast. Other leading black peppers are the *Tellicherry*, from the northern Malabar Coast, which are large, bold, handsome berries, traditionally the highest priced of the black peppers; the mild-flavored *Sarawak* from the former British colony of Sarawak, now part of the Federation of Malaysia, along the northwestern coast of Borneo; and the *Brazilian*, a relatively new trade quality from the state of Para on the Amazon river. Thanks largely to the efforts of Japanese settlers, the Brazilian has been produced in increasing quantities since 1946, and Brazil (the first country in the Western Hemisphere to produce pepper on a commercial basis) now has about 12,000 acres of this spice under cultivation.

The most important white pepper, known as *Muntok*, is exported through the highway center and port of Pangkalpinang on the island of Bangka, which lies off the southeastern coast of Sumatra. Chinese plantation owners have gradually developed, during the past eighty years, a major production center for white pepper on Bangka. Other prominent white peppers in the trade include the *Brazilian*, lighter in color and less pungent than the Muntok; and the *Sarawak*, usually blended in the renowned spice emporium of Singapore before being exported to Germany, England, and the Netherlands.

Most of the world's pepper is grown on small plots of land in the Far East. India and Indonesia between them account for roughly 65 percent of the world's output of about 156 million pounds per year. In recent years the average annual world exports of pepper have amounted to about $38,500,000, or just over 25 percent of the total volume of net world exports of all spices. The average price for both black and white pepper imported into the United States during 1971 was about 44 cents per pound.

The United States, with an average annual consumption per capita of about 4 ounces, is the largest consumer of pepper, followed by India, the Soviet Union, West Germany, France, and the United Kingdom. Black and white pepper rank as our number one spice import in total dollar value—at $26.4 million in 1971, more than three times that of the next spice, vanilla beans.

On steam distillation, black pepper yields from 1 to 2.4 percent of an essential oil that represents the aromatic odor of the spice. The sharp, pungent taste of pepper is said to be contributed by the resin chavicine and the burning aftertaste by the crystalline alkaloid piperine, both components of oleoresin of pepper, obtained from the ground dried berries through solvent extraction.

Both oil of pepper and oleoresin of pepper are utilized in the food industry to flavor sausages, table sauces, canned meats, and salad dressings.

Pepper was formerly employed in medicine as a stimulant, carminative, aid to digestion, and as a cure for diarrhea, cholera, and arthritis, among other ailments. But its chief use today is as the world's most important spice.

What is the basic reason for pepper's universal supremacy and popularity? The late Louis Diat, a famous master French chef, pointed out that no other spice can do so much for so many different types of food. It is often utilized three times in the same dish before the food is eaten: first, in the kitchen as an ingredient in the preparation; second, to correct or improve the overall seasoning during or after cooking; and finally at the dinner table if the diner should desire more seasoning.

Black pepper, characterized by a penetrating odor and hot, biting, and extremely pungent flavor, is preferred in the United States; milder-flavored white pepper is generally consumed in Europe. Although about seven times more black pepper is imported into the United States than white pepper, the good cook needs both kinds—white pepper is ideal in light-colored foods and sauces where dark specks would not be attractive.

Both black and white pepper are widely used in the foods of almost every nation on earth. They are available whole, cracked, coarsely ground, medium ground, or finely ground and may be used in almost all foods except those with a sweet flavor. Whole peppercorns are spicy additions to meats, soups, fish, and pickles. Ground pepper (black or white) is especially popular in eggs, salads, meats, soups, sauces, gravies, and vegetables. The tanginess of pepper provides welcome relief in salt-free diets.

In general, the flavor and aroma are more immediately available in the finer grinds, but these fine grinds have a short shelf life. If stored in a dry place in closed containers at a moderate temperature, the whole pep- percorns should keep for many years without any loss of quality.

Pepper Meat Balls

1 teaspoon instant minced
  onion
1 pound ground chuck
2 eggs
1 cup day-old bread cubes
1 teaspoon salt

½ teaspoon ground black
  pepper
½ teaspoon prepared
  horseradish
¼ teaspoon ground nutmeg
1 tablespoon cooking oil

Mix instant onion with 1 teaspoon water; let stand 5 minutes to soften. Combine with remaining ingredients. Shape into 1-inch balls or into bite-sized balls and brown on all sides in hot oil. Serve with spaghetti or on tooth- picks as cocktail balls.

**Yield: 12 one-inch balls or
         30 small cocktail balls**

Fricassee of Lamb, Polish Style

3 pounds boneless shoulder
  of lamb
1 teaspoon salt
½ teaspoon ground black
  pepper
2 tablespoons butter or
  margarine
¼ teaspoon instant garlic
  powder
1 teaspoon grated lemon
  peel

1 teaspoon lemon juice
8 medium-sized fresh
  mushrooms, sliced
4 anchovy fillets, chopped
2 cups beef stock or 2 beef
  bouillon cubes in 2 cups
  hot water
2 tablespoons flour
3 tablespoons water
4 cups cooked rice

Pour hot water over meat and then drain on paper towels to dry. Cut into 1-inch pieces. Mix the 1 teaspoon of salt with *black pepper* and rub into the meat. Brown in butter or margarine. Add garlic powder, lemon peel, lemon juice, mushrooms, anchovies, and stock. Cover and cook 1½ hours or until meat is tender. Blend flour with water until smooth and add to meat. Mix well. Stir and cook 1 minute or until slightly thickened. Serve with cooked rice.

Yield: 6 servings

Black Pepper Fried Chicken

1 broiler-fryer chicken,	*1 teaspoon salt*
cut in serving pieces	*½ cup flour*
1 cup milk	*Fat for deep frying*
2 teaspoons ground black	*Milk*
pepper	*¼ cup flour*

Place chicken in shallow dish. Combine milk, 1 teaspoon of the *pepper,* and ½ teaspoon of the salt. Pour over chicken. Cover and refrigerate 2 hours. Combine the ½ cup of flour and remaining *pepper* and salt. Coat chicken pieces in mixture. Reserve leftover milk for gravy. Refrigerate chicken 1 hour. Cook chicken in deep fat which has been heated to 350°F. 15 to 20 minutes or until brown and tender. To make cream gravy, measure leftover milk and add more milk to make 2½ cups. Place ¼ cup of the fat from deep frying in saucepan. Blend in the ¼ cup of flour. Add milk. Stir and cook until medium thick. Season to taste with salt and *ground black pepper.* Serve with chicken.

Yield: 4 servings

English Pepper Pasties

2 packages (10 oz. each)	*2 tablespoons parsley flakes*
pie crust mix	*1 teaspoon salt*
½ cup instant minced	*½ teaspoon* ground black
onion	pepper
1 pound lean boneless round	*2 tablespoons butter or*
or sirloin steak, cut into	*margarine*
¼-inch cubes	*1 egg white*
1½ cups finely diced raw	*1 tablespoon water*
potatoes	

Prepare pie crust according to package directions. Cover

and chill. Mix onion with ¼ cup water; let stand 5 minutes for onion to soften. Combine onion with steak, potatoes, parsley, salt, and *black pepper*. Divide pastry into 7 parts. Roll 6 of the parts into 7-inch rounds. Roll remaining part into 3- by 6-inch rectangle; cut into 6 strips, each ½ inch wide. Reserve. Place about ½ cup of meat mixture in center of each round. Dot each with 1 teaspoon butter. Moisten edges of dough, fold dough over filling and press edges together to form a ridge across the top. Twist reserved pastry strips to cover length of edge on each pasty; press firmly. Cut slits on each side of pasties. Brush with egg white blended with water. Bake in preheated hot oven (400°F.) for 15 minutes. Reduce heat to moderate (350°F.) and bake 45 minutes longer. Serve hot or cold.

Yield: 6 servings

Steak Au Poivre

4¾- to 5-pound boned
    sirloin steak, cut 1½
    to 2 inches thick

2 tablespoons freshly
    cracked whole black
    pepper
1 teaspoon salt

Press *cracked black pepper* into both sides of meat with palm of hand. Let steak stand at room temperature about half an hour. Lightly grease a 10- or 12-inch cast-iron skillet. Sprinkle with salt and place over high heat until salt begins to brown. Add steak and cook 8 to 10 minutes on each side.

Yield: 4–6 servings

Black Pepper Pot Roast

4½- to 5-pound bottom
    round of beef
1 can (6 oz.) tomato paste
1 small bay leaf
1½ teaspoons whole black
    pepper
1½ teaspoons salt

1 teaspoon instant minced
    onion
½ teaspoon ground black
    pepper
8 small new potatoes
6 medium carrots

Brown meat on all sides in large heavy kettle. Add tomato paste, 1½ cups water, bay leaf, *whole pepper,* salt, and minced onion. Cover and simmer 3 hours, basting frequently. Add *ground black pepper,* potatoes, and carrots, and continue cooking 30 minutes or until meat is tender.

Yield: 8 servings

Quick Hamburger Onion Hash

¼ cup instant minced
  onion
¼ cup water
1 pound ground lean beef
1 tablespoon butter or
  margarine
3 cups finely chopped
  cooked potatoes

1½ teaspoons salt
¼ teaspoon ground black
  pepper
⅛ teaspoon instant garlic
  powder

Soften instant minced onion in water. Set aside. Brown meat in butter or margarine. Add softened onion, potatoes, salt, *black pepper,* and garlic powder. Stir and cook 4 to 5 minutes. Serve hot as the main dish.

Yield: 6 servings

POPPY SEED

Papaver somniferum L.

A. Flowering branch of white variety
B. Flower of red variety
1. Vertical section of flower showing stamens and pistil
2. Various views of stamens
3. Pollen grain
4. Pistil
5. Transverse section of ovary
6. Mature fruit (capsule)
7. Seed
8. Vertical section of seed
9. Transverse section of seed

POPPY SEED

Family: Papaveraceae

LATIN	• Papaver somniferum L.
SPANISH	• Adormidera
FRENCH	• Pavot
GERMAN	• Mohn
SWEDISH	• Vallmo
ARABIC	• Khashkhash
DUTCH	• Slaapbol
ITALIAN	• Papavero
PORTUGUESE	• Dormideira
RUSSIAN	• Mak
JAPANESE	• Keshi
CHINESE	• Ying-Shu

POPPY SEED

POPPY, *Papaver somniferum,* also known as the opium or oil poppy, is a tall, robust annual belonging to the poppy family and is indigenous to the eastern Mediterranean region, Asia Minor, and central Asia. Since ancient times the red poppy flower has been the symbol of fallen warriors in many countries, alleged to have derived its color from the blood of heroes slain in battle. Following World War I the red poppies of Flanders' fields (*P. dubium*) were adopted as the official emblem to commemorate Armistice Day in the United States.

The botanical epithet *somniferum* means "sleep-bearing," and refers to this plant's narcotic qualities. "Opium" comes from *opion,* a diminutive of the Greek word for juice; the word morphine, a constituent of opium, is derived from Morpheus, the Greek god of dreams.

The tiny poppy seeds, which have an agreeable nutty flavor and no narcotic properties, are used as a condiment on rolls, pastry, and baked goods, and are crushed to produce an edible oil.

The drug opium, containing (among more than twenty other constituents) the alkaloids morphine and codeine, is an ingredient in the dried milky juice which is obtained from incisions made in the nearly ripe poppy capsules, ten to twenty days after flowering. Although coming from the same plant that produces opium, the poppy seed is not narcotic because it is not formed until after the capsule has lost its opium-yielding potential. Although the tissues of the ovary are richly laced with opium-containing lactiferous vessels, there are no lactiferous ducts between the ovary and the ovules (or immature seeds); hence no opium can reach the seeds.

The history of poppy—one of the Egyptian medicinal plants listed as a sedative in the Ebers Papyrus—goes back to earliest times.

The women of Crete cultivated poppy plants for opium as early as 1400 B.C., as evidenced by the statue of a poppy goddess from a sanctuary at Gazi. Homer, the legendary poet of early Greece, alluded to poppy as an ornamental garden plant about 800 B.C.

Hippocrates, the father of medicine, mentioned the medicinal virtues of opium wine about 400 B.C. Theophrastus in the third century B.C. described how opium could be obtained by scratching the unripe poppy pods. Dioscorides, in A.D. 77 clarified in precise detail the difference between the juice of the poppy capsule and that of the entire plant, the extract of the capsule being the more active.

Opium was employed for many years by physicians in Athens and Alexandria as a legitimate drug to combat dysentery. By the time of Mohammed (A.D. 570–632) the medicinal as well as the narcotic qualities of the drug were appreciated in Arabia. During the succeeding centuries Islamic traders and missionaries progressively spread the cultivation of the opium poppy to Persia, India, China, and Southeast Asia. When used in moderation, it brought relief from pain to those suffering from cholera, dysentery, and malaria. Unfortunately, the drug then fell into evil hands and began to be used excessively as a habit-forming, nerve-benumbing, body-destroying narcotic, first in India, then in China. Initially the drug was eaten in the Orient, but in the seventeenth century the nefarious opium-smoking habit was introduced to China, which seduced millions of additional addicts and spread like a plague over that vast empire. Production and sales of Oriental opium increased tremendously.

As the frenzied demand for opium intensified, the Portuguese, Dutch, and British merchants in the Far East, in turn, managed to make enormous profits by trafficking in the pernicious commodity, either legally or by contraband dealings. By the nineteenth century the struggle between the British trade interests importing or smuggling opium into China and the Chinese government, attempting to keep it out, culminated in the two so-called Opium Wars of 1840 and 1855, both very sordid chapters in the history of Western trade and diplomacy in the Orient. China lost both of these wars, having tried in vain to prevent the legalization of opium trade in that country.

Compared with the brutal history of opium, the story of the benevolent and innocent poppy seed is very tame. Nevertheless, it has a past worthy of record, even though no country ever waged war over it. The earliest use of poppy seeds dates from a remote period, as poppy capsules believed to be *Papaver setigerum* have been found near the lake dwellings in Switzerland.

During the second millennium B.C. the Egyptians had cultivated poppy not only as a medicinal plant, but also to produce an edible oil by crushing the seeds. Pliny, in the first century A.D., described a savory mixture of parched poppy seeds and honey popular in that era. Galen, a Greek physician who came from Asia Minor in the second century A.D., recommended mixing the seeds with flour to prepare a flavorsome bread.

The use of poppy seeds as a condiment on bread spread to Europe during the Middle Ages. Old German herbals referred to it as a pleasing bread spice and called it *Oelsamen*, or oil seed, because of its vegetable oil content.

Poppy seed cultivation has been extended to most temperate regions of the world, its geographical growing range extending from about 55 degrees north in Russia to 40 degrees south in Argentina. The principal producing countries today include Holland, Poland, Iran, Romania, Russia, Turkey, Czechoslovakia, and Argentina. The best quality Dutch poppy seed, slate blue in color, is imported into the United States.

The poppy plant is a stiff, erect annual with bluish-green stems that grows to a height of 3 to 6 feet. Propagation is by seeds drilled shallowly at close spacing, at the rate of about 1 pound per acre, so the mature plants will be about 1 foot apart. A well-manured soil, adequate moisture, and plenty of sunshine are recommended.

Seeds planted in March produce flowering plants in July, which are ready for harvest in September. The large flowers, 4 to 5 inches across, vary in color from white to mauve, with dark blotches at the base of the petals. After the flowers wither, the familiar egg-shaped poppy capsule, with a diameter of $1\frac{1}{2}$ to 3 inches, matures.

The harvest begins when the fruits first turn yellowish-brown. In Holland, following a mechanized harvest the poppy plants are stacked in windrows to dry. The poppy heads may also be cut off and spread out to dry. Normally the seed capsules do not shatter. Selected varieties of poppy, with pale lilac petals and dark gray seeds, have been developed for high seed production rather than for high opium yields.

The kidney-shaped seeds are minute, about $\frac{3}{64}$ inch long; approximately 900,000 make a pound. Their color ranges from white to blue to black. The seeds yield, by expression, about 50 to 60 percent of a fixed, tasteless, pale yellow vegetable oil that is commercially important for culinary purposes as a salad oil, being less liable to rancidity than is olive oil. Poppy seed oil is also used by artists as a drying oil.

Poppy seed is usually available as a condiment in whole form, to be used as a topping for rolls, breads, cookies, cakes, and baked goods, or as a garnish. Toasting or baking the seeds brings out the pleasant nutty flavor and crunchy texture. The crushed seeds mixed with sweetening are used as a filling for coffee cakes and pastries. Poppy seed butter lends an appetizing aroma to noodles, rice, vegetables, or broiled fish.

Poppy Seed Cake

1 cup poppy seed
⅓ cup honey
1 cup butter or shortening
1½ cups sugar
4 eggs, separated
1 teaspoon pure vanilla
  extract

1 cup sour cream
2½ cups sifted all-purpose
  flour
1 teaspoon baking soda
1 teaspoon salt

Cook *poppy seed* with honey and ¼ cup water in small saucepan for 5 to 7 minutes. Cool. Cream butter and sugar until light and fluffy. Add *poppy seed* mixture. Add egg yolks, one at a time, beating well after each addition. Blend in vanilla and sour cream. Sift together flour, baking soda, and salt; add gradually to *poppy seed* mixture, beating well after each addition. Beat egg whites until stiff. Fold into batter. Pour into greased and lightly floured 9-inch tube pan. Bake in moderate oven (350°F.) about 1 hour and 15 to 20 minutes or until done. Cool in pan for 5 minutes. Remove from pan and cool on wire rack. Frost with vanilla frosting.

FROSTING

2 tablespoons butter or
  margarine
1¾ cups sifted
  confectioners' sugar

2 tablespoons milk
Pinch of salt
¾ teaspoon pure vanilla
  extract

Cream butter until soft and fluffy. Add confectioners' sugar alternately with milk until mixture is of spreading consistency. Blend in salt and vanilla. Spread over top of cake; let icing dribble down sides of cake. Sprinkle *poppy seed* over top.

Yield: One 9-inch tube cake

Poppy Seed Crescents

4 cups all-purpose flour
1½ teaspoons double-acting
   baking powder
½ teaspoon salt
1¼ cups butter or
   margarine

2 packages active dry yeast
¼ cup lukewarm water
4 egg yolks, beaten
½ pint sour cream

POPPY SEED FILLING

2 cups poppy seed, ground
½ cup sugar
¼ cup milk
¼ cup butter or
   margarine

1 egg, beaten
¼ teaspoon cinnamon

Sift flour with baking powder and salt; with pastry blender cut butter into flour mixture. Dissolve yeast in lukewarm water; let stand for 5 minutes. Add beaten egg yolks and sour cream to yeast; mix thoroughly. Add to flour mixture, mixing lightly until dough is not sticky. Wrap in waxed paper; refrigerate 12 hours or overnight. To prepare filling, combine all ingredients in medium saucepan and cook over low heat for 5 minutes. Stir constantly to prevent scorching. Cool. Divide dough into 4 parts. Roll on lightly floured board to ¼-inch thickness; cut into 2-inch squares. Place 1 teaspoon *Poppy Seed* Filling in center of each square of dough. Roll and shape into crescents. Place on ungreased cookie sheets. If desired brush top of each crescent with beaten egg. Bake in a preheated hot oven (425°F.) for 10 minutes until lightly browned. Cool on wire racks.

Yield: Approximately 9 dozen

Poppy Seed French Dressing

2 tablespoons powdered
   mustard
¾ cup sugar
⅓ cup vinegar
1 cup olive oil

3 tablespoons finely
   chopped onion
1 tablespoon poppy seed
1 teaspoon salt

Blend mustard with 2 tablespoons warm water; let stand 10 minutes for flavor to develop. Combine all ingredients in a mixing bowl. Beat with a rotary beater until thickened. Serve over fruit or vegetable salad.

Yield: 1¾ cups

Poppy Seed Coffee Roll

¼ cup milk
1 package active dry yeast
1 teaspoon sugar
2½ cups sifted all-purpose flour

3 tablespoons sugar
¼ teaspoon salt
⅓ cup butter or margarine
1 egg, slightly beaten
Poppy Seed *Filling*

Scald milk; cool to lukewarm. Sprinkle yeast over ¼ cup warm water. Add 1 teaspoon sugar and stir until dissolved. Let stand 5 minutes. Sift flour with the 3 tablespoons of sugar and salt. Cut butter in with pastry blender or two knives until mixture resembles coarse meal. Add milk and egg to yeast mixture; gradually add to flour mixture and blend well. Knead until dough is smooth on lightly floured board. Place in greased bowl. Cover, let rise in warm place until doubled in bulk. Punch dough down and roll out on lightly floured board to a rectangle 10 by 16 inches. Spread with *Poppy Seed* Filling. Roll in jelly-roll fashion. Seal ends. Bake in preheated moderate oven (350°F.) 30 to 40 minutes or until done.

POPPY SEED FILLING

1 cup poppy seed
½ cup milk
2 tablespoons butter or margarine
2 tablespoons honey

1 tablespoon sugar
1 teaspoon ground cinnamon
½ cup raisins

Grind *poppy seed* in blender, if available, or use whole. Combine with remaining ingredients in small saucepan. Bring to boil, then simmer for 10 to 12 minutes. Cool mixture thoroughly before spreading on dough.

Yield: One 16-inch roll

Quick Poppy Seed Snails

1 package (14½ oz.) hot   1 tablespoon butter or
   roll mix   margarine, melted
Poppy Seed *Filling*

Prepare hot roll mix and let rise according to directions. Punch down dough and knead it on a lightly floured board 1 minute. Roll dough ⅛ inch thick in a 14- by 22-inch rectangle. Spread with *Poppy Seed* Filling. Roll up in jelly-roll fashion, starting at the long side. Cut roll into crosswise slices 1 inch thick. Place them in buttered 2½ inch cupcake pans. Brush tops with melted butter or margarine. Cover and let rise in a warm place (80° to 85°F.) 30 minutes or until rolls have doubled in size. Bake in a preheated moderate oven (375°F.) 12 to 15 minutes or until browned.

POPPY SEED FILLING

1 cup poppy seed   ½ teaspoon ground
½ cup sugar   cinnamon
1 cup water   1 teaspoon grated lemon
2 tablespoons honey   peel
½ cup raisins

Crush *poppy seed,* about ¼ cup at a time, by rolling seeds with a rolling pin between sheets of waxed paper or blend ¼ cup at a time in a blender. Mix sugar and ½ cup water in a saucepan. Bring to boiling point and boil 5 minutes or until it is the thickness of syrup. Add remaining water and the next 3 ingredients. Cook 3 minutes. Remove from heat and stir in lemon peel. Cool.

Yield: 24 rolls

ROSEMARY

Rosmarinus officinalis L.

Family: Labiatae

LATIN	• **Rosmarinus officinalis L.**
SPANISH	• **Romero**
FRENCH	• **Romarin**
GERMAN	• **Rosmarin**
SWEDISH	• **Rosmarin**
ARABIC	• **Iklil Al-Jabal**
DUTCH	• **Rozemarijn**
ITALIAN	• **Ramerino**
PORTUGUESE	• **Alecrim**
RUSSIAN	• **Rozmarin**
JAPANESE	• **Mannenrô**
CHINESE	• **Mi-Tieh-Hsiang**

ROSEMARY

ROSEMARY, *Rosmarinus officinalis,* is a small evergreen shrub of the mint family native to the Mediterranean region. Its small, narrow, aromatic leaves resemble curved pine needles when dried and are used as a fragrant seasoning herb. The fresh leaves and tender tops are distilled to produce an essential oil used in perfumery and medicine.

As its botanical designation indicates (*ros,* dew, and *marinum,* of the sea), *Rosmarinus officinalis* is often found near the coast, where it thrives under conditions of fog and salt spray, and frequently is encountered growing wild on the chalk hills of southern France and the Mediterranean. However, it also grows inland and may be found in the Sahara Desert.

An intriguing if unverified legend accompanies the history of how rosemary got its familiar name and how its flowers became blue. The Virgin Mary, fleeing from Herod's soldiers with the Christ Child to Egypt, hung her blue cloak one night on a rosemary bush with

ROSEMARY, 1487

a white flower. The next morning the flower had turned blue like Mary's garment and the herb was thereafter known as the "rose of Mary."

In the first century A.D. Pliny, in his writings on natural science, ascribed numerous medicinal properties to rosemary. It was much esteemed in the Middle Ages and cultivated on the imperial farms in central Europe by order of Charlemagne in the ninth century.

It was probably already in cultivation in England before the Norman Conquest, as it is recommended for use as a medicinal herb in an Anglo-Saxon herbal of the eleventh century.

In the Middle Ages rosemary was the customary condiment for European salted meats. Oil of rosemary was one of the first essential oils distilled, having been produced by vaporization and condensation about 1330 by Raymundus Lullus.

Much superstition surrounded rosemary in medieval times. It was believed to grow only in the gardens of the righteous and was used as a magic charm for protection from witchcraft and evils and against the "evil eye" in particular. More pragmatically, the burning twigs were employed at banquets as an incense or in courtrooms in seventeenth-century England to protect the judges from the pestilences and jail fevers of the prisoners brought before them.

In ancient Greece rosemary was renowned for its alleged ability to fortify the brain and refresh the memory. Greek students of that era would braid rosemary wreaths in their hair when taking examinations. In this manner rosemary became associated with remembrance and became the symbol for fidelity in lovers, living or dead, at weddings or funerals. It was the custom for the bridesmaids to present the bridegroom with a bunch of rosemary on his wedding day, so he would remember to be faithful. Ophelia alludes to this symbolism in *Hamlet,* Act IV, Scene V:

> There's rosemary, that's for remembrance; pray
> you, love, remember. . . .

At funerals rosemary sprigs were distributed among the mourners, to be thrown into the grave. In *Romeo and Juliet,* Act IV, Scene V, this practice is mentioned:

> Dry up your tears, and stick your rosemary
> On this fair corse, and, as the custom is,
> In all her best array bear her to the church. . . .

Most rosemary today is grown commercially in France, Spain, Portugal, Yugoslavia, and North Africa; some is produced in California.

Rosemary grows to a height of 5 feet or more. Its narrow leaves with in-rolled margins are about 1 inch long, dark glossy green above, pale or whitish beneath. The small flowers are light blue. The stem is woody with brown, tough bark. Commercially it is propagated by seeds or by cuttings, but the latter method is generally recommended. It does best when grown on a light, rather dry chalky soil, in a sheltered position in full sun with good drainage.

The plants are transplanted to field position in rows 4 feet apart, with about 18 inches between the plants in the row. They are divided frequently to promote the development of the young shoots, to be cut for distillation or for their foliage. When they have reached their maximum size but before they become woody, these shoots should be pruned back several inches, once or twice each season. By the end of the second year the rosemary plant is a dense shrub 2 feet in diameter and 3 to 4 feet high.

If the rosemary leaves are to be used for culinary purposes, they must be dried as soon as possible after being harvested to avoid loss of the volatile oil. When dried carefully on trays in a well-ventilated, dark, sheltered place, the leaves retain their green color and their clean, fresh, bittersweet flavor.

In days gone by rosemary was in demand for medicinal purposes as a carminative, stimulant, tonic, stomachic, and cure for headaches; to remove bruises; and to relieve head colds and nervous tension. It has also been used as a fragrant moth repellent.

No longer important as a medicine, rosemary is cultivated today as a condiment and for the distillation of its pale yellow essential oil, of which the fresh plant may yield from 0.5 to 1.5 percent. Oil of rosemary, with its pleasantly tenacious, clean, woody odor, is employed in the preparation of cosmetics, soaps, perfumes, deodorants, and hair tonics.

The spice is available either whole or ground and may be utilized in lamb dishes, stews, and soups, and in boiling potatoes or other vegetables.

In recent years, rosemary has been one of the most inexpensive of all the spices and herbs. The average price of Portuguese rosemary imported into the United States in 1971 was approximately 10 cents per pound.

Rosemary Bridal Punch

4 cups sugar
¼ cup lemon juice
3 tablespoons rosemary
   leaves
2 quarts strawberries

3 quarts cold water
2 cups lime juice
1¾ cups lemon juice
1 bottle (1 pt. 12 oz.)
   ginger ale

Combine sugar with 1 quart water, lemon juice, and *rosemary*. Bring to boiling point; boil 5 minutes. Strain out *rosemary leaves*. Cool. Meantime wash, cap, and slice strawberries. Force through a fine sieve. Add to cooled mixture with lime juice and lemon juice. Pour into punch bowl over ice. Add ginger ale and serve.

Yield: Approximately 9 quarts

Rosemary Fried Chicken Casserole

1 package (2½ lbs.) frozen
   fried chicken
1 can (10½ oz.) cream of
   mushroom soup

½ cup milk
½ teaspoon onion salt
½ teaspoon whole rosemary
   leaves, *crumbled*

Place chicken in a 1½-quart casserole. Place in a pre-heated hot oven (400°F.) to heat. Meanwhile mix soup with milk, onion salt, and *rosemary*. Heat thoroughly and pour over chicken. Cover and bake 45 to 50 minutes or until hot. Remove cover the last 10 minutes of baking period.

Yield: 4–5 servings

Rosemary Shrimp Pastry Loaf

Pastry made from 2½ cups
   flour
2½ pounds shrimp, peeled
   and deveined
1 cup white wine
1 tablespoon instant minced
   onion
2 eggs
1 egg yolk
1 cup heavy cream

2 tablespoons brandy
2 tablespoons lemon juice
2 teaspoons salt
½ teaspoon rosemary
   leaves, *crushed*
½ teaspoon ground nutmeg
⅛ teaspoon ground black
   pepper
⅛ teaspoon cayenne
1 egg, lightly beaten

With part of pastry, line 9- by 5- by 3-inch loaf pan; reserve remainder for top crust. Poach shrimp in seasoned court bouillon made with white wine and 2 cups water. Drain and cool. Put shrimp through fine blade of grinder or mince in blender. Combine shrimp with remaining ingredients except 1 egg. Mix well. Spoon shrimp mixture into pastry-lined pan. Cover with top crust, sealing edges well. Brush top with beaten egg. To allow steam to escape, make 2 holes the size of nickels on top. To set crust, bake in preheated very hot oven (450°F.) for 10 minutes. Reduce heat to 350°F. and continue baking for 65 minutes. Remove to rack and let cool. Refrigerate overnight before removing from pan. Slice and serve cold.

Yield: 10–12 servings

Rhubarb Rosemary Parfait

3½ pounds diced fresh
  rhubarb
2½ cups sugar
1½ teaspoons rosemary
  leaves, *crushed*
¼ teaspoon salt
4 packages unflavored
  gelatin

1 cup orange juice
1 pint strawberries, sliced
1 tablespoon confectioners'
  sugar
¾ cup heavy cream,
  whipped

Place rhubarb in deep saucepan with ¼ cup boiling water, sugar, *rosemary,* and salt. Cook, covered, over low heat, until rhubarb is tender, about 35 minutes. Transfer part of rhubarb to the container of an electric blender and blend until smooth. Depending on the size of blender, work small amounts at a time until it is all blended. Strain and pour back into saucepan; heat. Sprinkle gelatin over orange juice. Stir to dissolve. Add to hot rhubarb mixture. Stir until blended. Cool until mixture mounds slightly when dropped from spoon. Fold in sliced strawberries. Spoon mixture into parfait glasses. Refrigerate. Before serving, garnish with whipped cream sweetened with confectioners' sugar.

Yield: 12 servings

Spiced Fruit Salad Mold

1 envelope unflavored
  gelatin
¼ cup water
2¾ cups pineapple-
  grapefruit juice
¾ teaspoon rosemary
  leaves, crushed
½ teaspoon whole allspice
  berries
½ teaspoon whole cloves
2 whole ginger, each 1 inch
  long
1 tablespoon sugar

1 tablespoon fresh lemon
  juice
½ teaspoon pure vanilla
  extract
1 cup pineapple tidbits,
  drained
1 cup sliced canned peaches,
  drained
¾ cup chopped pecans or
  walnuts
Salad greens
Mayonnaise

Soften gelatin in water. Combine fruit juice, spices, and
sugar in a saucepan. Bring to a boil and simmer 10
minutes. Strain out spices and pour liquid over softened
gelatin. Stir in lemon juice and vanilla. Chill until mixture begins to thicken. Fold in fruit and nuts. Turn into
a lightly oiled 1-quart ring mold. Chill until firm and
ready to serve. Just before serving, turn out onto a serving plate. Garnish with salad greens. Serve with mayonnaise.

Yield: 8 servings

Spiced Fresh Fruit Medley

1 cup sugar
¾ cup water
¹⁄₁₆ teaspoon salt
½ teaspoon rosemary
  leaves, crushed
2 sticks cinnamon, 2 inches
  each
¼ teaspoon whole cloves

¼ teaspoon whole allspice
2 cups pineapple wedges
2 cups sliced strawberries
4 cups orange sections
2 tablespoons lemon juice
Grape clusters
Whole strawberries

Combine first 7 ingredients in a saucepan. Bring to boiling point and simmer 10 minutes. Remove from heat
and cool. Strain. In a mixing bowl combine pineapple,
strawberries, orange sections, and lemon juice. Pour

strained syrup over fruit and mix well. Chill. Just before serving, spoon into parfait glasses or sherbet dishes. Top with a small cluster of grapes or a whole strawberry.

Yield: 12 servings.

SAFFRON

Crocus sativus L.

SAFFRON

Family: Iridaceae

LATIN	• <u>Crocus sativus L.</u>
SPANISH	• Azafrán
FRENCH	• Safran
GERMAN	• Safran
SWEDISH	• Saffran
ARABIC	• Za'farãn
DUTCH	• Saffraan
ITALIAN	• Zafferano
PORTUGUESE	• Açafrão
RUSSIAN	• Shafran
JAPANESE	• Safuran
CHINESE	• Fan-Hung-Hua

SAFFRON

THE slender dried stigmas of the flowers of *Crocus sativus* constitute the true saffron of commerce, the world's most expensive spice. At the present time saffron costs spice dealers from $80 to $120 a pound in large lots in New York and London. The retail price at a fine food store is about 80 cents a gram, that is, about $365 a pound.

The English word "saffron" is derived from the Arabic *za'faran*, meaning yellow, and before the advent of coal-tar dyes saffron was popular as a magnificent yellowish-orange natural dyestuff. Traditionally saffron has been the Western colorant corresponding to turmeric in the East. In recent years, however, saffron has gone the way of such other natural colorings as indigo, madder root, and cochineal.

Crocus sativus, native to southern Europe and Asia Minor, is a small, showy, bulbous perennial, 6 to 10 inches high, and is cultivated for the vivid orange-red, funnel-shaped stigmas in the center of its violet to bluish, lily-shaped flowers. It is one of the familiar garden species of crocus of the iris family.

The plants grow best in a moderate climate and in a rich sandy or loamy soil with excellent drainage. Heavy rains or frost at flowering time may be disastrous. A low annual rainfall, about 15 to 18 inches, is desirable. Major saffron-producing countries include Spain, Turkey, and India.

Saffron plants are propagated vegetatively by planting at 6- by 6-inch intervals the young cormlets that form annually at the base of the bulblike mother corm. The soil should previously be plowed, harrowed, and well cultivated. While the plants may live and bloom for twelve to fifteen years, the progressive deepening of each year's corm in the soil so delays flowering time and so weakens the plant that few commercial plantings are kept for more than five years.

Under favorable conditions an annual per-acre yield of 8 to 12 pounds of dried saffron may be obtained from an established planting. The maximum yield occurs in the third year after planting. In France saffron beds are uprooted and replanted after three years, while in Spain this is done every four years. In Italy saffron is cultivated as an annual, mature corms being set every autumn, but in India the corms remain in the field planting for ten to fifteen years.

When the plants begin to bloom the harvesting commences immediately, for the flowering period may last only fifteen days. The brilliantly colored tripartite stigmas are picked by hand daily, just as the flowers open. About 210,000 dried stigmas, gleaned from about 70,000 flowers, are required to make one pound of true saffron—which is why the cost of production is excessively high. On drying, either in the sun or by artificial heat, the stigmas lose about 80 percent of their weight. In southeastern Spain, where the finest quality saffron is produced, the stigmas are "toasted" or dried in sieves over low heat. Saffron is the only economic product supplied by the stigma, the female organ of

SAFFRON, 1865

flowers.

When fully dried, the saffron must be stored immediately, preferably in tightly covered or sealed tin containers, and protected from light to avoid bleaching. The final product is a compressed, highly aromatic, matted mass of narrow, threadlike, dark orange to reddish-brown strands about an inch long.

As long ago as the first century A.D. Pliny warned that saffron was the most frequently falsified commodity. Ever since, its very high price has led to adulteration of the product by various cheap substitutes—particles of colored wax, shreds of meat, willow roots, safflower flowers, marigold petals, corn silk, and more recently miscellaneous coal-tar-dyed adulterants. Sometimes low-grade saffron has even been treated with urine to give it more color.

True saffron has a pleasantly spicy, pungent, bitter taste and a peculiarly tenacious odor. To be classified as unadulterated in the United States, the product must meet the standards of the Federal Food, Drug and Cosmetic Act of 1938, including regulations subsequently promulgated, defining saffron as "the dried stigma of *Crocus sativus* L. It contains not more than 10 per cent of yellow styles and other foreign matter, not more than 14 per cent of volatile matter when dried at 100° C., not more than 7.5 per cent of total ash, not more than 1 per cent of ash insoluble in hydrochloric acid."

The genuine commodity is a rich source of riboflavin and contains crocin, a reddish-yellow pigment. The coloring power of crocin is so potent that one part of pure crocin is capable of coloring up to 150,000 parts of water unmistakably yellow.

Saffron as a condiment, medicine, and natural dyestuff has been known since remote antiquity, but was used to a much greater extent in olden times than today. It is mentioned in the Old Testament in Song of Solomon 4:13–14:

> Thy plants are an orchard of pomegranates, with pleasant fruits; camphire, with spikenard, Spikenard and saffron; calamus and cinnamon. . . .

In the Graeco-Roman era, saffron was scattered on the floors of the theaters and public halls as a perfume. The extravagant Heliogabalus, Roman emperor in A.D. 220, is said to have bathed in saffron-scented water.

By 960 the Arabs were cultivating saffron in Spain. It is believed that saffron was introduced into Italy, France, and Germany during the thirteenth century by Crusaders who brought back corms from Asia Minor.

As this expensive spice became popular in Europe for coloring and flavoring food, adulteration increased and flourished until the severest laws were enacted. In Nürnberg, Germany, a strict saffron inspection (*Saf-*

ranschau) was organized in 1358 to check on falsification. All spice dealers were required to submit their saffron to critical examination. In 1444 an unfortunate debaser of the product named Findeker was apprehended and burned alive, together with his adulterated saffron. In 1456 Elss Pfragnerin was buried alive in Nürnberg for the same malpractice. Later the German penalty was modified to severe fines instead of death, but the very rigid examination of the spice remained in force until 1797. Similar inspections of saffron were carried out elsewhere in Germany and also in France, where King Henry II, while encouraging the growing of saffron corms, decreed in 1550 that any person who adulterated saffron would be sentenced to corrective corporal punishment.

The plant is said to have been smuggled into England at the end of the fourteenth century by a pilgrim from the Holy Land, who, at the risk of his life, hid a corm in his hollow staff. Whether or not this legend is true, by the sixteenth century saffron was being extensively cultivated in Essex, near the town later to be named Saffron Walden, in recognition of the crop that was to flourish in that region for over four hundred years. Saffron growers there were known as "crokers."

In Shakespeare's time saffron was widely used to color and flavor various foods, such as cakes and pies. In *The Winter's Tale*, Act IV, Scene III, the clown plans what he must buy for the sheep-shearing feast:

. . . I must have saffron, to colour the warden pies. . . .

In the Orient saffron has been used for centuries in the form of a perfume to be sprinkled over the clothing of arriving guests, as a gesture of welcoming hospitality. In India saffron coloring was traditionally employed for caste markings of wealthy individuals.

In times past saffron tea has been thought to revive the spirits and make one optimistic. In sixteenth-century England a cheerful, jolly individual was said to have "slept in a bagge of saffron." Saffron tea was put in canaries' drinking water, and Irish women dyed their sheets with saffron to strengthen their limbs.

Highly esteemed as a medicine three hundred years ago, saffron was considered efficacious as a stimulant, antispasmodic, emmenagogue, and as a remedial treatment for dysentery, measles, and jaundice.

The year 1670 marked the apogee of the medicinal use of saffron. In that year J. F. Hertodt published in Jena, Germany, a thick volume entitled *Crocologia*, to extol its effective potency as a therapeutic cure-all. According to Hertodt saffron could eradicate all sickness, from a simple toothache to the plague.

In recent years, however, the use of saffron as a medicine has declined in the West to insignificance, although it is still used in India and other Far Eastern countries as a tonic and stomachic.

Saffron oil is not readily available commercially, for steam distillation of the dried botanical material yields very little essential oil, 0.6 of 1 percent or less. Meager amounts of tincture of saffron are used in the preparation of Oriental-type perfumes.

The major use for saffron today is in coloring and flavoring foods such as cheeses, butter, pastry, and confectionery. In the culinary department it is an essential ingredient of French bouillabaisse (a mixture of shellfish and fish) and of the well-known Spanish favorites Arroz con Pollo (chicken and rice), Bacalao a la Vizcaina (codfish, Spanish style), and *paella* (meat, fish, rice, and vegetables).

Since its odor is sharp and penetrating, a little saffron goes a long way with foods such as rice, for which it has an affinity. Suggested amounts in recipes should not be exceeded, to avoid a medicinal flavor.

Saffron is available whole, and the individual strands may be used intact or crushed.

Rice Milan Style

½ cup chopped onions
6 tablespoons butter or
   margarine
1½ cups long-grained rice,
   uncooked
3½ cups chicken broth or
   4 chicken bouillon
   cubes in 3½ cups
   boiling water

1 teaspoon salt
⅛ teaspoon ground black
   pepper
1 cup tomato sauce
1⁄16 teaspoon saffron
½ cup grated Parmesan
   cheese

Sauté onions in 3 tablespoons of the butter until golden brown. Add rice and stir constantly 10 minutes or until rice is well coated and translucent. Add chicken broth and salt. Cover and bring to boiling point. Lower heat and simmer 20 minutes or until tender, stirring occasionally to prevent sticking. Add remaining butter, black pepper, tomato sauce, and *saffron*. Sprinkle Parmesan cheese over top. Serve at once.

Yield: 6 servings

Seafood Pilaf

⅓ cup olive or salad oil
1 3-pound chicken, cut
   into serving pieces
½ cup onion rings
1 tomato, diced
1½ cups long-grained rice
3 cups chicken stock
2 tablespoons salt
1 tablespoon paprika
½ teaspoon ground black
   pepper
¼ teaspoon cayenne
⅛ teaspoon crumbled
   saffron

1 pound diced uncooked
   fish
1 package (12 oz.) frozen
   cooked shrimp
6 ounces frozen or canned
   lobster meat
1 package (10 oz.) frozen
   peas
⅓ cup pimiento strips
1 can (1 lb.) artichoke
   hearts

Heat oil in deep saucepan or Dutch oven. Add chicken and brown on all sides. Add onions and brown lightly. Add tomato and cook 2 to 3 minutes. Stir in rice and mix well. Add chicken stock, salt, and spices. Mix well. Cover and cook 10 minutes, stirring frequently. Add fish, shrimp, lobster, and peas. Cook, covered, 10 minutes or until rice is done. Stir in pimiento and artichoke hearts. Cook 5 minutes. Serve at once.

Yield: 8 servings

Holiday Saffron Cake

1 cup mashed potatoes
1½ cups sugar
1 package active dry yeast
¼ teaspoon saffron
1 cup milk
½ cup shortening

2 eggs, well beaten
½ teaspoon salt
8 cups all-purpose flour,
  approximately
Cinnamon Topping

Mix thoroughly potatoes and ½ cup of the sugar. Dissolve yeast in 1 cup lukewarm water, add to potato-sugar mixture, cover, and let rise in warm place about 2 hours. Meantime, pour ¼ cup boiling water over *saffron* to draw out color and flavoring. Bring milk to boiling point, add shortening, eggs, remaining 1 cup sugar, and salt. Carefully drain *saffron water* into this mixture; when this is lukewarm add the yeast mixture and 4 cups of the flour. Beat well. Cover and let rise until bubbly, from 1 to 1½ hours. Add remaining flour or enough to make a dough that can be kneaded until smooth. Place in greased bowl. Cover and let rise about 4 hours or until doubled in bulk and light. Roll about ⅓ inch thick and place in four greased 9-inch baking pans. Brush tops with either melted butter, cream, or beaten egg; cover with cinnamon topping. Let rise about 1 hour. Bake in preheated moderate oven (325°F.) 20 to 25 minutes.

CINNAMON TOPPING

2½ cups flour
2 cups light brown sugar
1 teaspoon ground
  cinnamon

1/16 teaspoon saffron
1 cup shortening

Mix well with hands.   **Yield: Four 9-inch cakes**

Arroz Con Pollo

2½- to 3-pound chicken,
  cut into serving pieces
⅓ cup olive or salad oil
1 cup finely chopped onion
1 green pepper, chopped
2½ teaspoons salt
1 teaspoon oregano leaves
½ teaspoon ground black
  pepper
½ teaspoon instant garlic
  powder

1 can (1 lb. 12 oz.)
  tomatoes, chopped
½ cup chopped smoked
  ham
¼ cup sliced green olives
1 teaspoon salt
¼ teaspoon crushed saffron
1 cup long-grained rice
1 package (12 oz.) frozen
  peas

In large kettle brown chicken on all sides in hot oil about 15 minutes. Add onion and green pepper; sauté about 5 minutes or until limp. Add seasonings, tomatoes, ham, and olives. Cover and simmer until chicken is tender (about 35 to 40 minutes). Bring 3 cups water, salt, and *saffron* to boil. Add rice. Reduce heat; cook until water is absorbed, about 25 minutes. Cook peas according to package directions. Add rice and peas to chicken. Place in serving casserole. Serve hot with pimiento strips, if desired.

Yield: 6 servings

SAGE

Salvia officinalis L.

A. **Flowering branch**
1. **Flower, side view**
2. **Vertical section of flower**
3. **Corolla opened out**
4, 5. **Stamen showing elongated connectives**
6. **Sterile stamens (staminodia)**
7. **Pollen grain**
8. **Calyx opened showing pistil**
9. **Pistil showing style**
10. **Transverse section through fruit showing 4 nutlets**
11. **Vertical section of fruit**
12. **Calyx**
13. **Cluster of 4 nutlets**
14. **Single nutlet**
15. **Nutlet enlarged**
16. **Transverse section of nutlet**
17. **Vertical section of nutlet**
18. **Nutlet with pericarp removed**

SAGE

Family: Labiatae

LATIN	• <u>Salvia officinalis L.</u>
SPANISH	• Salvia
FRENCH	• Sauge
GERMAN	• Salbei
SWEDISH	• Salvia
ARABIC	• Mariyamiya
DUTCH	• Salie
ITALIAN	• Salvia
PORTUGUESE	• Salva
RUSSIAN	• Shalfey
JAPANESE	• Sêji
CHINESE	• Ching-Chieh

SAGE

SAGE, *Salvia officinalis,* is a hardy, erect, much-branched, evergreen shrub of the mint family indigenous to the Mediterranean region. The condiment is prepared from the dried leaves of this plant.

The generic name *Salvia* may have been derived from the Latin *salvere*, to save or to heal, referring to the healing powers ascribed to this medicinal herb in antiquity. In ancient Greece and Rome sage was generally not used as a seasoning in classical cookery, but rather as a heroic medicinal remedy alleged to cure snake bites, invigorate the brain, and act as a general tonic for mind and body, thus promoting longevity. Its therapeutic virtues were mentioned and praised by such ancient naturalists and scholars as Theophrastus, Dioscorides, and Pliny.

The Romans called it the *herba sacra*, and the Italian medical school at Salerno declared: "Cur moriatur homo cui salvia crescit in horto?" (Why should a man die who grows sage in his garden?)

During the Middle Ages herbalists considered sage an indispensable medicine for the cure of, among other maladies, constipation, cholera, the common cold, fevers, the palsy, liver trouble, and epilepsy. It was taken as a tonic to promote the flow of fresh, new blood in the body, strengthen the muscles, and calm the nerves. In medieval England this proverb prevailed:

> He that would live for aye,
> Must eat sage in May.

Charlemagne in the ninth century included sage among the herbs to be grown on the imperial farms in Germany. The herb gradually became well known throughout Europe, and when introduced to China it became the chief ingredient in a highly esteemed beverage in that country. During the seventeenth century the Chinese would exchange three or four pounds of their tea to Dutch traders in the Far East for one pound of European sage leaves.

In sixteenth-century England, years before tea was known, an infusion of sage leaves, later to be called sage tea, was a popular pleasant and healthful beverage.

By the early nineteenth century the herb had been introduced to American gardens, while in England Charles Lamb, in his "A Dissertation upon Roast Pig," recommended the use of sage in the preparation of pig stuffing.

Over the centuries and especially during the past three hundred years the use of sage as a condiment in cooking has increased, more or less commensurate with the decrease of its use as a medicinal cure-all. It is no longer officially recognized as a drug in the U. S. Pharmacopeia.

Although for many years sage was the most popular American culinary herb, since World War II it has been challenged by oregano and now must share top honors with the "pizza herb."

Sage is a well-established culinary herb in most

countries of the world with a temperate climate. The best quality sage has traditionally been grown near the Adriatic Sea, in Dalmatia, a region of Yugoslavia. It is also produced in Albania, Italy, the Soviet Union, Turkey, and Greece; in the United States it is cultivated commercially in California, Washington, and Oregon.

There are more than five hundred species of the genus *Salvia,* of which the most important for culinary purposes is *Salvia officinalis,* also known as "garden sage" or "true sage." This wiry-stemmed plant grows to about 2 feet high, its oblong leaves are $1\frac{1}{2}$ to 2 inches long, grayish-green, and hairy and have a pebbly texture above. The flowers are pale blue or purplish and usually appear in July or August of the second season. The popular sage honey owes its distinctive flavor to their aromatic bouquet.

Other species of sage in culinary use include *Salvia sclarea* L. (clary), and *Salvia pratensis* L. (meadow). The flowers and seeds of clary, sometimes called "clear eye," have been used medicinally in a limited way for the treatment of inflammation of the eye.

Although garden sage (*S. officinalis*) can be grown from seed, commercial propagation is by cuttings. The plants grow under a wide range of conditions, but do best on a rich clay loam with good drainage, in a sunny location.

For commercial crops the plants are spaced about 18 inches apart, with 3 feet between the rows. The first year's crop is small, but in the second and succeeding years a harvest of 1,200 to 2,000 pounds per acre of dried sage leaves is to be expected from two cuttings. Light cultivation is necessary to eliminate weeds that would spoil the flavor of the herb. The harvested crop consists of the top eight inches of growth, cut just before the flower spikes are produced. Careful drying in the shade for six or seven days is recommended to preserve the essential oil content and retain the natural gray-green color of the leaves. The dried leaves are then separated from the stems and should be stored in airtight containers. After some four years of growth, the plants become woody, and the planting is reestablished.

During World War II domestic production of sage became commercially important in the United States. High domestic labor costs of harvesting have led, in recent years, to increased importation of Dalmatian sage, and some 2,800,000 pounds of sage are imported annually into the United States from Yugoslavia.

On steam distillation the dried sage leaves yield from 1.5 to 2.5 percent of a pale yellow, spicy essential oil used extensively for flavoring sausages, canned meats, seasonings, and liqueurs. Sage oil is used in perfumery for blending with other essential oils in colognes and men's toilet lotions. Its limited bactericidal qualities have led to its being used also in mouthwashes and gargles.

The odor of the dried sage leaves is highly aromatic and fragrant. The taste is pungent and slightly bitter.

Sage is available whole, rubbed (crushed), or ground. Because it has an unusual flavor affinity for fats, abundant in pork and other meats, it is an important ingredient in sausages and in poultry seasoning. The meat-packing industry consumes large quantities of sage.

The chopped fresh leaves may be used to flavor salads, pickles, and cheese.

Sage Walnut Squash

3 large acorn squash
¼ cup butter or margarine, melted
½ teaspoon ground sage
⅛ teaspoon ground thyme
⅛ teaspoon ground black pepper
½ teaspoon salt

2 cups unflavored croutons
1 cup toasted walnuts, coarsely chopped
1 can (6 oz.) chopped mushrooms, drained
1 tablespoon butter or margarine, melted

Wash squash, cut in half lengthwise, and with a spoon scrape out seeds and stringy portion. Place, cut side down, in a baking pan. Pour in boiling water to depth of ¼ inch. Bake in a preheated hot oven (400°F.) 30 minutes. In the meantime, blend together the ¼ cup of melted butter or margarine, *sage,* thyme, black pepper, and salt. In a large bowl combine croutons and walnuts. Add drained mushrooms and butter mixture; toss lightly to blend. Turn cooked squash cut side up and fill with walnut mixture. Brush cut surface with 1 tablespoon of melted butter or margarine. Place in baking pan and bake in a preheated moderate oven (375°F.) 40 minutes or until squash is tender.

Yield: 6 servings

Sage-Stuffed Turkey

¾ cup butter or margarine	12 cups toasted bread cubes
1 cup chopped onion	¾ cup turkey stock or
1 cup diced celery	water
½ cup parsley flakes	2 eggs, beaten
4 teaspoons poultry	12- to 15-pound ready-to-
seasoning	cook turkey
3 teaspoons salt	Salt
½ teaspoon ground black	Butter or margarine for
pepper	basting
¾ teaspoon sage leaves	

Melt butter in large skillet. Add onions and cook until limp. Blend in remaining ingredients except turkey, salt, and basting butter. Sprinkle inside of turkey lightly with salt. Fill body cavity and crop loosely with stuffing. Fasten neck skin to back with skewer. Fold wings flat against body. Lace body cavity with skewers and string to hold stuffing. Tie legs together and fasten to tail. Brush outside skin with melted butter or margarine. Roast using favorite turkey-roasting method.

Yield: Sufficient stuffing for 12–15 pound ready-to-cook turkey

Cheese-Filled Celery

1 carton (8 oz.) creamy
  cottage cheese
1 package (3 oz.) cream
  cheese
2 tablespoons sour cream
1 teaspoon instant minced
  onion

½ teaspoon salt
¼ teaspoon ground sage
⅛ teaspoon ground black
  pepper
9 ribs celery, cut into
  3-inch pieces

Combine cottage cheese, cream cheese, and sour cream.
Blend in onion, salt, *sage,* and black pepper. Fill crisp
celery ribs neatly with knife or press through cake
decorator tube. Serve chilled as an appetizer or salad
accompaniment.

Yield: 27 3-inch pieces

Minestrone

2 pounds beef soupbone
1½ teaspoons salt
3 slices bacon, diced
2 cups shredded cabbage
½ cup celery flakes
2 tablespoons onion flakes
2 tablespoons parsley flakes
1 cup sliced carrots
2 cups diced potatoes
1 package (9 oz.) frozen
  Italian-style green beans
1 package (10 oz.) frozen
  zucchini

1 can (20 oz.) red kidney
  beans
1 can (1 lb.) tomatoes
1 tablespoon salt
1 teaspoon ground sage
½ teaspoon celery salt
¼ teaspoon ground black
  pepper
¼ teaspoon instant garlic
  powder
Grated Parmesan cheese

Place soupbone, 2 quarts water, and the 1½ teaspoons
of salt in a large kettle. Cover. Simmer until meat is
tender, 2 to 3 hours. Remove bone, trim off meat, discard bone, and add meat to stock. In skillet sauté bacon
with cabbage. Add to stock with celery, onion, and
parsley flakes, vegetables, and seasonings. Cover. Simmer 30 minutes or until vegetables are tender. Serve
with Parmesan cheese sprinkled over the soup if desired.

Yield: 12–16 servings

Bavarian Ham and Cabbage

2 tablespoons instant
  minced onion
2 tablespoons water
3 tablespoons butter or
  margarine
1 teaspoon ground sage
1½ teaspoons caraway seed

⅛ teaspoon ground black
  pepper
2-pound head cabbage,
  shredded
¾ pound slivered cooked
  ham
1 teaspoon salt

Combine onion with water and allow to stand for 10 minutes to soften. Melt butter or margarine in a large, heavy skillet. Add *sage,* caraway, black pepper, and onion and sauté 2 minutes. Stir in cabbage. Cover and cook 10 to 15 minutes or until crisp-tender, stirring once. Toss in ham and salt and cook until ham is hot. Serve immediately.

Yield: 6 servings

Sage Chicken Supreme

4- to 5-pound fricassee
  chicken, cut into serving
  pieces
2 teaspoons salt
2½ teaspoons sage leaves

⅛ teaspoon instant onion
  powder
Dash instant garlic powder
1 envelope unflavored
  gelatin

Place chicken on a rack in a 5-quart Dutch oven or kettle. Add 2 cups cold water, salt, and *sage.* Cover. Bring to boiling point. Lower heat and simmer until tender (about 2 hours). Remove chicken. Skim off fat and strain broth. Stir in onion and garlic powder. Soften gelatin in ¼ cup cold water and stir into hot broth. Pour into 8- by 8- by 2-inch pan or into individual molds. Chill until ready to serve. Remove skin from chicken. Cut in slices and arrange on platter. Cut the jellied broth into squares and arrange on platter with chicken.

Yield: 6–8 servings

SAVORY
Satureja hortensis L.

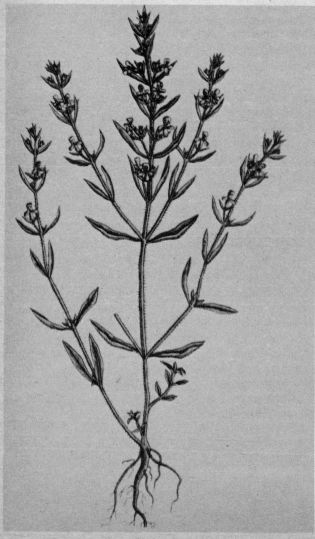

Family: *Labiatae*

LATIN	• **Satureja hortensis L.**
SPANISH	• Ajedrea
FRENCH	• Sarriette
GERMAN	• Bohnenkraut
SWEDISH	• Kyndel
ARABIC	• Nadgh
DUTCH	• Bonenkruid
ITALIAN	• Santoreggia
PORTUGUESE	• Segurelha
RUSSIAN	• Chabyor
CHINESE	• Hsiang Po Ho
JAPANESE	• Saborî

SAVORY

SUMMER savory, *Satureja hortensis,* the savory of commerce, is a small slender herbaceous annual of the mint family indigenous to southern Europe and the Mediterranean region. Winter savory, *Satureja montana* L., is a hardy woody perennial less popular as a culinary herb than is the more delicately flavored summer savory. The highly aromatic leaves and tender tips, used either fresh or dried, provide the condiment.

Savory was renowned in ancient Rome as a potherb and seasoning. Mixed with vinegar it was served as a sauce during feasts. Early records indicate that savory, which is peppery in flavor, was known to the Romans before the first lot of true pepper had been imported from India.

As the Latin name *Satureja* implies, the genus was supposed to have been the chosen plant of the satyrs, and may explain why the plant was once regarded as an aphrodisiac. The herb, reputed to have medicinal value as a tonic and stomachic, was also recommended for the treatment of bee and wasp stings. Virgil, in the first century B.C. grew savory as ambrosia for his bees and mentioned it as one of the most fragrant of condimental herbs.

The Romans brought savory to England, where it was called "savorie" in old Anglo-Saxon cooking recipes, and it became an important ingredient in "farsing" or stuffing.

By Shakespeare's time, this herb was widely known, and is mentioned in *The Winter's Tale*, Act IV, Scene IV:

> *Perdita:* Here's flow'rs for you:
> Hot lavender, mints, savory, marjoram. . . .

Savory was one of the first plants introduced to America by the colonists. Today the principal commercial plantings of summer savory in the United States are in California. European countries that export savory to the United States include Yugoslavia, France, and Spain.

Summer savory has slender, hairy, erect, branching stems that grow to 15 inches in height. The narrowly ovate leaves are soft dark green, about $\frac{1}{4}$ to $\frac{1}{2}$ inch long and blunt-tipped. The small flowers are lavender, pink, or white.

Propagation is usually by seed. Savory grows well in most temperate climates, in full sun on light, rich, well-drained loams. Commercially the seed is sown in April in rows 30 inches apart, with plants at 6-inch intervals within the rows. The harvest should take place just before flowering, about 75 to 120 days after sowing. The cut herbage is usually dried in the shade and then stored in closed containers to avoid loss of the aromatic essential oil.

Savory is known as the "bean herb" in Europe. In German it is called *Bohnenkraut* or *Pfefferkraut* ("pepper herb"), an allusion to its fragrant piquant flavor, reminiscent of pepper, which makes it blend well with beans, peas, and lentils.

The dried leaves, brownish-green in color, are available whole or ground. Savory blends well with other herbs, as in a mixture of Italian seasoning or *fines herbes*, bringing out their flavor without overpowering them. Used alone or in combination with other condiments, it makes an excellent flavoring for poultry seasoning, meats, soups, eggs, salads, and sauces. For garnishing it may be used as a refreshing substitute for parsley.

Savory was formerly used in medicines as a carminative and expectorant, but its importance today is almost entirely culinary.

On steam distillation, savory leaves yield up to about 1 per cent of a pale yellow, spicy essential oil. Savory oil has a sharp bitter flavor and is of limited use in the food industry for flavoring canned meats, seasonings, and pickles. Small quantities of the oil are also employed in perfumery for blending with other essential oils in the preparation of colognes.

Savory, an herb of minor importance, is also one of the least expensive. In recent years the price of savory imported from Yugoslavia has occasionally been as low as 7 cents per pound.

Savory Green Beans

1 package (9 oz.) frozen
  cut green beans
2 tablespoons butter or
  margarine
½ teaspoon ground savory

⅟₁₆ teaspoon salt
⅟₁₆ teaspoon ground
  black pepper
1 teaspoon lemon juice

Cook beans according to package directions. Meanwhile, melt butter in a small skillet; stir and cook until dark brown. Add remaining ingredients. Drain beans; pour brown butter sauce over beans and toss lightly.

Yield: 3–4 servings

Fisherman's Chowder

¼ pound salt pork, sliced
⅛ inch thick
2 medium potatoes, peeled
and sliced ¼ inch thick
¼ cup onion flakes
1 package (1 lb.) frozen
flounder fillets

2 teaspoons parsley flakes
1½ teaspoons salt
1 teaspoon ground savory
⅛ teaspoon ground black
pepper
2 cups milk

In a large saucepan fry pork until crisp. Remove cracklings from fat; reserve. Add 2 cups boiling water, potatoes, and onion flakes. Bring to boiling point. Reduce
heat and simmer, covered, 8 minutes. Add frozen fish
and seasonings and cook until fish flakes (about 10 to
12 minutes). Add reserved pork cracklings and milk.
Heat only until hot. Do not boil.

Yield: 6 cups or 6 servings

Confetti Salad Dressing

2 teaspoons instant minced
onion
⅔ cup salad oil
⅓ cup white vinegar
2 tablespoons dry white
wine
1 tablespoon chopped
pimiento

1½ teaspoons savory,
crumbled
1¼ teaspoons salt
½ teaspoon sugar
⅛ teaspoon ground black
pepper

Mix minced onion with 2 teaspoons water; let stand 10
minutes to soften. In a small jar combine softened onion
with remaining ingredients. Shake well. Serve over lettuce wedges, chilled green beans, or cold asparagus
spears.

Yield: Approximately 1¼ cups

SESAME SEED

Sesamum indicum L.

SESAME SEED

Family: Pedaliaceae

LATIN	• <u>Sesamum indicum</u> L.
SPANISH	• Ajonjolí
FRENCH	• Sésame
GERMAN	• Sesam
SWEDISH	• Sesam
ARABIC	• Simsim
DUTCH	• Sesam
ITALIAN	• Sesamo
PORTUGUESE	• Gergelim
RUSSIAN	• Kunzhut
JAPANESE	• Goma
CHINESE	• Hu-Ma

SESAME SEED

SESAME, *Sesamum indicum,* is an erect annual herb 2 to 4 feet high of the Pedaliaceae (sesame family). Although indigenous to Indonesia and tropical Africa, it has been cultivated since earliest times in most hot countries of the Old World for its small seeds, which contain about 50 percent of a fixed vegetable oil used in cooking. The seeds and leaves traditionally have been eaten as a food in Africa and India, while in most other countries sesame has been and still is grown for its oil.

Sesame may be the oldest condiment known to man. In any event, it is probably the oldest crop grown for its edible oil, for records of sesame production in the Tigris and Euphrates valleys date back to 1600 B.C.

The Egyptian name for sesame, *sesemt,* is mentioned in the list of medicinal drugs recorded in the sixty-five-foot long scroll of the Ebers Papyrus, dated about 1550 B.C.

Recent archeological diggings in Turkey indicate that between 900 and 700 B.C. in the empire of Urartu (now Armenia) sesame seed was grown and pressed to extract its oil. Now, 2,700 years later, some sesame seed mash has been found in one of the chambers excavated in the ruins of a fortified town of this kingdom, known in the Old Testament as Ararat.

In the tale of Ali Baba and the forty thieves, in *The Thousand and One Nights,* a password was needed to open the door of the robbers' den. The magical command "Open Sesame" may have been chosen because sesame was a common word that would have been familiar to early readers of *The Arabian Nights.* Or perhaps it was chosen because the sesame seeds when ripe burst from their pods suddenly with a sharp pop, like the springing open of a lock.

During the first century A.D. sesame oil was imported from Sind (Pakistan) and India to Europe via the Red Sea. By the Middle Ages the plant was grown in Egypt and exported from Alexandria to Venice. Marco Polo reported in 1298 that in Persia, where they had no olive oil, they were using oil of sesame for cooking purposes.

Meanwhile, the use of sesame as a food as well as an edible oil became widespread in Africa, and during the seventeenth and eighteenth centuries sesame seeds, then known as *benne,* were brought to America by the slaves. The seeds were looked upon as tokens of good luck, and the comforting oil was used as an all-round medicine and a laxative. In parts of the American South sesame is still known as benne.

An annual plant, sesame is grown only from seed. It thrives best in light, friable, sandy, well-drained loam in warm temperature with moderate rainfall and needs a fairly long growing season (about four months) to mature its seed.

The seed may be broadcast or planted with a seed drill in rows 2 to 4 feet apart, at the rate of 8 to 10 pounds per acre. The capsule, about 1 inch long and containing numerous seeds, tends to shatter very early in its maturation. The pods commence to ripen at the base instead of the top of the plant. The delicate harvesting operation should start when the upper pods are well formed but still green if seed loss due to shattering is to be minimized. The crop is cut, tied in bundles, and shocked like corn. After threshing, drying, and cleaning, the seed is stored in a protected place to prevent rodent depredation. Under favorable conditions seed yields of 500 to 750 pounds per acre are normal. In an effort to obtain higher yields, selected nonshattering varieties of sesame have been developed through plant breeding in Venezuela and other Latin American countries.

The seed is small, flattish, glossy, and oval-shaped, about $\frac{1}{8}$ inch in length, $\frac{1}{20}$ inch thick, and is usually available hulled or unhulled but seldom ground. The hulled seed is pearl white in color. The unhulled seed varies in color, depending on the variety, from yellowish-white through red and brown to black.

Total world production of sesame seed is close to 4 billion pounds per year, most of which is converted to oil. China is the world's largest producer. Other important producing countries include India, Ethiopia, Nicaragua, the Sudan, Mexico, Guatemala, and the United States. In this country sesame is grown extensively in the Southwest, especially in Texas, Louisiana, California, and Arizona.

The primary demand for sesame seed is for its fixed oil, obtained by expression. The yield varies from 44 to 57 percent. This nearly tasteless oil, pale yellow in color, is clear and rarely becomes rancid. It is usually expressed commercially in three steps. The first cold pressing produces the best oil, which is ready to use after filtering; the next two pressings of the residue, employing heat, yield murky, inferior oils that must be purified. After expression, the remaining cake is used as a high-protein cattle food or as a fertilizer.

In Europe and the United States sesame oil is of great

importance in the production of margarine and such other food products as salad oil and good quality cooking oils.

The recent emphasis on low cholesterol diets has caused sesame oil to enjoy an increase in demand, for it is one of the important sources of polyunsaturated fats.

The seed itself is used by bakers as a decorative condiment sprinkled on rolls and bread and in the preparation of such other baked goods as biscuits and crackers. The toasted seeds give sesame sauce its tasty, nutty flavor.

Considerable tonnage of hulled sesame seed is used in the Jewish candy halvah and other sweet confections. In the Middle East sesame paste is used in cooking and spread on bread instead of butter.

Niu bi tang, a sweet, gummy malt candy heavily covered with sesame seed, is a popular confection in Chinese restaurants throughout the world. Sesame seed is extensively utilized in China in preparing many different candies and sweets.

Sesame oil has been used traditionally in India.as a ghee substitute, for anointing the body, and in medicine as a tonic and laxative. In France the oil is used in the preparation of perfumes, soaps, and cosmetics. In China, Africa, and India it is used as an illuminant.

Since sesame seeds do not contain an essential oil, they cannot strictly be included in the category of aromatic spices, although they are a versatile condiment with a mild, sweet, nutlike flavor.

Quick Sesame Blueberry Coffee Cake

2 tablespoons all-purpose flour
¼ cup brown sugar, packed
½ teaspoon ground cinnamon

2 tablespoons butter or margarine
1 package blueberry muffin mix
2 tablespoons sesame seed, toasted

Combine flour, brown sugar, cinnamon, and butter; mix lightly with a fork until crumbly. Set aside. Combine blueberry muffin mix with *sesame seed* and prepare according to package directions. Turn into greased and lightly floured 8-inch square baking pan. Sprinkle with crumb topping. Bake in preheated hot oven (400°F.) 20 to 25 minutes, or until cake tester inserted in center comes out clean. Remove to rack; cut in squares; serve warm.

Yield: One 8-inch cake

Chocolate Pie With Sesame Seed Crust

3 envelopes no-melt chocolate
2¼ cups milk
1 cup sugar
¼ teaspoon salt
½ teaspoon ground cinnamon
¼ teaspoon ground cloves
4 tablespoons cornstarch
2 tablespoons butter or margarine

3 large egg yolks
1 teaspoon pure vanilla extract
8-inch baked pie shell made with 2 tablespoons sesame seed
2 tablespoons sesame seed, toasted*
Chocolate for garnish

In the top of double boiler, over boiling water, empty envelopes of chocolate and gradually stir in 2 cups of the milk. In a bowl mix ½ cup of the sugar and salt, cinnamon, cloves, and cornstarch. Blend in the ¼ cup of milk. Add mixture to heated chocolate and milk. Continue to stir and cook for 6 minutes, or until very thick. Cover and continue cooking 12 minutes. Stir twice. Blend in butter or margarine. Beat egg yolks lightly and blend with remaining ½ cup of sugar. Blend in a little of the hot mixture and stir into remaining hot filling. Cook over hot (not boiling) water 10 minutes, or until very thick. Remove from heat and add vanilla. Cool. Pour into cold *sesame seed* pie shell. (If commercial pie shell is purchased, sprinkle with *sesame seed* and lightly press in before baking.) Top with chocolate curls and toasted *sesame seed* before serving.

Yield: One 8-inch pie

Sesame Cheese Wafers

1 cup sifted all-purpose
 flour
1 cup grated Parmesan
 cheese
¼ cup butter or margarine
¾ teaspoon powdered
 mustard

¾ teaspoon water
6 tablespoons sour cream
¹⁄₁₆ teaspoon ground
 black pepper
2 teaspoons sesame seed
2 tablespoons butter or
 margarine, melted

In a large bowl combine sifted flour and grated cheese.
With a pastry blender or two knives, cut in the ¼ cup
butter or margarine until mixture resembles corn meal.
Combine powdered mustard and water; let stand 10 minutes for flavor to develop. Combine mustard with sour
cream, black pepper, and *sesame seed*. Add to flour
mixture; blend well. Shape mixture into a roll about 9
inches long. Wrap in waxed paper and chill in coldest
part of refrigerator for several hours or overnight. Cut
roll into very thin slices (about ⅛ inch thick). Arrange
on cookie sheets; brush with melted butter or margarine
and bake in a preheated moderate oven (350°F.) 12 to
15 minutes or until lightly browned. Remove to racks to
cool.

Yield: Approximately 5 dozen wafers

Fillet of Sole With Shrimp-Sesame Sauce

1½ cups soft bread crumbs,
 toasted
4 tablespoons sesame seed,
 toasted*
1 tablespoon instant minced
 onion
½ teaspoon salt
½ teaspoon ground thyme
⅛ teaspoon ground white
 pepper

3 tablespoons butter or
 margarine, melted
1½ pounds fillet of sole
 (cut into 6 serving
 pieces)
2 packages (1⅝ oz.)
 hollandaise sauce mix
½ pound peeled and
 deveined cooked shrimp

Combine bread crumbs, 2 tablespoons of the *sesame
seeds,* onion, salt, thyme, pepper, butter, and 2 tablespoons water. Mix well. Spoon equal amount on each

piece of fish fillet; roll and fasten with toothpick. Place fish in buttered baking dish. Prepare hollandaise sauce according to package directions. Add remaining 2 tablespoons *sesame seed.* Spoon over fish rolls. Bake in preheated moderate oven (350°F.) 20 to 25 minutes or until fish is flaky. Garnish with shrimp, spooning sauce over some of the shrimp.

Yield: 6 servings

* To toast *sesame seed,* bake in a preheated moderate oven (350°F.) 20 to 22 minutes. Stir once or twice to toast uniformly.

Sesame Seed Bologna Casserole

1 tablespoon instant minced onion
⅛ teaspoon instant minced garlic
1 tablespoon water
3 cups bologna, cut in small cubes
3 tablespoons butter or margarine
1 can (10½ oz.) cream of celery soup
3 tablespoons sesame seed, toasted
½ teaspoon salt
⅛ teaspoon ground black pepper
1 package (8 oz.) broad noodles
1 tablespoon sweet pepper flakes
½ cup buttered soft bread crumbs
2 tablespoons sesame seed, toasted

Mix minced onion, minced garlic, and water. Let stand 10 minutes. Sauté softened onion and garlic and bologna in butter or margarine until vegetables are lightly browned. Add next 4 ingredients. Mix well. In the meantime, cook noodles and sweet pepper flakes in boiling salted water according to noodle package directions. Drain. Fill a greased 1½-quart casserole with alternate layers of noodles and bologna mixture, beginning with noodles and ending with bologna. Sprinkle with combined bread crumbs and the 2 tablespoons of *sesame seed.* Bake in a preheated moderate oven (350°F.) for 35 minutes or until crumbs are brown.

Yield: 6 servings

Sesame Halibut Steaks

1¼ teaspoons salt
6 halibut steaks, serving-
  sized
3 teaspoons salad oil
2 cups soft bread crumbs
¾ teaspoon ground black
  pepper

2 tablespoons sesame seed,
  toasted
1 teaspoon grated dried
  orange peel
⅓ cup salad oil

Rub salt on both sides of fish. Arrange in an oiled 11½- by 7½- by 2-inch baking pan. Rub ½ teaspoon salad oil into the top of each piece of fish. Combine remaining ingredients. Sprinkle over fish. Bake in a preheated moderate oven (350°F.) 30 minutes or until bread crumbs are brown. Serve hot.

Yield: 6 servings

TARRAGON
Artemisia dracunculus L.

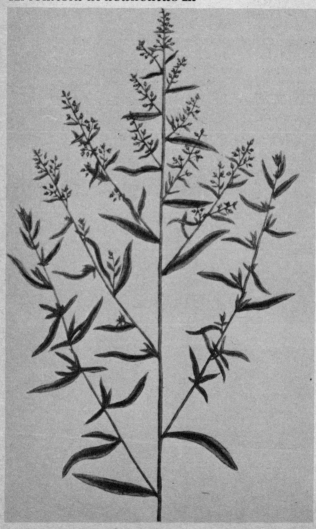

TARRAGON

Family: Compositae

LATIN	• <u>Artemisia dracunculus L.</u>
SPANISH	• Estragón
FRENCH	• Estragon
GERMAN	• Estragon
SWEDISH	• Dragon
ARABIC	• Tarkhūn
DUTCH	• Dragon
ITALIAN	• Targone
PORTUGUESE	• Estragão
RUSSIAN	• Estragon
CHINESE	• Ai-Hao
JAPANESE	• Esutoragon

TARRAGON

TARRAGON, *Artemisia dracunculus,* is a small herbaceous perennial plant of the *Compositae* (sunflower family) indigenous to southern Russia and western Asia.

The fragrant leaves, fresh or dried, are used as a condimental seasoning in salads, soups, stews, sauces, and vinegar. Tarragon's peculiar bittersweet flavor has made it one of the most popular of culinary herbs, expecially in Europe.

The English word tarragon is a corruption of the French *estragon*, or "little dragon," derived from the Arabic *tarkhūn*. Some writers believe that the herb was given this name because of its supposed efficacy in curing bites of venomous reptiles, while others claim the designation alludes to the coiled serpentlike roots of the plant.

Historically, tarragon is a relative Johnny-come-lately among the culinary herbs. Apparently it was virtually unknown in the Graeco-Roman era, and only rarely is it mentioned in works of medieval times. Although alluded to briefly in the thirteenth century by Ibn-al-Baytar, an Arabian botanist and pharmacist of Spain, as a seasoning for vegetables and as a sleep-inducing drug and breath sweetener, it really did not become well known as a condiment until the sixteenth century.

About 1548 it was introduced to England, and by 1597 John Gerard mentioned it in *Gerard's Herball*.

John Evelyn (1620–1706) an eminent diarist of his era, described the tops and young shoots of tarragon as "highly cordial and friendly to the head, heart, and liver."

By 1806 the herb had been introduced to the United States, where it is now grown commercially in California. Currently tarragon is grown in the Soviet Union and throughout most of Europe, and it is especially popular in France. The United States imports tarragon from France and Yugoslavia.

The two cultivated species of tarragon are the piquant French *Artemisia dracunculus*, sometimes called the "true" tarragon, and the less flavorsome Russian *Artemisia dracunculoides* Pursh. Both species are shrubby erect perennials; the former grows to about 2½ feet in height while the hardier Russian species may grow to 5 feet. The French tarragon leaves are smoother, glossier, darker in color, and more pungent and aromatic than are the Russian. Most commercial production is of the more popular French tarragon.

Tarragon grows well in most temperate climates, although it does best in warm, dry, well-drained, light soils in a sunny location. Since the small, inconspicuous green flowers of the cultivated plant seldom set fertile seed, propagation is normally by cuttings or root divisions. Early spring planting is recommended, at a spacing of about 18 by 30 inches. Two or three crops of the young herbage may be harvested annually. Care must be taken to protect the plants from severe frost and excessive moisture. "Wet feet" must be avoided. In northern climates, mulching is recommended in the winter.

When the plants are well established, the green leaves and tender top growth may be harvested at intervals during the growing season by cutting the stems a few inches above ground level. The freshly cut crop is shade-dried to preserve the leaf color and is then stored in closed containers to retain as much as possible of the warmly aromatic, licorice-anise aroma.

After three or four years the planting should be renewed by digging up, dividing, and replanting the roots of the older plants.

On steam distillation the herb yields about 0.3 to 1 percent of a pale yellow essential oil with an anise-like odor. Tarragon oil, also known as estragon oil, is produced mainly in southern France for use in perfumery, in the manufacture of scented toilet preparations, in canning pickles, and in flavoring vinegar and liqueurs.

Tarragon is a versatile and distinguished gourmet's herb. Available whole or ground, it blends well with tomato juice, *fines herbes*, and fish sauces, or may be sprinkled on fresh salads, meats, and stews. It has a special affinity for chicken and lobster. Its flavor is so pungently distinctive, however, that it is best to use it sparingly.

Tarragon vinegar, a favorite of culinary connoisseurs, is prepared by saturating the fresh or dried herb in wine vinegar. It creates a tasty salad dressing or adds distinctive flavor to sauces such as béarnaise, tartare, and hollandaise.

Roast Tarragon Chicken

5- to 6-pound roasting
  chicken
2 tablespoons lemon juice
2½ teaspoons salt

½ cup butter or margarine,
  softened
1½ teaspoons tarragon
  leaves

Brush chicken, inside and out, with lemon juice and salt. Mix butter with *tarragon* and generously rub skin of chicken, saving some *tarragon* butter to place in cavity of chicken. Place chicken on rack in roasting pan; roast in moderate oven (375°F.) for 1 hour and 20 minutes or until done. Baste occasionally with pan drippings. Serve with roasted potatoes, cooked carrots, green beans, and white onions.

Yield: 4 servings

Sauce Tarragon

¼ cup white wine
2 tablespoons wine vinegar
2 tablespoons tarragon
  leaves
1 teaspoon coarse ground
  black pepper
4 egg yolks

2 tablespoons butter or
  margarine
½ cup melted butter or
  margarine
⅛ teaspoon salt
1/16 teaspoon cayenne

In small saucepan cook together wine, vinegar, 1 tablespoon of the *tarragon leaves,* and black pepper until reduced by three quarters (about 10 minutes). Strain. Place thickened mixture in top of double boiler. Add egg yolks and 1 tablespoon water. Place double boiler top over hot water. With wire whip, beat yolk mixture until thick and lemon-colored. Slowly add the 2 tablespoons butter, 1 tablespoon at a time, then the ½ cup of melted butter, very slowly, beating constantly until all butter is added and sauce is thick. Remove from heat and beat in the remaining 1 tablespoon of *tarragon* and remaining ingredients until well blended. Sauce may be served with any of the following: boiled new potatoes, green beans, cooked carrots, broccoli, tomatoes, fish, sliced chicken.

Yield: Approximately 1½ cups

Pickled French Button Mushrooms

1 tablespoon wine vinegar
1 tablespoon olive or salad oil
½ teaspoon sugar
¼ teaspoon tarragon leaves
¼ teaspoon instant garlic powder
⅛ teaspoon salt
⅛ teaspoon powdered mustard
¼ teaspoon ground black pepper
1 can (4 oz.) French button mushrooms

Combine vinegar, oil, sugar, *tarragon,* garlic powder, salt, mustard, and black pepper. Heat to boiling point. Drain mushrooms and add to hot marinade. Toss lightly. Refrigerate at least 24 hours before serving. Serve on toothpicks with cocktails or as a pickle for dinner, lunch, or supper.

Yield: ½ cup

Easy Meat Pie

2 cans (20 oz. each) beef stew
1 can (1 lb. 4 oz.) mixed vegetables, drained
1 tablespoon instant minced onion
1 teaspoon parsley flakes
1 teaspoon salt
½ teaspoon ground tarragon leaves
¼ teaspoon ground black pepper
⅛ teaspoon instant garlic powder
1 can (8 oz.) prepared biscuits

Combine all ingredients except biscuits. Pour into 1-quart casserole. Top with biscuits. Bake in preheated oven (425°F.) 45 minutes or until biscuits are brown and thoroughly cooked. (Cover with aluminum foil if biscuits brown on top too much before lower part is cooked.)

Yield: 6 servings

407

Stuffed Baked Tarragon Tomatoes

4 large tomatoes
1 teaspoon salt
¾ cup grated cheese
½ cup dry bread crumbs

½ teaspoon tarragon leaves
⅛ teaspoon ground black pepper

Cut tops off tomatoes. Scoop out centers. Sprinkle with salt. Mix pulp with remaining ingredients and spoon into tomatoes. Bake in a preheated moderate oven (375°F.) 20 minutes.

Yield: 4 servings

Green Goddess Salad Dressing

1 tablespoon instant minced onion
2 teaspoons dried chives
1½ cups mayonnaise
1 tablespoon milk
1 anchovy fillet, minced

1 tablespoon tarragon vinegar
1 teaspoon parsley flakes
1 teaspoon tarragon leaves
½ teaspoon coarse ground black pepper

Place instant onion and chives in 1 tablespoon water; let stand 3 to 5 minutes to soften. Add onions and chives to remaining ingredients and blend until smooth. Serve on green salad or cold meat or fish.

Yield: 1¾ cups

THYME

Thymus vulgaris L.

A. Flowering plant	8. Stamens
1. Leaf showing oil glands	9. Stamens in anthesis
2. Calyx, side view	10. Pollen grain
3, 4, 5. Various views of flower	11. Calyx opened to show pistil
6. Flower showing exserted style	12. Pistil showing style
7. Flower showing exserted stamens	13. Calyx
	14. Seed
	15, 16. Seed sectioned

THYME

Family: *Labiatae*

LATIN	• **Thymus vulgaris L.**
SPANISH	• **Tomillo**
FRENCH	• **Thym**
GERMAN	• **Thymian**
SWEDISH	• **Timjan**
ARABIC	• **Sa'tar**
DUTCH	• **Tijm**
ITALIAN	• **Timo**
PORTUGUESE	• **Tomilho**
RUSSIAN	• **Tim'yan**
CHINESE	• **Pai-Li-Hsiang**
JAPANESE	• **Taimu**

THYME

THYME, *Thymus vulgaris,* is a diminutive perennial herbaceous shrub of the mint family native to the Mediterranean region and Asia Minor. Admirable for ornamental effects in rock gardens and edging paths and lawns, it is also grown as an herb for seasoning foods and for an essential oil that is used in medicine.

The condiment consists of the dried herbage, available whole or ground. Freshly cut branch tips may be used as garnishes.

Thyme is now grown in most countries having subtropical or temperate climates. Much of today's commercial production is in southern Europe, including France, Spain, Portugal, and Greece. It is also grown in California, although most thyme consumed in the United States is imported from France. The related species wild thyme, *Thymus serpyllum* L., has become naturalized as an escape from cultivation in many countries including England, Belgium, and the United States.

More than one hundred species of thyme are known, most of which are indigenous to the Mediterranean area, plus so many hybrids between them and different

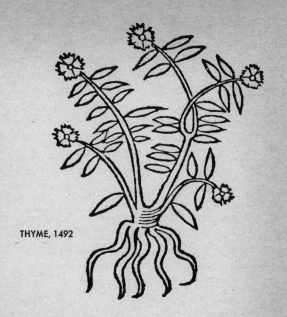

THYME, 1492

varieties of them that they are extremely difficult to classify.

Thymus vulgaris, common or garden thyme, is the kind most frequently found in herb gardens. It is sub-erect, with numerous stems 8 to 18 inches high and a woody fibrous root. The tiny grayish-green narrow leaves rarely exceed $\frac{1}{4}$ inch in length by about $\frac{1}{10}$ inch in width. The small lavender flowers are favorites of the honeybee. The seeds are minute and globose.

Among the other fragrant useful thymes are the creeping "mother of thyme" which grows in thick mats, the lemon, the mint, the orange, the golden-lemon, the caraway-scented, the woolly-stemmed, and the silver, to name a few. The leaves vary in form from broad-leaved to narrow-leaved. There are upright as well as prostrate, trailing species.

The two most important commercial varieties, both of which are grown in California, are the narrow-leaved French thyme *(Thymus vulgaris)*, and the variform lemon thyme *(Thymus citriodorus)*.

Thyme prefers a mild climate and a well-drained, sunny location. It can be propagated from seeds or cuttings, which are planted in the field at a spacing of about 3 feet by 1 foot. Thorough weeding is essential. The planting should be renewed every three years or so, for the plants become woody with age and then produce a lower proportion of tender shoots.

The herbage is harvested when the plants are in bloom. The flowering tops are cut off, together with several inches of the tender, leafy stem. This herbage is shade-dried to preserve the grayish-green color.

Sometimes two crops are cut in one season. One may expect a 1,000 to 2,000 pound yield per acre of dried thyme from a well-established planting.

Thyme's flavor is distinctively warm, pleasant, aromatic, and pungent. As a condiment it is used in flavoring clam and fish chowder, sausages, meats, poultry dressing, fish sauces, croquettes, fresh tomatoes, and the liqueur Benedictine. When recipes call for "a sprig of thyme," use half a teaspoon of ground thyme.

The dried herb yields about 1 percent of an essential oil on distillation. This thyme oil is used extensively in flavoring food products and in perfumery. Thymol, a white crystalline phenol having antiseptic and fungicidal properties as well as aromatic qualities, occurs in thyme oil. Thymol is utilized in pharmaceutical preparations such as gargles, coughdrops, dentifrices, and mouthwashes. It is also used to preserve meat and as a vermifuge to cure hookworm in horses and dogs. Commercially, it is the fungicidal ingredient in many antimildew preparations.

The name thyme, derived from the Greek, has been assigned various meanings and interpretations, including "courage," "sacrifice," and "to fumigate." Thyme was used as an incense to perfume and purify the temples. The herb was considered to have invigorating qualities and was also a symbol of courage and bravery—a compliment of the highest grade two thousand years ago in Greece was to tell someone he "smelled of thyme." Thyme blossoms have been famous for many centuries for scenting the incomparable honey from Mount Hymettus in Greece.

According to tradition, thyme was in the hay and straw bed of the Virgin Mary and the Christ Child.

The Romans used thyme to flavor cheeses and liqueurs. Their soldiers would bathe in water infused with thyme to gain vigor, courage, and strength.

This association of thyme with courage lasted well into the Middle Ages, when in the days of chivalry it was the custom for fair ladies to embroider a sprig of thyme into the scarves they gave to their knights-errant.

In herbal medicine thyme was a cure for nightmares and melancholy, an aid to menstrual flow, and a means of bringing on abortion and actuating urination. It was supposed to be good for strengthening the lungs and improving digestion.

By the sixteenth century thyme, having been introduced to England by the Romans, had become naturalized in Britain; in *A Midsummer-Night's Dream*, Act II, Scene I, Oberon mentions:

. . . I know a bank where the wild thyme blows.

In the eighteenth century the great Swedish botanist and father of modern systematic botany, Carl Linnaeus, recommended thyme as a cure for a hangover.

Beef and Vegetables Stew

3 pounds boneless top round
⅓ cup all-purpose flour
½ teaspoon salt
⅓ cup butter or margarine
2 tablespoons olive or salad
   oil
½ cup instant minced onion
2½ cups beef stock or
   consommé

1 bay leaf
5 carrots, quartered
½ pound mushrooms
   (caps and stems)
2 tablespoons parsley flakes
¼ teaspoon ground thyme
¼ teaspoon ground black
   pepper

Trim and discard excess fat from meat; cut into 1½-inch cubes. Mix flour with salt, add meat, and mix well to coat all sides with flour. Heat butter and oil in Dutch oven or heavy saucepan. Add meat and brown well on all sides. Stir in onion, stock, bay leaf; cover and simmer meat 1½ hours or until meat is almost tender. Add carrots. Cover and cook about 15 to 20 minutes. Add mushrooms, parsley, *thyme,* and pepper. Cook, covered, 10 minutes. Serve hot with baked or mashed potatoes.

Yield: 8–10 servings

Hot Quahog Canapes

⅓ cup cottage cheese
1 package (3 oz.) cream
   cheese
2 teaspoons lemon juice
½ teaspoon salt
½ teaspoon ground thyme

⅛ teaspoon instant garlic
   powder
1/16 teaspoon cayenne
¾ pound fresh clams
12 slices bread
Paprika

Combine cottage cheese, cream cheese, lemon juice, salt, *thyme,* garlic powder, and cayenne. Remove clams from shells by running a knife around the edges. Put clams through a food chopper, using a medium blade. Blend with cheese mixture. Trim crust from bread slices and cut each slice into 4 squares. Spread with clam mixture. Sprinkle paprika over the tops. Broil until bubbly and hot. Serve hot as a cocktail accompaniment.

Yield: About 48 canapés

New England Clam Chowder

¼ pound salt pork, diced
3 cups diced potatoes
¼ cup instant minced
  onion
1½ teaspoons salt
¼ teaspoon ground black
  pepper

18 fresh clams with liquid
  or 4 cans (7½ oz. each)
  clams
1 quart hot milk
1¼ teaspoons ground
  thyme
2 tablespoons butter or
  margarine

In 4-quart saucepan fry salt pork until crisp. Add 2 cups boiling water, potatoes, minced onion, salt, and black pepper. Cover and cook until potatoes are almost tender, 10 to 12 minutes. If fresh clams are used, drain off liquid and reserve. Chop clams and add to potatoes; cook 5 minutes. Stir in clam liquid, milk, *thyme,* and butter. Cover, simmer 5 minutes or until potatoes are tender. Serve in bowls with crackers, if desired.

Yield: 3 quarts

Half Moon Chicken Pies

6 tablespoons butter or
  margarine
6 tablespoons all-purpose
  flour
2 cups chicken stock
1 cup milk
1¾ teaspoons salt

1 teaspoon ground thyme
¼ teaspoon ground black
  pepper
2 cups diced chicken
Pastry, using 2 cups flour
Milk
Mushroom Gravy

Melt butter in a saucepan. Blend in flour. Cook until lightly browned. Add chicken stock and milk. Stir and cook until medium thick. Add salt, *thyme,* and black pepper. Measure 1 cup of sauce and blend with chicken. Save remaining sauce to use in mushroom gravy. Roll half the pastry at a time ⅛ inch thick. Cut pastry in circles, using a saucer for a pattern. Spoon ⅓ cup chicken mixture in center of each. Fold over the pastry and crimp edges with a fork. Brush the tops lightly with milk. Bake in a preheated hot oven (400°F.) 40 minutes or until pastry has browned. Serve with Mushroom Gravy.

Yield: 6 servings

MUSHROOM GRAVY

Sauté ½ cup sliced fresh mushrooms in butter or margarine until tender. Add to remaining cream sauce. Serve over Half Moon Chicken Pies.

Yield: 1½ cups sauce

Shrimp Creole

¼ cup olive or salad oil
3 tablespoons flour
1 can (1 lb. 12 oz.)
   tomatoes
¼ cup onion flakes
¼ cup sweet pepper flakes
¼ cup celery flakes
1 tablespoon parsley flakes
1 bay leaf
1 teaspoon salt

½ teaspoon sugar
½ teaspoon thyme leaves
⅛ teaspoon ground black
   pepper
⅛ teaspoon cayenne
1 pound large shrimp,
   cooked, peeled, and
   deveined
Cooked rice

In large saucepan heat oil; stir in flour. Cook, stirring, until lightly browned. Add tomatoes and ½ cup water. Bring to boil. Add onion, sweet pepper, celery, and parsley. Cover; simmer over low heat 10 minutes. Add remaining ingredients except shrimp and rice; continue to cook 10 minutes longer. Just before serving add shrimp. Cook about 5 minutes or until shrimp are heated. Serve over cooked rice.

Yield: 6 servings

Barbecued Sea Kebabs

2 (8 oz. each) frozen lobster
   tails, cooked
1 pound cooked large
   shrimp

1 medium-sized zucchini,
   cut into ½-inch slices
¾ pound mushroom caps
Cherry tomatoes

Cut lobster meat into chunks. String on skewers alternating with shrimp, zucchini, and mushrooms. Place cherry tomatoes on end of skewers. Broil, basting with barbecue sauce, 3 minutes or until shrimp are lightly browned.

Yield: 6 servings

BARBECUE SAUCE FOR SEA KEBABS

¼ cup salad oil
3 tablespoons cider vinegar
1 tablespoon lemon juice
¾ teaspoon garlic salt
½ teaspoon thyme leaves,
  crushed

½ teaspoon onion salt
½ teaspoon salt
¼ teaspoon ground black
  pepper

In small saucepan combine all ingredients. Heat to boiling. Cool. Brush sauce on kebabs.

Yield: ½ cup sauce

TURMERIC

Curcuma longa **L.**

A. **Entire plant**
B. **Leaf**
C. **Inflorescence**
1. **Flower**
2. **Vertical section of flower**
3. **Portion of flower showing fertile stamen**
4. **Stamen, side view**
5. **Vertical section of base of flower showing ovary and sterile stamens**
6. **Transverse section of ovary**

TURMERIC

Family: Zingiberaceae

LATIN	• <u>Curcuma longa L.</u>
SPANISH	• Cúrcuma
FRENCH	• Curcuma
GERMAN	• Kurkuma-Gelbwurzel
SWEDISH	• Gurkmeja
ARABIC	• Kurkum
DUTCH	• Geelwortel
ITALIAN	• Curcuma
PORTUGUESE	• Açafrão-da-India
RUSSIAN	• Zholty Imbir'
JAPANESE	• Ukon
CHINESE	• Yü-Chin

TURMERIC

TURMERIC, *Curcuma longa,* is a robust perennial tropical herb of the ginger family indigenous to southern Asia. Like ginger, turmeric has a thick, round rhizome, or underground stem, with short blunt "fingers." The thin leaves are 2 to 3 feet long and light green in color. Six to ten leaves may grow from a node with several tufts of them from a rhizome. The yellowish-white flowers are borne in dense cone-shaped spikes that arise from the tufts of leaves. Turmeric fruits are inconspicuous, and some cultivated strains are nearly sterile.

Turmeric is usually propagated vegetatively by "fingers" or small portions of the rhizomes of the previous season's growth. Its cultural requirements are similar in general to those of ginger. It thrives in a hot, moist, tropical climate in well-drained friable soil, from sea level up to about 3,500 feet. The "fingers" are planted 3 inches deep at 1-foot intervals.

The harvest commences when the stems begin to fade, about ten months after planting. The yield per acre may range from 10,000 to 20,000 pounds of raw turmeric. The rhizomes are carefully dug, then cured and prepared for the market by being boiled, cleaned, dried in the sun for about ten days, and polished. During the curing process the product loses about three-quarters of its original weight.

Cured turmeric is graded and sorted into "fingers," "rounds," and "splits," the best quality being "fingers."

Tumeric spice is made by grinding these orange-yellow, waxy, short rhizomes into a fine aromatic yellowish powder, which is used as a condiment and as an essential ingredient of curry powder.

Turmeric is a colorful, versatile product, combining the properties of a spice and a brilliant yellow dye-stuff. This coloring matter, known as curcumin and contained in the plant's rhizomes, has for many centuries been used as a vegetable dye in the Far East to give a rich yellow color to silks, cottons, foods, and at times people.

Turmeric was listed as a coloring plant in an Assyrian herbal dating from about 600 B.C. Marco Polo in 1280 mentioned turmeric as growing in the Fokien region of China: "There is also a vegetable which has all the properties of true saffron, as well the smell as the color, and yet it is not really saffron."

The trade in saffron has traditionally been from West to East—that of turmeric from East to West. In medieval times turmeric was known in Europe as "Indian saffron." Since then turmeric has been employed as a cheap coloring substitute for saffron and has been regarded in the spice trade as a poor relative of ginger.

Yet in Asia it has been highly esteemed as a condiment, dyestuff, and medicine. In Indonesia rice dyed with turmeric has traditionally formed part of the wedding ritual, as has the custom of the bride and groom tingeing their arms with curcuma coloring. In Malaysia turmeric is smeared on the abdomen of women after childbirth and applied as an ointment to the cut umbilical cord of a baby, both for healing purposes and also as a protection against evil spirits. In Indonesia tumeric water is rubbed on the body much as we would use cologne or alcohol. In many parts of the Far East women apply turmeric to their faces as a cosmetic—they prefer an appealing golden complexion to pink cheeks. In India it is alleged that the external application of turmeric tends to suppress the unwelcome growth of hair on female skin.

In many Asian countries turmeric is still used medicinally as a stomachic, carminative, and as a cure for liver troubles. It may be taken internally as a tonic for treating ulcers or externally as an ointment to heal skin sores. Boiled with milk and sugar, it is taken as a remedy for the common cold. (Turmeric is no longer of importance as a drug in Western medicine.)

Although still used in Asia as a coloring agent, turmeric has been replaced by coal-tar compounds as a fabric dye in the West. However, since it is nontoxic turmeric, like saffron, is used in alcoholic solutions for coloring such foods and beverages as margarine, butter, cheese, fruit drinks, and liqueurs.

On steam distillation the dried turmeric tubers yield from 2 to 6 per cent of an essential oil, oil of curcuma, which has a limited use today in flavoring spice products and in perfumery. Its spicy, peppery odor, like the flavor of turmeric powder, is reminiscent of mustard, with a cleaner, fresher aroma than that of ginger.

Turmeric is imported to the United States from India, Haiti, Jamaica, and Peru. India is by far the largest producer in the world, with over 100,000 acres under cultivation, mostly in the states of Andhra Pradosh,

Maharashtra, Madras, and Orissa. About 100,000 tons of cured Indian turmeric are produced annually, of which 98 percent is consumed internally; the remaining 2 percent is exported, mainly to the United States, Ceylon, and Japan.

An unusual characteristic of imported turmeric is its very low moisture content, usually about 3 to 4 per cent. Most spices, when imported, have a moisture content of 8 to 12 percent, and nutmeg's may be as high as 15 percent.

Ground turmeric lends color and flavor to prepared mustard and is included in many pickle and relish formulas. Its outstanding use, however, is as a highly important ingredient of most curries, primarily because of the vivid yellow color it imparts together with a distinctive pungent flavor.

Curry powder, the most common seasoning for curries, is not made from a single spice but is a blend or combination of a number of different spices and herbs; it may include as few as three or as many as thirty. On the average it contains fifteen or twenty. In addition to turmeric, most curries include coriander seed, cumin seed, chilies, black pepper, cardamom, cinnamon, cloves, ginger, fennel seed, celery seed, fenugreek seed, caraway seed, nutmeg, mace, mint leaves, mustard seed, poppy seed, sesame seed, saffron, and "curry leaves." This latter product comes from the small "curry-leaf tree," *Murraya koenigii*, which produces a hard, useful wood and fragrant, aromatic leaves. It is indigenous to tropical Hindustan, at the foot of the Himalayas in India. Despite the confusion sometimes caused by their name, these curry leaves are but one—and by no means the most important—of the many ingredients that may be included in curry blends.

A wretched, impoverished Asiatic might use a curry consisting of only three of the above spices and herbs to flavor his meager ball of cold rice. A prosperous gourmet, on the other hand, could utilize twenty or more, including a substantial portion of expensive saffron, in his curried Chicken Biriana.

Other curry seasonings, popular in the Orient, include curry paste and curry sauce, prepared traditionally with fresh spices and herbs. Since most of these tropical products are not readily available to the American housewife in a fresh state, the most practical way for her to prepare curry is to use a blend of curry powder that has been subdued to become more acceptable to the average American palate. If an authentic Far Eastern curry is desired, a few dashes of cayenne pepper may be added to capture the pungency so typical of the Orient. The strength or "hotness" of the curry will then depend on the amount of cayenne pepper added.

The word curry is also a general term for the seasoned dish itself, which includes the curry ingredients and is usually the entrée of the meal. For example, there are meat curries, stew curries, poultry curries, vegetable curries, curried eggs, fish curries, and shellfish curries such as "Shrimp Curry."

Curry powders should be stored in a dark cupboard to avoid discoloration, for turmeric is extremely sensitive to light.

Madras Rice

2½ cups chicken broth
2 teaspoons curry powder
½ teaspoon ground
   turmeric

½ teaspoon salt
1 cup regular-cooking rice
½ cup raisins

In medium-sized saucepan combine chicken broth, curry powder, *turmeric,* and salt. Bring to boiling point. Sprinkle in rice. Cover. Cook over low heat until rice is tender, about 25 minutes. Add raisins and toss lightly.

Yield: 4–6 servings

Shrimp Curry

3 tablespoons instant
   minced onion
2 tablespoons shortening or
   salad oil
½ cup water
1 tablespoon ground
   coriander seed
1 teaspoon ground cumin
   seed
¾ teaspoon ground
   turmeric

½ teaspoon ground
   cardamom seed
½ teaspoon curry powder
¼ teaspoon ground red
   pepper
1 pound uncooked shrimp,
   peeled and deveined
¼ cup water
1 teaspoon salt
¼ cup evaporated milk
Hot cooked rice

Soak onion in 3 tablespoons water 5 minutes. Heat
shortening in skillet. Add onion and sauté. Add spices.
Add the ½ cup of water and blend with mixture. Cook
slowly 20 minutes. Add shrimp, the ¼ cup of water,
and salt. Simmer 20 minutes. Stir in evaporated milk
just before removing from heat. Serve over hot cooked
rice, with chutney if desired.

Yield: 3–4 servings

Indian Curried Chicken

3- to 4-pound ready-to-cook
   roasting chicken
½ cup instant minced onion
2½ tablespoons ground
   coriander seed
1 tablespoon ground
   turmeric
2½ teaspoons ground
   cumin
1 teaspoon ground ginger
¾ teaspoon ground black
   pepper

¾ teaspoon ground red
   pepper
½ teaspoon instant minced
   garlic
2 tablespoons cider vinegar
1 tablespoon salad oil
2 bay leaves
1 stick cinnamon, 2 inches
   long
2½ teaspoons salt
¼ cup salad oil

Cut chicken into serving pieces. Make a paste by blending
together onion, coriander seed, *turmeric,* cumin, ginger,
black pepper, red pepper, garlic, cider vinegar, and 1
tablespoon of salad oil. Rub paste over all surfaces of

chicken pieces. Put seasoned chicken in covered pan and marinate in refrigerator overnight. When ready to cook, place bay leaves, cinnamon, salt, and the ¼ cup of oil in Dutch oven or large skillet and heat before adding chicken pieces. Brown on all sides. Add 1 cup hot water, cover, and simmer until chicken is tender (about 45 minutes). Serve hot or cold.

Yield: 6 servings

Far Eastern Seafood Kebabs

1½ pounds shrimp	*2 teaspoons curry powder*
3 packages (8 oz. each) frozen lobster tails	*1½ teaspoons ground cumin*
3 cups boiling water	*1 tablespoon ground turmeric*
1½ teaspoons salt	*½ teaspoon ground black pepper*
¾ teaspoon instant minced onion	*3 tablespoons lemon juice*
18 peppercorns	*6 wedges lemon or lime*
⅔ cup butter or margarine	*Cooked rice*
1 teaspoon salt	

Place shrimp and lobster tails in boiling water with the 1½ teaspoons of salt, onion, and peppercorns. Bring to boiling point, reduce heat, and simmer, covered, for 8 minutes. Remove from heat. Drain. Remove shells from fish and devein shrimp. Melt butter or margarine. Blend in the 1 teaspoon of salt, remaining spices, and lemon juice. Add fish to mixture. Coat well. Marinate in refrigerator 2 to 3 hours. String on skewers. If desired alternate with pieces of raw vegetables. Broil 3 minutes or until shrimp are slightly brown at edges. Serve with lemon or lime wedges and hot cooked rice.

Yield: 6 servings

VANILLA

Vanilla planifolia **Andr.**

A. Flowering branch	**7.** Fertile stamen open at tip
1. Lip or labellum of flower	**8.** Vertical section of stamen
2, 3. Views of upper portion of lip	**9.** Pollen
	10. Transverse section of ovary
4. Column of pistil	**11.** Fruit (capsule or "bean")
5. Upper portion of column	**12.** Seed
6. Unopened stamen	**13.** Section of seed

VANILLA

Family: Orchidaceae

LATIN	• <u>**Vanilla planifolia Andr.**</u>
SPANISH	• **Vainilla**
FRENCH	• **Vanille**
GERMAN	• **Vanille**
SWEDISH	• **Vanilj**
ARABIC	• **Wanila**
DUTCH	• **Vanille**
ITALIAN	• **Vaniglia**
PORTUGUESE	• **Baunilha**
RUSSIAN	• **Vanil'**
JAPANESE	• **Banira**
CHINESE	• **Hsiang-Ts'ao**

VANILLA

VANILLA, *Vanilla planifolia,* formerly known by the rather appropriate name *V. fragrans* (Salisb.) Ames, is a large green-stemmed creeping or climbing perennial plant of the orchid family. The vine has a fleshy, succulent stem; smooth, thick, oblong-lanceolate bright green leaves; and numerous twining aerial roots arising opposite each leaf, by which it clings to trees. It is native to the humid tropical rain forests of southeastern Mexico, Central America, the West Indies, and northern South America. In its wild state the vine may grow to a length of 80 feet or more, climbing to the top of tall forest trees.

The popular flavoring material is obtained from the dried, cured, full-sized but not fully ripe fruits—commercially called "beans"—which resemble pods. These pods have no flavor when picked, for the fragrant aroma develops during the curing process.

The generic name *Vanilla* is derived from the Spanish *vainilla,* a diminutive of *vaina,* a pod; its specific epithet, *planifolia,* refers to the broad, flat leaf of the plant.

Vanilla is the outstanding contribution of the Western Hemisphere to the spices of the world. Although the *Orchidaceae*, with approximately 35,000 species known, represents the largest family of flowering plants, with the exception of ornamentals vanilla is its only important commercial product.

For many centuries prior to the discovery of America, the Aztec Indians in Mexico used vanilla as a flavoring, having developed a crude fermentation process for curing the pods. These vanilla beans were employed also by the Aztecs as a medium of exchange to pay tribute to their emperor, as a source of perfume, and as an herbal medicinal tonic.

When the Spanish conquistadores led by Hernán Cortés were in Mexico in 1520, one of their officers, Bernal Díaz, observed that the emperor Montezuma was drinking *chocolatl,* a beverage consisting of powdered cocoa beans and ground corn, flavored with *tlilxochitl* (ground black vanilla pods) and honey.

Much impressed, the Spanish took vanilla back to their motherland, where by the end of the sixteenth century factories were established to manufacture chocolate with vanilla flavoring. This use of vanilla spread to other parts of Europe. In 1602 Hugh Morgan, apothecary to Queen Elizabeth I, recommended that vanilla be used as an exquisite flavoring in its own right, following the example of the Aztecs. By 1700 vanilla was employed in France for flavoring chocolate and scenting tobacco.

For more than three centuries after the time of Cortés, Mexico was the leading vanilla-producing country in the world, enjoying a complete and lucrative monopoly. A few attempts were made to grow the crop in tropical Far Eastern countries, including an experimental planting in Buitenzorg, Java, in 1819; but although the vines would flower, no fruit was produced. This baffling mystery was not solved until 1836 when

A SEVENTEENTH-CEN-
TURY ILLUSTRATION
OF VANILLA, KNOWN
AS *TLILXOCHITL* BY
THE AZTECS

the Belgian botanist Charles Morren found the answer
by hand-pollinating the vanilla flowers. He pointed out
that the plants could not produce fruit naturally unless
the Mexican or Central American pollinating insects
were present. In the vanilla-growing areas of Mexico
the *melipone* bees and certain species of humming-
bird, not present in tropical Asia, were found to be the
pollinating agents. Morren observed that the lemon-
yellow orchid flower stayed in bloom less than twenty-
four hours, so that pollination at just the right time was
necessary if fertilization and fruit development were
to follow.

In 1841 Edmond Albius, a former slave on the French
island of Réunion, perfected a quick pollination method:
With the pointed tip of a small bamboo stick, he picked
up the adhesive pollen masses, and prying up the flaplike
rostellum inside the flower, he pressed the male pollen
mass into contact with the sticky female stigma. This
same method of artificial pollination of vanilla is used
commercially today.

Vanilla plantings were established in Réunion, Java,
Mauritius, Madagascar, Tahiti, the Seychelles, Tanzania
(Zanzibar), Brazil, and Jamaica and other islands in

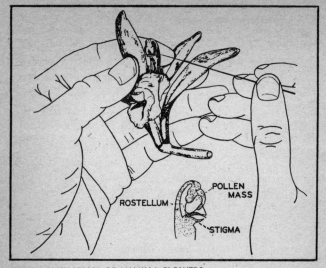

HAND-POLLINATION OF VANILLA FLOWERS

To obtain commercial production of vanilla beans, it is necessary to pollinate the flowers by hand, since a fleshy lip, or rostellum, lies between the male and female organs. The worker lifts this rostellum with a sharp bamboo stick, so that the pollen grains from the anther (male organ) may be smeared with the left thumb upon the stigma (female organ).

the West Indies. The French colonies became leaders in world vanilla production. Today the Malagasy Republic (Madagascar), the Comoro Islands and Réunion grow about 90 percent of the world's crop of vanilla beans. The remaining production comes largely from the Seychelles, Mexico, French Polynesia, Indonesia, and Uganda.

Vanilla thrives in a hot, humid tropical climate where it is protected from the wind, at elevations from sea level to 2,500 feet, with good drainage, adequate humus, and an annual rainfall of about 75 to 100 inches.

Live supports for the vines are usually grown, and many species of trees and shrubs have been so utilized. The most desirable live supports are small-leaved and fast-growing, with low branches to which the vanilla vines can cling. Normally the supports are planted a year before the vanilla cuttings, at a spacing of about 8 feet by 8 feet, or 680 to the acre. Occasionally, support for the vines is provided by means of wooden trellises.

Plantation vanilla is propagated by cuttings from 1 to 4 feet long, planted close to the base of the young supporting tree. The upper end of the vanilla cutting may be tied loosely to the stem or hung over one of its low branches. In ten to twelve weeks the cuttings should strike root. The vine must be pruned constantly so that it will not grow beyond the reach of the workers who must hand-pollinate the flowers and harvest the pods. The first crop is harvested in about three years, with maximum yields reached in the seventh or eighth year. Vines are abandoned after ten to twelve years, when they have usually ceased to be commerically productive.

A healthy, fully developed vine may bear as many as 1,000 pale yellow flowers, of which 40 to 50 selected blossoms (but no more than 6 to 8 flowers in one cluster) are artificially hand-pollinated. The flowering period may extend over two months, but each blossom lasts only one day, from early morning to late afternoon. Therefore, the hand-pollination must be carried out early in the morning on which the flower opens. An expert will pollinate from 1,000 to 1,500 blossoms a day.

Following fertilization the pods mature in four to nine months. They are picked before they are ripe, just as their color starts to change from green to yellow. At this time, they may be from 5 to 10 inches long and about 1 inch in circumference. The longer beans are the more desirable.

In the Malagasy Republic shortly before the harvest most green vanilla beans are tattoed by pinpricks with the initials or identification mark of the owner of the vine. This "brand" to discourage theft does not affect the flavor or quality of the bean, but provides positive and permanent identification.

After harvesting, the troublesome, time-consuming fermentation or curing process commences. In the Malagasy Republic the pods are dipped in hot water (about 135°F.) for two or three minutes and are then successively sweated and dried; in Mexico the sweating and drying operation commences without the initial immersion in hot water.

During the sweating period, which may last for ten to twenty days, the pods are spread in the sun daily for several hours until hot and are then folded in blankets to sweat until the following morning. This process is repeated until they become pliable and are deep brown in color. Drying is then continued for many more weeks, either in the sun or in heated rooms. By this traditional method five to six months may be required to complete the curing and drying.

As the sweating process goes on, fermentation accelerates the formation of a white crystalline compound known as *vanillin*, the peculiar and very fragrant constituent of the cured vanilla pods (vanillin does not occur in the growing plant). When the curing has been completed, the pods are covered with this crystalline efflorescence, the presence of which is an indication of high quality.

The pods are sorted and graded according to quality, length, aroma, color, flexibility, and luster. The most desirable pods are those about 7 to 10 inches in length, highly aromatic, free of any trace of mildew, dark brown, fleshy, supple, free of blemishes and insect infestation, somewhat oily in appearance, and shaped like a long, slim cigar. After being sorted and graded they are tied in bundles and packed in tin containers to conserve their aroma. Well-cured vanilla beans protected in this manner should keep indefinitely.

During the curing and drying process, the beans lose considerable weight. About 5 pounds of fresh green vanilla pods are required to produce 1 pound of dried beans of marketable quality. Healthy vines in full production should yield about 120 pounds of cured, dried vanilla beans per acre.

In recent years a new process by which the vanilla beans are cured in a few days instead of months has been developed and is now used in Uganda. This revolutionary method, although fundamentally similar to natural curing and fermentation, accelerates the necessary enzyme activity, for the beans are first chopped and then mechanically processed under intense heat. Beans of all lengths and sizes are used, and much of the tedious hand labor required in the traditional method is eliminated, thus drastically reducing production costs. For political reasons, however, it has not been accepted enthusiastically in most vanilla-producing countries, where labor is cheap and gainful employment is necessary.

Vanillin, the crystalline component, was first isolated from vanilla pods by Gobley in 1858. By 1874 it had been obtained from glycosides of pine tree sap, temporarily causing an economic depression in the natural vanilla industry.

The year 1891 brought another difficult period for natural vanilla, for in that year two other processes for producing artificial or synthetic vanillin were instituted. One used eugenol, an aromatic substance obtained by fractional distillation of clove oil; the other was a patented electrolytic method of producing vanillin from sugar (sucrose). Subsequently other syntheses of vanillin were developed from lignin (in wood pulp), waste paper pulp, oil of sassafras, and coal tar. Coumarin, a white crystalline compound of vanillalike flavor found in the tonka bean (*Dipteryx odorata* Willd.), has also been used as a cheap substitute for vanilla. Recent technical studies, however, indicate that coumarin has a dangerously high level of toxicity, and its use in foods or for food additives has been barred in the United States by regulations promulgated under the Food, Drug and Cosmetic Act and revisions thereof.

Extract of vanilla, made from the beans, may be twenty times more expensive than a flavoring of comparable strength made with synthetic vanillin. The true vanilla beans, however, possess a pure, delicate, spicy flavor and peculiar bouquet that is not duplicated exactly by the synthetic product. Vanillin or imitation vanilla, because it is a chemically pure substance lacking certain secondary scents and minor flavor constituents found in the natural product, imparts a harsh odor and rank, bitter aftertaste. Consequently, the demand for pure vanilla extract for high-quality flavoring purposes has continued, even though the synthetic product is used in cheaper flavorings. In the United States the Food and Drug Administration standards require that the label read "Imitation Vanilla" if the product contains any synthetic ingredients. If the label states "Vanilla Extract," the product must be derived from vanilla beans.

Vanilla extract is obtained from the cured beans by hydroalcoholic extraction in much the same way that coffee is percolated. The vanilla beans are finely chopped, then enclosed in large stainless steel baskets that are immersed in a warm alcohol-water solvent (at least 35 percent alcohol by volume) in glass-lined or stainless steel percolators. The solvent, which has been piped in from the top of the vat, percolates down through the beans and on reaching the bottom is recirculated to the top to continue percolation until the maximum of vanilla flavor has been extracted. The freshly percolated extract is drawn off, filtered, aged for about three weeks, and bottled. Each batch must be tested and standardized since all vanilla beans are not alike in flavor.

The vanillin content of the vanilla pods may vary, according to the country of origin, from about 1.5 to 2 percent for Mexico to about 2.6 percent for Bourbon (the Malagasy Republic and Réunion). The dried, cured vanilla pods, on steam distillation, give negligible yields of essential oil. Although the characteristic aroma and taste of vanilla are due not to an essential oil but to vanillin, the quality of the beans is not necessarily commensurate with the percentage of vanillin content, for other subsidiary substances (such as gums, fixed oils, and resins) likewise contribute to the delicately sweet, rich, spicy, and persistent aroma. The Mexican vanilla, for example, although relatively low in vanillin content, is nonetheless considered by the trade to be one of excellent quality.

The commercial term "vanilla oleoresin" refers to a dark brown liquid that is really not an oleoresin but a resinoid obtained from the pods through solvent extraction. It is utilized in products requiring a very concentrated vanillalike flavor or when solubility in oil is necessary.

During the sixteenth and seventeenth centuries vanilla was considered by European physicians to have various medicinal properties, including those of a stimulant, stomachic, aphrodisiac, and antidote to poison. For many years it was listed in the British and German pharmacopoeias, and was official in the U. S. Pharmacopeia from 1860 to 1910. Its medicinal use has gradually declined, however, and today it is not regarded as a drug but rather as the world's most popular flavoring for sweetened foods.

Since none of the aroma and taste of vanilla is due to an essential oil, this condimental plant is sometimes not classified as a spice. But as its principal use, like that of true spices, is for the flavoring of food, vanilla is being accepted as a spice in this book in the broad sense of the term.

Vanilla sugar is the finely ground cured bean mixed with sugar and is used in the manufacture of sweet chocolate. Vanilla is the main flavoring in most chocolates and tends to reinforce the characteristic chocolate taste. Some European chefs and French housewives prefer to use the actual bean rather than the extract, and recipes in most French cookbooks call for it.

Most vanilla flavor is marketed, especially in the United States, in the form of pure vanilla extract, widely used as a flavoring par excellence for ice cream, soft drinks, eggnogs, chocolate confectionery, candy, tobacco, baked goods, puddings, cakes, cookies, liqueurs, and as a fragrantly tenacious ingredient in perfumery.

Eggnog Mexicana

2 eggs, separated
⅓ cup sugar
¼ teaspoon salt

3 cups milk
2 teaspoons pure vanilla
extract

Beat egg yolks lightly. Gradually add sugar and salt and continue beating until thickened. Add milk and *vanilla extract*. Beat thoroughly for one minute. Beat egg whites to form soft peaks. Spoon equal amounts into each glass of eggnog. Chill and serve.

Yield: 4 servings

Vanilla Cottage Cheese Cupcakes

1 teaspoon soda
1 teaspoon salt
½ cup shortening
1½ cups light brown sugar,
packed
2 teaspoons pure vanilla
extract

2 eggs
2¼ cups sifted all-purpose
flour
½ cup milk
1 carton (8 oz.) creamy
cottage cheese
¾ cup chopped raisins

Mix together soda, salt, and shortening. Gradually blend in sugar and *pure vanilla extract*. Beat in eggs, one at a time. Add flour alternately with milk. Stir in cottage cheese and raisins. Spoon batter into cupcake pans filling them ⅔ to ¾ full. Bake in preheated moderate oven (375°F.) 20 to 25 minutes or until a cake tester inserted in center comes out clean. Cool. Sprinkle tops with confectioners' sugar.

Yield: 30 cupcakes

Vanilla Party Cookies

3 cups sifted all-purpose
  flour
2¼ teaspoons baking
  powder
½ teaspoon salt
¾ cup butter or margarine,
  softened

1¼ cups sugar
1¼ teaspoons pure vanilla
  extract
1 egg
2 tablespoons milk

Sift flour, baking powder, and salt together; set aside. Cream butter, sugar, and *vanilla extract* together. Beat in egg. Stir in flour mixture and milk. Mix well (dough will be stiff). Shape into 1-inch balls. Place on ungreased cookie sheets 1 inch apart. Flatten in crisscross fashion with a fork. Bake in a preheated hot oven (400°F.) 10 minutes.

Yield: 4½ dozen cookies

Blond Brownies

1 cup sifted all-purpose
  flour
1½ teaspoons ground
  cinnamon
½ teaspoon baking powder
½ teaspoon salt
¼ teaspoon ground nutmeg
⅓ cup butter or margarine

1 cup brown sugar
1 egg
1 egg yolk
1 teaspoon pure vanilla
  extract
½ cup chopped nuts
Confectioners' sugar
  (optional)

Sift flour with cinnamon, baking powder, salt, and nutmeg. Melt butter or margarine in large saucepan; remove from heat. Add brown sugar, stirring until dissolved. Cool. Add egg, egg yolk, and *vanilla;* beat well. Stir in sifted dry ingredients and nuts; mix well. Spread batter in greased 8-inch square pan. Bake in preheated moderate oven (350°F.) for 25 to 30 minutes. Cool. Cut into bars. Serve plain or dusted with confectioners' sugar.   **Yield: 24 bars**

Vanilla Chocolate Cookies

2 cups sifted all-purpose
 flour
½ teaspoon salt
½ cup butter or margarine
1 cup sugar
1 teaspoon ground
 cinnamon

1 egg
2 tablespoons milk
1 teaspoon pure vanilla
 extract
2 squares (2 oz.)
 unsweetened chocolate,
 melted

Sift flour with salt. Cream butter in mixing bowl. Gradually add sugar and cinnamon; continue creaming until light and fluffy. Add egg, milk, and *vanilla extract;* beat well. Blend in chocolate. Add sifted dry ingredients gradually; mix well. Press a small amount of dough at a time through cookie press onto ungreased cookie sheet, shaping as desired. Bake in preheated moderate oven (350°F.) 6 to 9 minutes.

Yield: About 12 dozen cookies

Browned Sugar Vanilla Sauce

½ cup sugar
⅛ teaspoon salt
1 teaspoon butter or
 margarine

2 teaspoons pure vanilla
 extract
1 tablespoon cornstarch

Heat sugar in heavy pan over moderate heat until just melted, stirring constantly (sugar turns brown as it melts). Add 1 cup boiling water and salt; reduce heat. Add butter and *vanilla.* Cook and stir until smooth. Remove a little of the liquid and mix with cornstarch to form a smooth mixture. Add to pan and stir until blended and thickened. Remove from heat. Serve on waffles, pancakes, ice cream, or cake.

Yield: ⅔ cup sauce

APPENDIX

SPICE-PRODUCING COUNTRIES OF THE WORLD
(Summarizing present sources of spices and herbs)

ALBANIA
Sage

ALGERIA
Coriander

ARGENTINA
Coriander
Fennel
Poppy Seed
Fenugreek
Mint Leaves

AUSTRALIA
Ginger
Mustard Seed
Poppy Seed

BELGIUM
Basil
Parsley
Tarragon

BRAZIL
Pepper
Sesame Seed
Fennel
Cloves

BULGARIA
Basil
Paprika
Coriander
Mustard Seed
Mint Leaves
Fennel
Onions
Garlic

CAMBODIA
Pepper
Cardamom
Chili Peppers

CANADA
Mustard Seed
Oregano
Parsley
Coriander

CHILE
Marjoram
Paprika
Chili Peppers
Mustard Seed
Cumin

CHINA (MAINLAND)
Chili Peppers
Cassia
Star Anise
Cumin Seed
Dill Seed
Fennel
Ginger
Garlic Powder
Sesame Seed
Turmeric
Onions
Mustard Seed

COSTA RICA
Cardamom
Chili Peppers

CYPRUS
Bay Leaves
Cumin
Oregano
Sage

CZECHOSLOVAKIA
Coriander
Sage
Paprika

DENMARK
Mustard Seed
Poppy Seed
Caraway Seed

DOMINICAN REPUBLIC
Oregano
Parsley

EL SALVADOR
Sesame Seed
Cardamom
Chili Peppers

ETHIOPIA
Sesame Seed
Chili Peppers
Fenugreek
Mustard Seed

FIJI
Ginger

FRANCE
Celery Seed
Oregano
Fenugreek
Marjoram
Mint Leaves
Parsley
Rosemary
Savory
Basil
Thyme
Fennel
Chervil
Tarragon

FRENCH POLYNESIA
Vanilla

GREECE
Chili Peppers
Bay Leaves
Oregano
Sage
Thyme
Marjoram
Basil

GRENADA
Nutmeg
Mace

GUATEMALA
Cardamom
Allspice
Sesame Seed
Chili Peppers
Vanilla

HAITI
Ginger
Chili Peppers
Turmeric

HONDURAS
Allspice

HONG KONG
Ginger

HUNGARY
Paprika
Basil
Parsley
Onions
Garlic

INDIA
Pepper
Turmeric
Chili Peppers
Fenugreek
Celery Seed
Coriander
Cumin
Cardamom
Ginger
Dill
Fennel
Sesame Seed
Cassia
Cinnamon

INDONESIA
Pepper
Nutmeg
Mace

Chili Peppers
Cumin
Vanilla
Cassia
Cloves

IRAN
Cumin
Poppy Seed
Fenugreek
Saffron

ISRAEL
Onions
Coriander
Cumin

ITALY
Mustard Seed
Oregano
Fennel
Sage

IVORY COAST
Pepper
Chili Peppers

JAMAICA
Allspice
Ginger
Turmeric

JAPAN
Chili Peppers
Cumin Seed
Horseradish

KENYA
Chili Peppers
Cinnamon

LEBANON
Fenugreek
Sage
Sesame Seed
Marjoram
Cumin

LEEWARD ISLANDS
Allspice
Nutmeg
Mace

MALAGASY REPUBLIC
Vanilla
Cloves
Pepper
Cinnamon

MALAYSIA
Pepper
Chili Peppers
Vanilla
Cloves
Cardamom
Cassia
Nutmeg

MEXICO
Chili Peppers
Allspice
Anise Seed
Paprika
Dill Seed
Marjoram
Oregano
Cumin
Vanilla
Sesame Seed

MOROCCO
Coriander
Paprika
Cumin
Fenugreek
Mint Leaves

MOZAMBIQUE
Vanilla
Cloves

NETHERLANDS
Caraway Seed
Poppy Seed
Mustard Seed
Tarragon

NICARAGUA
Sesame Seed
Chili Peppers

NIGERIA
Chili Peppers
Ginger
Coriander

PAKISTAN
Turmeric
Coriander
Chili Peppers
Celery Seed

PERU
Marjoram
Turmeric
Ginger

POLAND
Poppy Seed
Caraway Seed
Coriander

PORTUGAL
Rosemary
Bay Leaves
Chili Peppers
Paprika
Oregano
Thyme
Marjoram

REUNION
Vanilla

ROMANIA
Fennel
Paprika
Mint Leaves
Coriander
Poppy Seed
Marjoram

SARAWAK
Pepper

SEYCHELLES
Cinnamon

Vanilla
Paprika
Cassia

SIERRA LEONE
Chili Peppers
Ginger

SOUTH AFRICA
Mint Leaves

SOUTH VIETNAM
Cassia
Ginger
Chili Peppers

SPAIN
Paprika
Saffron
Anise Seed
Oregano
Rosemary
Savory
Thyme
Parsley
Onions
Garlic

SRI LANKA (CEYLON)
Cinnamon
Pepper
Cardamom
Turmeric
Cassia
Nutmeg
Mace

SUDAN
Sesame Seed
Chili Peppers

SYRIA
Anise Seed
Sesame Seed
Cumin
Caraway Seed

TAIWAN
Ginger

Chili Peppers
Cassia
Garlic

TANZANIA
Cloves
Chili Peppers
Cardamom
Cinnamon
Anise Seed

THAILAND
Ginger
Cardamom
Chili Peppers

TRINIDAD
Nutmeg
Mace

TURKEY
Paprika
Oregano
Anise Seed
Cumin
Bay Leaves
Chili Peppers
Poppy Seed
Sage
Marjoram

UGANDA
Chili Peppers
Vanilla

UNITED ARAB REPUBLIC
Sesame Seed
Saffron
Mint Leaves
Onions
Garlic
Caraway Seed
Cumin

UNITED KINGDOM
Mustard Seed
Parsley
Mint Leaves

UNITED STATES
Chili Peppers
Mustard Seed
Sesame Seed
Rosemary
Celery Seed
Garlic Powder
Horseradish
Tarragon
Mint Leaves
Bay Leaves
Onions
Paprika
Dill
Thyme
Sage
Parsley
Basil
Savory
Marjoram
Chervil
Coriander

U. S. S. R.
Anise Seed
Caraway Seed
Coriander
Sesame Seed
Poppy Seed
Mustard Seed
Parsley
Horseradish
Onions
Garlic
Paprika
Mint Leaves
Sage

WEST GERMANY
Mustard Seed
Oregano
Fennel
Parsley
Dill
Thyme

YUGOSLAVIA
Coriander
Sage

Anise Seed	Rosemary
Paprika	Savory
Bay Leaves	Dill
Fennel	Thyme

STATISTICS

The following table summarizes the prices and volume of United States imports of specified spices and herbs during 1971 (based on U.S.D.A. Foreign Agriculture Circular FTEA 1-72 March 1972).

	AVERAGE PRICE PER LB.*	IMPORTS (in LBS.)	VALUE (in $ U.S.)
Allspice	.79	900,000	711,000
Anise Seed	.23	551,000	129,000
Basil	.52	293,000	153,000
Bay (Laurel) Leaves	.18	572,000	105,000
Capsicum Peppers (Chilies)	.28	11,592,000	3,244,000
Caraway Seed	.26	6,099,000	1,596,000
Cardamom Seed	2.73	163,000	445,000
Cassia	.60	9,590,000	5,811,000
Celery Seed	.28	4,205,000	1,188,000
Cinnamon	.30	4,852,000	1,448,000
Cloves	1.34	3,027,000	4,071,000
Coriander Seed	.09	2,787,000	246,000
Cumin Seed	.26	5,145,000	1,356,000
Dill	.12	885,000	109,000
Fennel Seed	.16	1,235,000	196,000
Ginger Root	.32	4,528,000	1,469,000
Mace	.56	578,000	327,000
Marjoram	.37	556,000	208,000
Mint Leaves	.56	113,000	64,000
Mustard Seed	.05	95,081,000	4,360,000
Nutmegs	.40	3,629,000	1,443,000
Origanum Leaves	.26	3,867,000	1,019,000
Paprika	.33	9,432,000	3,075,000
Parsley (Manufactured)	.33	21,000	7,000
Pepper, Black	.44	54,941,000	24,204,000
Pepper, White	.44	4,915,000	2,149,000
Poppy Seed	.27	5,042,000	1,367,000
Rosemary	.12	462,000	57,000
Saffron	100.00	(est.) not available	not available
Sage	.28	2,810,000	783,000

Savory	.33	116,000	38,000
Sesame Seed	.17	45,442,000	7,832,000
Tarragon	.93	31,000	29,000
Thyme	.20	860,000	176,000
Turmeric	.15	3,137,000	488,000
Vanilla Beans	4.46	1,875,000	8,368,000

* Prices per pound in country of origin, exclusive of import duty, freight, and insurance charges; given in $ U.S.

While there are many spices, trade is concentrated for the most part in a few. The following nine tropical spices, ranked according to estimated average annual exports during the ten-year period 1961–1970, account for about two-thirds of the total world trade in spices:

WORLD TRADE IN MAJOR SPICES, 1961–1970
(based on statistics received from the Commonwealth Secretariat, Plantation Crops Section, London)

SPICE	AVERAGE ANNUAL WORLD EXPORTS (in LBS.)	ESTIMATED AVERAGE ANNUAL EXPORT VALUE (in $ U.S.)
1. PEPPER	150,000,000	45,000,000
2. CAPSICUMS AND CHILIES	100,000,000	35,000,000
3. VANILLA	2,500,000	17,000,000
4. CLOVES	32,500,000	17,000,000
5. CINNAMON AND CASSIA	30,500,000	14,000,000
6. CARDAMOM	5,500,000	13,000,000
7. NUTMEG AND MACE	12,500,000	6,000,000
8. GINGER	22,000,000	6,000,000
9. ALLSPICE (PIMENTO)	5,000,000	4,000,000

* Includes re-exports from Singapore and Hong Kong

The ten most important spice-producing countries, ranked according to estimated average annual dollar volume of net exports of spices during the period 1961–1970 (based on statistics received from the Commonwealth Secretariat, Plantation Crops Section, London):

PRODUCING COUNTRY	PRINCIPAL SPICES EXPORTED	ESTIMATED ANNUAL NET EXPORTS (in $ U.S.) 1961–1970
1. INDIA	Pepper, cardamom, chilies, ginger, turmeric, sesame seed, coriander seed	37,500,000
2. INDONESIA	Pepper, nutmeg, mace, cassia, vanilla, cloves	17,500,000
3. MALAGASY REPUBLIC	Vanilla, pepper, cloves, cinnamon	12,500,000
4. MALAYSIA	Pepper, ginger	12,500,000
5. TANZANIA	Cloves, chilies	9,000,000
6. SRI LANKA (CEYLON)	Pepper, cinnamon, cardamom, cloves	6,000,000
7. SPAIN	Paprika, saffron	6,000,000
8. JAMAICA	Ginger, allspice, turmeric	5,500,000
9. BRAZIL	Pepper, sesame seed	3,500,000
10. MEXICO	Vanilla, allspice	3,000,000

GLOSSARY

A

Alkaloid An organic, nitrogen-containing, often bitter constituent of many plants, usually with marked biological activity.

Annual A plant of one year's duration from seed to death.

Anther The pollen-producing portion of the stamen.

Antibacterial Any substance that has the ability, even in dilute solutions, to destroy or inhibit the growth or reproduction of bacteria and other microorganisms; used especially in the treatment of infectious diseases of man and other animals, and plants.

Antidote A remedy that counteracts or removes the effects of poisons.

Antiseptic A substance which prevents sepsis, putrefaction, or decay by arresting the growth or action of noxious microorganisms, either by inhibiting their activity or by destroying them. The term antiseptic generally refers to agents applied to living tissue, the term disinfectant to those used on inanimate objects such as floors, walls, or clothing.

Antispasmodic Any drug that prevents or counteracts spasms (muscular, intestinal, bronchial, etc.).

Aphrodisiac A drug or food that arouses sexual desire.

Aril An accessory appendage of certain seeds (ex.: mace around the nutmeg seed).

Axil The upper angle formed where a leafstalk joins a stem.

B

Biennial A plant of two years' duration from seed to death, flowering and fruiting only in the second year.

Binomial nomenclature Provision of a name of two Latinized words; the first is that of its genus, the second is the specific epithet. For example, in the case of black pepper, *Piper nigrum* L., *Piper* is the name of the genus and *nigrum* identifies the species. (L. is the abbreviation of Linnaeus, the person who first gave the species this binomial.)

Bud The immature or unopened state of a branch, leaf, or flower.

Bulb A modified underground stem usually consisting of overlapping fleshy scales (ex.: onion).

Bulblet A small bulb or bulblike body usually borne on the stem (ex.: garlic).

C

Calyx The outer circle of the floral envelope, the bracts or cup (usually green) enveloping the flower when in bud. (*See* COROLLA.)

Capsule A dry fruit that splits open at maturity (ex.: sesame).

Carminative A drug that relieves flatulence and assuages the pain associated with it.

Carpel A seed vessel; one of the units of the female element of a flower (*See* GYNOECIUM.)

Catkin A slender, spikelike inflorescence (ex.: black pepper).

Chavicine One of the most active and pungent alkaloids of black and white pepper and of oleoresin of pepper.

Condiment A substance used to give relish to food; a seasoning.

Coppicing The periodical cutting back of trees, as practiced with cinnamon and cassia.

Corm An underground stem, usually fleshy.

Corolla The inner of the two envelopes of certain flowers, composed of united petals, forming a bell, trumpet, tube, or similar shape. (*See* CALYX.)

Cover Crop A crop sown to protect and enrich the soil (especially in orchards).

Cultivar A variety that has originated in cultivation (ex.: the Southport White Globe onion).

Cuneiform Wedge-shaped, as the characters in ancient Assyrian and Babylonian inscriptions.

Cutting A segment of a stem or root used to propagate a plant such as horseradish.

D

Dioecious Having the male and female flowers on separate plants (ex.: the nutmeg tree). (*See* MONOECIOUS.)

Distillation A purification process in which a liquid is converted to vapor by the external application of heat and the vapor is condensed to the purified liquid by some means of cooling, usually a water-cooled condenser.

Diuretic A drug that increases the output of urine by the kidneys.

Drupe A one-seeded ("stone"), fleshy fruit.

Duct A conductive tube.

E

Embryo The rudimentary plantlet fully formed within the seed.

Emetic A drug that causes or promotes vomiting.

Emmenagogue A drug or physical measure that induces menstruation.

Enfleurage The extraction of flower scents from picked flowers with cold fat (lard and tallow). The alcoholic washings of the perfumed fat (floral extracts) may be concentrated to any strength desired.

Entrepôt A warehouse or depot for commercial goods

(especially for transshipment); a trading center.

Enzymes Organic substances, frequently proteins produced by living cells, that promote chemical reactions in the metabolism of plants and animals. When outside of living cells, many enzymes are still capable of functioning and exerting a catalytic effect, as in fermentation.

Escape A cultivated or introduced plant that has "escaped" from cultivation and grows spontaneously.

Essential Oils Volatile oils, which evaporate readily and usually leave no stain. They occur in various parts of plants, especially in the flowers and leaves, and may be isolated from plants by distillation, extraction, and enfleurage (the essential oils of most spices are obtained through steam distillation). The characteristic odor and flavor of spices are usually due to the presence of essential oils; ex.: oil of peppermint and oil of cloves. (*See* FIXED OILS.)

Eugenol A colorless liquid, of spicy aroma, contained in oil of bay, oil of cloves, and other essential oils; widely used as a dental antiseptic.

Expectorants Remedial agents (including hot vapors) that promote bronchial secretion and facilitate its ejection.

Expression The action of squeezing out fixed oils by pressing the seeds of certain plants such as sesame.

F

Family A group of related plants forming a category higher than a genus and lower than an order. The family names in plants usually end in *–aceae,* such as *Liliaceae* (onions, garlic, and chives) or *Zingiberaceae* (cardamom, ginger, and turmeric) among the spices.

Federal Food, Drug and Cosmetic Act of 1938 This act and its subsequent revisions set up the standards of identity and quality for edible spices in the United States; the Food and Drug Administration enforces these regulations.

Fixed Oils Fatty oils, usually bland, that leave a stain and do not evaporate (ex.: sesame oil); may be obtained by expression or solvent extraction, but not through distillation as with essential oils. (*See* ESSENTIAL OILS.)

Flower The reproductive part of any "higher" plant having a short axis which, when the flower is complete, bears the calyx, the corolla, the stamens, and the pistil (or pistils).

Fruit The ripened or matured ovary (often with fused associated parts) normally containing the seeds (ripened ovules).

G

Genus (plural, genera) A major category of plants ranking next above the species, and next below the family. Among spices examples of genera are *Foeniculum, Papaver,* and *Myristica.*

Gland A secretory part or organ, such as the nectar gland of a flower.

Glycosides Physiologically active substances found in plants; when treated with acids or enzymes, they yield glucose or other sugars as well as nonsugar components.

Gynoecium The female parts of a flower collectively, including the carpels; the pistils as a unit.

H

Habitat The home of a plant; where it grows naturally or is indigenous.

Herb A soft-stemmed plant that dies back to the ground at the end of its growing season; also a plant used for the sweet scent of its herbage or flowers.

Herbaceous Pertaining to herbs. Not woody.

Hermaphroditic Having both male and female organs in the same flower, that is, perfect (ex.: the clove tree). (*See* IMPERFECT.)

Hull The outer covering, or husk, of certain fruits or seeds.

I

Imperfect Said of a flower which contains the organ(s) of only one sex; that is, lacks either anthers or carpels (*See* HERMAPHRODITIC.)

Indigenous Native to a given place.

Inflorescence Flower-bearing branch, or the arrangement in which the flowers are borne.

L

Labellum The specialized petal (lip) of an orchid which may be tubular (as in vanilla), pouchlike, or otherwise shaped differently from the other petals.

Lactiferous Producing a milky substance (ex.: the nearly ripe poppy capsule).

Lip One of the parts (there are usually two—the upper and lower lips) of an irregular calyx or corolla, as in the mint family.

M

Menthol Peppermint camphor; a white crystalline alcohol similar to thymol, with a characteristic peppermint-like odor. May be obtained from peppermint oil, by hydrogenation of thymol, or by a more complicated but economical synthesis from citronellal. Used in many cosmetics such as shaving creams, because when applied to the skin it stimulates the nerves for the perception of cold, but depresses those for the perception of pain—thus substituting a cool sensation for that of itching.

Mericarp One-half of the dry, dehiscent (splitting-open) fruit (schizocarp) found in most members of the parsley family.

Monoecious Having the male and female flowers separate, but some of each sex on the same plant. (*See* DIOECIOUS.)

Myristicin A toxic substance found in the fruit of certain plants of the nutmeg family. Together with other constituents it is responsible for the hallucinogenic action of nutmeg. In large doses these substances produce excitement and stupor, but in small amounts they act as carminatives and local stimulants to the intestinal tract.

N

Node The point of attachment of a leaf to a stem.

Nutlet A small or diminutive nut, or nutlike fruit.

O

Oleoresins Viscid or liquid pharmaceutical preparations consisting of natural resins and oils obtained by percolation. Oleoresins contain a high concentration of volatile oils, giving them a definite fragrance.

Ornamental A plant cultivated for decorative purposes.

Ovary The female reproductive organ; in a flower the ovule-bearing portion of the gynoecium or pistil.

Ovule The egg-containing organ within the ovary which in a plant, following fertilization, develops into the seed.

P

Perennial A plant of several years' duration, as distinct from annuals (one year) and biennials (two years).

Petal One of the segments of the corolla of a flower.

Petiole The stalk of a leaf, absent if the leaf is sessile.

Pigment (as used in this book) Any of various coloring matters found in the cells and tissues of plants or animals.

Piperine A colorless, crystalline alkaloid found in black and white pepper. It has a milder taste than chavicine.

Pistil The female reproductive unit of a flower, comprised of ovary, style and stigma; sometimes designated the gynoecium.

Pod A general term for a dry fruit that splits open at maturity; applied usually to the legume of the bean family (Leguminosae).

Pollen The male chromosome-bearing grains produced within the anther of a stamen; the basic male element of a flower.

Polygamous Having both perfect and imperfect flowers on the same plant (ex.: the bay tree).

Pomander A ball of mixed aromatic substances — including spices such as cloves, cinnamon, nutmeg, and cardamom—formerly worn as a supposed protection against infection or as a perfume. Enclosed in a small bag or perforated container, carried in the pocket or suspended by a chain from the neck, pomanders were in vogue in Europe from the Middle Ages up to the nineteenth century.

Pubescent Covered with soft, short hairs.

R

Restorative A remedy that aids in restoring health and vigor, such as a tonic; any agents (including gases) that promote a return to consciousness.

Rhizome A creeping underground, rootlike, often fleshy stem (ex.: ginger).

Rootlet A small root.

Rubefacient A cream or ointment containing one or more active ingredients (such as mustard) that produce temporary redness and warmth of the skin.

Runner A slender horizontal stem that may produce roots at the leaf nodes (ex.: peppermint).

S

Schizocarp The dry dehiscent fruit of most members of the parsley family that splits vertically into two halves (mericarps), each borne on a slender wiry stalk.

Sedative A drug that produces a calming or quieting effect.

Seed The ripened or matured ovule, consisting of two coats, an embryo, and reserve food.

Sessile Without a stalk or petiole, said of a leaf.

Sinigrin A sulfur-containing glycoside found in black mustard seeds, horseradish roots, and allied plants.

Species A category of plants subordinate to a genus but above a variety.

Stamen The male pollen-bearing unit of a flower, usually comprised of filament (stalk) and anther (the pollen sacs).

Staminodium A sterile stamen, that is, one that produces no pollen, often a filament only.

Stigma The terminal part of the gynoecium (pistil) that receives the pollen.

Stimulant In the usual meaning of the word any substance, natural or synthetic, which exerts a stimulating effect upon the central nervous system and thereby promotes wakefulness.

Stomachic A drug, herb, or extract that acts as a tonic for the stomach and promotes gastric digestion.

Style The usually elongated portion of the pistil between the ovary and the stigma.

T

Tonic A remedial agent, usually in the form of a palatable liquid, that increases body tone by stimulating the nutrition of tissues within the body.

U

Umbel An inflorescence (often flat-topped) in which all of the flower stalks originate from a common point (ex.: parsley).

United States Pharmacopeia (U.S.P.) The official U.S. code describing the composition of basic drugs and preferred medicaments, regulating their preparation, standards of purity and potency, and dispensation. The first U.S. Pharmacopeia was published in 1820, and listed many spices and herbs considered worthy of recognition. During the past fifty years pure, whole spices and herbs have been almost entirely deleted. In the latest U.S. Pharmacopeia (the seventeenth revision, of 1965) certain essential oils of spices (including oil of anise, oil of cinnamon, oil of cloves, and oil of peppermint) are recognized.

V

Vanillin A colorless, crystalline compound, the fragrant constituent of vanilla; also produced synthetically from wastes of the wood pulp and paper industry.

Variety A category of classification subordinate to a species; a subdivision of a species.

Vedic Pertaining to the Vedas, a collection of sacred Hindu writings that date from the second millennium B.C.

Vermifuge Any agent that expels intestinal worms and similar intestinal parasites upon ingestion or repeated ingestion.

Volatile Oils (*See* ESSENTIAL OILS.)

BIBLIOGRAPHY

ADAMSON, A. D. *Oleoresins Production and Markets With Particular Reference to the United Kingdom.* Report No. G56. London: Tropical Products Institute, 1971.

AIKEN, JOHN. *Select Works of the British Poets.* Philadelphia: Wardell, 1844.

AIYADURAI, S. G. *A Review of Research on Spices & Cashewnut in India.* Ernakulam, India: E. K. Balasundaram, 1966.

ALLPORT, NOEL L. *The Chemistry and Pharmacy of Vegetable Drugs.* Brooklyn: Chemical Publishing Company, Inc., 1944.

AMERICAN SPICE TRADE ASSOCIATION. *A History of Spices.* New York: American Spice Trade Association, 1966.

——. *What You Should Know About Cinnamon.* New York: American Spice Trade Association, 1961.

——. *What You Should Know About Dehydrated Onion.* New York: American Spice Trade Association, Inc., 1967.

——. *What You Should Know About Paprika.* New York: American Spice Trade Association, 1966.

——. *What You Should Know About Pepper.* New York: American Spice Trade Association, 1964.

ANDREWS, ALFRED C. "Marjoram as a Spice in the Classical Era." *Classical Philology,* Vol. 56, No. 2 (April, 1961).

——. "Sage as a Condiment in the Graeco-Roman Era." *Economy Botany,* Vol. 10, No. 3 (1956).

ARBER, AGNES. *Herbals: Their Origin and Evolution.* Cambridge, England: Cambridge University Press, 1953.

ARCTANDER, STEFFEN. *Perfume and Flavor Materials of Natural Origin.* Elizabeth, New Jersey: By the Author, 1960.

AULT, WARREN O. *Europe in the Middle Ages.* Boston: D. C. Heath and Company, 1932.

BAILEY, L. H. "Origanum," *The Standard Cyclopedia of Horticulture,* II, The Macmillan Company, 1935.

BARRY, DODIE. "A Faint Trail of Perfume." *Perfumery and Essential Oil Record,* Vol. 59, No. 3 (March 1968).

BARTON, BENJAMIN H., and CASTLE, THOMAS. *The British Flora Medica: A History of the Medicinal Plants of Great Britain.* London: Chatto and Windus, 1877.

BAUMANN, BILL B. "The Botanical Aspects of Ancient Egyptian Embalming and Burial." *Economic Botany,* Vol. 14, No. 1 (January–March 1960).

THE BIBLE (authorized King James Version).

BLAKE, SIDNEY F. *Economic Plants of Interest to the Americas: Cassia and Cinnamon.* United States Department of Agriculture. Washington: U. S. Government Printing Office, 1943.

BOIS, D. *Les Plantes Alimentaires chez Tous les Peuples et à travers les Âges.* Paris: Paul Lechevalier, 1934.

BOXER, C. R. *The Dutch Seaborne Empire 1600–1800.* London: Hutchinson of London, 1965.

BREASTED, JAMES HENRY. *Ancient Times: A History of the Early World.* Boston: Ginn and Company, 1944.
———. *The Conquest of Civilization.* New York: The Literary Guild of America, Inc., 1938.

BROWN, E. *Note on the Production of Cardamoms.* Tropical Products Institute Report No. G26. London: Ministry of Overseas Development, 1966.

BROWNLOW, MARGARET. *Herbs and the Fragrant Garden.* New York: McGraw-Hill Book Company, 1963.

BURKILL, I. H. *A Dictionary of the Economic Products of the Malay Peninsula.* London: Crown Agents for the Colonies, 1935.

CADY, JOHN F. *Southeast Asia: Its Historical Development.* New York: McGraw-Hill Book Company, 1964.

CALPOUZOS, LUCAS. "Botanical Aspects of Oregano." *Economic Botany,* Vol. 8, No. 3 (July–September 1954).

CHALFIN, ELEANOR P. *Herbs Described.* Virginia: The Mutual Press, 1955.

CHAPMAN, C. P. "A New Development in the Agronomy of Pimento." *Caribbean Quarterly,* Vol. 2 (1965).

CHILDERS, NORMAN F., and CIBES, HECTOR R. *Vanilla Culture in Puerto Rico.* United States Department of Agriculture Circular No. 28. Washington: U. S. Government Printing Office, 1948.

CLAIBORNE, CRAIG. *An Herb and Spice Cook Book.* New York: Harper & Row, Publishers, 1963.

CLAIR, COLIN. *Of Herbs & Spices.* London: Abelard-Schuman, 1961.

CLARKSON, ROSETTA E. *Herbs: Their Culture and Uses.* New York: The Macmillan Company, 1961.

CLAUS, EDWARD P., and TYLER, VARRO E., JR. *Pharmacognosy.* Philadelphia: Lea & Febiger, 1967.

Cloves and Kretek. Indonesia Economic Studies Bulletin No. 2, 1966.

COBLEY, LESLIE S. *An Introduction to the Botany of Tropical Crops.* London: Longmans, Green and Co., 1956.

COLIN, JANE. *Herbs and Spices.* London: Arlington Books, 1962.

COLLINS, RUTH PHILPOTT. *A World of Curries.* New York: Funk & Wagnalls, 1967.

Commercial Growing of Horseradish. United States Department of Agriculture Circular. Washington: U. S. Government Printing Office, 1968.

CORRELL, DONOVAN S. "Vanilla, Its Botany, History, Cultivation and Economic Import." *Economic Botany*, Vol. 7, No. 4 (1953).

COUNCIL OF SCIENTIFIC & INDUSTRIAL RESEARCH. *The Wealth of India.* Vols. 2 and 3, *Raw Materials.* New Delhi: Council of Scientific & Industrial Research, 1950 and 1952.

CREECH, JOHN J. "Propagation of Black Pepper." *Economic Botany*, Vol. 9, No. 3 (1955).

CROCKER, ERNEST C. *Flavor.* New York: McGraw-Hill Book Company, Inc., 1945.

CROFTON, R. H. *A Pageant of the Spice Islands.* London: John Bale Sons & Danielsson, Ltd., 1936.

Culinary and Medicinal Herbs. Ministry of Agriculture, Fisheries and Food Circular. London: Her Majesty's Stationery Office, 1960.

[CULPEPER, NICHOLAS.] *Culpeper's Complete Herbal.* London: Foulsham, W. & Co. Ltd., n.d.

DATTA, P. R., SUSI, H., HIGMAN, H. C., and FILIPIC, V. J. "Use of Gas Chromatography to Identify Geographical Origin of Some Spices." *Food Technology* (October 1962).

DAVIES, C. COLLIN. *An Historical Atlas of the Indian Peninsula.* Madras, India:

Oxford University Press, 1965.

DAVIES, D. W. *A Primer of Dutch Seventeenth Century Overseas Trade.* The Hague: Martinus Nijhoff, 1961.

DAY, AVANELLE, and STUCKEY, LILLIE. *The Spice Cookbook.* New York: David White Company, 1964.

DAY, CLIVE. *A History of Commerce.* New York: Longmans, Green and Co., 1917.

DECANDOLLE, ALPHONSE. *Origin of Cultivated Plants.* New York: Hafner Publishing Company, 1964.

DEWAARD, P. W. F. "Pepper Cultivation in Sarawak." *World Crops*, Vol. 16, No. 3 (September 1964).

DEWEY, LYSTER H., and BAILEY, L. H. "Mentha," *The Standard Cyclopedia of Horticulture,* II, The Macmillan Company, 1935.

DILLON, GORDON W. *The Story of Vanilla.* American Orchid Society Bulletin, Vol. 10, No. 11 (1942).

DONAHUE, ROY L. *Agriculture in India,* Vol. 2, *Crops.* London: Asia Publishing House, 1963.

DORRANCE, ANNE. *Green Cargoes.* New York: Doubleday, Doran & Co., Inc., 1945.

DREANY, JOSEPH. *The Magic of Spices.* New York: G. P. Putnam's Sons, 1961.

ELLACOMBE, HENRY N. *The Plant-Lore & Garden-Craft of Shakespeare.* Exeter, England: William Pollard, 1878.

ELVEHJEM, C. A., and BURNS, C. H. "Sodium Content of

Commercial Spices." *The Journal of the American Medical Association,* Vol. 148, No. 12 (March 22, 1952).

FAEGRI, KNUT. *Krydder.* Oslo: J. W. Cappelens Forlag, 1966.

FAZLI, F. R. Y., and HARDMAN, R. "The Spice, Fenugreek, (*Trigonella foenumgraecum* L.): Its Commercial Varieties of Seed as a Source of Diosgenin." *Tropical Science,* Vol. 10, No. 2 (1968).

FINNEMORE, HORACE. The *Essential Oils.* London: Ernest Benn Limited, 1926.

FISHER, CHARLES A. *South-East Asia.* London: Methuen Co., Ltd., 1964.

FLACH, M. *Nutmeg Cultivation and Its Sex-Problem.* Wageningen, The Netherlands: Agricultural University, 1966.

FLÜCKIGER, FRIEDRICH A., and HANBURY, DANIEL. *Pharmacographia: A History of the Principal Drugs of Vegetable Origin, Met With in Great Britain and British India.* London: Macmillan and Co., 1879.

FORBES, R. J. *Short History of the Art of Distillation.* Leiden, the Netherlands: E. J. Brill, 1948.

FREEMAN, MARGARET B. *Herbs for the Mediaeval Household.* New York: The Metropolitan Museum of Art, 1943.

GARRISON, FIELDING H. *History of Medicine.* Philadelphia: W. B. Saunders Company, 1967.

GEMMILL, CHALMERS L. *Silphium.* Bulletin of the History of Medicine, Vol. 40, No. 4 (July–August 1966).

GENTRY, HOWARD SCOTT. "Introducing Black Pepper into America." *Economic Botany,* Vol. 9, No. 3 (1955).

[GERARD, JOHN.] *Gerard's Herball.* Ed. Thomas Johnson. London: Spring Books, 1964 (originally published 1636).

GIBBONS, EUELL. *Stalking the Healthful Herbs.* New York: David McKay Company, Inc., 1966.

GIBBS, W. M. *Spices and How to Know Them.* Buffalo: The Matthews-Northrup Works, 1909.

GLATZEL, H. "Neuere Untersuchungen über die Wirkung von Gewürzen auf die Verdauungsorgane." *Fortschritte der Medizin,* 85. Jg., Nr. 10 (May 25, 1967).

GÖÖCK, ROLAND. *Das Buch der Gewürze.* Hamburg: Mosaik Verlag, 1965.

GOODSPEED, GEORGE STEPHEN. *A History of the Babylonians and Assyrians.* New York: Charles Scribner's Sons, 1909.

GRAY, FREDERICK D. *Spice trends in the United States. National Food Situation. Economic Research Service.* Washington: U.S. Department of Agriculture (November 8, 1972).

GRIEVE, MRS M. *A Modern Herbal.* New York: Hafner Publishing Co., 1967.

GUENTHER, ERNEST. *The Essential Oils,* Vols. 1, 4, and 5. New York: D. Van Nos trand Company, Inc., 1952.

HAMILL, KATHARINE. "The Spices' New Life." *Fortune*, Vol. 64, No. 6 (December 1961).

HAYES, ELIZABETH S. *Spices and Herbs Around the World*. New York: Doubleday & Company, Inc., 1961.

HEEGER, E. F. *Handbuch des Arznei und Gewürzpflanzenbaues, Drogengewinnung*. Leipzig: Deutscher Bauernverlag, 1956.

HEISER, CHARLES B., JR., and SMITH, PAUL G. "The Cultivated Capsicum Peppers." *Economic Botany*, Vol. 7, No. 3 (July–September 1953).

HENDRICKSON, RUTH M., and JOHNSON, FRANCES M. *Herbs and Their Culture*. Circular 149. New Haven: Agricultural Experiment Station, November 1941.

Herbs. Ministry of Agriculture and Fisheries Circular. London: His Majesty's Stationery Office, 1938.

HERRMANN, PAUL. *Conquest by Man*. New York: Harper & Brothers, 1954.

HILL, ALBERT F. *Economic Botany*. New York: McGraw-Hill Book Company, Inc., 1952.

HITTI, PHILIP K. *History of the Arabs*. New York: St. Martin's Press, 1968.

HODGKIN, THOMAS. "Alaric," *Encyclopaedia Britannica* (1946), I.

HOLMES, EDWARD MORELL. "Opium," *Encyclopaedia Britannica* (1946), XVI.

HOWE, SONIA E. *In Quest of Spices*. London: Herbert Jenkins Limited, 1946.

HUMPHREY, SYLVIA WINDLE. *A Matter of Taste*. New York: The Macmillan Company, 1965.

IRISH, H. C. "Capsicum," *The Standard Cyclopedia of Horticulture*, The Macmillian Company, 1935.

IRVING, WASHINGTON. *Columbus's Voyages of Discovery*. London: Simpkin, Marshall, Hamilton, Kent & Co., 1841.

JAYNE, K. G. *Vasco da Gama and His Successors: 1460–1580*. London: Methuen & Co., Ltd., 1912.

JONES, HENRY A., and MANN, LOUIS K. *Onions and Their Allies*. London: Leonard Hill [Books] Limited, 1963.

JONES, LESTER W. (ed.). *A Treasury of Spices*. New York: American Spice Trade Association, 1956.

KAINS, M. G. "Horse-radish," *The Standard Cyclopedia of Horticulture*, II, The Macmillan Company, 1935.

KEATS, JOHN. *Selected Poems*. Ed. Edmund Blunden. London: Collins, 1964.

KEVORKIAN, A. G. *Pepper, Vanilla and Other Spices: The Yearbook of Agriculture 1964*. Washington: U. S. Government Printing Office, 1964.

Kostbarkeiten ferner Länder eine Gewürz-und Teepflanzenkunde von Alba. Bielefeld, West Germany: Gehring & Neiweiser, 1951.

KREMERS, EDWARD, and URDANG, GEORGE. *History of Pharmacy*. Revised by Glenn Sonnedecker. Philadelphia: J. B. Lippincott Company, 1963.

KRUTCH, JOSEPH WOOD. *Herbal.* New York: G. P. Putnam's Sons, 1965.

LANGER, WILLIAM L. *An Encyclopedia of World History.* Boston: Houghton Mifflin Company, 1948.

LAWALL, CHARLES H. *Four Thousand Years of Pharmacy.* Philadelphia: J. B. Lippincott Company, 1927.

LEHNER, ERNST, and LEHNER, JOHANNA. *Folklore and Odysseys of Food and Medicinal Plants.* New York: Tudor Publishing Company, 1962.

——. *Folklore and Symbolism of Flowers, Plants and Trees.* New York: Tudor Publishing Company, 1960.

LEYEL, MRS. C. F. *Herbal Delights.* Boston: Houghton Mifflin Company, 1938.

——. *The Magic of Herbs.* New York: Harcourt, Brace & Company, 1926.

LLOYD, JOHN URI. *Origin and History of All the Pharmacopeial Vegetable Drugs with Bibliography.* Cincinnati: The Caxton Press, 1929.

LOEWENFELD, CLAIRE. *Herb Gardening.* Newton, Massachusetts: Charles T. Branford Company, 1965.

LONGFELLOW, HENRY WADSWORTH. *Complete Poetical Works.* Boston: Houghton Mifflin Co., 1893.

LOPEZ, ROBERT S., and RAYMOND, IRVING W. *Medieval Trade in the Mediterranean World.* New York: Columbia University Press, 1961.

LUDWIG, EMIL. *The Mediterranean.* New York: Whittlesey House, 1942.

McCormick Spices of the World Cook Book. New York: McGraw-Hill Book Company, 1964.

MACKAY, ALASTAIR. *Farming & Gardening in the Bible.* Emmaus, Pennsylvania: Rodale Press, 1950.

MACMILLAN, H. F. *Tropical Planting and Gardening.* London: Macmillan & Co., Ltd., 1962.

McNAIR, JAMES B. *Spices and Condiments.* Chicago: Field Museum of Natural History, 1930.

MADAN, C. L., KAPUR, B. M., and GUPTA, U. S. "Saffron." *Economic Botany,* Vol. 20, No. 4 (December 1966).

MAISTRE, JACQUES. *Les Plantes à Épices.* Paris: G.-P. Maisonneuve & LaRose, 1964.

The Market for Vanilla Beans. Tropical Products Institute Report No. 22/61. London: Ministry of Overseas Development, 1961.

MASEFIELD, G. B. *A Handbook of Tropical Agriculture.* Oxford: The Clarendon Press, 1949.

MASSELMAN, GEORGE. *The Cradle of Colonialism.* New Haven: Yale University Press, 1963.

MATHIEU, ROSELLA F. *The Herb Grower's Complete Guide.* Silverton, Ohio: Fragrant Herb Farm, 1949.

MEILINK-ROELOFSZ, M. A. P. *Asian Trade and European Influence in the Indonesia Archipelago between 1500 and about 1630.* The Hague: Martinus Nijhoff, 1962.

Memorandum on Ginger. Tropical Products Institute Report No. 13/62. London:

Ministry of Overseas Development, 1962.

The Merck Index of Chemicals and Drugs. Rahway, New Jersey: Merck & Co., Inc., 1960.

The Merck Manual of Diagnosis and Therapy. Rahway, New Jersey: Merck & Co., Inc., 1966.

MILLER, J. INNES. *The Spice Trade of the Roman Empire.* Oxford: The Clarendon Press, 1969.

MILORADOVICH, MILO. *The Art of Cooking with Herbs and Spices.* Garden City, New York: Doubleday & Company, Inc., 1950.

MITCHELL, J. LESLIE. *Earth Conquerors.* New York: Simon and Schuster, 1934.

MOLDENKE, HAROLD N., and MOLDENKE, ALMA L. *Plants of the Bible.* New York: The Ronald Press Company, 1952.

MORISON, SAMUEL ELIOT. *Admiral of the Ocean Sea.* Boston: Little, Brown and Company, 1942.

MUENSCHER, WALTER CONRAD, and RICE, MYRON ARTHUR. *Garden Spice and Wild Pot-Herbs.* New York: Comstock Publishing Associates, 1955.

MUÑOZ FLORES, IGNACIO, and PINTO CORTÉS, BENITO. "Taxonomía y distribución geográfica de los chiles cultivados en Mexico," *Proceedings,* Caribbean Region, American Society of Horticultural Science, 1967.

NICHOLLS, H. A. ALFORD. *A Text-Book of Tropical Agriculture.* London: Macmillan and Co., Limited, 1897.

NORTHCOTE, LADY ROSALIND. *The Book of Herbs.* London: The Bodley Head, 1912.

Note on the Preparation of Turmeric. Tropical Products Institute Report No. 62/62. London: Ministry of Overseas Development, 1962.

Note on the Production of Caraway. Tropical Products Institute Report No. 64/62. London: Ministry of Overseas Development, 1962.

Note on the Production of Coriander. Tropical Products Institute Report No. 66/62. London: Ministry of Overseas Development, 1962.

OCHSE, J. J., SOULE, M. J., JR., DIJKMAN, M. J., and WEHLBURG, C. *Tropical and Subtropical Agriculture,* Vol. 2. New York: The Macmillan Company, 1961.

OLMSTEAD, A. T. *History of the Persian Empire.* Chicago: The University of Chicago Press, 1948.

Onions. Ministry of Agriculture, Fisheries and Food Circular. London: Her Majesty's Stationery Office, 1965.

The Oxford Classical Dictionary. Oxford: The Clarendon Press, 1966.

PARRY, J. H. *The Age of Reconnaissance.* New York: The New American Library, 1964.

PARRY, JOHN W. *The Story of Spices.* Brooklyn: Chemical Publishing Co., Inc., 1953.

———. *The Spice Handbook.* Brooklyn: Chemical Publishing Co., Inc., 1945.

———. *Spices, Their Mor-*

phology, Histology and Chemistry. Brooklyn: Chemical Publishing Co., Inc., 1962.

PEATTIE, DONALD C. *Cargoes and Harvests*. New York: Appleton-Century, 1936.

The Periplus of the Erythraean Sea, trans. Wilfred H. Schoff. New York: Longmans, Green, and Co., 1912.

PHILLIPS, JAMES DUNCAN. *Pepper and Pirates*. Boston: Houghton Mifflin Company, 1949.

———. *Salem and the Indies*. Boston: Houghton Mifflin Company, 1947.

PHILLIPS, WENDELL. *Qataban and Sheba*. London: Victor Gollancz Ltd., 1955.

PIRENNE, HENRI. *Mohammed and Charlemagne*. London: George Allen & Unwin Ltd., 1965.

Plantation Crops: A Review. Commonwealth Secretariat. London: Her Majesty's Stationery Office, 1968.

PLINY, *Natural History,* trans. H. Rackham. London: William Heinemann Ltd., 1960.

POLO, MARCO. *Travels*. Ed. Milton Rugoff. New York: New American Library, 1961.

Production of Drug and Condiment Plants. Farmer's Bulletin No. 1999, United States Department of Agriculture. Washington: U. S. Government Printing Office, 1948.

PURSEGLOVE, J, W. *Tropical Crops: Dicotyledons,* Vols. 1 and 2. New York: John Wiley & Sons, Inc., 1968.

RABINOWITZ, L. *Jewish Merchant Adventurers*. London: Edward Goldston, 1948.

REDGROVE, H. STANLEY. *Scent and All About It*. Brooklyn: Chemical Publishing Company, Inc., 1928.

———. *Spices and Condiments*. London: Sir Isaac Pitman & Sons, Ltd., 1933.

REED, HOWARD S. *A Short History of the Plant Sciences.* New York: The Ronald Press Company, 1942.

REINHARDT, LUDWIG. *Kulturgeschichte der Nutzpflanzen*. Munich: Verlag von Ernst Reinhardt, 1911.

A Review of the Hong Kong Ginger Industry. Hong Kong: The Hong Kong Preserved Ginger Distributors, Ltd., April 1957.

RIDLEY, HENRY N. *Spices*. London: Macmillan and Co., Limited, 1912.

RIMMEL, EUGENE. *The Book of Perfumes*. London: Chapman and Hall, 1865.

ROBBINS, WILFRED W., and RAMALEY, FRANCIS. *Plants Useful to Man*. Philadelphia: P. Blakiston's Sons & Co., Inc., 1937.

[ROLFE, R. A.] "Vanillas of Commerce." *Bulletin of Miscellaneous Information,* Royal Gardens, Kew, England; Vol. 467, No. 104 (August 1895).

ROLFS, P. H. "Onions," *The Standard Cyclopedia of Horticulture,* II, The Macmillan Company, 1935.

ROUK, HUGH F., and MENGESHA, HAILU. *Fenugreek: Its Relationships, Geography and Economic Importance*. Experiment Station Bulletin No. 20. Diredawa, Ethiopia: Imperial Ethiopian College of Agriculture and Mechanical Arts, April 1963.

SAMARAWIRA, I. S. E. "Cinnamon." *World Crops,* Vol. 16, No. 1 (March 1964).

SAMHABER, ERNST. *Merchants Make History.* London: George G. Harrap & Co., Ltd., 1963.

SANFORD, EVA MATTHEWS. *The Mediterranean World in Ancient Times.* New York: The Ronald Press Company, 1951.

Savory Herbs: Culture and Use, Farmer's Bulletin No. 1977, United States Department of Agriculture. Washington: U. S. Government Printing Office, 1948.

SCHERY, ROBERT W. *Plants for Man.* London: George Allen & Unwin, Ltd., 1956.

SCHULTES, RICHARD EVANS. "The Genus *Quararibea* in Mexico and the Use of Its Flowers as a Spice for Chocolate." *Botanical Museum of Harvard University Leaflet.* Vol. 17, No. 9 (January 22, 1957).

SELFRIDGE, H. GORDON. *The Romance of Commerce.* London: The Bodley Head Ltd., 1923.

SHAKESPEARE, WILLIAM. *The Comedies.* New York: The Heritage Press, 1958.

——. *The Histories.* New York: The Heritage Press, 1958.

——. *The Tragedies.* New York: The Heritage Press, 1958.

SIMMONS, ADELMA GRENIER. *Herb Gardening in Five Seasons.* Princeton: D. Van Nostrand Company, Inc., 1964.

SINGER, CHARLES. *From Magic to Science.* London: Ernest Benn Ltd., 1928.

The Spice Islands Cook Book. California: Lane Book Company, 1963.

SPICES EXPORT PROMOTION COUNCIL. *Indian Spices* (Overseas Edition). Ernakulam. India: Spices Export Promotion Council, 1966.

——. *Report of the Spices Trade Delegation to the Middle East, Continent and U. K.* Ernakulam, India: Spices Export Promotion Council, 1963.

——. *Spices Bulletin, Seminar Number.* Ernakulam, India: Spices Export Promotion Council, 1965.

STANFORD, ERNEST ELWOOD. *Economic Plants.* New York: D. Appleton-Century Company, Incorporated, 1934.

STEARNS, FOSTER. "Spice Caravans." *The Herbarist,* No. 14 (1948).

STEFANSSON, VILHJALMUR (ed.). *Great Adventures and Explorations.* New York: The Dial Press, 1952.

STEINMETZ, E. F. *Codex Vegetabilis.* Amsterdam: By the Author, 1957.

[STURTEVANT, E. LEWIS.] *Sturtevant's Notes on Edible Plants.* Ed. U. P. Hedrick. Albany, New York: J. B. Lyon Company, State Printers, 1919.

TAYLOR, NORMAN. *Herbs in the Garden.* New York: D. Van Nostrand Company, Inc., 1953.

THOMPSON, C. J. S. *The Mystery and Art of the Apothecary.* London: The Bodley

Head Limited, 1929.

THOMPSON, R. CAMPBELL. *The Assyrian Herbal*. London: Luzac and Co., 1924.

THORWALD, JÜRGEN. *Science and Secrets of Early Medicine*. New York: Harcourt, Brace & World, Inc., 1963.

TIDBURY, G. E. *The Clove Tree*. London: Crosby Lockwood & Son, Ltd., 1949.

TOUTAIN, JULES. *The Economic Life of the Ancient World*. London: Kegan Paul, Trench, Trubner & Co., Ltd., 1930.

TREASE, GEORGE EDWARD. *Pharmacy in History*. London: Bailliere, Tindall & Cox, 1964.

———. *A Textbook of Pharmacognosy*. London: Bailliere, Tindal and Cassel, 1966.

TSCHIRCH, A. *Handbuch der Pharmakognosie*. Leipzig: Verlag von Bernhard Tauchnitz, 1930.

UNITED NATIONS, FOOD AND AGRICULTURE ORGANIZATION. *Spices—Trends in World Markets*. Rome, 1962.

UPHOF, J. C. Th. *Dictionary of Economic Plants*, 2nd ed. Würzburg, West Germany: Verlag von J. Cramer, 1968.

USHER, GEORGE. *A Dictionary of Botany*. Princeton: D. Van Nostrand Company, Inc., 1966.

VANILLA INFORMATION BUREAU. *Make Mine Real Vanilla*. New York: Bernard L. Lewis, Inc., 1964.

VAUGHAN, J. G., and HEMINGWAY, J. S. "The Utilization of Mustards." *Economic Botany*, Vol. 13, No. 3 (1959).

VERDOORN, FRANS (ed.). *Plants and Plant Science in Latin America*. Waltham, Massachusetts: Chronica Botanica Company, 1945.

VERRILL, A. HYATT. *Perfumes and Spices Including an Account of Soaps and Cosmetics*. Clinton, Massachusetts: L. C. Page & Company, 1940.

WALKER, WINIFRED. *All the Plants of the Bible*. London: Lutterworth Press, 1964.

WARD, J. F. *Pimento*. Kingston: Jamaican Ministry of Agriculture and Lands, 1961.

WARBURG, O. *Die Muskatnuss*. Leipzig: Verlag von Wilhelm Engelmann, 1897.

WARMINGTON, E. H. *The Commerce Between the Roman Empire and India*. Cambridge, England: Cambridge University Press, 1928.

WATT, SIR GEORGE. *The Commercial Products of India*. India: Today & Tomorrow's Printers & Publishers, 1966.

WEBSTER, HELEN NOYES. *Herbs: How to Grow Them and How to Use Them*. Newton, Massachusetts: Charles T. Branford Company, 1959.

———. "Those Herbs Called Chervils." *The Herbarist*, No. 13 (1947).

WEBSTER'S BIOGRAPHICAL DICTIONARY. Springfield, Massachusetts: G. & C. Merriam Co., 1961.

WEBSTER'S GEOGRAPHICAL DICTIONARY. Springfield, Massachusetts: G. & C. Merriam Co., 1962.

WILLIS, J. C. *A Dictionary of the Flowering Plants and Ferns,* 7th ed. Ed. H. K. Airy Shaw. Cambridge, England: Cambridge University Press, 1966.

WINTON, ANDREW L., and WINTON, KATE BARBER. *The Structure and Composition of Foods,* Vol. 4. New York: John Wiley & Sons, Inc., 1939.

WONG, K. CHIMIN, and LIEN-TEH, WU. *History of Chinese Medicine.* Shanghai, China: Chinese National Quarantine Service, 1936.

WOOTTON, A. C. *Chronicles of Pharmacy,* Vols. 1 and 2. London: Macmillan and Co. Limited, 1910.

WREN, R. C. *Potter's New Cyclopedia of Botanical Drugs and Preparations.* London: Sir Isaac Pitman & Sons, Ltd., 1956.

YOUNG, THOMAS B., and TRUE, RODNEY H. *American-Grown Paprika Pepper.* United States Department of Agriculture Bulletin No. 43. Washington: U. S. Government Printing Office, 1913.

YULE, HENRY. *The Book of Ser Marco Polo.* London: John Murray, 1875.

——. "Marco Polo," *Encyclopaedia Britannica* (1946), XVIII.

ZWEIG, STEFAN. *Conqueror of the Seas: The Story of Magellan.* New York: The Literary Guild of America, Inc., 1938.

ILLUSTRATION ACKNOWLEDGEMENTS

Color photographs of 40 spices: Lewis/Neale, Inc., New York.

page

24, Spices used in early Egypt as aromatic pomades: J. G. Wilkensen, *Manners and Customs of the Ancient Egyptians.* London: 1837.

25 top, Perfuming the embalmed body; Eugene Rimmel. *The Book of Perfumes.* London: Chapman and Hall, 1865.

25 bottom, Egyptian bearers with fruits: Roland Göock. *Das Buch der Gewürze.* Hamburg: Mosaik Verlag, 1965. (Copy of an ancient Egyptian relief adapted from Forrer. *Reallexikon der prähistorischen, klassischen und frühchristlichen Altertümer.* Berlin/Stuttgart, 1907.)

27, Collection of Frankincense: Ambroise Paré. *De Distillationibus.* Paris, 1582. (Courtesy of the National Library of Medicine, Bethesda, Maryland.)

28 bottom, Egyptian ships: Roland Göock. *Das Buch der Gewürze.* Hamburg: Mosaik Verlag, 1965. (Adapted from a carving in the temple at Deir-el-Bahri, Egypt.)

30 top, Transporting a Myrrh tree: The Mansell Collection, London. (Adapted from a carving in the temple at Deir-el-Bahri, Egypt.)

30 bottom, A pimitive incense offering: Eugene Rimmel. *The Book of Perfumes.* London: Chapman and Hall, 1865.

31 bottom, Measuring heaps of incense: E. Neville. *The Temple of Deir-el-Bahri.* London, 1896. (Courtesy of the Wellcome Trustees, London.)

32 top, Camel, 1477: Aesop. *Fabulae et Vita.* Ulm: J. Zainer, 1477.

34, Ancient Spice Trade Routes: Outline map based on *An Historical Atlas of the Indian Peninsula* by C. Collin Davies. (Courtesy of Oxford University Press, 1949.)

35, Hindu Perfumer Mixing Spices: Eugene Rimmel. *The Book of Perfumes.* Chapman and Hall. London, 1865.

465

BOTANICAL PRINT CREDITS

RECIPE INDEX

INDEX

(Boldface numerals indicate principal references in the text.)